# JUNIORPLOTS 4

# JUNIORPLOTS 4

## A Book Talk Guide
## for Use with Readers Ages 12–16

By JOHN T. GILLESPIE
and CORINNE J. NADEN

R. R. BOWKER®

A Reed Reference Publishing Company
New Providence, New Jersey

Published by R. R. Bowker,
A Reed Reference Publishing Company
Copyright © 1993 by Reed Publishing (USA) Inc.
*All rights reserved*
Printed and bound in the United States of America

**Library of Congress Cataloging-in-Publication Data**
Gillespie, John Thomas, 1928–
    Juniorplots 4 : a book talk guide for use with readers, ages 12–16
/ by John T. Gillespie and Corinne J. Naden.
        p.  cm.
    Includes bibliographical references and indexes.
    ISBN 0-8352-3167-4
    1. Teenagers—United States—Books and reading.  2. Young adult
literature—Stories, plots, etc.  3. Book talks.  I. Naden, Corinne
J.  II. Title.
Z1037.G514   1992
028.5'5'0973—dc20                                              92-35670
                                                                    CIP

ISBN 0 - 8352 - 3167 - 4

9  780835  231671

# Contents

# Preface

The first three volumes in the *Juniorplots* series appeared at ten-year intervals: *Juniorplots* in 1967, *More Juniorplots* in 1977, and *Juniorplots 3* in 1987. As a gap of ten years brings a wealth of quality literature, it was decided that new editions would appear every five years, thus the 1992 date on this volume.

Helping youngsters select books for their reading pleasure is one of the most enjoyable responsibilities of teachers and librarians. There are many methods that can be used, but perhaps the most potent is actually talking about the books one wishes to recommend to either an individual patron or to groups. This technique is known as "booktalking."

The primary purpose of this volume is to help librarians and teachers supply reading guidance by way of the book talk. A secondary purpose is to serve as a collection-building tool. The introduction, "A Brief Guide to Booktalking," is reprinted from the companion volume *Seniorplots* (Bowker, 1989) and provides hints and aids for the would-be booktalker.

Another feature of this edition is the special indexes that follow the regular author, title, and subject indexes. These additions are cumulative indexes (author, title, and subject) to the books summarized in this and the preceding three volumes in the series. These indexes will facilitate the use of the volumes as an integrated set.

The eighty-one plots in *Juniorplots 4* have been divided by subjects or genres popular with adolescent readers. They are (1) Teenage Life and Concerns; (2) Adventure and Mystery Stories; (3) Science Fiction and Fantasy; (4) Historical Fiction; (5) Sports Fact and Fiction; (6) Biography and True Adventure; (7) Guidance and Health; and (8) The World Around Us.

Various methods were used to choose the books to be highlighted. A basic criterion was that each had to be recommended for purchase in several standard bibliographies and reviewing sources. In addition to criteria involving quality, an important consideration was the desire to provide materials covering a variety of interests and needs at different reading levels. In spite of these concerns, some of the selections remain personal and, therefore, arbitrary. Particular emphasis was placed on titles published between 1987 and the end of 1991.

The individual titles are analyzed under six headings:

1. *Plot Summary.* Each plot briefly retells the entire story. The summary includes all important incidents and characters, while trying to retain the mood and point of view of the author.

2. *Thematic Material.* This section enumerates primary and secondary themes that will facilitate the use of the book in a variety of situations.

3. *Book Talk Material.* Techniques are given on how to introduce the book interestingly to young adults. Passages suitable for retelling or reading aloud are indicated and pagination is shown for these passages for the hardcover edition. It was found that pagination in the hardcover edition was usually the same in the paperback.

4. *Additional Selections.* Related books that explore similar or associated themes are annotated or listed with identifying bibliographic information. Approximately seven titles are given per book.

5. *About the Book.* Standard book reviewing sources (for example, *Booklist*) are listed with dates and pages of reviews. Also, listings in *Book Review Digest* and *Book Review Index* are given when available so that additional reviews can be located if needed.

6. *About the Author.* Standard biographical dictionaries (for example, *Something about the Author* and *Contemporary Authors*) were consulted to locate sources of biographical information about the author. When this section does not appear, no material was found. However, the user also may wish to consult other sources, such as periodical indexes (*Readers' Guide, Education Index, Library Literature*), jacket blurbs, and material available through the publisher.

The detailed treatment of the main titles is not intended as a substitute for reading the books. Instead, it is meant to be used by teachers and librarians to refresh their memories about books they have read and to suggest new uses for these titles.

This volume is not meant to be a work of literary criticism or a listing of the best books for young adults. It is a representative selection of books that have value in a variety of situations.

# Introduction: A Brief Guide to Booktalking

by John T. Gillespie

There is basically just one purpose behind booktalking—to stimulate reading and a love of literature through delivering tantalizing, seductive introductions to books. There are, however, often many different secondary purposes, for example, to introduce specific authors, titles, or themes of books; to develop a specific aspect of literary appreciation; to further a particular school assignment; to present yourself to students; or to encourage visits to and use of the library.

Book talks generally fall into two main categories, informal and formal. The informal book talk consists of the spontaneous introduction to books that goes on every day in the library with single or small groups of students often in reply to such questions as "Could you suggest some good books for me to read?" The formal book talk is explored here in this brief introduction.

Before preparing a specific book talk, three "knows" are helpful. First is to know your audience as well as possible—age and grade levels, the range of abilities and interests, and levels of maturation and sophistication. Second is a knowledge of books. This comes in time through reading about books, in book reviewing journals and other secondary sources, but more importantly from reading the books themselves. It is wise to begin a card file with brief notes on each book read. Although these are never as detailed as the coverage of each title in *Juniorplots 4*, certain topics should be covered. Basically these are: a brief plot summary; a list of a few key passages, particularly at the beginning of the book, that would be suitable for retelling or rereading to an audience; a note on the major subjects or themes covered; and other related book titles that come to mind. As this file grows it can be used to refresh one's memory of books and thus save rereading time and also serve as a source to create new book talks by "mixing and matching" titles to create a variety of interesting new combinations of titles and themes.

Third is a knowledge of the many aids, such as *Juniorplots 4*, available to help in preparing and delivering a book talk. Some of the most valuable aids are described at the end of this introduction.

Before choosing the books to be presented, a preliminary framework should be established. First, the physical conditions should be studied (place, time, purpose, number of attendees). Second, the length of the talk should be determined. Most book talks last 15 to 25 minutes depending on such factors as the number of books to be introduced and the attention span of the audience. An average length is about 20 minutes. In a classroom period of 40 to 45 minutes this allows time for housekeeping chores (for example, announcements, attendance taking), the book talk itself, browsing through the books presented and additional titles, checking out books, and so on.

Deciding on the number of titles to be presented is next. Some booktalkers like to give short one- or two-minute "quickies" whereas others feel more comfortable spending longer periods on each title, supplying more details of plot or character and perhaps retelling or reading a key self-contained incident. Still others mix both techniques. The conditions of the book talk and the preference of the booktalker in the end determine the style used. Also, if a large number of books is to be introduced, a bibliography can be prepared and distributed to students to prevent confusion and give them reading guidance for future visits to the library. This bibliography should contain names of authors, titles, and a brief "catchy" annotation for each.

In preparing the talk, a connecting link or theme should be identified. This could be as general as "Books I think you would enjoy reading" or "Some titles old and new that are favorites of young people your age" to something more specific such as American Civil War novels or family crises as portrayed in fiction. The more specific topics are often suggested by a classroom teacher and are assignment-oriented. Regardless of the nature of the theme or subject, it supplies a structure and connecting link to give a oneness and unity to the book talk. It is used to introduce the talk, act occasionally as a bridge from one book to the next, and serve as a conclusion to round out the presentation.

Next choose the books themselves. Although this seems an obvious point, each book should have been read completely. The ultimate outcome or denouement in a book will often determine the material to be presented in introducing the book. Lacking this knowledge, the booktalker might misrepresent the contents or give an inaccurate or incorrect interpretation. One should believe in the value of each title to be presented—feel that the book is worthy of being introduced and that it will supply enjoyment and pleasure to the intended audience. The booktalker does not necessarily have to dote on each title and must at times introduce examples of a genre he or she does not like. It is sufficient that one choose good books that will enlighten and entertain the audience regardless of the personal preference of the presenter. Be sure the selection represents the interests and reading levels of the group—some difficult, some average, some easy; some old titles, some new; some fiction, some nonfiction; and so forth.

One should determine the method and content of each book introduction after choosing the theme and the books themselves. There are several ways of introducing books. The most frequently used is a brief description of the plot to a certain climactic moment. Words of caution: Do not give away too much of the plot, stick to essential details (for example, avoid introducing subplots or subsidiary characters), and try not to overwork this technique or else students will find the "cliffhanger" endings ultimately frustrating. The second method is by retelling or reading a specific self-contained incident or incidents that give the flavor of the book. This can be the most satisfying for the audience because a "complete" story has been told and yet one hopes a desire for more has also been implanted. One must be very cautious about reading from the book and use this technique sparingly, only when the author's style cannot be produced otherwise. Some booktalkers eschew reading from the book entirely and instead memorize the passages because reading from the book interrupts the immediate eye contact with the audience and can lessen or destroy the rapport one has with the group. Therefore, passages to be read must be chosen very carefully, and should be short and fulfill a specific purpose when simple retelling will not suffice. A specific interesting character can be introduced fully and placed within the context of the book. This is a suitable technique for booktalking such works as *Goodbye, Mr. Chips* or *Breakfast at Tiffanys*. Using the setting or atmosphere of the novel is a fourth method. Science fiction or fantasies with their often exotic, fascinating locales lend themselves frequently to such introductions.

Make sure you are honest in interpreting the book. To present, for example, *The Red Badge of Courage* as an exciting, action-filled war story is both a disservice to the book and a misrepresentation to the audience.

Some people write down their book talks and memorize them; others simply prepare them mentally. A rehearsal, however, is necessary to test pacing, presentation, timing, and sequencing. Perhaps friends, family, or colleagues can be an initial test audience. Tape recorders, or better yet video recorders, are also helpful in preparation. Though rehearsals are necessary, always try for sincerity, naturalness, and a relaxed atmosphere in the delivery. Because initial nervousness can be expected, be particularly careful to know thoroughly the beginning of the talk. Once one becomes used to the audience and the surroundings nervousness usually disappears. Introduce the theme quickly in a way that bridges the gap between the experience and interests of the audience and that of the contents of the books you wish to introduce. Be sure to mention both the author and the title of the book (often twice—once at the beginning and once at the end of the presentation), show off the book (dust jacket and covers can help sell a book and supply a visual reminder of the book), and then display the book (usually by standing it up on the desk). Try to adhere to principles of good public speaking—include the entire audience in your eye contact; don't fidget, rock, play with elastic bands or create other distractions; speak slowly with good intonation and use pauses effectively; and move quickly from one book to the next.

Fortunately there are many excellent guides to help one become a good booktalker. Joni Richards Bodart, a master booktalker, has written extensively on the subject. Bodart's *Booktalk! 2* (Wilson, 1985), an update of *Booktalk!* (Wilson, 1980), gives extensive guidance in preparation and delivery of book talks and supplies many brief examples. Sequels, *Booktalk! 3* (Wilson, 1988) and *Booktalk! 4* ( Wilson, 1992) give additional sample book talks. Bodart's 30-minute videotape *Booktalk* (also available from Wilson) supplies both tips and actual presentations.

Hazel Rochman, staff reviewer for young adult books at *Booklist*, also has a fine book and videotape on booktalking (both released in 1987). They are called *Tales of Love and Terror: Booktalking the Classics Old and New*, and are available from the American Library Association, as are two old standbys on the subject by Elinor Walker, *Book Bait* (ALA, 1988) and *Doors to More Mature Reading* (ALA, 1981). Some general books on teenage literature such as Alleen Pace Nilsen and Kenneth L. Donelson's *Literature for Today's Young Adults* (Scott, Foresman, 1989) also contain valuable sections on the subject. *Primaryplots* by Rebecca L. Thomas (Bowker, 1989; new edition forthcoming in 1993) is a book talk guide containing 150 recommended books for use with children ages 4 to 8. Also suggested are my own series of book talk guides. They are *Juniorplots* (Bowker, 1967), written with Diana Lembo and containing an introduction on booktalking by Doris Cole; *More Juniorplots* (Bowker, 1977), with a special section on booktalking by Mary K. Chelton; *Juniorplots 3* (Bowker, 1977) and *Seniorplots* (Bowker, 1989)—for use with readers ages 15 to 18—coauthored with Corinne J. Naden. *Middleplots 4*, also by Gillespie and Naden (Bowker, forthcoming 1993) is a selection guide for use with readers ages 8 to 12, and is a successor to *Introducing Books* (Bowker, 1970) by Diana Spirt, *Introducing More Books* (Bowker, 1978) by Gillespie and Lembo, and *Introducing Bookplots 3* (Bowker, 1988) by Spirt.

# 1

# Teenage Life and Concerns

TEENAGERS enjoy reading about their counterparts and in so doing explore the concerns, problems, and joys of adolescence. These novels explore various facets of growing up and delve into themes such as friendship, getting along in the family, school relationships, responsibility, first love, and reaching maturity.

**Ames, Mildred.** *Who Will Speak for the Lamb?*
   Harper, 1989, $13.95 (0-06-020111-8)

Mildred Ames has dabbled with both the occult and science fiction in such earlier young adult novels as *Conjuring Summer In* (Harper, 1986, $12.89) and *Anna to the Infinite Power* (pap., Scholastic, 1985, $2.50). In the present novel, however, she deals with the grim reality of the ill usage of animals and the animal rights movement. Julie, the central character, a senior high school student and former model, makes for an interesting heroine with whom readers can easily identify. This novel will interest readers in grades 7 through 10.

### Plot Summary
At the age of seventeen, Julie Peters has already worked as a successful model for nine years. The stress and pace of life on the modeling circuit caused her to have a nervous breakdown, so the family left New York and her father, a scientist, took a research job in a small college town on the West Coast. Julie has enrolled in Kennedy High School to spend her senior year as a normal teenager. She is relieved but fearful. Her psychiatrist back east told her that she needed to do things on her own. This is extremely difficult for Julie; her strong-willed mother has guided her life and career for many years, and even now Julie is aware that her

1

mother is very disappointed at having to end her daughter's successful career, with the money and fame it brought.

On the very first day of school, Julie gets caught up in a protest march. Laura Ryder is leading a student demonstration against the slaughtering of a lamb in an agricultural science class. Julie also meets Laura's college freshman brother, Jeff, who deliberately draws Julie into the protest, knowing that her name will make news and gain recognition for their animal rights group.

Julie's mother is furious at the notoriety, and Julie is annoyed at Jeff for exploiting her in this way. However, the two meet again when Laura arranges for Jeff to make some extra money giving Julie driving lessons. Despite their differences, Julie and Jeff are slowly drawn to one another. She tells him that although she knows her mother wants her to continue her modeling career, she herself is not at all sure that she is interested. Yet she knows how persuasive her mother is and feels that she cannot go against her wishes.

Surprisingly, Jeff has something of the same problem. Since his father's death, he has tried to placate his mother, who wishes him to continue in his father's work as a wildlife biologist. Jeff has discovered a fondness for the law, and secretly wishes to go to law school. His uncle has promised to help him get a scholarship to Stanford University.

Julie applies to a few colleges, Stanford among them, although her mother is insistent that she go to school in the East, Yale being the favorite. Her romance with Jeff progresses, much against her mother's wishes.

On a trip east for a few days, Julie learns that her mother is already making plans for her return to modeling after school. When the acceptance comes in the mail from Yale University, her mother assumes the matter is settled.

Jeff is urged by a friend in the animal rights group to take a menial job in the experimental research lab where Julie's mild-mannered father works. Jeff is horrified to see firsthand the deplorable conditions and torturous experiments that some of the animals endure for what seem to him frivolous reasons. Cats are caged with no litter pans; dogs stand in their own urine on bare cement floors; monkeys are given drugs until they are stoned out of their minds and die. The laboratory is filthy and barbaric. Jeff tells Julie what he has seen and accuses her father of inhumane behavior. Julie is shocked and angry at Jeff and the two part.

Soon after, the research lab is broken into and many animals are rescued. Julie is sure that Jeff is behind the break-in. When she tries to talk to her father about his work, she is dismayed to learn that this somewhat absentminded scientist she has adored seems unaware of the pain and suffering of the animals in his charge. To her father, any means seems to justify his ends.

Julie is confused and heartsick. She realizes that her father truly believes that the work he does is of benefit to humans and therefore acceptable. Part of Julie understands that, but the other part fights against it.

Julie and Jeff run into each other near the end of the school year. He apologizes for criticizing her father. She tells him that the unwanted publicity about the research lab has caused her father to consider taking a position back east, so the family will return and Julie will probably go to Yale. They talk about the lack of independence that each feels when dealing with their families.

That evening Jeff and his mother talk about the future. She expects him to spend the summer with her. Jeff chooses this moment to assert himself. He tells her he has decided to work in his uncle's law firm. He also tells her that he has been accepted at Stanford; he will go there and study law. Jeff is sorry about the lost, unhappy look in his mother's eyes when she reminds him that his father wanted him to study wildlife biology, but he says, "I can't do it just because it was what Dad wanted. I've got to find my own way."

Julie's conversation with Jeff has made an impression on her. After a talk with an avid animal rights advocate whom she met through Jeff, Julie returns home to learn from her mother that the family is planning to head back to New York as soon as Julie graduates. She will be going to Yale, they will live in New York City, and they will spend the summer in Scotland, where Julie can begin to resume her modeling career. Her mother directs her to send the acceptance letter to Yale.

As Julie goes to her room, she asks herself, "What about me? Is there any me?"

Julie writes the letter and then confronts her mother with the news that she will not be going to Yale; she has also been accepted at Stanford and that is where she will go. Her mother is horrified and indignant, but Julie stands her ground. It is even harder to stand up to her mother than it was to face a camera, but she is doing it. I'm not a child anymore, Julie thinks. I do have a voice. I just have to learn to use it.

It is graduation time at Kennedy High. After the ceremony, Julie meets Jeff again. They tell each other the surprising news that each will be at Stanford in the fall.

Julie and Jeff realize that they have taken a big step toward maturity. Each has found a voice in his or her destiny and is learning how to use it. For Julie the future is suddenly radiant.

### Thematic Material

This is an interesting and somewhat complicated story of coming of age that deals with many levels of social contact. Both Julie and Jeff are dominated by their mothers for different reasons; both are fearful of voicing their own desires and needs. Julie's father is portrayed as a decent, loving man who keeps himself somewhat removed both from his family and from any sense of responsibility that interferes with what he believes to be justified and proper work. The animal rights advocate friend of Jeff is shown as a reasonable person who firmly believes in her cause but understands the social and human problems that come into play concerning animals and medical experiments. The discussions of laboratory experiments and descriptions of lab conditions are graphic and distressing.

### Book Talk Material

Two strong themes dominate the book: the inability of both Julie and Jeff to voice their own feelings and concerns and the treatment of animals in lab experiments. See: Julie talks to the school principal about the demonstration (pp. 23–26); Julie and her mother discuss Laura and Jeff Ryder (pp. 60–61); Jeff listens while his mother makes plans (pp. 62–64); Jeff is shocked by the lab conditions (pp. 159–64); and Julie talks to her father about his work (pp. 185–86).

### Additional Selections

Paul Ross, editor of a school newspaper, embarks on a crusade to end drug dealing and vandalism in his school in Gloria D. Miklowitz's *The Emerson High Vigilantes* (Delacorte, 1988, $14.95).

School spirit gets out of hand when a rival school is attacked and Beth is arrested in Elaine Scott's *Choices* (Morrow, 1989, $12.95; pap., Archway, $2.95).

David and Lizzie adopt a reclusive neighbor for a school assignment with fatal results in Jenny Davis's *Sex Education* (Orchard, 1988, $13.95; pap., Dell, $2.95).

The son of an unpopular high school teacher is unable to live up to his father's great expectations in Alden R. Carter's *Wart, Son of Toad* (Putnam, 1985, $13.95; pap., Pacer, $2.50).

Twelve high school students attend a special writing seminar and also learn a great deal about themselves in Barbara Cohen's *Tell Us Your Secret* (Bantam, 1989, $13.95).

Brenda and a friend try to revolutionize the school newspaper in Jill Pinkwater's *Buffalo Brenda* (Macmillan, 1989, $13.95).

The controversy concerning a nuclear waste dump divides an English town and Lucy's family in Robert Swindells's *A Serpent's Tooth* (Holiday, 1989, $13.95).

Three teenagers are confused about the Vietnam War and draft resistance in Margaret Rostkowski's *The Best of Friends* (Harper, 1985, $14.95).

Barbara A. Lewis's *The Kid's Guide to Social Action* (Free Spirit, 1991, $14.95) is a manual on how people can make a difference by voicing opinions and influencing decisions on social issues.

### About the Book
*Booklist*, March 15, 1989, p. 1274.
*Center for Children's Books Bulletin*, April 1989, p. 187.
*Kirkus Reviews*, April 15, 1989, p. 620.
*School Library Journal*, March 1989, p. 191.
*VOYA*, June 1989, p. 97.
See also *Book Review Digest*, 1990, pp. 44–45; and *Book Review Index*, 1989, p. 21.

### About the Author
Commire, Anne, ed., *Something about the Author*. Gale, 1981, Vol. 22, pp. 14–15.
Evory, Ann, and Metzger, Linda, eds., *Contemporary Authors* (New Revision Series). Gale, 1984, Vol. 11, p. 22.
Holtze, Sally Holmes, ed., *Sixth Book of Junior Authors and Illustrators*. Wilson, 1989, pp. 6–7.

**Blume, Judy.** *Just as Long as We're Together*
Watts, 1987, $12.95 (0-531-05729-1); pap., Dell, $3.50 (0-440-40075-9)

This novel once again demonstrates Judy Blume's amazing knack of capturing the concerns and the language of early adolescence. Here, a group of girls face problems involving friends, family, first dates, and physical changes. The narrator, Stephanie, is a thirteen-year-old in her first year of junior high. Through her candid account of a series of crises, the episodic plot gains realism and cohesion. It is enjoyed by readers in grades 6 through 8.

**Plot Summary**

This is a warm and funny story about being almost thirteen and starting the seventh grade. It is also about changes and friendships and secrets and boys and heartaches.

As the school year begins, Stephanie finds herself with two best friends. There is Rachel, who is *very* smart and who has been Stephanie's best friend since second grade, and there is also Alison, recently moved to Connecticut from California. Alison is Vietnamese and adopted; her mother is a famous television personality. Stephanie's family consists of her mother and father and younger brother, Bruce, who has nightmares and is worried about the possibility of nuclear war.

Stephanie's father is away on business trips until Thanksgiving. When he returns and the family and relatives gather, Stephanie learns that her parents are in the midst of a trial separation. She is upset that they have tried to keep this problem from her.

Everything goes wrong for Stephanie. Rachel is put into an enriched ninth-grade math class and doesn't even tell her. How can you be best friends if you keep secrets? Rachel tries to explain that she didn't want to tell her because she was afraid Stephanie would be mad. Stephanie tends to take out her anger in eating. Her mother notices that she is gaining weight and decides that Stephanie should go on a diet.

For Christmas vacation, Stephanie and Bruce visit their father, who has temporarily settled on the West Coast. They meet his "friend" Iris, and Stephanie realizes her father is having what she terms a "fling." She behaves outrageously to the woman.

Back home after the disastrous trip, Stephanie talks with her mother about the possibility of her parents' divorce, something Stephanie does not want to face. Events reach a pinnacle of unhappiness for Stephanie on the day Max Wilson comes to class for the first time and Stephanie's friend Eric Macaulay introduces her to the new boy as "El Chunko." It is time for a diet.

One bright spot in the year occurs when Bruce wins second place in a "kids for peace" contest and is invited to the White House to meet the president. Disaster strikes again for Stephanie when she has a fight with Rachel. During the argument, the subject of keeping things from one another comes up. Rachel accuses Stephanie of doing that very thing concerning her parents' separation. "You don't see anything you don't want to see," Rachel says. "You don't face reality. You live in some kind of sick fantasy world."

No amount of urging by her mother will get Stephanie to make up with Rachel. On Stephanie's thirteenth birthday, she attends the Ground Hog Day dance at school and is surprised to find that some of the boys actually know how to dance. She also gets her first period that night.

Weeks pass and Stephanie and Rachel are still not speaking. Rachel's mother meets Stephanie and tells her how much Rachel needs her friendship. She says she understands how difficult her parents' separation must be, but that Stephanie should not take her anger out on her best friend. Could that possibly be what she is doing?

Soon after, her father calls from the West Coast to announce that he has broken off his friendship with Iris and will be moving to New York, so they will be seeing more of each other. Stephanie approaches her mother and asks if this means they will be getting back together. Her mother says that this is possible but not likely. This angers Stephanie once again.

March comes around and everyone seems to have the flu. Before Alison keels over with it, she tells Stephanie that her adopted parents are "pregnant," and instead of being happy, Alison is terrified that they won't love her as much. Stephanie talks to her mother and they both agree that from now on they will say just what they feel. "It's not good to hold in feelings . . . anger and resentment build up that way."

Seven weeks after the fight between Rachel and Stephanie, Alison is recovering from the flu and has come to terms with the news of the impending birth. She is even helping to pick a name. After all, she tells Steph, if things don't work out, she can always run away after the baby is born.

Later, Stephanie runs into Rachel. The two old friends begin to walk together, quietly at first. Then they begin to explain their feelings and how hurt each has been because of the actions of the other. The two girls part with assurances of seeing each other the next day.

Stephanie wonders what Alison will say when she tells her that she and Rachel are speaking, that maybe they are even friends again. Probably she'll be glad, Stephanie thinks. With that, she breaks off a sprig of forsythia and rings Alison's bell.

### Thematic Material

This is a standard, readable story filled with the humorous aspects of coming of age. Stephanie is a likable young heroine with all the insecurities and needs of a normal almost-thirteen-year-old. Her stubborn attitude about the impending breakup of her parents' marriage is understandable, and her passionate ups and downs about friendship and boys offer an enjoyable story of teenage life.

### Book Talk Material

Stephanie's conversations with "best friends" Rachel and Alison serve as a fine introduction to this teenage novel. See: Stephanie and Rachel discuss her bedroom posters and walk each other home (pp. 4–8); Stephanie meets Alison (pp. 9–14); school begins (pp. 23–26); and Rachel and Stephanie go to see Alison's talking dog (pp. 32–36).

### Additional Selections

Three children discover that their mother's new baby-sitter is really their father in disguise in Anne Fine's *Alias Madame Doubtfire* (Little, Brown, 1988, $12.95; pap., Bantam, $3.50).

When Holly's mother proposes that she and her seventh-grade daughter leave New York City and return to Iowa, Holly goes to outlandish ends to prevent the move in Jan Greenberg's comic *Just the Two of Us* (Farrar, 1988, $12.95; pap., $3.95).

A self-styled high school shrink, Adriana Earthlight, decides to work on herself in Bonnie Zindel's *Dr. Adriana Earthlight* (Viking, 1988, $11.95).

Marilyn, a seventh-grader, feels the first rush of romance in Merrill Joan Gerber's *I'd Rather Think about Robby* (Harper, 1989, $11.95; pap., $3.50).

Members of an eighth-grade English class bring two shy students together in a comic production in *Romeo and Juliet Together (and Alive!) at Last* by Avi (Orchard, 1987, $11.95; pap., Avon, $2.50).

Shirley secretly and against her mother's wishes begins a catering business in Judie Angell's *Leave the Cooking to Me* (Bantam, 1990, $13.95; pap., $3.50).

Jessica enters junior high school and is ridiculed by friends who say her dress looks like a Wonder Bread wrapper in *Wonder* (Orchard, 1991, $13.95) by Rachael Vail.

**About the Book**
*Book Report,* January 1988, p. 31.
*Booklist,* August 1987, p. 741.
*Center for Children's Books Bulletin,* September 1987, p. 3.
*Horn Book,* January 1988, p. 66.
*Kirkus Reviews,* July 1987, p. 987.
*New York Times Book Review,* November 1987, p. 33.
*School Library Journal,* September 1987, p. 177.
*VOYA,* February 1988, p. 278.
See also *Book Review Digest,* 1988, pp. 167–68; and *Book Review Index,* 1987, p. 79, and 1988, p. 85.

**About the Author**
Chevalier, Tracy, ed., *Twentieth-Century Children's Writers* (3rd ed.). St. James, 1989, pp. 99–101.
Commire, Anne, ed., *Something about the Author.* Gale, 1983, Vol. 31, pp. 28–34.
de Montreville, Doris, and Crawford, Elizabeth D., eds., *Fourth Book of Junior Authors and Illustrators.* Wilson, 1978, pp. 46–47.
Estes, Glenn E., ed., *American Writers for Children since 1960: Fiction* (Dictionary of Literary Biography: Vol. 52). Gale, 1986, pp. 30–38.
Kirkpatrick, D. L., ed., *Twentieth-Century Children's Writers* (2nd ed.). St. Martin's, 1983, pp. 93–95.
Lee, Betsey, *Judy Blume's Story.* Dillon, 1989.
Riley, Carolyn, ed., *Children's Literature Review.* Gale, 1976, Vol. 2, pp. 15–19.
Senick, Gerard J., ed., *Children's Literature Review.* Gale, 1988, Vol. 15, pp. 57–82.
Ward, Martha, ed., *Authors of Books for Young People* (3rd ed.). Scarecrow, 1990, pp. 68–69.
Weidt, Maryann. *Presenting Judy Blume.* Twayne, 1989.

## Carter, Alden R. *Up Country*

Putnam, 1989, $15.95 (0-399-21583-2); pap., Scholastic, $2.95
(0-590-43638-4)

Alden Carter writes nonfiction books on such subjects as national and international affairs as well as realistic fiction in which young adults achieve growth through facing and overcoming personal problems. For example, in *Growing Season* (Putnam, 1984, $13.95; pap., $2.25), Rick, a high school senior, learns to accept responsibility when his parents move from a big city to a Wisconsin dairy farm. In *Up Country,* a somewhat similar situation is presented as sixteen-year-old Carl Staggers is sent to stay with country relatives. It is read and enjoyed by youngsters in grades 7 through 10.

### Plot Summary

When the Milwaukee police knock on his door, sixteen-year-old Carl Staggers has two reasons to worry. For one thing, there are on his work-bench half a dozen stolen car stereos he has been repairing. For another, there is his mother, thirty-eight-year-old Veronica, who has a drinking problem and a habit of bringing strange men home at night.

This time it turns out to be Mom. She got involved in a fight in a bar and nearly killed someone by hitting him over the head with a bottle. Carl, who can't remember his father though in a snapshot the man looks something like a cowboy, digs into his "Plan" money and bails her out.

Carl's Plan stems from his discovery that he can fix just about anything electric. The Plan money is going to get him away from this place and this life. "The plan [is] going to get me out," Carl says. "I'm going to be valedictorian of my class and land the biggest scholarship around. Then I'm going to get an engineering degree and find a life I can stand. Because I can't stand the one I've had. I'm sorry my mother's a drunken whore, but it ain't my problem. I'm going to get what I want. And I really don't care if I have to run over people and rules to get it." The rules that Carl runs over involve his pal Steve, who steals stereos from cars. He brings them to Carl, who fixes them up. They then sell them, and Carl stashes away his share for the Plan.

After the bailout, Mom stays clean until Christmas vacation and then is picked up for drunk driving. Carl can't bail her out because she is sent away for treatment at a rehabilitation center. Carl says he can take care of himself but both the law and social worker Mullan say no. It is decided to send Carl to Blind River in northern Wisconsin—up country—to his mother's brother and sister-in-law, Uncle Glen and Aunt June, whom Carl hasn't seen in years. He will stay with them and attend school until his mother's rehabilitation is finished.

Reluctantly, Carl takes the bus to Blind River, a small rural community north of Green Bay, Wisconsin. He figures that life will be boring, but he'll just hang on for a couple of months until Mom is through with the treatment and he can get back to Milwaukee and the Plan.

Carl is slowly and reluctantly drawn into life in the north country. His aunt and uncle are kind and fair and his cousin Bob, their youngest son and about Carl's age, is tolerable. Still, Carl resists any involvement with school or new friends, even the friendship of Signa Amundsen, who takes an obvious interest in him. He is determined to get back to Milwaukee.

However, weekly phone conversations with his mother make it clear that Veronica is not responding to treatment. For the first time, Carl begins to think that perhaps his Plan is not going to work out—that when he and his mother return to Milwaukee it will start all over again: the drinking, the men, the bailing her out of trouble. It does not, however, appear to Carl that he has any other choice; she is his mother and it is his responsibility to help her. It is as though he is responsible for her drinking problem, or at least guilty of not being able to help her. He even refuses Aunt June's offer to talk it over.

Little by little, Carl is drawn into life in the rural community, including a budding romance with Signa. The school principal, Mr. Dowdy, tries to tell Carl that he is not responsible for his mother's drinking problem.

More complications occur when the Milwaukee police summon Carl back home to the city. They are looking for Carl's old buddy Steve, the one who stole all the car stereos. Carl thinks that his involvement with the theft ring will be uncovered, but the police are more interested in locating Steve, which they do, for a bigger crime. With his mother still in rehabilitation, Carl is given a choice of going to a foster home or returning up country. He goes north once again.

Back in the rural environment, he begins to think hard about what Dowdy, the principal, and Mullan, the social worker, have been trying to tell him. Carl begins to see that he has almost been programmed by the alcoholism of his mother. He has been a robot, not an individual. He might as well have the initials C.A.—Child of an Alcoholic—stamped across his chest. He tells himself that it doesn't have to be that way.

Carl checks out every available book in the library on alcohol and drug abuse. He also confides in Signa about the Plan and about his fears for the future. Because of his involvement with the stolen car stereos, he believes he will be sent either to reform school or back home with his mother. Either way, he loses; either way he loses his dream.

Mullan telephones from Milwaukee with the news that he will recommend that Carl not be sent away. Instead, Mullan will suggest a supervised environment with the stipulation that Carl make restitution for the stereos—a total of about $3,000, which he will have to earn. Assuming that the judge will go along with these proposals, Mullan asks Carl what he wants to do with his future. Where will he go? Carl takes a deep breath and replies, "Back to my mother's. I've got to help her if I can," Carl tells the social worker.

In a Milwaukee courtroom with his mother, Carl receives a warning from the judge: If he follows society's rules, he has a promising future. If he breaks the rules, he will come back before the court to pay for that decision.

Carl returns to his seat beside his mother, but facing a return to his old life, something newly born in him makes him speak up: "I can't do it," he tells the court. "I can't go back to her," he says to the social worker. "I just can't risk everything on her. She might start drinking, and I can't live through that again."

With Carl's mother at his side, the court rules that he be allowed to live up country with his aunt and uncle. When Carl says good-bye to his mother, she tells him she will see him when she gets straightened out. "I'm never coming back," he tells her honestly. "I know, baby, I know," she replies.

Carl goes home to his new family, to school, to Signa, and to a new life up country.

**Thematic Material**

This story presents an interesting, realistic picture of how alcohol abuse by a parent can turn a child's life upside down. Carl accepts his mother's alcoholism as though he is somehow responsible for it; because he is unable to stop her from drinking, he feels in some way guilty of encouraging her. Carl is a bright, talented young man; he is aware that what he is doing with the car stereos is wrong, but he rationalizes that his Plan for giving himself a better life outweighs other considerations. It is only when he is able to let down the barriers that prevent other people from reaching him with their caring and their love that he can truly understand right from wrong and see that he can love his mother and still not allow her to ruin his dreams and his chance at life.


### Book Talk Material

The contrast between Carl's life in Milwaukee and life in Blind River can serve as an excellent introduction to this study of a boy in turmoil. See: the police knock on the door (pp. 8–10); meeting Mom in the courtroom (pp. 15–20); Mom brings a stranger home for Christmas (pp. 45–49). Also see: Carl arrives in Blind River (pp. 82–87); meeting the principal (pp. 90–93); and Carl takes over the lesson on electricity (pp. 114–16).


### Additional Selections

A ten-year-old girl is sent to live with an eccentric uncle and a quarrelsome aunt whom she grows to despise in Paula Fox's *The Village by the Sea* (Orchard, 1988, $13,95; pap., Dell, $3.50).

During a family reunion to celebrate her grandmother's birthday, sixteen-year-old Laura confronts complex relationships involving her grandmother, her mother, and herself in Norma Johnston's *The Potter's Wheel* (Morrow, 1988, $12.95).

During the Depression, Amanda leaves her working-class home to live with a sophisticated aunt in Memphis in George Ella Lyon's *Borrowed Children* (Orchard, 1988, $12.95; pap., Bantam, $2.95).

Thirteen-year-old Lisa finds she has time on her hands when her retarded brother is sent to school and her attention becomes focused on Robert, a new boy in school, in Joseph McNair's *Commander Coatrack Returns* (Houghton, 1989, $13.95).

Bernie, age sixteen, proves her worth through a friendship with a rock singer in Marc Talbert's *Rabbit in the Rock* (Dial, 1989, $14.95).

Salina's placid life in the mountains of Tennessee is disrupted by the arrival of a new girl, Scooter Russell, in Alana J. White's *Come Next Spring* (Clarion, 1990, $13.95).

Thirteen-year-old Tommy (a nickname for Tamara) is sent to Maine to live with a father she doesn't know in Deborah Moulton's *Summer Girl* (Dial, 1992, $15).

For stories of male teenagers being uprooted, see Additional Selections under S. E. Hinton's *Taming the Star Runner*.

**About the Book**
*Booklist,* July 1989, p. 1891.
*Center for Children's Books Bulletin,* July 1989, p. 270.
*Horn Book,* July 1989, p. 486.
*Kirkus Reviews,* June 15, 1989, p. 913.
*School Library Journal,* June 1989, p. 121.
*VOYA,* August 1989, p. 155.
See also *Book Review Digest,* 1989, pp. 260–61; and *Book Review Index,* 1989, p. 137.

**About the Author**
Commire, Anne, ed., *Something about the Author.* Gale, 1992, Vol. 67, pp. 40–43.
Senick, Gerard J., ed., *Children's Literature Review.* Gale, 1991, Vol. 22, pp. 16–23.

---

**Cole, Brock.** *The Goats*
Farrar, 1987, $13.95 (0-374-32678-9); pap., $3.50 (0-374-42575-2)

---

When *The Goats,* the author's first novel for young adults, first appeared in 1987, Brock Cole was already known as a writer and illustrator of several successful picture books for children. This novel was a great critical success and was followed two years later by *Celine* (Farrar, 1989, $13.95), the story of a confused high school junior who, like Holden Caulfield before her, is trying to distinguish between the phony and artificial in life and the sincere and genuine. During this quest, she befriends a lonely second-grader named Josh, who, because of his parents' separation, feels isolated and unwanted. The story's subject matter and thematic material make it suitable for slightly more advanced readers. *Celine* is recommended for readers in grades 8 through 10 and *The Goats* for upper-elementary through junior high grades. The title, *The Goats,* refers to two thirteen-year-olds—a boy and a girl—who are victims of a cruel practical joke while at summer camp. The locale is a rural area that, one gathers, is a few hours outside Chicago. The action takes place over a period of five days.

**Plot Summary**
Howie cannot believe what is happening to him. What was to have been an evening cookout on Goat Island with some of his companions at summer camp turns into a nightmare. Boys he thought were friends grab him, strip him, and head back for shore in the canoes. Scared and

confused, he discovers a tent platform and inside it a girl named Laura, wrapped in a blanket and sobbing. She, too, has been stripped and left behind. The two realize that they are this year's camp goats—the misfits and outsiders who are so socially immature and vulnerable that they become easy victims of the other campers' cruelty.

Soon the two hear the distant voices of camp counselors, who have come to the island to rescue them. Both are determined not to face the humiliation of returning to camp. Instead, they find a log on the beach, roll it into the water, and, clinging desperately to it, paddle toward the shore.

They are hours in the water and Laura, who is unable to swim, escapes drowning only with Howie's help. At daybreak they reach shore and Howie drags Laura onto the beach. They break into a boarded-up summer cottage where they find some clothes and ease their hunger with canned goods. They also learn a little about each other. Laura lives alone with her mother, a businesswoman who has sent Laura to camp to learn how to make friends. Howie's parents are archaeologists, currently excavating sites in Turkey.

They decide that Laura must ask her mother to come and get them. They clean up the cottage before leaving, try to repair the break-in damage, and then head for the municipal beach, where they know there are telephones.

Laura guiltily steals some money from the change compartment of a parked pickup truck and calls her mother, Maddy Golden. Laura is unable to explain coherently what has happened and begins crying. Maddy, unaware of her daughter's desperate situation, promises to come two days later, during Parents' Weekend, but shortly after she hangs up, she is contacted by camp officials who say that her daughter has disappeared. She leaves work immediately to help find her daughter.

Pretending to be an assistant to the beach attendant, Howie secures the keys to the clothes lockers of two teenage bathers. After a quick change, the two look a little less conspicuous but decide to leave the beach area, where they are certain camp counselors will be searching for them.

At a gas station, they see two parked school buses and mingle with a group of inner-city youngsters, mostly black, who are headed for camp. Two of them, Tiwanda and Calvin, befriend them and offer to help. In the general confusion of departure, Howie and Laura board the bus undetected and soon find themselves at another summer camp. Nicknamed "Bonnie and Clyde" by their new friends, Howie and Laura are accepted into the group, who share their possessions and accommodations with them and keep their presence secret. Only one, a street-smart boy named Pardoe, gives them a little trouble, but the rest are friendly and show a refreshing excitement and delight in life.

The following morning, Tiwanda gives the youngsters $5 before they leave. Laura makes another phone call to her mother and, receiving no answer, leaves a message on her answering machine. In the meantime, Maddy, now at the camp, checks on her messages and discovers to her relief that Laura and Howie are alive and wandering about somewhere in the vicinity.

Laura's period starts and she is forced to spend most of their remaining money on tampons. Outside a motel, they see a husband, wife, and daughter vacating their room. Laura has a brilliant idea. Before the vacationers depart, she finds out that they are the Hendricks family, then after entering the suite and retrieving the key, she phones the switchboard and, pretending to be the daughter, tells the operator that her parents are at a local garage with car trouble and want to stay an extra night. She and Howie, who is now suffering from a bad cold, move in. The two are exhausted. Laura innocently crawls into bed with Howie to help end his attack of shivers, but unknown to them, they are being spied on by a cleaning lady, Mrs. Purse, who suspects the worst.

That evening the two go to the motel's restaurant and have a good meal, intending to charge it on their motel bill. At the cash register, Laura is confronted by Mrs. Purse, who escorts her back to the motel for an explanation of the whereabouts of the Hendrickses and of her unseemly behavior that afternoon. Luckily Howie is able to activate a fire alarm and they both escape. They spend the night in an unlocked parked car.

The following day is Saturday, the day of the promised rescue. A major problem is getting to camp some ten miles away. On the highway, they are picked up by a scruffy man who offers them a ride. He claims to be a deputy sheriff, but the youngsters become frightened when he pulls off the main highway, stops at a pay phone, and locks them in his Jeepster. Howie notices that the keys are in the car. While driving off they accidentally run over the foot of a very surprised deputy sheriff, who was only trying to notify his boss that he had located the two missing children.

After abandoning the truck, the two borrow some money from an old man at a farmstand to make phone calls. From the camp headquarters, Laura learns that her mother is staying at a local motel. When they reach her by phone, Laura tries to explain how much she and Howie mean to each other and that they must not be separated until after his parents return from Turkey. Her mother promises and is soon on her way to pick them up. Howie, however, is so fearful of being left alone and sent back to camp that he runs into the woods. Laura chases after him and reassures him that no one will ever come between them. Hand in hand, they return to the highway.

**Thematic Material**

This is a novel of both survival and discovery. Two unwanted, unattractive losers not only find ways to live by their own wits and intelligence, but also discover inner resources and self-worth that they did not know they had. The growing respect and love that the two feel for each other is touchingly portrayed. The fact that the author refers to the two principal characters as "the boy" and "the girl" and keeps geographical details to a minimum adds universality to the story. The episode with the inner-city children shows that even among those with few possessions, kindness, understanding, and sharing are still possible and that there is a "oneness" with all who are abused and forgotten. The emergence of Maddy's deeper feelings concerning her daughter's welfare is an important subtheme. Other ideas explored are the unthinking cruelty people can inflict on others, the problem of outsiders, the discovery of the power to love, and the excitement that accompanies accomplishing something worthwhile. On another level, this is also a rousing, suspenseful adventure story.

**Book Talk Material**

An explanation of the title (perhaps it could have been called *The Sacrifical Lambs?*) should interest readers. The novel is filled with brief self-contained episodes suitable for book talks. Some are: abandonment on the island and beginning the trip to shore (pp. 3–16); the stay at the beach cottage (pp. 18–31); stealing clothes at the beach (pp. 41–47); meeting Calvin and Tiwanda and the episode with Pardoe (pp. 69–86); and gaining entry to the motel (pp. 113–23).

**Additional Selections**

Wil Newton is mysteriously drawn to an island in the middle of a beautiful lake in the isolated northwoods in Gary Paulsen's *The Island* (Orchard, 1988, $13.95; pap., Dell, $3.50).

The timid son of a businessman and an abused sixteen-year-old girl work out their problem while sharing quarters in London in *The Other Side of the Fence* (Delacorte, 1988, $14.95) by Jean Ure.

Summer camp is not the fun and games expected by twelve-year-old Betsy, who has a weight problem, in *Bathing Ugly* (Orchard, 1989, $13.95; pap., Dell, $3.50) by Rebecca Busselle.

Marina escapes into silence after her father accidentally disfigures her in *So Much to Tell You* (Little, Brown, 1989, $13.95) by John Marsden.

In *Circle of Light* (Harper, 1989, $13.95) by Elaine Corbeil Roe, an eighth-grade girl reluctantly trains for a scholarship competition.

Wardy Spinks, a fourteen-year-old nerd, finds comfort in the friendship of a German exchange teacher who, unfortunately, demands total devotion in Susan Coryell's *Eaglebait* (Harcourt, 1989, $14.95).

At age thirteen, Chester is given the terrible task of choosing which parent he should live with in Marc Talbert's *Pillow of Clouds* (Dial, 1991, $14.95).

In Vivien Alcock's *A Kind of Thief* (Delacorte, 1992, $14), a thirteen-year-old girl must take charge of her household when her father is sent to prison awaiting trial for fraud.

**About the Book**
*Booklist*, November 15, 1987, p. 564.
*Center for Children's Books Bulletin*, October 1987, p. 24.
*Horn Book*, January 1988, p. 68.
*Kirkus Reviews*, September 1, 1987, p. 1318.
*New York Times Book Review*, November 8, 1987, p. 31.
*School Library Journal*, November 1987, p. 113.
*VOYA*, April 1988, p. 22.
*Wilson Library Bulletin*, January 1988, p. 75.
See also *Book Review Digest*, 1988, p. 336; and *Book Review Index*, 1987, p. 152, and 1988, p. 163.

**About the Author**
Holtze, Sally Holmes, ed., *Sixth Book of Junior Authors and Illustrators*. Wilson, 1989, pp. 62–63.
Senick, Gerard J., ed., *Children's Literature Review*. Gale, 1989, Vol. 18, pp. 81–85.

**Collier, James Lincoln.** *Outside Looking In*
Macmillan, 1987, $13.95 (0-02-723100-3); pap., Avon, $2.95 (0-380-70961-9)

Adult readers probably know James Lincoln Collier best as a writer of books about jazz including biographies of Benny Goodman and Duke Ellington. In the field of juvenile literature, he leads a double life. With his brother, the historian Christopher Collier, he has written excellent novels dealing with American history such as *My Brother Sam Is Dead* (Four Winds, 1974, $14.95; pap., Scholastic, $2.50; condensed in *More Juniorplots,* Bowker, 1977, pp. 79–82), which tells the moving story of a family torn apart by the American Revolution, and *The Winter Hero* (pap., Scholastic, 1985, $2.75; condensed in *Juniorplots 3,* Bowker, 1987, pp. 210–14), a novel that uses Shays's Rebellion as a background. Independently he writes novels like this one that deal with contemporary issues. Among these are *When the Stars Begin to Fall* (Delacorte, 1986, $14.95; pap., Dell, $2.95) and *The Winchesters* (Macmillan, 1988, $13.95; pap., Avon, $2.95). *Outside Looking In* is a first-person narrative and, like the above-mentioned titles, is suitable for readers in grades 6 through 9.

**Plot Summary**
With each passing day, fourteen-year-old Fergy Wheeler is becoming more disheartened and despairing about the nomadic existence he and his eight-year-old sister, Ooma, endure with their parents, Gussie and J. P., and their companions, a black college dropout named the Wiz and his girlfriend, Trotsky. Ever since the Wheelers, with the Wiz and Trotsky, left their commune, stealing the two vans the commune shared, life has been an endless succession of parking lots, trailer parks, and public rest stops. At shopping centers and street corners, they engage in the same well-developed routine. Fergy and Ooma collect a crowd by singing and playing their guitars and then J. P. moves in to sell his bottles of honey ("a sure cure for high blood pressure") or cheap good-luck amulets. Provided the cops don't move them on, he will then distribute printed excerpts from his *Journal*—a series of diatribes against the materialism and fascism that, he religiously believes, permeate all aspects of contemporary American life. When cash is low, J. P. and his friends are not above stealing, an act that is regarded as reclaiming that which rightfully belongs to them.

Although J. P. seems to have been born a nonconforming hippie, this is not the case with Gussie. When Ooma and Fergy ask about her past, she sometimes recalls wistfully, in spite of J. P.'s protests, her life as the only child of very strict and very wealthy proper Bostonians, the Hamiltons of Cambridge. When she was only sixteen, now fifteen years ago, she met and became infatuated with J. P., who was in Boston organizing a peace rally. They ran away together and although her mother and father tried every stratagem to bring their daughter back, including having J. P. jailed temporarily, the two have remained a couple ever since. Unknown to J. P., Gussie, who like Fergy is increasingly discontent with this vagabond life, has maintained contact with her parents.

J. P. seems impervious to Fergy's unhappiness. Fergy longs for some structure in his life and a chance to attend school so he can learn to read and write. He also is concerned about his completely illiterate sister, Ooma, whose name means "filled with sweetness and light." Fergy sees that she is rapidly becoming a foul-mouthed hellion with an incurable urge to steal.

After fleeing a shopping mall in New Jersey because Ooma is caught stealing a Walkman, the six drive into New York City to try their luck. In Soho, J. P.'s pitch is once again interrupted by police. Ooma has been caught lifting $100 from a cash register. Later, in a New Jersey shopping mall, the young girl takes a portable radio from an appliance store, and while trying to escape the police, J. P. is involved in an accident that totals one of the vans.

Now all six are forced to share a single van. They find a pleasant federal campground in Pennsylvania and decide to use it as headquarters while working the towns and malls in the area. However, they all know that something must be done about their intolerable living conditions. Their neighbors are Mr. and Mrs. Clapper, a pair of retired schoolteachers who live in a spacious motor home. Fergy is surprised when J. P. encourages him and Ooma to become friendly with this kindly couple because the Clappers seem to epitomize all the middle-class values their father detests.

The two youngsters quickly grow to love the Clappers, who give them regular wholesome meals and seem genuinely concerned about their future. Returning to the campsite after a picnic with the children one day, the Clappers discover that their beautiful motor home has been stolen. Fergy also notices that Wiz has disappeared and that his father seems overly solicitious toward the elderly couple. The boy realizes with horror that his father is responsible for the theft.

A few days later, after the Clappers have returned to their permanent home, Fergy and family travel to North Carolina, where they find the Wiz and move into the repainted and disguised motor home. Fergy is so dismayed at these developments that he begins making plans to run away with Ooma to the grandparents he has yet to meet.

One night when they are in Kansas, he seizes the opportunity. Taking a few clothes, some road maps, and the money he finds in J. P.'s wallet, Fergy and his sister steal out of the motor home. After walking all night, they hitch a ride with a passing motorist but, when they stop for gas, Fergy realizes the driver is contacting the police. They escape and after hitching another ride are deposited at a shopping mall where, to their horror, they see in the distance the motor home and their parents, who are searching for them. The two dive into a truck that is delivering carpets at one of the loading docks. Suddenly the doors are closed, and the truck takes off. They travel overnight, destination unknown. When the truck is opened in the morning, they find themselves at the Acme Carpet Company in Washington, D.C. Using the last of their money, Fergy buys two bus tickets to Boston, and soon the two waifs are on the doorstep of the highly respected Hamiltons of Cambridge.

In the next few days, Fergy succeeds in his attempts to fit into the patrician ways of his grandparents, whom he discovers are far from being the ogres J. P. had portrayed. With Ooma, however, it is different. She longs to be back with her mother and shows her rebellious nature by stealing from one of the servants. To resolve this situation, the Hamiltons hire a detective to locate their daughter. Before he can report back, however, Gussie telephones. In an effort to locate her children, she had gone to the police, who, during their investigation, identified the stolen motor home. Now, she and J. P. are in jail being held for $10,000 bail. The Hamiltons wire the money and soon Gussie and J. P. are in Cambridge. J. P. demands his children in spite of Fergy's announcement that he will never go back to his father. Gussie knows that for the sake of her children she, too, must end this vagrant, dead-end life, particularly after she discovers that J. P. plans to skip bail rather than face a possible jail sentence. Until she can make more permanent arrangements, she moves in with her parents. A helpless and defeated J. P. leaves. Fergy at last has the home he longed for.

**Thematic Material**

Fergy's problems illustrate the need for structure and discipline in children's lives and the conflict that young people often have choosing between family loyalties and their own need for self-development. Two life-styles—one of radical rebellion and the other of conservative conformity—are explored in the novel. Other themes are personal courage, the need to accept responsibility for one's actions, various concepts of what constitutes freedom and dignity, and ethical and moral problems that arise when an individual is in conflict with society.

**Book Talk Material**

Some interesting passages that can introduce the book are: Ooma is caught stealing a Walkman (pp. 1–7); Fergy talks about his past (pp. 7–13); getting busted in Soho (pp. 20–26); Fergy tries to explain his problems to J. P. (pp. 29–35); Ooma and the stolen radio (pp. 40–46); and Fergy and Ooma meet the Clappers (pp. 53–60).

**Additional Selections**

Kate runs away to live with her Cherokee grandfather in *The Fledglings* by Sandra Markle (Bantam, 1992, $15).

Sixteen-year-old Sidonie and her older sister have difficulty adjusting to their mother's death in Martha Brooks's *Two Moons in August* (Little, Brown, 1992, $14.95).

In Robert Cormier's *Tunes for Bears to Dance To* (Delacorte, 1992, $15), an eleven-year-old boy is bribed by an evil man to destroy a Holocaust survivor's handiwork.

Thirteen-year-old Tommy is sent to live with her father whom she hasn't seen in ten years in Deborah Moulton's *Summer Girl* (Dial, 1992, $15).

During the summer of 1943, Henry, a thirteen-year-old orphan, is hired to work on an Ohio farm in *A Place to Claim as Home* by Patricia Willis (Clarion, 1991, $13.95).

In Jean Davies Okimoto's *Molly by Any Other Name* (Scholastic, 1990, $13.95), Molly, an Asian girl adopted by a white family, searches for her birth mother.

Shep, a fifteen-year-old boy, desperately wants reunion with his father in Cynthia D. Grant's *Keep Laughing* (Atheneum, 1991, $14.95).

A homeless eleven-year-old boy learns to survive on the streets of New York City in *Monkey Island* (Orchard, 1991, $14.95) by Paula Fox.

**About the Book**
*Book Report,* September 1987, p. 36.
*Booklist,* April 1, 1987, p. 1203.
*Center for Children's Books Bulletin,* May 1987, p. 164.
*Kirkus Reviews,* March 1, 1987, p. 371.
*School Library Journal,* May 1987, p. 96.
See also *Book Review Digest,* 1988, p. 343; and *Book Review Index,* 1987, p. 154.

**About the Author**
Chevalier, Tracy, ed., *Twentieth-Century Children's Writers* (3rd ed.). St. James, 1989, pp. 223–24.
Commire, Anne, ed., *Something about the Author.* Gale, 1977, Vol. 8, pp. 33–34.
Evory, Ann, ed., *Contemporary Authors* (New Revision Series). Gale, 1981, Vol. 4, pp. 149–50.
Holtze, Sally Holmes, ed., *Fifth Book of Junior Authors and Illustrators.* Wilson, 1983, pp. 78–80.
Kinsman, Clare D., ed., *Contemporary Authors* (First Revision). Gale, 1974, Vols. 9–12, p. 179.
Senick, Gerard J., ed., *Children's Literature Review.* Gale, 1987, Vol. 3, pp. 44–49.
Ward, Martha, ed., *Authors of Books for Young People* (3rd ed.). Scarecrow, 1990, p. 224.

---

**Conrad, Pam.**   *My Daniel*
Harper, 1989, $13.00 (0-06-021313-2); pap., $3.95 (0-06-440309-2)

---

Pam Conrad has written a series of fine realistic novels for young adults. Among them are *Holding Me Here* (Harper, 1986, $11.92; pap., Bantam, $2.95), about a young girl's futile attempts to help a divorced woman hide from her abusive former husband, and a story of two girls' friendship, *Taking the Ferry Home* (Harper, 1988, $11.95). In *My Daniel,* the author artfully constructs plot shifts between the present, in which a grandmother and her two grandchildren visit a natural history museum, and long ago, when the brother of Julia, now a grandmother, searched for dinosaur bones and encountered an evil fossil collector. It is suitable for readers in grades 6 through 9.

**Plot Summary**
As the story opens, eighty-year-old Julia Creath Summerwaite has just stepped off a plane from Nebraska. It is her first trip east. She is visiting her youngest son and her two grandchildren, twelve-year-old Ellie and

her younger brother, Stevie. Julia makes it clear that she has made the trip for only one reason. She wants to go to the Natural History Museum alone with her grandchildren. Her son suspects she wants to see the dinosaur bones.

A few days later, as requested, Ellie's father drives Grandma Summerwaite and the children to the Natural History Museum, promising to pick them up at the end of the afternoon. Once inside, the threesome slowly makes its way to the fourth floor and the dinosaurs. They stop now and again so that Grandma can rest or Stevie can explore some interesting site. As they proceed, the old lady seems to drift back in time.

What is history on the Nebraska prairie comes alive for her modern-day grandchildren as she tells them stories of long ago when she was a young girl on the farm. She talks of her brother, their long-dead Uncle Daniel, whom she loved, in her words, "with a white fire."

At sixteen, Daniel's passion in life was fossils. Grandma recounts the morning that she, just a little girl then, and her brother followed behind Ma and Pa working the fields. Suddenly Daniel dropped to his knees in delight. He pulled rocks from the dirt and, licking his fingers, cleaned them and brought to life the delicate designs of clams and tiny seashells. "Fossils," he told his fascinated sister.

Julia also remembers that Pa was outraged at first that Daniel was spending time picking up silly rocks when he should be working the fields. But she recalls that not long afterward Pa bought a chisel and a shovel for Daniel, so perhaps he wasn't so angry after all. Both she and her brother listened spellbound as Pa talked of dinosaur hunters, called paleontologists—men such as Howard Crow, who thought there might be dinosaur bones buried somewhere in the Nebraska soil. Daniel was intrigued with the thought of finding the bones of the "terrible lizards"—perhaps right in their own fields. When he heard that paleontologist Crow would pay a reward for any such discovery, he was determined to find the remains of a dinosaur on their own piece of Nebraska prairie.

Grandma Summerwaite's stories of Daniel and his search for dinosaur bones continue as she, Ellie, and Stevie go slowly toward the dinosaur collection. She tells the children of how Daniel met some prospectors who were also dinosaur hunting. They told him of the "dinosaur war" going on between Howard Crow and his former employer, Oswald Mannity. The two men were trying to outdo each other in the search for dinosaur bones. The prospectors claimed that Mannity was a dirty dog who would do anything to beat Crow. He had even hired Hump Hinton to do his searching. Hump Hinton had a wooden leg, traveled with a mysterious black woman, and owned a camel. The prospectors told Daniel that Hinton had been known to commit murder to get what he wanted.

Julia was frightened by such stories, but Daniel was more intrigued than ever. Day after day he set off with his chisel and pick, hunting the elusive dinosaur bones. Then one day after a rain, the unbelievable happened. In the mud of the creek bank, Daniel uncovered bones— huge dark-gray bones, the biggest Julia had ever seen. "I knew it!" Daniel shouted to his sister. "I knew it!"

Daniel and Julia covered up the bones and Daniel wrote a letter— dated April 23, 1885—to Howard Crow, telling him of the discovery. Daniel was certain it was a dinosaur.

They did not tell their parents of the find because they were convinced that the reward for the find would pay off the mortgage on the farm. What a surprise for Ma and Pa.

Daniel anxiously awaited the reply from Crow. Instead, a few weeks later Hump Hinton appeared, along with his woman companion and his camel. They hung around the area as Daniel frantically tried to keep secret his discovery of the bones near the creek. He watched with great anxiety as Hump Hinton and his companion traveled up and down the river bed, hunting and scraping for treasure.

After what seemed an eternity, a letter arrived from Howard Crow. It said, "I'm coming. Don't touch anything."

One afternoon young Julia watched as a fierce electrical storm swept over their Nebraska farm. She worried because Daniel was out by the creek guarding his dinosaur discovery. Her worst fears were realized when she found her brother dead, struck by lightning.

Julia told her grieving parents of Daniel's discovery and their expectations of Howard Crow's arrival. Pa's first action was to take out his rifle and scare off Hinton. Then they all waited for Howard Crow.

At this point in her story, Grandma Summerwaite, Ellie, and Stevie have reached the doorway of the Early Dinosaur Hall at the museum.

"Would you like to see what Crow did with Daniel's bones?" she asks the children. "I'm ready," answers Stevie. "So am I," the old woman murmurs.

The children enter the hall and stand in awe before the mighty structure of ancient bones—the dinosaur, resurrected and pieced together. Stevie reads from the plaque at its feet: "Brontosaurus, one hundred and forty million years old, sixty-seven feet long, thirty tons. Found near Dannebrog, Nebraska."

Grandma Summerwaite's memory goes back once more, to the day Howard Crow arrived on the Nebraska farm, to the day she saw his eyes light up at her brother Daniel's dinosaur bones.

It was months, of course, before the extent of Daniel's find was realized and the bones were unearthed. On the last night of Crow's dig, Julia brought him a sack. It contained all of Daniel's fossils, and she tried not to cry as she offered them to this man, who would take away her brother's treasures. Gently, one by one, Howard Crow took out Daniel's fossils and, like a storyteller, explained them to Julia. When he attempted to return them to her, she said no. "My brother would want you to have them." Crow nodded and said, "I'll see that they get put with the proper collections at the museum." It seemed a proper tribute for Daniel.

Of course, the reward was not quite what her brother had hoped. It turns out that $100 from the museum was the best Howard Crow could do.

Her story now done, Grandma Summerwaite is filled with a great peace. As her grandchildren watch in amazement, she approaches the dinosaur base and begins to climb it. The guard rushes to stop her, but Ellie clutches his sleeve. "It's hers," she explains. "She dug that dinosaur up herself. In Nebraska."

Ellie and Stevie and the guard stand in silence as the old woman slowly climbs toward the head of the dinosaur. Her laughter rings out across the vast room and she sounds like a young girl. "Oh, Daniel," she cries. "We did good, Daniel! We did real good."

The young Julia once again hears Daniel's voice, calling to her over the prairie grasses. She goes to meet him.

### Thematic Material

In many ways this is an old-fashioned story of a childhood dream, of family love and devotion, of memories, and of true adventure. It celebrates the bonds of family ties and praises the human spirit. It paints a warm portrait of a long-ago way of life, sprinkled with treachery and deceit but held together by a love and a dream that lasted a lifetime. The old woman's memories come vividly to life as she re-creates the wonder of her brother's discovery for her young grandchildren.

**Book Talk Material**

Grandma Summerwaite's descriptions of life on the prairie during the last century will serve as a fine introduction to this adventurous and loving tale. See: Daniel finds a fossil (pp. 18–20); the day their little brother dies (pp. 23–25); Daniel succumbs to the magic of dinosaur hunting (pp. 26–29); and Daniel digs a grave and talks about dinosaurs (pp. 37–42).

**Additional Selections**

In Kathryn Lasky's *The Bone Wars* (Morrow, 1988, $12.95; pap., Puffin, $4.95), two teenagers, one an orphan and the other an aristocrat's son, are involved in searching for fossils in the Montana of the late 1890s.

David and his ailing grandfather, Max, a Holocaust survivor, try to locate Max's artist friend Bernie, another survivor, in Gary Provost's *David and Max* (Jewish Publication Soc., 1985, $12.95).

Merkka's grandmother, who has sacrificed her life for her family, must now begin thinking about herself in Betty Levin's *The Trouble with Gramary* (Greenwillow, 1988, $11.95).

In George Ella Lyon's *Red Rover, Red Rover* (Orchard, 1989, $12.95), a twelve-year-old girl must cope with several problems, including the death of her grandfather.

Two new books about dinosaurs are *My Life with the Dinosaurs* (pap., Pocket, 1989, $2.75) by Stephen and Sylvia Czerkas, in which two dinosaur sculptors describe their search for fossil remains, and *The New Illustrated Dinosaur Dictionary* (pap., Morrow, 1991, $14.95) by Helen Roney Sattler, which contains entries in text and pictures for all dinosaurs of the Mesozoic Era.

Maggie, a thirteen-year-old, spends August in a New England cabin with her divorced father, his second wife, and their baby in Avi's *Blue Heron* (Bradbury, 1982, $14.95).

Kate is fearful that the extended drought will force her family off their Kentucky farm in Martha Bennett Stiles's *Kate of Still Waters* (Macmillan, 1990, $15.95).

**About the Book**
*Booklist*, April 15, 1989, p. 1464.
*Center for Children's Books Bulletin*, March 1989, p. 167.

*Horn Book*, March 1989, p. 374.
*Kirkus Reviews*, May 1, 1989, p. 688.
*School Library Journal*, April 1989, p. 117.
*VOYA*, June 1989, p. 98.

**About the Author**

Commire, Anne, ed., *Something about the Author*. Gale, 1988, Vol. 52, pp. 29–31.
Holtze, Sally Holmes, ed., *Sixth Book of Junior Authors and Illustrators*. Wilson, 1989, pp. 64–66.
May, Hal, ed., *Contemporary Authors*. Gale, 1987, Vol. 121, pp. 110–11.
Senick, Gerard J., ed., *Children's Literature Review*. Gale, 1989, Vol. 18, pp. 86–89.

---

**Cormier, Robert.**   *After the First Death*
  Pantheon, 1979, $12.99 (0-394-94122-5); pap., Dell, $3.95 (0-440-20835-1)

---

In many of his young adult novels, Robert Cormier explores the theme of an individual in conflict with some aspect of society. In *The Chocolate War* (Pantheon, 1974, $18.95; pap., Dell, $3.50; condensed in *More Juniorplots*, Bowker, 1977, pp. 28–32) and its sequel, *Beyond the Chocolate War* (Pantheon, 1985, $11.95; pap., Dell, $3.25; condensed in *Seniorplots*, Bowker, 1989, pp. 50–55), the societal institution is the school and its administrative structure. In *I Am the Cheese* (Pantheon, 1977, $18.95; pap., Dell, $3.95) and *After the First Death*, it is various aspects of government. The title of the latter is from a poem by Dylan Thomas, "After the first death there is no other." It is told from the standpoint of three teenage protagonists who become involved in the hijacking of a school bus by terrorists: Ben Marchand, the son of an army general; Kate Forrester, a substitute bus driver; and Miro, a young terrorist. The main action takes place over a period of about twenty-four hours. In alternating chapters, two points of view are explored. The first is Ben's point of view and tells of the army's resistance to the terrorist attack. The second is that of the terrorists and their captives on the bus. This powerful, often disturbing novel is read by better readers in grades 8 through 12.

**Plot Summary**

Kate Forrester, a blond, attractive teenager, has consented to help her sick uncle by driving his school bus with sixteen preschoolers to a summer day camp situated on the outskirts of their small Massachusetts town, close to the large army base at Fort Delta. On a lonely stretch of road, the bus is stopped by a van. Two of the four passengers in the van enter the bus brandishing pistols. The leader, a man about forty, is named Artkin. He is followed by a youth, Miro. They feed the children candy laced with drugs to tranquilize them and then force Kate to drive the bus to the middle of a rickety, abandoned railroad bridge. Kate is unaware that Artkin had promised Miro that at this point the young man could commit his first murder by killing the bus driver. However, to Miro's disappointment, Artkin decides that Kate should have a temporary reprieve so that she can help care for the children.

Gradually a terrified Kate is able to piece together details of the plot. Artkin and Miro, together with their colleagues Stroll, a black man, and the brutish Antibbe, are on a terrorist mission to strike a blow for the liberation of their homeland. They have already been involved in similar deadly attacks in other American cities. Particularly vivid in Miro's memory is the one in which his beloved brother Aniel was killed. Their present plan is to establish contact with Fort Delta and make three demands involving the release of political prisoners, payment of $10 million, and the dismantling of a secret international brainwashing operation named Inner Delta that has its headquarters at Fort Delta. If these conditions are not met, it will mean death for Kate and the children.

The demands have been sent to the leader of Inner Delta, General Rufus L. Briggs, actually the code name for General Mark Marchand, the renowned behavioral psychologist who has joined the army at his country's request to head this special project.

Soon army units and helicopters buzz around the hijacking site, but they cannot act for fear of reprisals. The first death is accidental, but it gives the terrorists a psychological edge. One of the children dies from the drugged candy. After displaying the body publicly, Artkin lowers it from the bridge to the soldiers below.

Miro is left in charge of the bus while the others remain in the van negotiating with the army and awaiting further instructions from Sedeete, the chief of their central terrorist command. Kate uses this opportunity to try to break down Miro's reserve and perhaps arouse some spark of humanity in this bitter teenager who, like his comrades, seems devoid of human feeling. She learns that Miro knows nothing about his parents and that he and his brother were found in a refugee camp by Artkin and were recruited into the terrorist organization. Artkin demanded and received slavish obedience from his two charges and instilled in them the idea that theirs was a holy crusade for freedom. Today Miro still regards Artkin as part savior and part god but Kate detects a glimmer of tenderness in this would-be killer.

Kate discovers that she has an extra key to the bus. Although filled with self-doubt concerning her own inner strength, she devises an audacious plan. When Miro makes one of his brief departures from the bus, she will back it off the bridge and drive to safety. She is fearful that she lacks the courage to carry out her plan, but when the opportunity comes, she rises to the situation and is able to move the bus back several feet before the engine stalls. The terrorists retake the bus. Kate's last hope of saving herself and the children is gone.

A trigger-happy soldier loses control and accidentally kills Antibbe. Artkin retaliates by taking one of the children—Kate's favorite, Benjamin—from the bus and performing a public execution.

By early morning, both sides are becoming increasingly desperate. Luckily, the army has been able to capture the ringleader, Sedeete, in Boston, but the hijackers refuse to believe this news, which, if true, would seriously weaken their position to negotiate. Artkin wants visual proof; he wants one of Sedeete's possessions, a small stone from their homeland, delivered to the van by some neutral unarmed person. General Marchand, who is anxious at all costs to save Inner Delta, can think of only one person to fulfill this operation: his son Ben. He summons Ben and explains what is needed of him. Ben, a sensitive, trusting young man, agrees. Although the army plans to attack the bus and van at 8:35 A.M., General Marchand gives the boy a series of incorrect clues to make him believe he has secret information that the attack will occur at 9:30.

In the early morning light, Ben approaches the van. Inside he is strip-searched and tortured unmercifully until he reveals what his father had known he would—the wrong information concerning the attack. As planned, the terrorists are taken by surprise. In the ensuing shootout, the bus is captured and the children are saved. Stroll is killed first, followed by Artkin, who before dying shoots Ben in the shoulder. Miro, using Kate as his shield, flees into the woods. In one last attempt to awaken some feelings of humanity in Miro, Kate again questions him about his past. She tells him that she believes Artkin is really his father. Miro realizes that this could be true. Suddenly the full significance of this concept registers, and he begins wailing like a mortally wounded beast. As Kate cradles him like a mother, he shoots her in the heart, before making his successful escape to the highway and freedom.

Ben survives his physical wound but his psychic wounds will not heal. He can neither cope with his belief that he acted like a coward under torture nor accept the extent of his father's duplicity and betrayal and the fact that he was willing to sacrifice his own son for an army security project. Ben unsuccessfully attempts suicide by taking sleeping pills. When he recovers he is enrolled in his father's military school, Castleton Academy, where it is hoped he will resume a normal life. But the extent of his disillusionment is not understood. General Marchand, hoping for reconciliation and forgiveness, goes to see his son at Castleton for a weekend. During the first brief meeting in his son's room, he is able to express his true feelings. When he returns for a second visit, it is too late—Ben's second suicide attempt has been successful.

### Thematic Material

This brutal story of terror and deception contains scenes of almost unbearable suspense and tension. However, each time the reader's hopes are aroused, the powers of evil triumph. It is a tale of deception and betrayal. Both Ben and Miro have been cruelly deceived by their fathers. Each father has placed his country's well-being over that of his son's and each father, in a sense, is in turn a victim of his own society. The novel questions how far basic human values can be sacrificed in the name of duty and patriotism. The vulnerability of the young and weak when challenging the existing power structure is explored as is the destructive potential of brainwashing. Various aspects of courage and bravery are well depicted—particularly when Kate, an average girl, successfully conquers her fears to defy the terrorists. In the end, however, this novel delivers the cynical truth that sometimes in life there are no winners, only survivors.

### Book Talk Material

This novel can be introduced by a brief discussion of international terrorism and the ethical questions it poses. Some passages of importance are: Miro and Artkin are introduced (pp. 17–23); hijacking the school bus (23–31); the death of the first child (pp. 41–46) and Artkin's display of the body (pp. 73–77); and Ben and his father discuss the hijacking (pp. 85–90).

**Additional Selections**

In trying to figure out why his friend Ashley committed suicide, Joey spends a week as a drifter in Hadley Irwin's *So Long at the Fair* (McElderry, 1988, $13.95; pap., Avon, $2.95).

Jackie McKee is abducted and imprisoned in a small dark cellar in Ouida Sebestyen's *The Girl in the Box* (Little, Brown, 1988, $13.95; pap., Bantam, $3.50).

Jim Taylor's life is in danger when he accidentally receives a computer disc filled with information about the mob in David Skipper's *Runners* (Viking, 1988, $11.95).

Anna feels important as a member of a secret gang but becomes troubled when the older boys impose increasingly cruel tasks in Vivien Alcock's *The Trial of Anna Cotman* (Delacorte, 1990, $13.95).

When Jed and Annie investigate their friend Charlie's suicide, they find that he had a secret past in *Face at the Edge of the World* (Clarion, 1985, $13.95; pap., $3.95) by Eve Bunting.

In *Blindfold* (Holiday, 1990, $13.95) by Sandra McCuiag, Sally must find out if she was really responsible for the death of two brothers.

A nonfiction account of hostage-taking and terrorism around the world is given in L. B. Taylor's *Hostage! Kidnapping and Terrorism in Our Time* (Watts, 1989, $12.90).

**About the Book**
*Booklist*, March 15, 1979, p. 1131.
*Center for Children's Books Bulletin*, June 1979, p. 172.
*Horn Book*, August 1979, p. 426.
*Kirkus Reviews*, April 1, 1979, p. 391.
*New York Times Book Review*, April 29, 1979, p. 30.
*School Library Journal*, March 1979, p. 146.
See also *Book Review Digest*, 1979, p. 273; and *Book Review Index*, 1979, p. 97, and 1980, p. 109.

**About the Author**
Campbell, Patricia J., *Presenting Robert Cormier*. Twayne, 1985; pap., Dell, $4.95.
Chevalier, Tracy, ed., *Twentieth-Century Children's Writers* (3rd ed.). St. James, 1989, pp. 237–38.
Commire, Anne, ed., *Something about the Author*. Gale, 1976, Vol. 10, p. 28; updated 1986, Vol. 45, pp. 58–65.

Estes, Glenn E., ed., *American Writers for Children since 1960: Fiction* (Dictionary of Literary Biography: Vol. 52). Gale, 1986, pp. 107–14.

Evory, Ann, ed., *Contemporary Authors* (New Revision Series). Gale, 1982, Vol. 5, pp. 130–32.

Holtze, Sally Holmes, ed., *Fifth Book of Junior Authors and Illustrators*. Wilson, 1983, pp. 85–86.

Kirkpatrick, D. L., ed., *Twentieth-Century Children's Writers* (2nd ed.). St. Martin's, 1983, p. 203.

Senick, Gerard J., ed., *Children's Literature Review*. Gale, 1987, Vol. 12, pp. 144–55.

Straub, Deborah A., ed., *Contemporary Authors* (New Revision Series). Gale, 1988, Vol. 23, pp. 87–94.

---

## Deaver, Julie Reece.   *Say Goodnight, Gracie*
Harper, 1989, pap., $3.50 (0-06-447007-5)

---

This touching novel, dealing with a young girl's painful adjustment to the death of a dear friend, is Julie Reece Deaver's first young adult novel. It has been joined by *First Wedding, Once Removed* (Harper, 1990, $13.89), the story of teenager Pokie, who is upset when her beloved brother becomes engaged. Both make fine reading for youngsters in grades 7 through 10.

**Plot Summary**

Morgan and Jimmy are seventeen years old. They have been friends forever, and they have loved each other forever—not romantic love but the kind that says "I know you better than anyone else in the world. I can't imagine life without you. We are best friends. For life." They don't actually say those words to each other, but they feel them. In fact, when one of them attempts to express an emotion, to actually *say* what he or she is feeling, the other is likely to interrupt with "Just say goodnight, Gracie"—the old line vaudeville/radio/television star George Burns used to end the run-on speeches of his wife and comedy partner Gracie Allen.

Tall, lanky Jimmy wants to be a dancer. When he was ten years old, he discovered Fred Astaire. He coaxed Morgan into being his Ginger Rogers, and he has been dancing ever since. When Jimmy drives his MG into Chicago's Loop district three times a week after school to study dance, Morgan goes to an acting workshop.

Jimmy gets an opportunity to audition for a dance part in a touring production of *Oklahoma!* He throws himself so single-mindedly into practice that Morgan is afraid he will be stale at the tryout. She skips school to see his audition.

As soon as Jimmy walks on center stage and Morgan hears the first few notes of the *Oklahoma!* overture, she knows her fears are confirmed. She mentally urges Jimmy to relax and be himself, but he moves around the stage like a scared amateur. He is stiff and wooden, not the wonderfully fluid, talented dancer she knows him to be. Not surprisingly, he doesn't get the part.

Following the audition, Morgan and Jimmy have perhaps their first really serious argument. She tells him that it isn't the end of the world; there will be a next time and he'll be more relaxed. He lashes back that she doesn't know what she's talking about. "What do you know about being a *professional?*" he snaps.

Morgan is devastated by Jimmy's flare-up. But later Aunt Lo, a hospital psychiatrist, helps Morgan to understand Jimmy's embarrassment at performing so badly in front of the one person in the world he wanted to impress. They make up verbally, then have a pillow fight.

That fall and winter Morgan joins Jimmy as an apprentice at a children's theater, where he performs. She experiences a strange twinge of—could it be?—jealousy when Jimmy is kissed by his onstage partner, a long-legged girl named Robin. Jimmy and Morgan have a half-kidding, half-serious talk about it. Jimmy says, "You don't have anything to worry about, Morgan." "I don't," she replies. Jimmy answers, "No, Robin's nothing compared to you." Somehow, Jimmy always knows what she wants to hear.

Then, in true show-biz tradition, Robin can't perform one night and Morgan makes her stage debut. She walks on stage, catches her toe on something, and literally falls flat on her face. Jimmy covers up for her, but she vows never to appear onstage again. They have another of their half-serious, half-kidding talks, and when Morgan tries to thank him for covering up for her, he replies, "Look . . . Morgan . . . I never know what to say when you talk like that."

"Very simple, Jimmy," she replies. "Just say goodnight, Gracie."

Shortly after Christmas, the two friends drive into Chicago for their classes. He is wearing the sweater she gave him for Christmas. She is not wearing a coat because she was late and ran out of the house without one. It is cold in Chicago. Jimmy drops her off, gives Morgan his jacket to wear, and says he will pick her up at 5:30.

For the first time in all their seventeen years, Jimmy is late picking her up. It isn't like him not to call if he has car trouble. When Morgan feels she is about to freeze to death, her mother arrives. There has been an accident. They don't know how badly he's been hurt.

When Morgan walks into the hospital and sees Aunt Lo holding the hands of Jimmy's mother, she doesn't have to be told about his injuries. She knows that Jimmy is dead. It was a drunk driver. Jimmy did not regain consciousness.

It has never occurred to Morgan that she would spend her life without Jimmy. As she says, who thinks about things like that when you're seventeen?

In the hospital, still wearing Jimmy's jacket, Morgan has a panic attack. Aunt Lo sedates her. In the days that follow, Morgan feels that she is handling Jimmy's death. She tells her father that everyone thinks she is going to fall apart, but she won't. As though to prove this, she throws Jimmy's jacket in the garbage can; later that night, when another panic attack begins, she retrieves the jacket, puts it on, and feels better. After that she wears it to bed every night. Aunt Lo tells her that when she really starts to deal with Jimmy's death, she won't feel the need to wear his jacket, but Morgan insists she *is* dealing with it.

Morgan goes to Jimmy's funeral, but finds she can't go in. She has another panic attack in school. She has trouble sleeping. When her father is late picking her up one day, she is terrified that he, too, is dead. She meets a young man who asks her to go for a cup of coffee, but she can't. She learns that Jimmy's mother is getting some therapy to help her deal with her loss. At least I don't need professional help, Morgan thinks; I'm coping. But Aunt Lo seems to think that it is Jimmy's mother who is coping.

One day Morgan and her father talk about depression, and Morgan admits that although she got through Jimmy's death—she never cried once—she can't figure out how to get through life without him. She tells her father that she wishes she had been the one to die because Jimmy could have made it without her, but she can't without him. Her father says that depression is a funny thing; the more you lie around, the more depressed you get. After that conversation, Morgan can laugh a little. She says she feels as though a shot of novacaine is starting to wear off. It hurts. Her father says that now she is beginning to cope.

However, when the pain of coping really starts, it takes another panic attack and her understanding aunt to make Morgan realize that all along she has been protecting herself from being hurt by Jimmy's death. Her life will never be the same without him, but she now will start to live again. Morgan knows that the healing has truly begun when she stops on a bridge over the Chicago River, where she and Jimmy once stood, and she tosses his jacket into the wind.

### Thematic Material

This book deals sensitively with love, friendship, and death; it portrays vivid, real relationships between people—the warmth between Morgan and her parents; the open affection and admiration between Morgan and her aunt; and, above all, the funny, close, and caring love between Morgan and Jimmy. It is an honest, unsentimental look at the stages of grief that humans endure when they suffer the loss of a loved one, and a sensitive portrait of grief and healing made more poignant by the youth of those involved.

### Book Talk Material

The following passages, which illustrate the relationship between Morgan and Jimmy, can serve as a good introduction: the pierced-ears discussion (pp. 6–7); one of their "Goodnight, Gracie" routines (pp. 15–17); Jimmy overpractices for *Oklahoma!* (pp. 33–35); and the makeup pillow fight (pp. 61–65). Morgan's reactions after Jimmy's death can prompt a discussion of the ways in which individuals deal, or fail to deal, with sorrow and disappointment in their lives; see: Morgan refuses to go to Jimmy's funeral (pp. 128–31); Morgan talks to Aunt Lo about wearing Jimmy's jacket to bed (pp. 150–51); Morgan and her father talk about depression (pp. 173–75); and another panic attack (pp. 200–6).

### Additional Selections

When the deaf younger brother of college freshman Jesse Harmon is killed by a drunk driver, his family is torn apart in Eve Bunting's *A Sudden Silence* (Harcourt, 1988, $14.95; pap., Fawcett, $3.50).

Gideon, a seventeen-year-old would-be country music star, tries to adjust to his best friend's suicide in Mary Blount Christian's *Singin' Somebody Else's Song* (Macmillan, 1988, $13.95; pap., Dell, $3.95).

Jessie finds the inner strength to cope with her sister's death from cancer in Cynthia D. Grant's *Phoenix Rising, or How to Survive Your Life* (Atheneum, 1989, $12.95).

The nonfiction *Teenagers Face to Face with Bereavement* (Messner, 1989,

$11.88; pap., $5.95) by Karen Gravelle and Charles Haskins offers seventeen interviews with young people from ages ten to eighteen who have had to adjust to the death of a loved one.

Jerry discovers that his girlfriend Sheila has incurable cancer in Alden Carter's tragic *Sheila's Dying* (Putnam, 1987, $13.95).

In Dawna Lisa Buchanan's *The Falcon's Wing* (Orchard, 1990, $13.95), Bryn moves to Canada after her mother's death to live with an aunt and uncle who have a daughter born with Down's syndrome.

Robin's life collapses after his mother dies and his father remarries in James D. Forman's *The Pumpkin Shell* (Farrar, 1981, $10.95).

**About the Book**
*Book Report*, September 1988, p. 33.
*Booklist*, April 1988, p. 1336.
*Center for Children's Books Bulletin*, February 1988, p. 114.
*Horn Book*, September 1988, p. 620.
*Kirkus Reviews*, February 1, 1988, p. 200.
*New York Times Book Review*, July 31, 1988, p. 33.
*School Library Journal*, February 1988, p. 84.
*VOYA*, April 1988, p. 22.
See also *Book Review Digest*, 1988, p. 418; and *Book Review Index*, 1988, p. 201.

---

**Doherty, Berlie.**   *Granny Was a Buffer Girl*
Orchard, 1988, $12.95 (0-531-05754-2)

---

The stories in this collection, as in the author's later *White Peak Farm* (Orchard, 1990, $12.95), were written originally for BBC Radio. In *White Peak Farm*, a family living on a farm in the north of England is so tyrannized by the father that one daughter marries in secret and a son's emotional development is destroyed. In both of these books, this prize-winning novelist has tellingly portrayed the bonds of family and the influence of locale on young people growing up. Both books are suitable for good readers in junior and senior high school.

**Plot Summary**
The title of this novel comes from the boring and dirty job that young girls once performed in large cutlery firms, in this case in England. They spent their days buffing cutlery, which meant to clean and polish these utensils, and the smell of it stayed forever in their clothes and their hair.

The story opens in modern-day England where Jess is just about ready to go to college. She is leaving the following day for a year's study in France and has already said good-bye to her boyfriend, Steve. Three generations of her family have gathered to see her off. There is Grandpa Jack, her Granny Dorothy, her own parents, her brother John and his girlfriend, Katie, who is also Jess's best friend, and, of course, the memory of her dead brother Danny. Jess goes into the room that used to be Danny's and looks once again at the photograph of him that is still on the wall: Danny with his head back, laughing.

There is so much to remember, so much of her family to take with her when she leaves. Slowly, family stories come spinning back; they tell of the growth, the triumphs and disasters, and the changes that occurred over the years to make them into the people, and the family, they are today.

The first story concerns Grandpa Jack and Grandma Bridie. He is old now and sometimes he talks as though Bridie were still with him, instead of dead for a year. When she was young, Bridie was a beauty, with strong Irish features and thick dark hair. Her Catholic mother and father were proud of and very protective of their daughters. Even so, they could not keep her from meeting Jack, son of a headmaster, whose elderly and Protestant parents bemoaned the fact that their only son seemed to care nothing for study and all for his motorbike. Oh well, they thought, as long as he's happy and a good boy, which meant, of course, not marrying a Catholic.

Warning and punishments could not keep the young couple apart. Though neither would change religion and though each realized the convictions of their families, they married in secret in the middle of a working day. When the marriage was revealed in Bridie's house, she was thrown out into the street. When the young bride and groom told his parents of their union, the groom's father handed him some money for a honeymoon and turned them out as well.

"And we called our first daughter Josephine, after my pa," said Grandpa Jack.

Granny Dorothy, the buffer girl, tells quite a different story. Oh, how bored she was in her dull and dirty job buffing cutlery. Then at a dance one night at Cutlers' Hall, she met Mr. Edward, who drove a motor car and told her she had eyes the color of bluebells. Of course, Mr. Edward did not know that she was a buffer girl at his father's factory, and when he found out, Dorothy's fleeting moment of romance and escape from a life of boredom was over. Soon after, Albert Bradley came to call and asked for her hand in marriage. In her heart, Dorothy said, "I'll never get away." To Albert, who would turn out to be Jess's grandfather, she said, "All right. But don't be late for work . . . we want all the money we can get now, if we're to be wed."

Dorothy and Albert's son, Michael, is Jess's father. When he was a lad, he was always in trouble, always out of work, always at loose ends. His family despaired. Still, young Mike worked just enough to get some dandy new clothes for the Saturday hop; he had his eye on Jennifer.

"What happened?" Jess asks him, knowing full well that her mother's name is not Jennifer. "Did you ever see Jennifer again?"

"Still do," her father replies with a wink at her mother. "I owe a lot to Jennifer."

It transpires that Mike became involved not with Jennifer, but with a friend of hers, lumpish and sniffy Lucy Cragwell. Then he was called into the army. He didn't care about Lucy really, but she was in love with him and he didn't want to break her heart. Wonders of wonders, before he had to leave, Lucy told him that she knew he really cared for Jennifer. On departure day, Jennifer arrived at the station to say good-bye. She pushed a young girl into Mike's train compartment, saying "This is my big sister Josie. She's going to college."

Josie is Jess's mother.

About three years later, Michael and Josie married. Their first child was Danny. Not long after his birth, they realized there was something wrong with him. Danny would in time be bound to a wheelchair and would not live past his teens. They decided to keep him at home and make his few years as happy as possible. What Danny wanted more than anything, he told his parents, was a baby sister, and even though there was the chance that another infant would have the same affliction, they decide on a second child. Jess's brother John was born. Then, finally, came Jess, whom Danny adored from the moment he first held her and until he died. Jess and Danny had a very special relationship until she was about eight years old and Danny's condition began to deteriorate rapidly. Afraid of what she could not understand, young Jess shouted one day that she hated her brother. When he died, she was guilt-ridden, feeling that she was the cause.

Young Jess and John could not cry after Danny's death, but when they buried the teddy bear that Danny gave her, both children began to sob. Their mother said, "Time for the living. I hope it's not too late."

There are other family stories, too, for Jess to take with her. They are about brother John and the wounded pigeon, and Granny Dorothy's sister and her booming giant of a husband, Uncle Gilbert. When Uncle Gilbert had a stroke and no one could understand him, it was Jess who told them that he wanted to be taken home once more. They did, and it was there that the old man died.

The last story is about Jess herself, her friendship with Katie, and how they would go to the disco on Saturday nights. It is there that she met Terry and realized she had never felt like this before in her life. They met a few times, drove in his car, held hands, and spoke romantic words. Jess was delirious with happiness until she asked Katie why she was acting so strangely when Jess mentioned Terry's name. Does she know him? Yes, Katie admitted; she baby-sits for him and his wife.

The family members all turn out to see Jess off at Midland Station. Even her boyfriend, Steve, is there. "I'll see you at Christmas," she tells him—but no promises.

Once on the train, Jess knows that when she returns she will no longer be a child. As though to underscore that, she opens the present her mother has given her to find the picture of Danny, laughing from the past. Danny, celebrating life.

### Thematic Material

This is a rich tapestry of family life through the generations. It traces one family's roots, emphasizing how the strengths and weaknesses, triumphs and disasters of their lives bring them together to form the love and warmth that they share.

### Book Talk Material

Many passages from the individual stories can be used to interest readers. See: Grandpa Jack and Grandma Bridie discuss religion and marriage (pp. 20–21); Bridie is thrown out of the house (pp. 23–24); the buffer girl resigns herself to her future (pp. 40–41); Jess's dad meets Jess's mother (pp. 69–70); Danny wants a baby sister and his parents make a decision (pp. 76–77); and brother John brings home a wounded bird (pp. 86–92).

**Additional Selections**

A shy thirteen-year-old girl tries to form a friendship with her ancient, difficult aunt in Georgess McHargue's *See You Later, Crocodile* (Delacorte, 1988, $14.95).

In Meredith Daneman's *Francie and the Boys* (Delacorte, 1989, $14.95), set in London, thirteen-year-old Francis accepts a role in a play that a nearby boys' school is producing.

In Ruth White's *Sweet Creek Holler* (Farrar, 1988, $13.95), a young girl along with her mother and older sister spend six years in a small Appalachian town during the 1950s.

Also set in Appalachia is Jim Wayne Miller's *Newfound* (Orchard, 1989, $13.95), the story of a boy's coming of age and his life with his divorced mother and grandmother.

Louise copes with the jealousy she feels for her talented twin sister in Katherine Paterson's *Jacob Have I Loved* (Harper, 1980, $12.70; pap., Avon, $2.95; condensed in *Juniorplots 3*, Bowker, 1987, pp. 85–90).

In Kit Pearson's *The Sky Is Falling* (Viking, 1990, $12.95), ten-year-old Norah is distraught when she and her young brother must leave England and her family during World War II and be relocated in Canada.

A handicapped girl finds friendship when an American family buys the island off the coast of Scotland on which she lives in Ian Strachan's *The Flawed Glass* (Little, Brown, 1990, $14.95).

Missy Cord's grandmother and uncle object to her fulfilling her great ambition of going to college in Suzanne Newton's *Where Are You When I Need You?* (Viking, 1991, $13.95).

**About the Book**

*Booklist*, March 1, 1988, p. 1130.
*Center for Children's Books Bulletin*, March 1988, p. 133.
*Horn Book*, May 1988, p. 357.
*Kirkus Reviews*, January 1988, p. 53.
*New York Times Book Review*, August 21, 1988, p. 25.
*School Library Journal*, April 1988, p. 111.
*VOYA*, June 1988, p. 84.

**About the Author**

Chevalier, Tracy, ed., *Twentieth-Century Children's Writers* (3rd ed.). St. James, 1989, pp. 292–93.
Senick, Gerard J., ed., *Children's Literature Review*. Gale, 1990, Vol. 21, pp. 55–61.

---

**Hall, Barbara.** *Dixie Storms*
Harcourt, 1990, $15.95 (0-15-223825-5)

---

In *Dixie Storms,* fourteen-year-old Dutch Peyton, who is the narrator, discovers her own strengths and weaknesses through a number of incidents including the sudden visit of Norma, a beautiful cousin from the city. This is also the story of a troubled family and of human conflict. The author uses the symbolism of a cleansing southern storm at the climax of this novel. Another fine title by the same author is *Skeeball and the Secret of the Universe* (Orchard, 1989, $12.99), about Matty's coming of age during the summer before his senior year. Both books are enjoyed by junior and senior high school readers.

### Plot Summary

Margaret "Dutch" Peyton finds life pretty good in the small farming town of Marston, Virginia, where she has spent all of her fourteen years. This summer is not going to be easy, however. It is blazing hot and the area is plagued by drought. Dutch knows that her family is having financial troubles running the farm, too. The family consists of her father, a quiet, gentle man; his sister, Aunt Macy, the lady of the house, Dutch's mother having died in childbirth; Dutch's much older brother, Flood; and Flood's young son, the irrepressible Bodean, whose conversation that summer seems limited to such expressions as "Do me a favor" and "Make me an offer." Bodean's mother, Becky, ran off when the boy was about a year old. Dutch misses her a great deal and she feels that the taciturn Flood has never gotten over his wife's disappearance.

Sometimes Dutch wonders why Becky never even writes to find out about Bodean or calls him, but mostly she is busy with farm chores and school and trying to decipher her feelings for red-haired Ethan Cole. However, the pleasant boredom of life in Marston is interrupted when Papa announces the arrival of Dutch's cousin Norma, his brother's child. Dutch is rather pleased to have a rare visitor and she is totally entranced at the arrival of Norma "from the big city," who exhibits all the sophistication and worldliness that Dutch feels she lacks. All the young men in town, including Bodean, fall hopelessly in love with her. Norma keeps a diary to record all the events of her life so that when she becomes famous no details will be lost, and Dutch is persuaded to do the same—although she can't imagine ever being famous enough for someone to read about.

What starts off as a good relationship, however, begins to pale for Dutch as more and more Norma makes her feel inadequate and unworldly, turning her sunny days into a "tire with a slow leak." Even her relationship with Ethan changes as she tries to follow Norma's advice to "make him jealous." Dutch is disturbed when she overhears a conversation between Norma and Flood indicating that Norma wants a closer relationship with him, which Flood refuses.

Events speed up in slow-living Marston. The bank repossesses Papa's tractor because he can't make the payments; Papa tells Dutch that Norma's parents are going to get a divorce, which Norma doesn't yet know; and Dutch finds letters sent to Bodean from his mother, letters that Flood has obviously hidden from the boy.

Dutch writes a secret letter to Becky, telling her that Bodean has never gotten her letters. Norma and Dutch have an argument in which Dutch loses her temper and blurts out to the girl that her parents are divorcing and is then ashamed of herself for causing such hurt. It isn't until Norma is leaving that it comes to Dutch that Norma is just as young and scared as she is, and she remembers her Papa's telling her that people aren't all good or all bad, but a little of both. When Norma boards the bus, Dutch starts to cry. "I really like Norma," she tells Papa, "I didn't know it till just now."

When they return home, a strange car is parked in the driveway. It is Bodean's mother, Becky! She doesn't reveal that Dutch wrote to her and she tells Flood that she has not come back to stay, but she wants to see her son. Flood is angry and refuses to talk to her. Bodean at first wants nothing to do with her either. But both Dutch and Bodean later overhear a conversation between Becky and Flood. She tells him that she was so young when Bodean was born and that Flood was never a person who could share his feelings. She tells him that love has to be worked out, not declared and then put on a shelf. Flood doesn't want to listen when she requests that Bodean come to visit her in the city, where she has an apartment; she is now a real estate agent.

Flood relents and allows Bodean to go to Norfolk with his mother for the rest of the summer. The appearance of Becky has made a change in Flood. He tells Papa about the money he has been saving, money that he planned to use to take himself and Bodean away and start a ranch out west somewhere. Now he has decided that perhaps his home in Virginia is best after all, and the money can be used to reclaim that tractor they need.

Soon after, Flood starts dating, which upsets Dutch, who is still hoping that he and Becky will get back together. In a conversation, her brother tells her that she is too hard on people, that she has "hard hopes." He tells her she has to let go of folks, that she can't make them do what she wants any more than she can make it rain when she wants to. Flood's words stay with Dutch as she thinks about Norma and Becky. Perhaps her brother is right.

Walking home one afternoon, she meets Ethan. Things have been strained between them, but Ethan gets up the courage to ask her if she wants to go steady. "If you don't want to, that's fine with me," he says, "but I figured I might as well ask."

Dutch thinks that it's not the romantic moment she'd always dreamed of, but as moments go, it isn't bad.

"All right," she says.

There in the country lane, Ethan slips an arm around her and they glance up into a darkening sky. It looks like the long drought is over. Ethan and Dutch stare at each other in the falling rain.

### Thematic Material

*Dixie Storms* is a warm novel of first love and family ties and a young girl's growing up in the security of a somewhat unconventional but caring family. Dutch is a likable heroine who learns a valuable lesson that summer about the futility of trying to put people into a mold created in one's mind. The relationship between father and daughter is well depicted—Papa is a caring man who gives his daughter advice but knows that in the end she must make up her own mind and stand by her decisions.

### Book Talk Material

Any of the scenes of interaction will make a fine introduction to this plausible family grouping. See: Bodean gets feisty (pp. 2–3); Papa tells Dutch about Norma's arrival (pp. 9–11); Dutch talks to Ethan and Kenny about the impending visit (pp. 16–18); the two cousins meet (pp. 23–27); and Norma talks about her diary (pp. 35–37).

### Additional Selections

In C. B. Christiansen's *A Small Pleasure* (Atheneum, 1988, $12.95; pap., Avon, $2.95), Wray Jean hides her feelings about her father's terminal illness by becoming an overachiever.

Cat watches her father sink into insanity and feels guilty when he commits suicide in Jean Thesman's *The Last April Dancers* (Harper, 1987, $13.95; pap., Avon, $2.75).

Amanda spends a summer on an island where she forms an attachment with a deaf boy in *Tell Me How the Wind Sounds* by Leslie Guccione (Scholastic, 1985, $12.95).

Aspiring artist Sus5an meets some unusual people when, after high school graduation, she spends a summer in Boston in Louise Plummer's *My Name Is Sus5an Smith: The 5 Is Silent* (Delacorte, 1991, $14.95).

During World War II, Margaret and her friend Elizabeth find a pacifist young man trying to escape fighting in the war in Mary Downing Hahn's *Stepping on the Cracks* (Clarion, 1991, $13.95).

In *Author! Author!* by Susan Terris (Farrar, 1990, $14.95), Valerie tries to determine if the celebrated poet Tekla Reis is really her mother.

Pokie, a young teenager, must let go of her dependence on her older brother when he goes to college and gets married in Julie Reece Deaver's *First Wedding, Once Removed* (Harper, 1990, $13.95).

In Alden R. Carter's *Robo Dad* (Putnam, 1990, $14.95), Shar must cope with a father who has changed radically since his stroke.

**About the Book**
*Booklist*, May 1, 1990, p. 1693.
*Center for Children's Books Bulletin*, July 1990, p. 261.
*Horn Book Guide*, January 1990, p. 252.
*Kirkus Reviews*, May 15, 1990, p. 729.
*School Library Journal*, September 1990, p. 250.
See also *Book Review Digest*, 1991, p. 773; and *Book Review Index*, 1990, p. 336, and 1991, p. 379.

---

**Hinton, S. E.**   *Taming the Star Runner*
Delacorte, 1988, $14.95 (0-440-50058-3); pap., Dell, $3.50 (0-440-20479-8)

---

Like Travis Harris, the protagonist of *Taming the Star Runner*, S. E. Hinton was interested in writing from her childhood. She also completed her first novel and had it accepted for publication when she was only sixteen. This was *The Outsiders* (Viking, 1967, $13.00; pap., Dell, $3.25; condensed in *More Juniorplots*, Bowker, 1977, pp. 60–63). This blockbuster about the violent life of street gangs was a publishing sensation when it appeared in 1967, particularly when it became known that the author was a teenage girl. This novel was followed by *That Was Then, This Is Now* (Viking, 1971, $13.95; pap., Dell, $3.25), *Rumble Fish* (Delacorte, 1975, $13.95; pap., Dell, $3.50), and *Tex* (Delacorte, 1979, $14.95; pap., Dell, $3.50). Alienation is the central theme of all of these novels but *Taming the Star Runner* has a very different locale. The story begins in a midwestern city (possibly Cleveland), but most of the action takes place on a ranch in rural Oklahoma. The time period of the novel is only a few weeks. The narrative is told in the third person, but the point of view is exclusively that of Travis, the central character. This novel is popular with readers in both junior and senior high school.

**Plot Summary**

Trouble and sixteen-year-old Travis Harris seem to go hand in hand. Good-looking, tall for his age, he is considered one of the coolest guys in his high school. His favorite sports are hanging out with his buddies Joe, Kirk, and the twins Billy and Mike, getting drunk, cruising for girls in the twins' Trans Am, and trying to avoid the bullying of his stepfather, Stan. He also has a decent, more serious side to his personality. For example, although he knows he is hooked on cigarettes, he has refused to get involved with serious drugs except for occasionally smoking grass. Travis has one driving ambition and that is to become a writer. Ever since grade school, he has been creating stories and telling them to his friends. In the sixth grade he taught himself to type, and now every spare moment, when he's not hell-raising, is spent writing. He has completed his first novel and secretly sent the manuscript to a publisher in New York.

Travis's father, Tim, was killed in Vietnam two months before Travis's birth and, out of loneliness more than love, his mother remarried. Stan is far from the ideal husband and he and Travis, who resent each other's presence in the home, are continually at odds. Ironically, it is Travis's writing that causes the final blowup. Stan considers the solitary hours Travis spends in his room writing a deliberate act of defiance. Seeking to assert his authority, he gathers the boy's manuscripts and begins burning them. Travis enters and is so blinded with rage that he attacks Stan with a fire poker and almost kills him. Travis is arrested on a complaint lodged by Stan and charged with attempted murder. Travis's mother appeals for help to Tim's surviving brother, Ken, who lives on a ranch in Oklahoma, and Travis is released under his uncle's cognizance.

The parting scene at the airport is somewhat pathetic. Travis, holding his valise and a cardboard box containing his beloved cat, Motorboat, is valiantly trying to hide his fear of flying and his doubts about living with an uncle he doesn't know. His mother is tearful and overly solicitous as if to compensate for the actions of her husband, and friends Joe and Kirk (the twins couldn't get off work), though unable to express their real feelings, are miserable at the impending loss of their dear friend.

Uncle Ken turns out to be something of an enigma to Travis. Though he welcomes Travis into his home, he seems to be detached from the situation and often almost oblivious to the boy's needs. At thirty-seven, Ken is a highly successful lawyer, a partner in his law firm, but something of an overachiever and workaholic. These characteristics have produced some personal problems. His wife, Teresa, has recently left him and Ken sees his young son, Christopher, only on weekends. Ken had once hoped to become a gentleman rancher, but, like his marriage, this dream also failed and he now rents out the barn and surrounding acreage.

One evening while sharing a pizza with Ken at a restaurant, Travis notices three girls in a neighboring booth. One appears to be about eighteen and the other two about his own age. He tries one of his usually successful ploys to get their attention but the oldest one snubs him. Ken intervenes and introduces Travis to Casey Kencaide, a horsetrainer who is lessee of Ken's barn, and two of her students, attractive Jennifer and sidekick Robyn, who also works for Casey as a groom.

Because Travis has found no friends at the high school he attends—in his opinion, his classmates are either hicks or nerds—he begins hanging out at the barn. Though continually rebuffed by Casey, he finds himself strangely attracted to her. Casey, however, is completely occupied with her horses and her training school. One of her major concerns is the huge gray horse she owns, the wild, seemingly untamable Star Runner.

Travis also gets to know Jennifer better and the troubled Robyn, whom he suspects of being on hard drugs. Two of the other students, thirteen-year-olds Kristen and Kelsey, are still at the giggly adolescent stage and something of a pain to Travis. Though he tries to make a good impression on perfectionist Casey and offer his help, he continually fails. For example, one day he hoses down the barn because he does not know that the term "watering the stalls" means simply filling the buckets. The way Casey manages the school and her handling of such crises as a riding accident in which Kristen breaks her leg increase his feeling of admiration and one day he realizes he has actually fallen in love with her.

News from home is mixed. Joe has written that he and the twins are working for Orson, a record-store operator who Travis knows makes shady deals. He wishes he could be there to protect his friends. Travis is torn between apprehension and anticipation when he learns that his mother is forwarding a letter to him from the New York publisher.

The letter arrives from editor Eleanor Carmichael. His manuscript has been accepted for publication. Travis phones Carmichael, who plans to visit him in Oklahoma to discuss details. Ecstatic, Travis wants to celebrate and tell the world of his success, but because no one is around to share his joy, he heads into town and sneaks into a tavern, where he manages to order several drinks. When he is discovered to be both underage and drunk, the bouncer beats him up and leaves him in a dark alley. Ken is summoned and, furious, takes Travis back to the ranch.

The next day, to escape a very chilly atmosphere in the house, Travis heads for the barn and encounters a half-naked Robyn, who is obviously stoned on cocaine. Casey arrives, fires Robyn, and offers the groom's position to Travis, who readily accepts. Later that day, he at last breaks through Casey's reserve and gains her admiration when, with the help of Motorboat, he kills a lethal water moccasin.

His mother phones and tells him that because he is underage she will have to co-sign on the book contract and Stan has forbidden her to do so until he approves of the contents of the novel. Furious, Travis rips the phone from the wall and throws it, narrowly missing Teresa and Christopher, who have just entered the room. A shaken Teresa threatens Ken with denying him visitation privileges with Christopher because she believes Travis is a menace to the child's safety. Ken's only recourse is to send Travis back home. Under the burden of the situation, Travis breaks down and sobs uncontrollably before his uncle. When Travis explains the circumstances behind the phone incident, he relents at the last moment and allows Travis to stay, hoping that in time Teresa will also change her mind.

In the last big horse show of the season, Casey rides the wild Star Runner to victory in spite of competing with broken ribs caused by a fall when the horse balked at a hurdle. Travis is so elated that he kisses Casey and confesses his love. Gently, Casey says that she genuinely likes him but that it is not the kind of love he feels for her.

Travis's meeting with Carmichael is successful and plans for publishing the book are completed. His temporary peace of mind is shattered when he receives a phone call from an extremely agitated Joe, who is in a local motel. When Travis arrives, Joe tells him how he fled their hometown and hitchhiked to Oklahoma after witnessing the cold-blooded shooting of the twins by a dope-crazed Orson after he discovered that they had double-crossed him. Travis calls on Ken for help and together they persuade Joe to surrender to the police and return home.

A severe electrical storm develops as they return to the ranch. The horses panic and Star Runner escapes from his paddock. Casey and Travis give chase but their Jeep overturns. Although they are not injured, Star Runner is killed by a bolt of lightning.

The death of Star Runner ushers in a period of calm for Travis. His mother has agreed to sign the book contract, and, as expected, Teresa allows Christopher to continue visiting Ken. Soon Travis will be transferring to a larger and (he hopes) more hospitable high school where he will be in classes with Jennifer, with whom he has become very friendly. Now he must follow Eleanor Carmichael's advice and begin novel number two. Who knows, maybe he'll even be able to give up smoking.

**Thematic Material**

This novel is essentially the story of two creatures—a teenage boy and a horse—who are in conflict with their environments. Neither can be tamed to conform to established behavioral patterns. It also portrays the agony of an outsider trying to maintain his own values and identity in a seemingly hostile world. Dedication to the development of one's talents and determination not to have goals thwarted are well depicted in Travis's attitude toward his writing. Various kinds of social relationships are explored in the novel, such as the problems that sometimes occur in step-families and those torn by divorce, various facets of getting along with the opposite sex, and the meaning of friendship. The gradual development of the relationship that links uncle and nephew is also well depicted. Drug abuse and its consequences are explored in the stories of Robyn and Orson. The reader also learns a great deal about horsemanship and the skills, discipline, and hard work that are required to succeed in this sport.

**Book Talk Material**

The booktalker might begin by pointing out the similarities in the lives of the author and her central character. After an introduction to Travis, his family, friends, and problems, one or more of the following incidents could be used: Travis's dedication to his writing and the calamitous quarrel with Stan (pp. 9–13); Travis is introduced to Casey by Ken (pp. 25–27); his reaction to his new high school (pp. 33–35); Casey confronts Travis about the "watering the stalls" fiasco (pp. 47–49); Kristen breaks her leg (pp. 60–65); Travis celebrates the acceptance of his novel by getting drunk (pp. 72–81); and he kills the water moccasin (pp. 90–92).

**Additional Selections**

Nick Miller enjoys hanging around his older brother's motorcycle gang until the members begin exploiting him in Gillian Cross's English novel *A Map of Nowhere* (Holiday, 1989, $13.95).

Fifteen-year-old Ben is caring for his father's animal preserve when snipers attack in Theodore Taylor's *Sniper* (Harcourt, 1989, $14.95; pap., Avon, $3.50).

In *The Search for Jim McGwyn* (Atheneum, 1989, $12.95) by Marcia Wood, a teenager, saddled with an alcoholic father, sets out to find the identity of a reclusive mystery writer.

Sixteen-year-old Marcus has a serious problem with his uncontrollable drinking in Stephen Roos's *You'll Miss Me When I'm Gone* (Delacorte, 1988, $13.95; pap., Dell, $2.95).

Three generations of black cowboys are brought together because of a beautiful black horse and a rodeo in Joyce Carol Thomas's *The Golden Pasture* (Scholastic, 1986, $11.95; pap., $2.50).

In Stephanie S. Tolan's *Plague Year* (Morrow, 1990, $12.95), Bran wears an earring and a ponytail to his new superuptight high school but it is the news that his father is an accused murderer that spells tragedy for him.

In Joyce Sweeney's *Face the Dragon* (Delacorte, 1990, $14.95), the friendship of two high school students, Eric and Paul, is tested by competition both in school work and for attractive Melanie.

During the 1930s, fourteen-year-old Roy and his ex-convict father hit the rails to find work in California in Pieter Van Raven's *A Time of Troubles* (Scribner, 1990, $13.95).

**About the Book**
*Book Report*, February 12, 1989, p. 9.
*Booklist*, October 15, 1988, p. 398.
*Center for Children's Books Bulletin*, October 1988, p. 39.

*Horn Book,* January 1989, p. 78.
*Kirkus Reviews,* August 15, 1988, p. 1241.
*New York Times Book Review,* April 2, 1989, p. 26.
*School Library Journal,* October 1988, p. 161.
*VOYA,* December 1988, p. 238.
See also *Book Review Digest,* 1989, p. 750; and *Book Review Index,* 1988, p. 371, and 1989, p. 376.

**About the Author**

Chevalier, Tracy, ed., *Twentieth-Century Children's Writers* (3rd ed.). St. James, 1989, pp. 454–55.
Commire, Anne, ed., *Something about the Author.* Gale, 1990, Vol. 58, pp. 96–106.
Daly, Jay. *Presenting S. E. Hinton.* Twayne, 1989.
de Montreville, Doris, and Crawford, Elizabeth D., eds., *Fourth Book of Junior Authors and Illustrators.* Wilson, 1978, pp. 176–77.
Garrett, Agnes, and McCue, Helga P., eds., *Authors and Artists for Young Adults.* Gale, 1989, Vol. 2, pp. 65–76.
Kirkpatrick, D. L., ed., *Twentieth-Century Children's Writers* (2nd ed.). St. Martin's, 1983, p. 377.
Locher, Frances C., ed., *Contemporary Authors.* Gale, 1979, Vols. 81–84, pp. 242–43.
Senick, Gerard J., ed., *Children's Literature Review.* Gale, 1978, Vol. 3, pp. 69–73.
Senick, Gerard J., ed., *Children's Literature Review.* Gale, 1991, Vol. 23, pp. 132–51.
Ward, Martha, ed., *Authors of Books for Young People* (3rd ed.). Scarecrow, 1990, p. 332.

---

**Kerr, M. E.**   *I Stay Near You: 1 Story in 3*
Harper, 1985, $12.89 (0-06-023105-X); pap., Berkley, $2.50 (0-425-08870-7)

---

Toward the end of this novel, which deals with three generations of male members of the Storm family, one of the characters states, "When a Storm falls in love, he *falls.*" This is the story of the ill-fated loves of the scions of this wealthy family who live palatially in upstate New York and of the many people whose destinies are changed by these attachments. The novel spans over forty years—from the early days of World War II through the mid-1980s—and is told in three separate but interconnected stories. The first is narrated by Laura Stewart, a casual friend of the central character, Mildred Cone. The second, told in the third person, focuses on Mildred's son, Vincent, and the last is a tape-recorded memoir by Powell, Vincent's son. This novel is enjoyed by readers in grades 7 through 10.

**Plot Summary**

*I Stay Near You: Mildred Cone in the Forties.* The year is 1942 and the setting is Cayuta, a small town in upstate New York. Although most of the members of the sophomore class of East High School in Cayuta rarely pay attention to their classmate Mildred Cone, when they do make reference to her, her name is usually preceded by the adjective "poor." In many respects, Mildred could accurately be called poor. She is the only girl in her class from the wrong side of the tracks (she had transferred from West High hoping to get a better education) and her family, including Mildred, all work at the White Lamb Laundry and live in a ramshackle house in back of the plant. Physically, she can be described, at best, as gawky. Her frizzy black hair and hand-me-down clothes only compound a sorry appearance, and the fact that she plays classical music on the harp at school assemblies does not endear her to her classmates. Mildred does not, however, feel sorry for herself. She is an independent, gutsy girl whose future plans involve competing for a music scholarship after graduation. The only person in her class who could remotely be called a friend is Laura Stewart, who pays attention to Mildred more from curiosity than affection.

In her junior year, the ugly duckling miraculously emerges as a swan and, though still not popular, Mildred gets more attention, particularly from the boys. As she adds some popular songs to her harp repertoire, her assembly appearances become less painful to endure.

During the following summer (it is now 1943), Mildred takes a job as a waitress at the Cayuta Yacht Club and there she meets Powell Storm, the handsome young son of the wealthiest family in the county. Powell is immediately attracted to this aloof, self-reliant beauty, and Mildred, in spite of an innate dislike of the rich, is also swept up in this love-at-first-sight situation. Although great differences separate them, they begin meeting secretly and their love for each other blossoms.

Powell has just enlisted in the navy. To commemorate his leaving for flight training, the Storms plan a gala July Fourth party at Cake, their huge mansion on Fire Hill overlooking Cayuta. In spite of obvious disapproval from both sets of parents, Powell invites Mildred as his date. For moral support, Mildred, in turn, invites Laura and another classmate, Horace (nicknamed Wormy) Haigney. At the party, Powell whisks Mildred away, leaving Laura and Wormy on their own. Although Laura briefly talks to Powell's older sister, Pesh, and her fiancé, Paul Spoonhour, she and Wormy are so out of their element that, in his discomfort, Wormy begins performing outlandish practical jokes. Powell's father, P. T. Storm, is outraged at this behavior and uses it as an excuse to order the three misfits off his property.

After Powell's departure for flight school, he and Mildred continue to communicate by letter. He showers her with presents, including a valuable family heirloom, a ring that contains an inscription in Basque, *Nagozu Aldean,* meaning "I Stay Near You." Powell obtains leave to return home in August to attend his sister Pesh's wedding. Once again he and Mildred are inseparable, although the Storms continue their campaign to break up the romance by various ploys—including embarrassing Mildred's parents during a formal dinner at Cake.

Wormy, who now calls himself Ace, enlists in the army during his senior year and is sent to Georgia for training. Unfortunately, Mildred is so preoccupied with Powell that her grades suffer and she loses the coveted scholarship. In August, Powell, now an ensign, again returns on leave to his family and Mildred. Their romance continues to cause family friction.

That November, Mildred discovers she is pregnant. She confides in Ace, who is on leave in Cayuta. Knowing that Mildred's pride will not allow her to ask help from the Storms, Ace proposes marriage so that her child will have a legitimate father. Mildred accepts and the two leave town for Ace's army base in the South. A few months later she has a baby boy whom she names Vincent after the poet she and Powell love, Edna St. Vincent Millay. Three months later news is received that Powell has been killed in action in the Pacific.

Laura attends the funeral. At the gravesite, she notices in the distance a young girl dressed in black accompanied by a soldier. Mildred and Ace have come to pay their last respects.

*Welcome to My Disappearance: Vincent Haigney in the Sixties.* Vincent has inherited his mother's musical talents. His instrument is not the harp, however, but the guitar and on it he has composed a number of fine original songs, some of which he sings as part of his act at the Cayuta Coffee House where he plays evenings after school. He is now sixteen and living in Cayuta with his father, Ace, who owns the local printing shop, and his mother, Mildred. His mother has promised that on his eighteenth birthday, he will inherit the beautiful gold ring that she owns with some strange writing on it. In the meantime, because he wants a ring to wear as part of his costume, he wanders into Paris Antiques where he meets Joanna Fitch, the seventeen-year-old daughter of the owners. From this first sight, he is completely captivated by this smooth-talking, tough, ambitious girl. His parents try to dissuade him and tell him that the Fitches are no-goods who actually sell stolen goods in their shop and that Joanna is a tramp with an unsavory reputation. But Vincent is hooked. He creates opportunities to be with Joanna. One day he shows her his mother's gold ring and she asks if he will give it to her when it becomes his.

Vincent's infatuation is so consuming that he decides to run away to New York City with Joanna. Before they can complete their plans, the police raid Paris Antiques and discover stolen goods. Joanna is sent to California to escape arrest. Vincent is devastated, particularly when he learns that the owner of the club where he plays has also gone to California to marry Joanna. He spends weeks in his room crying. One day, his mother comes to comfort him. She tells him about his real father and that he is actually part of the wealthy Storm clan. She also tells him how she was given the ring and, to console him, says he can now have it. It is too late. Before she left for California, Vincent had taken it from his mother's drawer and given it to Joanna.

*Something I've Never Told You: Powell Storm Haigney in the Eighties.* As part of an English assignment, Powell Storm Haigney, age fifteen, tape records a message to his father, once-famous rock star Vincent Haigney, now burned out from booze and drugs and out of the public eye. From these memoirs, Powell (also known as P.S.) continues the story of the Storm family and his grandmother Mildred.

After Vincent learned of his parentage, he moved to Cake to be with his Aunt Pesh and Uncle Paul. There he became a close friend of their son, Storm Spoonhour, but unfortunately both fall in love with Jackie, a beautiful local girl. When Vincent and Jackie marry, Storm is so distraught that he commits suicide. This death produces such a strain on the marriage that after Powell's birth, they are divorced. Powell lives with his mother until her untimely death in an automobile accident. Then he is sent to live with Pesh and Paul. Powell rarely hears from his father, who is caught up in a celebrity whirl, and the boy longs to be loved by the father he scarcely knows. While attending prep school in Boston, Powell is invited by Vincent to attend the Grammy Awards presentation in California. Anxious to be with his father, he leaves school without permission. During the ceremonies Vincent deserts his son when he sees still-attractive Joanna. Because of his absence, Powell is expelled from school. Pesh and her husband show such displeasure over this that Powell decides to move in with his widowed grandmother, Mildred, who now shares a house with another widow, her childhood friend Laura. Though he has left Cake, Powell still has his memories and also the beautiful gold ring with the strange inscription that Pesh gave him. (Many years before, she had been able to retrieve it from Joanna.) For now, Mildred proudly wears the ring on a chain around her neck but soon, when he comes of age, it will be time to give it back to her grandson.

**Thematic Material**

Through these stories that focus on three generations of teenagers, readers explore various aspects of love—how it can inspire, destroy, scar, elevate, cripple, and, most important, change the destinies of those who come after. Social relationships in a small town are interestingly depicted and the debilitating effects of class distinction and separation by different life-styles and financial backgrounds are well portrayed. The cause-and-effect continuity of life from one generation to the next is explored as well as a wide variety of personal relationships. Through the use of authentic details, the author has accurately re-created three different periods in contemporary American history. A secondary theme is that although times change, human emotions remain constant. Other themes explored are sacrifice, friendship, and father-son relations.

**Book Talk Material**

Showing the dust-jacket picture of the ring and its inscription and giving basic background plot information should interest young readers. Some incidents in the first story for reading or retelling are: Mildred and the Storm family are introduced (pp. 3–8); Mildred and Powell meet at the Cayuta Yacht Club (pp. 15–23); and the disastrous July Fourth party (pp. 37–48). In the second story, Vincent meets Joanna (pp. 83–88).

**Additional Selections**

Cassandra sees little of her famous rock-star mother and forms a friendship with street-wise Mollie in Hila Colman's *Rich and Famous Like My Mom* (Crown, 1988, $10.95).

In Cynthia Rylant's *A Kindness* (Orchard, 1988, $13.95; pap., Dell,

$3.25), Chip finds his single-parent mother is pregnant and refuses to name the father.

Bonnie is envious of her teenage friends, Linda and Ray, who are married, but later discovers that they, too, have problems in Margaret Willey's *If Not for You* (Harper, 1988, $11.95; pap., $3.25).

In her fantasy world, Australian teenager Sydney imagines herself the daughter of a famous rock star in Colby Radowsky's *Sydney, Herself* (Farrar, 1989, $12.95).

Fourteen-year-old Grayling enjoys hearing the life stories of her grandmother, an aunt, and two women cousins who all live together in a house in Seattle in Jean Thesman's *The Rain Catchers* (Houghton, 1991, $14.95).

In Margaret Shaw's *A Wider Tomorrow* (Holiday, 1990, $13.95), a British teenager must choose between attending college and following her boyfriend to America.

After a glorious senior year at high school, Hallie finds she is left behind by her college-bound friends and she gradually sinks into depression in *The Party's Over* (Scholastic, 1991, $13.95) by Caroline B. Cooney.

**About the Book**
*Booklist*, April 15, 1985, p. 1179.
*Center for Children's Books Bulletin,* June 1985, p. 188.
*Kirkus Reviews*, March 1, 1985, p. J 18.
*School Library Journal*, April 1985, p. 98.
*VOYA*, June 1985, p. 132.
See also *Book Review Digest*, 1986, p. 876; and *Book Review Index*, 1985, p. 339.

**About the Author**
Chevalier, Tracy, ed., *Twentieth-Century Children's Writers* (3rd ed.). St. James, 1989, pp. 523–25 (under Marijane Meaker).
Commire, Anne, ed., *Something about the Author*. Gale, 1980, Vol. 10, pp. 124–26 (under Marijane Meaker).
Commire, Anne, ed., *Something about the Author*. Gale, 1990, Vol. 61, pp. 117–27 (under Marijane Meaker).
de Montreville, Doris, and Crawford, Elizabeth D., eds., *Fourth Book of Junior Authors and Illustrators*. Wilson, 1978, pp. 210–12.
Garrett, Agnes, and McCue, Helga P., eds., *Authors and Artists for Young Adults*. Gale, 1989, Vol. 2, pp. 123–38.
Kerr, M. E., *Me Me Me Me Me*. Harper, 1983; pap., NAL.
Kirkpatrick, D. L., ed., *Twentieth-Century Children's Writers* (2nd ed.). St. Martin's, 1983, pp. 428–29.
May, Hal, ed., *Contemporary Authors*. Gale, 1983, Vol. 107, pp. 332–36 (under Marijane Meaker).

Nilsen, Alleen Pace, *Presenting M. E. Kerr.* Twayne, 1986.
Roginski, Jim, *Behind the Covers Volume II.* Libraries Unlimited, 1989, pp. 161–76.
Sarkissian, Adele, ed., *Something about the Author: Autobiography Series.* Gale, 1986, Vol. 1, pp. 141–54.
Ward, Martha, ed., *Authors of Books for Young People* (3rd ed.). Scarecrow, 1990, p. 392 (under Marijane Meaker).

---

**Koertge, Ron.** *The Arizona Kid*
Little, Brown, 1988, $14.95 (0-316-50101-8); pap., Avon, $3.50 (0-380-70776-4)

---

This is Ron Koertge's second novel for young adults. It was preceded by *Where the Kissing Never Stops* (Little, Brown, 1986, $14.95; pap., Dell, $2.95), the story of Walker, a teenager beset by sexual fantasies and yearnings who, while trying to adjust to the fact that his mother has become a stripper in a local roadhouse, finally has his first love affair. *The Arizona Kid* was followed by *The Man in the Moon* (Little, Brown, 1990, $14.95), also about a sexually obsessed seventeen-year-old boy who finds love with a compassionate girlfriend. The title comes from the hero's severe case of acne, which makes his face resemble a lunar surface. All three novels have been characterized as bawdy and irreverent because they often deal with sexual situations in frank, explicit language. In addition to naturalistic, authentic dialogue and situations, each is suffused with good humor, believable characterizations, fast-moving plots, and probing explorations of human relationships. Because of the candid treatment of sex in these novels, they are recommended for mature readers in the ninth grade and up.

**Plot Summary**

As the Amtrak train from Kansas City pulls into the station in Tucson, Arizona, on a hot June afternoon, an apprehensive young man of sixteen named Billy Kennedy disembarks. Billy has left his comfortable, secure home in the small midwestern town of Bradeyville to spend the summer with his Uncle Wes and he is feeling somewhat fearful about living with a gay uncle he scarcely knows and working at a local racetrack. A combination of heat and tension takes its toll and, as Billy moves along the platform to greet his uncle, he faints—hardly a propitious beginning. Nevertheless, Billy and Wes become friends immediately.

Wes is hardly a typical uncle. He is not only a gay activist and volunteer at an AIDS crisis center, but also the owner of one of the smartest craft and artifact shops in the entire city. He is also incredibly handsome, well-built, sophisticated, and, most important, a very nice guy.

Billy could also be classified as a nice guy. Coming from a loving and stable home, he is friendly, decent, and generally has good feelings about himself except for two conditions he regards as important deficiencies: his height (short) and his sexual status (virgin).

Wes's home is a perfect extension of the man himself—open, immaculate, tastefully furnished, and very chic. Billy is impressed but is also so exhausted from the trip that he retreats to his bedroom and almost sleeps around the clock.

The next day Wes takes Billy to the racetrack to meet his boss, Jack Ferguson, a respected local horse trainer. Billy will be working with an older (and much taller) teenager, Lew Coley, a veteran stable boy. Together they will be cleaning the stalls and feeding the horses that have been placed in Jack's care. Their relationship begins poorly when Lew calls Billy "Short Stuff" but when Billy stands his ground and refuses to answer other than to his correct name, Lew realizes that, though short, Billy is tough and spunky. Soon they develop mutual respect and a deep friendship. Billy gets to know Lew's girlfriend, Abby Dayton, daughter of a wealthy horse owner, and is immediately attracted to an aloof blond horse exerciser about his age named Cara Mae Whitney.

One of the troublesome horses in the stable is a mare, Moon Medicine, who could be a fine racehorse but is so nervous and high strung that she is a constant "stall walker," wasting all her energy before each race. Because Jack makes most of his money betting on the horses he tends, it is important not to divulge information about the condition of the horses in order that favorable odds can be maintained at the betting windows. Billy is not aware of this and two no-goods, the crooked trainer Fletcher Denman and his sidekick Grif, trick Billy into giving them information about Moon Medicine. Jack's anger teaches Billy a valuable lesson.

One evening Lew and Billy are joined at the track by Cara and Abby. After the races, the four drive in Lew's car to a butte overlooking Tucson. While Lew and Abby make out in the front seat, Billy and Cara have a chance to talk and soon Billy realizes that much of Cara's bravado is a bluff to hide her own anxieties and insecurities. Her mother left some ten years ago and she lives alone with her father, a racetracker who moves with the horses. Although Cara loves racetrack life, the scars of constant moving have left her confused and lonely. The two share stories of their pasts and hopes for the future: Billy to become a veterinarian and Cara a horse trainer.

With the help of Uncle Wes and his gift of western boots and a tall-crowned hat, Billy begins to look and act less like a tourist. Wes also gives him the use of a van for the remainder of the summer and, after learning about Cara, a handful of condoms.

At the stable Billy inadvertently discovers how to cure the Moon's jitters. A pet chicken placed in her stall miraculously acts as a tranquilizer and hope now rises for her future as a winner. But these hopes are short-lived as Fletcher and Grif gain training rights from the horse's owner and transfer her to their nearby stables. Several days later, Billy brings Chicken Little to visit the Moon and finds the mare dead in her stall. Jack thinks it is a heart attack, but Billy believes the cause of death was loneliness.

Meanwhile Billy and Cara grow closer and gradually realize they have fallen in love. With each date Cara and Billy's relationship deepens and becomes more intimate. They decide to sleep together. The opportunity comes one weekend when Wes is away. Although it is the first time for both, it is a beautiful and fulfilling experience.

From Uncle Wes, Billy learns about the alternate sexual life-styles of homosexuals. Though far from promiscuous, Wes occasionally participates in the life of bar cruising and one-night stands. Billy shares Wes's despair and agony at the illness and death of friends stricken with AIDS.

August rolls around and Billy realizes sadly that in one month he must leave Arizona. Everyone's attention at the racetrack is focused on the upcoming Labor Day Tucson Derby. A new batch of horses arrives for the races. Lew rashly accepts a $500 bet with Fletcher and Grif that The Dark Mirage, the new three-year-old filly sent to Jack for training, will beat their rival's new acquisition, French Bred. Billy and Lew dig deep into their precious savings to collect the necessary $500.

Unfortunately, The Dark Mirage suffers from the same impulsive nervousness as Moon's Medicine. At her first workout with Cara in the saddle, the horse bucks and races so violently that Cara faces the embarrassment of being rescued by one of the other riders.

As a last resort, Jack decides to send the horse to a small quiet training center outside town. The change in surroundings works and while the Dark's performance improves, news comes that French Bred's has not. When the Dark is returned to the stables at the racetrack, Jack is so afraid that Fletcher and Grif might try to harm the horse that he orders a twenty-four-hour watch, with Billy and Lew jointly taking the night shift.

The night before the big race, Lew doesn't show up. Billy learns that Lew's father, an eccentric survivalist, has "kidnapped" his son to go on maneuvers. On his own, Billy becomes nervous when he hears footsteps approaching. It is Cara, who has come to keep him company. Realizing with sadness that in only two days they will be parting, they once again declare their love. They are interrupted by the arrival of Fletcher and Grif. Courageously Billy confronts them and manages to scare them off by threatening to report them to the authorities. That night in the stables, Cara and Billy make love once more and promise that though separated they will always keep in touch.

On the day of the race, Cara and Billy are given the privilege of walking the horse from her stall to the jockey and giving tips on how to handle the horse properly. As expected, The Dark Mirage wins over French Bred. Lew and Billy collect the $500, but this moment of triumph suddenly becomes one of sadness as Billy says good-bye to his friends, including Cara.

The next day, Wes takes Billy to the train station. As a parting gesture Billy gives his uncle his hat for safekeeping. Wes promises to keep it in Billy's room so it will be there when he returns.

**Thematic Material**

With wit and understanding, the author has created a tender but unsentimental story of two young people coming of age. The necessity of accepting one's physical and emotional makeup is examined. Various types of love are explored and contrasted: for example, the casual physical relationship of Lew and Abby, the tender tentative feelings shared by Billy and Cara, and the homosexual life-style of Uncle Wes. All are portrayed honestly but with compassion. The need for tolerance and understanding of others is stressed and Billy's growing love and admiration for his uncle are well depicted. The description of gay life is refreshingly candid without being lurid and a serious message about AIDS is given. The reader also learns a great deal about behind-the-scenes racetrack life. Courage, the triumph of justice, and coping with parting are other themes that are developed in this novel.

**Book Talk Material**

A fine introduction to the novel would be to describe Billy's arrival in Tucson, his meeting with Uncle Wes, and the embarrassing fainting spell (pp. 1–5). Other interesting passages are: Wes takes Billy to his shop and they discuss AIDS (pp. 17–20); Billy meets Jack and Lew (pp. 24–28); Billy meets Lew's eccentric family (pp. 42–46); he learns a little about Cara and about racetrack betting (pp. 53–59); and Cara and Billy get to know one another (pp. 63–68).

### Additional Selections

For mature readers, Alice Childress explores the closeted life of a gay teenage boy and the cover-up of a rape in *Those Other People* (Putnam, 1989, $13.95).

After his girlfriend drops him, George finds a new romance via his sister's computer in Harry Mazer's *City Light* (Scholastic, 1988, $12.95; pap., $2.75).

Isabelle Holland's *Man without a Face* (Lippincott, 1972, $12.89; pap., Harper, $2.95) tells the story of a teenage boy who engages a disfigured gay man as a teacher.

An abandoned teenage Ute boy is sent to a ranch in Colorado to live with a lonesome old miner in Will Hobbs's *Bearstone* (Atheneum, 1989, $12.95).

In a novel for an older audience, Jack's divorced father tells his son that he is gay in A. M. Homes's *Jack* (Macmillan, 1989, $13.95; pap., Random, $8.95); and in Norma Klein's *Now That I Know* (Bantam, 1989, $13.99), Nina's father tells her that he is gay and that his lover is moving in.

Two excellent novels that deal with same-sex love affairs are Nancy Garden's *Annie on My Mind* (Farrar, 1982, $12.95; pap., $3.50), about Liza and Annie, two New York City high school seniors, and Sandra Scoppettone's *Trying Hard to Hear You* (Harper, 1974, $13.89), about the tragic love of Jeff and Phil, two Long Island teenagers.

The Cohens, Susan and Daniel, discuss both gays and lesbians from the standpoint of nongays seeking basic, authentic information in *When Someone You Know Is Gay* (Evans, 1989, $13.95).

### About the Book

*Book Report*, September 1988, p. 34.
*Booklist*, May 1, 1988, p. 154.
*Center for Children's Books Bulletin*, June 1988, p. 209.
*Kirkus Reviews*, May 1, 1988, p. 694.
*New York Times Book Review*, August 21, 1988, p. 25.
*School Library Journal*, June 1988, p. 118.

*VOYA*, October 1988, p. 183.
See also *Book Review Digest*, 1988, pp. 918–19; and *Book Review Index*, 1988, p. 458, and 1989, p. 458.

**About the Author**
Commire, Anne, ed., *Something about the Author*. Gale, 1988, Vol. 53, pp. 95–96.
May, Hal, and Straub, Deborah A., eds., *Contemporary Authors* (New Revision Series). Gale, 1989, Vol. 25, p. 253.

---

**Konigsburg, E. L.**  *Father's Arcane Daughter*
Atheneum, 1976, $12.95 (0-689-30524-9); pap., Dell, $3.25 (0-440-42496-8)

---

This novel, like so many by this author (such as *George* [pap., Dell, $3.25; condensed in *More Juniorplots*, Bowker, 1977, pp. 112–15] and *Journey to an 800 Number* [Atheneum, 1982, $13.95; pap., Dell, $3.25]), deals with family relationships complicated by special conflicts within the chief protagonist. Dictionaries define *arcane* as "mysterious, secret, esoteric" and "known or understood only by those having secret, special knowledge." Reading this book, one wonders whether the title refers to Caroline, the mysterious woman who appears after an absence of seventeen years, or to young Heidi, the troubled product of a second marriage. The surprise ending reveals the truth. The intricately structured plot shifts between two different time periods. The first takes the form of a recollection by the narrator, Winston, of events that took place in 1952. The second is told in fragments of a conversation between Winston and his sister Heidi, over twenty-five years later in the late 1970s. This short but complex novel is enjoyed by readers in grades 6 through 9.

**Plot Summary**
From early childhood, Winston Eliot Carmichael knew his family was rich—really rich. Living in the most fashionable area of Pittsburgh, surrounded by servants including a butler and a chauffeur, and attending the posh Wardhill Academy are all signs of the wealth that surrounds him. Now a seventh-grader, he lives with his father, the outwardly affable and industrious custodian of this great fortune; his mother, a typical grande dame of society who is extremely conscious of position and propriety; and a younger sister, Hilary, usually called Heidi, who at age ten

is strangely undeveloped for her age. She shuffles animal-like instead of walking, is always thumb-sucking, and often engages in strange behavior to gain attention. Although she shows flashes of intelligence, she usually acts so remote and vacant that Winston worries about this unusual sister whose erratic behavior is usually ignored by his parents.

Another subject not discussed in the Carmichael household is the tragic event that occurred seventeen years earlier, during Mr. Carmichael's first marriage. His daughter Caroline, a freshman at college, was kidnapped and held for $1 million ransom. The kidnappers' hideout caught fire during a police shootout, and it was believed that Caroline died in the fire, though positive identification of the charred bodies was not possible. The results of this traumatic experience caused Anne, Caroline's mother and heir to the vast Adkins fortune, to sink into alcoholism, the cause of her premature death, while her husband lives a life haunted by tragic memories and unresolved questions. Even now, in 1952, almost two decades after these events, the overly protective attitude of Mr. Carmichael and his second wife toward their children is a symptom of residual fears that cannot be erased.

Winston is a precocious, wildly imaginative youngster who has no real friends except Barney Krupp, whom he sees only at school. In his lonely, isolated world, Winston has developed a sensitivity and wisdom beyond his years, particularly in his relationship with Heidi, whom he alternately scorns and pities.

Only months from what would have been Caroline's thirty-fifth birthday, the deadline for her to claim the Adkins inheritance, a strange woman claiming to be Caroline appears at the Carmichael mansion. She passes test after test, infallibly remembering facts about family life before the kidnapping, including insignificant details about Finchley, the prep school she attended; its headmistress, Agatha Trollope; and dear friends like Bunny Miller. There can be no doubt that she is Caroline. She explains that after the nightmare of the kidnapping, she wanted a new life, and, assuming the name Martha Sedgewick, spent many years as a social worker in Ethiopia. After her recent return to the United States, she had deliberately taken a position in a nursing home where her partially senile grandmother, Flora Adkins, was a patient. Before her death, Mrs. Adkins, who realized Martha was really her granddaughter Caroline, persuaded her to resume her former life.

Caroline quickly establishes a friendship with Winston, who finds in this highly intelligent, astute, but somewhat enigmatic woman the confidante he always wanted. She also is concerned about Heidi's problems and secretly has her tested by her old friend Bunny Miller, now Bunny Walheim, who has a doctorate in child development. The tests confirm what both Winston and Caroline suspected. Heidi has above-normal intelligence but suffers from physical disabilities, including a severe hearing impairment. At first Mrs. Carmichael, who is actually ashamed of this daughter whom she secretly thinks is retarded, refuses to believe the diagnosis and denies Caroline access to Heidi. Caroline persists, and through appeals to her father, is able to get Heidi the treatment she needs.

Throughout all of these months with his newly found half-sister, whom he adores, Winston has inwardly questioned her identity. One day before Caroline leaves the city to begin the college career previously denied her, he asks her for the truth. She gives him a sealed envelope and tells him that the contents will reveal whether she really is Caroline Adkins Carmichael.

Twenty-five years later, Winston, now a writer, retains the unopened envelope. Caroline has just died and Winston is visiting his sister's office to make funeral arrangements. Hilary, who has discarded her childish nickname Heidi, has become a very successful business executive. Winston shows her the envelope and together they talk of Caroline and how she changed their lives. Not only did she end the torment of uncertainty and loss that had dominated their father's life, but she also gave Hilary the life that would have been denied her and freed Winston from the guilt about his sister that had impaired his development.

The mystery remains—who was this woman really, their sister or an imposter? From the envelope Hilary produces a document and asks Winston to read it. It is a lengthy statement signed by Headmistress Trollope, who has been promised a monetary gift for Caroline's alma mater, Finchley School, as a token of gratitude for supplying this information.

As part of her college admission requirements, Caroline had visited Agatha Trollope to obtain a transcript of her work at Finchley. The headmistress knew that the real Caroline had a below average I.Q. and that the woman with whom she was talking did not. Martha Sedgewick then told her the truth. She was an orphan who had indeed worked in Ethiopia and had later been the personal nurse of old Mrs. Adkins. In her muddled state of mind, the old lady confused her with her dead granddaughter, Caroline, and nightly told her in intimate detail about the Carmichael family. To please the dying woman in the weeks that followed, Martha gradually assumed this new identity. After Grand-mother Adkins's death, Martha decided to present herself as Caroline, not because of the inheritance, but as a way to help this tortured family.

Brother and sister decide to keep Martha's secret and bury these docu-ments with her. To them, she will always be their sister Caroline, the first of Mr. Carmichael's two arcane daughters.

**Thematic Material**

This novel explores the nature of truth, as both an abstract and a pragmatic entity. Defining truth as "that which works" explains the deci-sion to hide the deception involving Caroline's reappearance. Complex family relationships are explored in the interaction among a mother who, driven by concern for social status, is damaging her family's future, a father eager to believe lies to assuage ghosts from the past, a son who feels guilt that he is normal when his sister is not, and an intelligent daughter trapped in a malfunctioning body. The extent to which the past can dominate the present is explored, as is the theme that wealth does not necessarily produce happiness. This novel also depicts how the intervention of a single individual can change and reshape the lives of others.

**Book Talk Material**

A definition of the word *arcane* and a brief explanation of the family situation when Caroline appears should interest readers. Some interest-ing episodes are: a typical Saturday for Winston and Heidi (pp. 26–29); Winston tells about his only friend, Barney (pp. 24–26); a description of the kidnapping and its effects (pp. 14–19); Caroline and Winston get to know one another (pp. 37–40); and Caroline passes some truth tests administered subtly by Mrs. Carmichael (pp. 43–45).

**Additional Selections**

In a sequel to Mary R. Ryan's *Dance a Step Closer* (pap., Dell, 1988, $2.95), *I'd Rather Be Dancing* (Delacorte, 1989, $14.95), teenager Katie Kusik learns a great deal about herself during a summer at Manhattan's American Dance Conservatory.

Jane learns she has a new family resulting from her father's secret remarriage years before in Nina Bawden's *The Outside Child* (Lothrop, Lee & Shepard, 1989, $12.95).

Drew wonders if the witch that lives in his brain is real or the result of an LSD trip in Ruth Riddell's *Shadow Witch* (Atheneum, 1989, $13.95). In *Annie John* (Farrar, 1985, $18.95; pap., Plume, $6.95) by Jamaica Kincaid, a stubborn West Indian girl is continually at odds with her mother.

Mick searches for answers to questions about life as he realizes his father's mental condition is worsening in Phyllis Reynolds Naylor's *The Keeper* (Atheneum, 1986, $12.95; pap., Bantam, $2.95).

Sassy Jo spends a summer with her alcoholic mother, who had abandoned her years before, in J. P. Reading's *The Summer of Sassy Jo* (Houghton, 1989, $13.95).

When Stacy receives an unexpected legacy from an elderly actress, she sets out to find out the circumstances of the old lady's death in Norma Johnston's *The Time of the Cranes* (Four Winds, 1990, $13.95).

**About the Book**

*Booklist,* September 15, 1976, p. 177.
*Center for Children's Books Bulletin,* September 1976, p. 12.
*Horn Book,* October 1976, p. 504.
*Kirkus Reviews,* July 15, 1976, p. 795.
*New York Times Book Review,* November 7, 1976, p. 44.
*School Library Journal,* September 1976, p. 134.
See also *Book Review Digest,* 1977, p. 740; and *Book Review Index,* 1976, p. 243, and 1977, p. 244.

**About the Author**

Block, Ann, and Riley, Carolyn, eds., *Children's Literature Review.* Gale, 1976, Vol. 1, pp. 118–23.
Chevalier, Tracy, ed., *Twentieth-Century Children's Writers* (3rd ed.). St. James, 1989, pp. 541–42.
Commire, Anne, ed., *Something about the Author.* Gale, 1987, Vol. 48, pp. 140–47.
de Montreville, Doris, and Hill, Donna, eds., *Third Book of Junior Authors.* Wilson, 1972, pp. 164–65.
Konigsburg, E. L., *Throwing Shadows.* Atheneum, 1979.
Metzger, Linda, ed., *Contemporary Authors* (New Revision Series). Gale, 1986, Vol. 17, pp. 249–54.
Ward, Martha, ed., *Authors of Books for Young People* (3rd ed.). Scarecrow, 1990, p. 403.

**Korman, Gordon.** *A Semester in the Life of a Garbage Bag*
Scholastic, 1988, pap., $2.75 (0-590-40695-7)

Gordon Korman's zany humor and fast-paced plots seem to be inspired by a combination of comic strips like *Archie* and television sitcoms. Regardless of their origins, they have captured a wide range of young readers who identify with their hapless young heroes, who are usually faced with seemingly insurmountable problems often caused by adult intervention or stupidity. This Canadian author's first book was published when he was only thirteen. Since then he has written over a dozen novels for young readers, including *Don't Care High* (pap., Scholastic, $2.95) and *Son of Interflux* (Scholastic, 1986, $12.95; pap., $2.95). The "garbage bag" of this title is Raymond Jardine, one of the two protagonists, who maintains that his life is like one of those garbage bags in commercials where someone is always increasing the pressure to test its strength. This is a typical Jardinism, that is, a remark filled with exaggeration, jaundiced humor, and off-the-wall logic. As the title suggests, the action takes place during a single high school semester from September to December. This story is enjoyed by both junior and senior high readers.

**Plot Summary**
DeWitt High School, situated in a middle-class suburban New York community on Long Island, has begun the school year with an aura of distinction because it is the home of a $33 million experiment by the Department of Energy called the Solar/Air Current Generating System or SACGEN. For the students it represents a huge technological lemon. This conglomeration of solar panels and windmills situated on the roof like a mechanical garbage pile has been nicknamed "The Windmill." It malfunctions so frequently that the school is continually being plunged into darkness. Some areas are grossly overheated—the students now call the cafeteria "Miami Beach"—whereas others, like the indoor swimming pool, resemble an arctic environment. Q. David Hyatt, the school principal (a.k.a. Q Dave), and the two supervising engineers, Sopwith and Johnson, refuse to admit any faults in the system. To them SACGEN is comparable to the miracle of sliced bread.

Not so for Sean Delancey, a student in his junior year. Bitter experience at home has taught him to doubt, indeed fear, modern gimmicks because his father, a New York businessman, and mother, a school-teacher, slavishly worship modern technology. They continually invest in such mechanical breakthroughs as the superefficient dishwasher that recently reduced the family crockery to a fine powder and the high-voltage air purifier that produced only a toxic blue cloud. Sean's fresh-man sister Nikki remains neutral on the subject, but his eighty-eight-year-old grandfather, recently transplanted to the Delancey household from Brooklyn, is firmly on the side of the nonrobots. Gramp Delancey has two obsessions: monitoring even the slightest climatic disturbance reported on the weather channel and smoking Scrulnick's, the world's most foul-smelling cigar.

Sean accurately considers himself to be an average, good-natured guy, with a fine record as guard on the school's basketball team. He has a lot of friends, including the school's hunk, Steve Semenski, and Howard Newman, the operator of the school's floating poker game. For betting purposes, they use toothpicks.

Into each life a little rain must fall, but when Raymond Jardine enters Sean's, it is comparable to a deluge. It begins when Mr. Kerr, the English teacher, organizes his class into pairs of students to study a modern poet of its choice and produce a lengthy term paper. Sean inherits Raymond, a new student at DeWitt. Raymond, who always refers to himself in the third person as Jardine, could be called an eccentric, a nonconformist, an oddball, or a kook—and each would be something of an understate-ment. His overriding ambition is to build his scholastic and service rec-ord during this semester so that he will be one of the six students at DeWitt High chosen to spend next summer on the Greek island of Theamelpos. This would provide him with access to Mediterranean beaches and beautiful vacationing Swedish girls and also supply him with an excuse to avoid his usual odious and odoriferous summer job gutting fish at his uncle's processing plant.

Mr. Kerr assigns another new student, the beautiful teenage model Ashley Bach, to Sean and Raymond's committee. Now the boys have another concern—how to keep the lovely Ashley to themselves and pre-vent her from meeting such jocks as Steve Semenski, whom Raymond refers to as Cementhead.

Raymond finds a strange three-lined poem called "Registration Day" written in 1949 by an obscure Canadian poet named Gavin Gunhold. In last-minute desperation, Gunhold's name is given to Mr. Kerr as the committee's topic. Unfortunately, when Sean and Raymond go to the

New York Public Library to do research, they find an obituary stating that before his death in a traffic accident, this promising author had completed only one poem, the aforementioned "Registration Day." Raymond, never at a loss for ideas, persuades Sean not to upset Ashley with this news and instead join him in writing some fictitious poems to flesh out the report. After hours of brainstorming, only three suitably enigmatic quatrains have been added to the Gunhold canon.

Raymond's bad luck continues to dog him. For social studies, his laudatory report on the stability of the government of Pefkakia is submitted on the day on which there is a revolution during which their king is beheaded. Undaunted, Raymond decides to better his school service record and persuades Ashley and Sean to join him in organizing the school's Halloween Party. On the night of the event, all goes well until "The Windmill" malfunctions, turning on the sprinkler system and sending hundreds of soaking students into the night. To add injury to insult, Raymond falls during one of SACGEN's blackouts and breaks his ankle.

To delay submitting the English report, Raymond announces in class that Gunhold now lives in New York and has consented to an interview. Ashley is excited at the thought of meeting a real poet and unconditionally demands to be part of the interview. Desperate to produce a Gunhold, Raymond persuades Sean's grandfather to assume the role. He is so convincing and charming that Ashley contacts some of her showbusiness friends and "Gunhold" is offered a spot on the talk show *Spice of Life*. Gramp, who loves both the deception and the notoriety, eagerly accepts and is such a great hit reading his poems (now five in number) and doing his yo-yo tricks that more offers pour in. Soon he has become such a celebrity that preventing the family from seeing Gramp on television becomes an almost full-time job for Sean, who decides that this deception should be put to good use. For an evening when he knows his parents will be in New York, he organizes, with the consent of Q Dave, a special student-teacher-parent meeting in the auditorium with guest speaker poet Gavin Gunhold. Hoping to strike a blow for justice and truth, Sean has persuaded his grandfather to publicly expose SACGEN for the imperfect boondoggle it is. However, the plan misfires. The audience takes sides, and during the subsequent riot, Gramp, Sean, Raymond, Ashley, and Steve (in spite of all efforts, he and Ashley have become an item) are nabbed by the police and brought to the station. The deception is revealed, parents are summoned, and finally everyone is allowed to return to their homes. The exertion of heating and lighting the auditorium for a whole evening proves too much for SACGEN, however, and that night it explodes.

The next morning the four students are summoned to Q. David Hyatt's office. He tells them that this July the government will rebuild SACGEN and that he certainly doesn't want any of them around to disturb construction. His solution? Send them all to Theamelpos. Perhaps Raymond's garbage-bag days are over.

**Thematic Material**

This is basically a zany comedy of errors that also gently spoofs modern technology, the misguided devotion to it, pretentiousness in poetry criticism, and the use of hype to create and sell a product. The theme of student-versus-the-establishment is an important one. Many high school institutions and activities are also held up to courteous ridicule. It is also a story of friendship, perseverance, and ingenuity. The growth of friendship between the two completely dissimilar protagonists is believably developed.

**Book Talk Material**

Explaining the title (see p. 19) and showing the dust jacket (which depicts Raymond with his foot in a cast) should interest readers. Some interesting passages: Q. Dave's pride over SACGEN (pp. 4–6); the Delanceys and modern technology (pp. 10–14); Raymond discovers Gavin Gunhold (pp. 53–57); the Halloween dance (pp. 84–99); seeing the obituary of Gavin Gunhold (pp. 103–08); and poetry writing (pp. 108–13).

**Additional Selections**

Seven commuting students spend their weeknights at a motel near their school in Thelma Hatch Wyss's amusing *Here at the Scenic-Vu Motel* (Harper, 1988, $13.95; pap., $3.50).

A high school sophomore falls hopelessly in love with a self-centered heartthrob in Robert Kaplow's humorous *Alessandra in Love* (Lippincott, 1989, $11.95; pap., $3.50).

Conte Mark takes advantage of a computer error and doubles his class load in Sonia Levitin's *The Mark of Conte* (pap., Macmillan, 1976, $2.95).

J. D. Landis has written a fast-paced, bouncy teenage romance in *Looks Aren't Everything* (Bantam, 1990, $13.95; pap., 3.50).

In Laura A. Sonnenmark's *Something's Rotten in the State of Maryland*

(Scholastic, 1990, $12.95), Marie finds that being a look-alike of Snow White has disadvantages even though she has been honored by having her adaptation of *Hamlet* produced at school.

Adrian Mole has problems growing up as revealed in his hilarious journal, *Secret Diary of Adrian Mole, Aged 13 3/4* by Sue Townsend (pap., Avon, 1984, $3.95).

Becky and Nemi's friendship becomes more serious as they rehearse for a high school play in Marilyn Singer's *The Course of True Love Never Did Run Smooth* (Harper, 1983, $12.95).

**About the Book**
*Booklist*, August 1987, p. 1738.
*Horn Book*, November 1987, p. 744.
*Kirkus Reviews*, July 1, 1987, p. 994.
*School Library Journal*, October 1987, p. 140.
*VOYA*, December 1986, p. 219.
See also *Book Review Digest*, 1988, p. 961; and *Book Review Index*, 1987, p. 432, and 1988, p. 460.

**About the Author**
Commire, Anne, ed., *Something about the Author*. Gale, 1987, Vol. 49, pp. 146–50.
May, Hal, ed., *Contemporary Authors*. Gale, 1985, Vol. 112, p. 289.
Senick, Gerard J., ed., *Children's Literature Review*. Gale, 1991, Vol. 25, pp. 98–112.

---

**Lowry, Lois.** *Rabble Starkey*
Houghton, 1987, $12.95 (0-395-43607-9); pap., Dell, $3.25 (0-440-40056-2)

---

One of the highlights of Lois Lowry's distinguished literary career occurred in 1990 when she received the Newbery Medal for *Number the Stars* (Houghton, 1989, $12.95; pap., Dell, $3.50), a novel based on the Danish underground's efforts to save Jewish families during the Nazi occupation in World War II. Before that she had written many fine novels for the middle grades, including those about the untamable Anastasia Krupnik, plus a number at the junior high level such as *Find a Stranger, Say Goodbye* (Houghton, 1978, $14.95; pap., Dell, $3.50) and *A Summer to Die* (Houghton, 1977, $13.95; pap., Bantam, $2.95). *Rabble Starkey* straddles both groups. Although its heroine is a sixth-grader, the concept and interest levels of the novel are such that the book has appeal to readers from sixth to ninth grades. It is a first-person narrative, told candidly and often in ungrammatical English (e.g., "we was going") by a feisty, intelligent young girl from rural West Virginia. The action takes place over a single school year (from September to June). During this time, Rabble's grammar improves somewhat partly because of her own efforts and partly because of corrections from her dearest friend, Veronica (e.g., "we *were* going, Rabble").

## Plot Summary

For the past four years, twelve-year-old Rabble and her loving mother Sweet-Ho (short for Sweet-Hosanna) Starkey have lived in a small two-room apartment with bath above the Bigelows' garage in the town of Highriver, West Virginia. Sweet-Ho serves as housekeeper to the Bigelows with responsibilities involving cooking, cleaning, and taking care of the Bigelow family. This includes daughter Veronica, also twelve and Rabble's best friend, the sickly but good-natured four-year-old brother, Gunther, and Mrs. Bigelow, who, though harmless and quiet, is obviously losing hold of reality and sinking into insanity. Norman Cox, the obnoxious son of the local minister and classmate of Rabble and Veronica, even publicly calls Mrs. Bigelow "one of the crazies." Phil Bigelow, the father, is a kindly, understanding real estate agent who, in spite of these family difficulties, is good-natured and attentive to both his own family and the Starkeys.

One of the first assignments given to Rabble and Veronica by their sixth-grade teacher, Mrs. Hindler, is to construct family trees. This gives Rabble and Veronica an opportunity to review their past histories. Sweet-Ho loves to retell the story of the day she was sent by her mother, the widow Naomi Jones, to buy molasses at Appleby's General Store and saw an attractive ginger-haired man of about twenty sitting in a pickup truck outside the store. It was love at first sight. Impulsive fourteen-year-old Sweet-Ho ran off to get married to Ginger Starkey and her mother never did get the molasses. However, when their baby arrived, Ginger deserted them and Sweet-Ho returned home. It was Naomi who named the baby Parable Ann, but this soon was shortened to Rabble. It was also Gnomie (Rabble's version of Naomi) who raised the child. When Naomi's health declined and Sweet-Ho found the job with the Bigelows, Rabble moved with her mother to Highriver, shortly before her grandmother's death. The Joneses were numerous and when drawing her family tree

Rabble finds she has so many cousins that she lends some to Veronica, who unfortunately has only her immediate family to claim. Veronica is Rabble's age but is maturing faster physically, much to her embarrassment. She is more gentle than the boisterous Rabble, but the two are close friends. Both love the young brother, Gunther, who because of his many ailments and allergies exists on bananas, hard-boiled eggs, and Chef Boyardee spaghetti.

One hot Saturday afternoon, Rabble and Veronica decide to take Gunther to the creek to cool off. They pass the house of old Millie Bellows, the town grouch, who seems immune to any show of kindness or civility. At the creek they are tormented by the bully Norman Cox, who throws rocks at them, one of which injures Gunther. While giving chase, they hear Gunther's frantic screams. Mrs. Bigelow, who has followed them to the stream, has Gunther in her arms. After licking the blood from the wound, she tries to breast-feed him and then enacts a mock baptism scene that half drowns the child before the girls can rescue him and escort a passive Mrs. Bigelow home. News of the breakdown speeds through town. Even crotchety Millie Bellows sends over a Jell-O salad to help. Reluctantly, Mr. Bigelow commits his wife to the local mental hospital, Meadowhill. Veronica is so troubled and embarrassed by the situation that at one point she wants to erase her mother's name from her family tree. Mr. Bigelow invites the Starkeys to move into the family house and suddenly Rabble begins to feel part of a real family.

Halloween comes and the two girls in gypsy disguises dress Gunther as a mini-ballerina and go out trick-or-treating. Millie Bellows is slow to answer her bell and when she does, she is hit in the face by a stone thrown from the shrubbery. Rabble runs after the attacker, and though he escapes, he drops a hat that is later identified as belonging to Norman Cox.

Out of pity, the two girls begin visiting and cleaning house for a still grumpy and ungrateful Millie Bellows. Some of the chores require a boy's strength, and Rabble decides to blackmail Norman into helping them by using the threat of revealing him as the guilty stone-thrower. Veronica, who would rather forgive and forget, suggests a milder method of persuasion. She knows that Norman is secretly attracted to her and, by applying some of her charms, tames Norman into becoming a willing helper. Rabble, however, is so jealous of the attention Veronica pays Norman and so fearful that her friend no longer cares for her that she becomes distant. The rift is mended when, at a birthday party the two girls attend, Rabble deliberately passes up a chance to reveal Norman as the culprit and, as a result, regains Veronica's respect.

Mr. Bigelow believes that Sweet-Ho has great untapped potential. Gradually he is able to build her self-confidence sufficiently for her to obtain a high school equivalency diploma and make plans to enroll as a part-time student in the local junior college. He and Veronica are also encouraged by the progress they see when visiting Mrs. Bigelow.

Christmas comes and the three Bigelows and two Starkeys celebrate as one happy family. Late that night, Rabble sees Mr. Bigelow and Sweet-Ho kiss beside the tree.

Spring brings many changes. Millie Bellows dies suddenly and a new family, the Elliots, with a son Gunther's age, buy her house. Sweet-Ho does so well at college that she becomes impatient to accelerate her studies. The most surprising news of all comes from Meadowhill—Mrs. Bigelow has recovered enough to be sent home in the middle of June. Rabble is both happy and dismayed because she knows that when Mrs. Bigelow returns, she will lose her new home and family and will have to return to the cramped garage. But there are further surprises in store. Sweet-Ho tells Rabble that they will be moving. She has saved enough money so that, by taking a part-time evening job, she can enter the university at Clarkburg as a full-time student in a teacher's training program. Mr. Bigelow has given them an old car and Sweet-Ho has already rented a small apartment for them. Once more Rabble has conflicting reactions but in time she realizes that this is best for all. Sweet-Ho tells Rabble that at one time she thought she was romantically in love with Phil Bigelow but that this feeling changed into the same kind of close friendship and affection that Rabble has always felt for all the Bigelows. Together they pack the car with their few belongings and set out for a new life.

**Thematic Material**

This novel contains a sensitive portrait of a charming, feisty, honest young girl who faces change and the problems of growing up with both humor and common sense. It is also a portrait of various kinds of love: romantic love as felt temporarily by Mr. Bigelow and Sweet-Ho; familial love as shown by the tender relationship between Sweet-Ho and Rabble, and by Mr. Bigelow and his family; love that stems from deep friendships like that shared by Veronica and Rabble; and love that develops through nearness and compassion such as that felt by Rabble for Millie

Bellows and Gunther. A realistic picture of mental illness and its effects on families is presented and the novel also contains a touching portrayal of the meaning and importance of home and family in the lives of young children. The importance of growing up and moving on when necessary is underlined. The episodes involving Rabble, Veronica, and Norman illustrate the destructive power of jealousy and the constructive power of forgiveness.

### Book Talk Material

Some passages that could be read or retold are: the family tree assignment (pp. 1–6); Sweet-Ho tells of her life with Ginger and the naming of Rabble (pp. 9–13); the Starkeys move into the garage (pp. 18–23); the incident at the creek with Mrs. Bigelow (pp. 38–45); Rabble uses a thesaurus on her composition about home (pp. 59–67); and trick-or-treating at Millie Bellows's house (pp. 78–86).

### Additional Selections

In Kristi Holl's *No Strings Attached* (Atheneum, 1988, $12.95), a sequel to *Just Like a Real Family* (Atheneum, 1983, $12.95), seventh-grader June and her mother move in with Franklin, an old man who needs someone to take care of him.

Patty Dillman, an eighth-grader, grows up while working in a shelter for the homeless in Susan Wojciechowski's *Patty Dillman of Hot Dog Fame* (Orchard, 1989, $13.99). This is a sequel to *And the Other, Gold* (Orchard, 1987, $12.95).

When the father of thirteen-year-old Lily takes off to New York to sell his paintings, she must learn independence in Mary Haynes's *Catch the Sea* (Bradbury, 1989, $12.95).

When her husband is killed, Emily's mother tries to run an inn in rural Wisconsin in Barbara Joose's *Pieces of the Picture* (Lippincott, 1989, $12.95).

A young girl who is epileptic is sent to live with her father, who operates a dog kennel, in *Halsey's Pride* (Scribner, 1990, $12.95) by Lynn Hall.

In Sheri Cooper Sinykin's *Next Thing to Strangers* (Lothrop, Lee & Shepard, 1991, $12.95), two misfits, each visiting grandparents in a retirement trailer park, form an unusual friendship.

Alice, the heroine of several of Phyllis Reynolds Naylor's novels, finds during the second half of the seventh grade that having everything going for her can be boring in *All But Alice* (Atheneum, 1992, $12.95).

**About the Book**
*Book Report,* September 1987, p. 40.
*Booklist,* March 15, 1987, p. 1128.
*Center for Children's Books Bulletin,* March 1987, p. 40.
*Horn Book,* July 1987, p. 130.
*Kirkus Reviews,* March 1, 1987, p. 374.
*New York Times Book Review,* May 17, 1987, p. 33.
*School Library Journal,* April 1987, p. 99.
*VOYA,* April 1987, p. 31.
See also *Book Review Digest,* 1987, p. 1157; and *Book Review Index,* 1987, p. 477.

**About the Author**
Chevalier, Tracy, ed., *Twentieth-Century Children's Writers* (3rd ed.). St. James, 1989, pp. 610–11.
Commire, Anne, ed., *Something about the Author.* Gale, 1981, Vol. 23, pp. 120–22.
Estes, Glenn E., ed., *American Writers for Children since 1960: Fiction* (Dictionary of Literary Biography: Vol. 52). Gale, 1986, pp. 249–61.
Holtze, Sally Holmes, ed., *Fifth Book of Junior Authors and Illustrators.* Wilson, 1983, pp. 198–99.
Metzger, Linda, ed., *Contemporary Authors* (New Revision Series). Gale, 1984, Vol. 13, pp. 333–36.
Senick, Gerard J., ed., *Children's Literature Review.* Gale, 1984, Vol. 6, pp. 192–97.
Ward, Martha, ed., *Authors of Books for Young People* (3rd ed.). Scarecrow, 1990, p. 451.

---

**Mahy, Margaret.** *Memory*
McElderry, 1988, $14.95 (0-689-50446-2); pap., Dell, $3.50 (0-440-20433-X)

---

Margaret Mahy is probably the most distinguished and best known of contemporary New Zealand writers of books for children and young adults. Two of her books for the latter audience have won the Carnegie Medal: *The Haunting* (McElderry, 1982, $12.95), about an eight-year-old boy and his encounter with a wizard, and *The Changeover* (McElderry, 1984, $14.95; pap., Scholastic, $2.95; condensed in *Juniorplots 3,* Bowker, 1987, pp. 132–37), another novel that deals with witchcraft and the occult. Like her other novels, *Memory* is multilayered in its meanings. It takes place (except for a brief epilogue) over a period of a few days in a city in present-day New Zealand. Except for a few local references, however, the situation and events could easily be transposed to contemporary America. This thoughtful novel is suitable for better readers in grades 8 through 12.

**Plot Summary**

At nineteen, Jonny Dart believes he is washed up, a has-been. As a child growing up in New Zealand, he had shown great talent as a tap dancer. Prodded by his mother, he and his older sister, Janine, had achieved fame and fortune dancing on television in a commercial for Chickenbits. That was before the terrible accident that filled him with remorse and depression. On the high cliffs of the Seacliff Heights Reserve five years ago, he, his sister, and her best friend, Bonny Benedicta, were on an outing when Janine lost her footing and fell to her death. Somehow Jonny feels responsible for his sister's death and guilty that he survived. Since that time he has been drifting—continuing his formal education but with no goal in sight.

It is now exactly five years to the day since the accident occurred. Jonny goes to the local pub, gets roaring drunk on wine and brandy, and is beaten up during a fight that the police break up. His father is called and after a stern lecture from him, Jonny, still high on booze, wanders off into the night. He is intent on finding Bonny, the only witness to the accident and the one, he feels, who can help assuage his anxieties. He has not seen her since the funeral, but Jonny was always attracted to her. Bonny, who has delved into the occult, gave prophecies and advice to the young boy and dressed so oddly that he always called her his Pythoness. At the Benedictas' home, he finds a party in progress celebrating a rally for Maori land rights that occurred earlier in the day. Bonny's mother tells Jonny that her daughter has moved into town to be closer to the university she is attending. She refuses to give him further information but he notices a handwritten entry in Benedicta's telephone book and discovers that she lives in the downtown area of Colville on Marribel Road. The name Colville brings back painful memories to Jonny. He and his family lived there for many years and, while there, he was cruelly victimized at school by a sadistic bully, Nev Fowler, who had been rejected as a suitor by his sister.

After being driven into town by a friend of the Benedictas, Jonny falls asleep on a traffic island and wakes up in the middle of the night thoroughly hung over. In a parking lot attached to a shopping center, he is approached by a shabby old lady, obviously in her eighties, wearing a strange red hat shaped like a flower pot and pushing a shopping cart.

She begins talking to Jonny and tells him her name is Sophie. The young man soon realizes that she is completely dotty and that she has mistaken him for someone else. She invites him home. They wander together through the predawn streets of the city until, on Marribel Road, they arrive at two ancient houses separated from the surrounding buildings. Number 113 has a gigantic model water tap protruding from its upper story above a balcony and a sign that says Tap House; Errol West: Master Plumber. Sophie ushers Jonny into this house. The stench that assaults his nostrils on entering is so strong that Jonny is scarcely able to find the bathroom before he becomes violently sick. The cause is a multitude of untended cats. The interior of the house is a shambles, filth everywhere, a dead blackbird in the refrigerator, moldy cheese in the soap dish, and soap in the butter dish. Sophie is obviously in an advanced state of senility. She utters non sequiturs with many references to her deceased husband, Errol.

In the morning, Jonny tries to leave Sophie, but something about her pathetic good nature and her vulnerability draws him back to Tap House. Together they go to the Post Office and after drawing money from their savings accounts shop for provisions, including a great deal of cat food. Back at the house, Jonny begins a process of cleaning up and airing out. In a knife drawer, he discovers a pile of receipts, all recent, signed with the name Spike. He wonders if Sophie, in her addled state, is being exploited by someone in the neighborhood.

The next day he vows to leave Sophie and go home. At a local pub where he stops for some food, he is accosted by Nev Fowler, his former nemesis, who is as threatening and malicious as before. The presence of people like Nev in the neighborhood again arouses in Jonny concern and sympathy for the defenseless Sophie. Once more he returns to her home.

In a package of faded photographs he finds a picture of a distant cousin of Sophie's, named Alva Babbitt. He is dressed in the same type of blazer that Jonny is wearing. The mistaken identity problem is solved. Sophie believes he is her cousin, an old flame whom she loved before meeting Errol but was forbidden by her family to marry. He also finds an unopened letter, obviously brought in by mistake, that is addressed to Bonny Benedicta at 115 Marribel Road, the house next door. He rushes to 115 and finds Bonny, no longer the Pythoness in exotic garb, but still the charming open girl he remembered. He tells her about the plight of Sophie, the neighbor Bonny had regarded as a nuisance, and she suggests that he seek help from the Aged Citizen's Council. In spite of having many assignments to complete, she consents to have dinner with Jonny and Sophie the following night.

Later that night, Jonny wakens to find a naked Sophie standing over him, tears streaming down her cheeks, bemoaning the loss of her true love, Alva. Gently, Jonny takes her back to her bedroom.

The following day Jonny visits the Aged Citizen's Council. An official, Mr. Dainton, listens to Jonny's story and suggests that Sophie may have Alzheimer's disease. He believes that eventually she will have to be institutionalized, but in the meantime he will supply some visiting nurse care and a cleaning service. When Jonny returns to Sophie's laden with groceries for the evening meal, the mysterious Spike is there taking money from the old lady. Even though Sophie owns her house, he has persuaded her that she owes rent and for months has been extorting money from her. Furious, Jonny orders him from the house with threats of arrest if he ever reappears.

That evening, the meal with Sophie and Bonny goes well, but Jonny impulsively kisses Bonny, although she resists his advances. After Bonny leaves, Jonny is on the balcony when a van stops in front of Sophie's house carrying Nev, Spike, and another hood out for revenge. From below, they taunt Jonny, until in desperation he thinks of his sister's last act and jumps from the balcony onto them. His shoulder is badly injured, but he is able to continue the fight until police are summoned by Bonny. Before he is driven to the hospital, he asks Bonny the question that has been tormenting him for five years. She tells him that he was in no way responsible for his sister's death. Jonny breaks down, sobbing tears of pain and relief.

Six months pass and Jonny reappears at Sophie's house on Marribel Road. After a stay in the hospital coupled with some help from a therapist, he is once again healthy and is now anxious to make something of his life. He tells Bonny, whom he now realizes can be no more than a dear friend, that he has a job in construction and that he plans on caring for Sophie until the inevitable separation. Sophie's reaction after her usual string of "oh dears" is a simple, "that's nice."

**Thematic Material**

This novel explores the interrelationship of past and present. Both Jonny and Sophie are prisoners of memory: She is trying to recall the past and he to forget it. In both cases, memory has distorted reality.

Sophie, though ill, emerges as a dignified, loving person and through his caring for her Jonny learns to care about himself. His reorientation and return to health result jointly from his emerging sense of responsibility and his confrontation with the past. The corrosive nature of guilt is explored, as is the nature of friendship.

### Book Talk Material

A discussion of the nature of memory could serve to introduce this thoughtful novel. With small groups, the dust jacket, showing a vacant Sophie, a bruised Jonny, and, in the background, Tap House, could also be used. Specific passages are: Jonny and the Benedictas (pp. 5–22); his first meeting with Sophie (pp. 33–36) and his introduction to Tap House (pp. 42–48); the two have tea and Jonny spends the night (pp. 52–58); and the morning after (pp. 61–69).

### Additional Selections

In William Mayne's challenging novel *Gideon Ahoy!* (Delacorte, 1989, $13.95), readers meet a seventeen-year-old English tourboat worker who is both deaf and brain-damaged as a result of a childhood accident.

In Gail Radley's *The Golden Days* (Macmillan, 1991, $12.95), for a younger audience, an eleven-year-old foster home misfit and a former circus trouper, Carlotta, form an unusual friendship.

After her mother's death, fourteen-year-old Lara moves in with her father and stepmother, where she encounters a strange wild dog in Libby Hathorn's *Thunderwith* (Little, Brown, 1991, $15.95), a novel set in Australia.

Merry Moonbeam Flynn, sixteen, is annoyed by the interference in her life by all the ex-hippies from the commune where she and her parents once lived in Marsha Qualey's *Everybody's Daughter* (Houghton, 1991, $13.95).

When Nick Herrera saves a young girl from being killed by an oncoming subway train, he begins to think that his mission in life is to save people in Neal Shusterman's *Speeding Bullet* (Little, Brown, 1991, $14.95).

The fairy tale "Rapunzel" is retold as a realistic young adult novel set in an English girls' boarding school in Adele Geras's *The Tower Room* (Harcourt, 1992, $15.95).

In Barbara Corcoran's *Annie's Monster* (Atheneum, 1990, $13.95), a thirteen-year-old girl finds a mentally ill woman living in an isolated shed in a park.

**About the Book**
*Booklist,* April 15, 1988, p. 1419.
*Center for Children's Books Bulletin,* April 1988, p. 160.
*Horn Book,* May 1988, p. 360.
*Kirkus Reviews,* February 1, 1988, p. 202.
*New York Times Book Review,* May 8, 1988, p. 24.
*School Library Journal,* March 1988, p. 214.
*VOYA,* June 1988, p. 88.
See also *Book Review Digest,* 1988, p. 1090; and *Book Review Index,* 1988, p. 520.

**About the Author**
Bowden, Jane A., ed., *Contemporary Authors.* Gale, 1978, Vols. 69–72, pp. 391–92.
Chevalier, Tracy, ed., *Twentieth-Century Children's Writers* (3rd ed.). St. James, 1989, pp. 626–29.
Commire, Anne, ed., *Something about the Author.* Gale, 1978, Vol. 14, pp. 129–31.
de Montreville, Doris, and Crawford, Elizabeth D., eds., *Fourth Book of Junior Authors and Illustrators.* Wilson, 1978, pp. 248–50.
Kirkpatrick, D. L., ed., *Twentieth-Century Children's Writers* (2nd ed.). St. Martin's, 1983, pp. 504–6.
Senick, Gerard J., ed., *Children's Literature Review.* Gale, 1984, Vol. 7, pp. 176–88.
Ward, Martha, ed. *Authors of Books for Young People* (3rd ed.). Scarecrow, 1990, p. 475.

---

**Marino, Jan.** *The Day That Elvis Came to Town*
Little, Brown, 1991, $14.95 (0-316-54618-6)

---

This novel appeared on all of the major young adult "best books" list for 1991. It is a touching story about a young girl who is growing up in Georgia in the 1960s. Beset by such personal problems as an alcoholic father, the heroine, thirteen-year-old Wanda, gravitates toward a friendship with a female jazz singer who comes to live in the boarding house run by Wanda's mother. The book is enjoyed by students in grades 7 through 10.

**Plot Summary**
*The Day That Elvis Came to Town* is a song of the South set in the 1960s when the pace of life was slower and Elvis swayed the hearts of teenage girls. Such is the case with thirteen-year-old Wanda Sue Dohr, whose life in Claxton tends to border on the humdrum.
Wanda generally resents the fact that her mother takes in boarders.

For one thing, it means work for Wanda. It also means that she has to give up her own room and is now relegated to the sun porch off her parents' bedroom. But at least she can go in there, close the glass door draped with a shade, and put on her Elvis records. While she sings along with the words of her idol, she thinks about her life—about Poppa, whom she loves for his gentle ways but who she knows has a problem with alcohol; about Momma, whose brisk manner helps her keep one eye on her boarders and the other on her husband; about her mean-spirited aunt, April May, who is their star boarder and now occupies Wanda's old room. Wanda once asked her mother why Aunt April May, Poppa's sister, had two names. Momma replied that April May "was slow even then. She took her time and didn't arrive fully until ten minutes after twelve on May first."

And then, Mer-*say*-des Washington comes to town and rents a room. With her arrival, Wanda has something new to think about. Mercedes, a professional jazz singer, is the most beautiful creature Wanda has ever seen. She arrives with four suitcases and Wanda is instantly enchanted. Mercedes has skin the color of homemade coffee ice cream, big green eyes, black hair, and a warm, friendly manner. The two become instant friends.

Mercedes has a gig in nearby Savannah, which is why she will be staying at Wanda's house for a time. She tells Wanda all about life on the jazz circuit, but the biggest thrill for the young girl is when Mercedes says that she went to high school with Elvis Presley—*the* Elvis Presley! Wanda can't believe it. She pressures Mercedes into telling her all she can about the great Elvis. Mercedes says that they weren't really friends, of course, just that she knew him and that somewhere she has a picture taken with him and other school friends. Wanda begs her to find it and Mercedes tells her that in time she will.

Life takes on new meaning for Wanda with the presence of Mercedes in the house, even though Momma and Aunt April May are not so taken with the singer. But Momma has enough to think about. For instance, Poppa doesn't come home one payday. A few days later he returns, carrying a huge stuffed bear for Wanda. He'd had a few drinks and got on a plane for New York. He promises his wife that he will reform, but Wanda knows that he always promises that.

About the biggest thrill in Wanda's life comes when Mercedes needs to be driven to Savannah to get to her performance on time. Mr. Gingrich, another boarder, agrees to drive her, and Wanda begs Momma to let her go along. Momma reluctantly agrees and then decides to go with them. They leave the house without telling Poppa; he has come home drunk again.

Wanda has never been to Savannah and she is enthralled watching Mercedes at work. "Mercedes Washington—Georgia's Own Sweet Lady of Jazz—Appearing Nightly (Except Sunday) 7 and 9 P.M.—Limited Engagement."

Before they return home, Momma asks Wanda to call Poppa and let him know where they are. Poppa, it turns out, has been frantic over their disappearance.

On the return trip, Wanda sees an ad announcing an Elvis Presley concert in the city coming up in September. The ad gives a number to call for tickets. Wanda tells Mercedes that she will write a letter to Elvis and sign Mercedes's name; surely Elvis will send them tickets. Mercedes says he won't even remember her. Wanda writes the letter and settles down to wait for the tickets.

While she waits, life at the house takes some unexpected turns. For one thing, Wanda learns that Momma is going to have a baby and she is understandably concerned about what this news will do to an already unstable husband. Almost more shocking to Wanda is Aunt April May's angry statement that Mercedes is "as colored as I am white." Wanda is furious with her aunt for making such an accusation.

Soon afterward, Wanda walks home one evening with Poppa. He tells her that he knows about the baby, and she tells him what Aunt April May said about Mercedes. Poppa replies, "Does it matter if she is?" Wanda thinks about that for a while. "What about Momma?" Wanda asks. April May told Wanda that Momma could get in trouble for having "colored boarders." Poppa tells Wanda that her mother has been aware of the situation since the night they all went to Savannah. That was also the night, it turns out, that Poppa decided to do something about his drinking because he was so frightened when he didn't know what had happened to his wife and daughter.

Wanda and Mercedes have a talk during which the jazz singer gives the young girl a lesson in prejudice. She says that her mother was white, her father black, and she is often, she explains, not wanted by either world. Why does it have to be like this for her, Wanda asks. It's not fair.

Things begin to look up for Wanda—Aunt April May is going to get married and that means she will leave the house.

Wanda gets a reply to her letter to Elvis, but it's just a form letter telling her where to get tickets. She decides Mercedes has lied to her and there is an angry scene.

At Aunt April May's wedding, someone spikes the punch without thinking about Poppa. When he goes missing, they all fear the worst, but there is no time to worry about Poppa, for Momma is suddenly stricken and must be rushed to the hospital. As the ambulance drives off, Mercedes is there to wrap the crying girl in her arms and comfort her.

Wanda's baby brother is born prematurely and may not live. But Poppa is at the hospital and he is sober. It turned out that he was helping a friend; he hadn't had any of the spiked punch; he hadn't been drinking at all.

Small as he is, the baby will make it. He and Momma come home, Aunt April May is gone, and Mercedes gets Wanda and her girlfriend Sarah tickets to see Elvis in Savannah. After the performance, Mercedes asks Wanda if Elvis was all she expected. Wanda nods. She still loves him, but she now realizes that there are many other beautiful things in her life. Momma, the baby, Poppa not drinking and going to meetings in the evening—and Mercedes.

Before Mercedes leaves at the end of her gig, she tells Wanda the truth about "going to high school" with Elvis. She did go to the same high school as Elvis Presley, but they found out she wasn't white, so she had to leave.

Wanda holds on to her and says she will never forget her. "Please come back," she whispers.

### Thematic Material

This is a story rich in the many ways that love and friendship can show themselves. The characters are warm and alive, with obvious faults and weaknesses, and drawn with realism. The reader is so firmly transported back into the 1960s that the question of the color of Mercedes's skin becomes totally understandable through the eyes of young Wanda, as is the depth of Mercedes's pain.

### Book Talk Material

A number of incidents relate the full flavor of life in this small town in Georgia in the 1960s. See: Wanda sings along with Elvis in her glass bubble bedroom (pp. 6–8); Wanda meets the jazz singer (pp. 10–14); Poppa comes home with a teddy bear (pp. 34–37); and Mercedes tells Wanda about going to school with Elvis (pp. 43–44, 49–51).

**Additional Selections**

In Christi Killien's *Fickle Fever* (Houghton, 1988, $13.95), a sequel to *Putting On an Act* (Houghton, 1986, $12.95; pap., Dell, $2.95), fifteen-year-old Skeeter experiences many infatuations before she learns what true love is all about.

Angie, a black youngster, is trying to succeed in spite of appalling conditions at home, at school, and in the community in Camille Yarbrough's *The Shimmershine Queens* (Putnam, 1989, $13.95; pap., Knopf, $3.50).

In Jean Ferris's *Looking for Home* (Farrar, 1989, $12.95), an abused teenage girl's need for love leads to her pregnancy in her junior year of high school.

A blind prejudiced teenager and an elderly black man are marooned on a Caribbean island in Theodore Taylor's *The Cay* (Doubleday, 1987, $12.95; condensed in *More Juniorplots*, Bowker, 1977, pp. 146–49).

In need of a confidant, Terry writes to "the Boss" in Kevin Major's *Dear Bruce Springsteen* (Delacorte, 1988, $14.95; pap., Dell, $2.95).

Talley, a black student, falls in love with David, a white boy, in Virginia Hamilton's *A White Romance* (Philomel, 1987, $14.95).

Fat, fourteen-year-old Bridget, the only adopted one in her family, works out some personal problems with the help of a reclusive artist in Isabelle Holland's *The House in the Woods* (Little, Brown, 1991, $15.95).

**About the Book**
*Book Report*, May 1991, p. 46.
*Booklist*, December 15, 1990, p. 817.
*Center for Children's Books Bulletin*, February 1991, p. 147.
*Kirkus Reviews*, January 1, 1991, p. 48.
*School Library Journal*, January 1991, p. 114.
*VOYA*, April 1991, p. 31.
See also *Book Review Index*, 1991, p. 585.

**Mazer, Norma Fox.** *Silver*
Morrow, 1988, $12.95 (0-688-06865-0); pap., Avon, $2.95 (0-380-75026-0)

In her many distinguished novels for teenagers, Norma Fox Mazer explores the problems and pleasures of the period of maturation and self-discovery known as adolescence. In addition to themes related to growing up, she often delves into complex family relationships. For example, in an earlier novel, *After the Rain* (Morrow, 1987, $12.95; pap., Avon, $3.50), teenager Rachel feels responsible for caring for Izzy, her terminally ill grandfather. However, Izzy is completely unlovable. He is a tyrannical, demanding, selfish old man. The conflicts that Rachel feels in this situation are realistically portrayed. In *Babyface* (Morrow, 1990, $12.95; pap., Avon, $3.50), a later novel, fourteen-year-old Toni is complacent about her life when, after her father has a heart attack, she must stay with her older sister. There she discovers an unpleasant secret about her parents. In *Silver*, Sarabeth, the central character, has only a single parent, her mother, and many of her friends who are children of divorce also face family problems. *Silver* is told from a first-person point of view, takes place over a period of four months, and is suitable for readers in grades 6 through 10.

**Plot Summary**

Sarabeth's mother, Janie, was only sixteen when she discovered she was pregnant and had to marry her boyfriend, Ben Silver. It was a marriage filled with love in spite of poverty and family opposition. Both left school to find work. However, after only three and a half years together, Ben was killed in an automobile accident. Since then Janie has been cleaning houses to earn enough to feed and clothe Sarabeth and herself and pay the rent on their small trailer in the Roadview Trailer Park. Sometimes they exist on spaghetti for days, and their clothes, bought at local thrift shops, look shabby, but there is great love in the household and both Sarabeth and her mother have learned to accept their situation and feel grateful that they have each other. They are also fortunate in having many close friends in the park, including Cynthia, a café singer, and her husband, Billy, a staff sergeant in the army who lives on base except on weekends. Janie also has a boyfriend who visits regularly. He is Leo, a chimney sweep by trade, who owns a most unusual automobile covered with a collection of hood ornaments. It is nicknamed the Goldmobile. Rounding out the family in more ways than one is Tobias, their fifteen-pound cat, who is an amazing hunter.

Shortly before Sarabeth is due to enter junior high school, Janie discovers that the local school district boundaries cut through the trailer park. When a trailer in the upper part of the park becomes vacant, she and her daughter move so that Sarabeth can attend the much superior Drumline schools, where most of the students come from upper-middle-class homes. From the first day at school, Sarabeth is drawn to a classmate, Grant Varrow, a beautiful, composed girl of obvious wealth. Sarabeth daydreams that the two will become friends, but Grant seems content with the friends she has: Asa Goronkian, whose father is a prominent judge; Jennifer Rosen, an outgoing redhead; and the beautiful but somewhat moody Patty Lewis.

In spite of some qualms, Sarabeth attends the first school dance and there meets a somewhat rabbity-looking boy, Mark Emelsky, an espouser of unpopular causes (like vegetarianism). He impresses Sarabeth because they share similar open, friendly attitudes toward people and life. Unfortunately, Mark attends a neighboring private school, but, at the end of the evening, he and Sarabeth exchange phone numbers.

Sarabeth accidentally learns that her mother has had to borrow money from Cynthia. In an effort to help, she secretly takes a job cleaning a neighbor's trailer. When Janie finds out, there is a terrible scene, which ends with Janie losing control and slapping her daughter. Only through Cynthia's intervention is there a reconciliation. It is difficult for Sarabeth to understand that this violence was really a sign of her mother's need to protect her.

Gradually her social life improves. Mark calls her and she is so ecstatic at this attention that, when he hangs up, she grabs a pillow and, pretending it is Mark, imagines what his kisses would be like. She slowly becomes friends with Grant, whom, she discovers, is also missing a father. Since her parents' divorce and her mother's remarriage, she has seen very little of her real father, who has also remarried. Sarabeth begins having lunch with Grant and her friends Asa, Jennifer, and Patty. One day while talking about boys, Sarabeth lets it slip that Mark has kissed her, but, before she can explain it was really only a pillow, she suddenly has assumed such great status with the group that she is too embarrassed to tell the truth. A social breakthrough occurs when Grant insists that she come to a pajama party at Patty's that Asa and Jennifer will also attend. The five have a splendid time. However, Patty, who lives with her divorced mother at the home of her wealthy and highly respected Uncle Paul, lets slip that there are problems within this household. During this confession time, Sarabeth, whom the group have nicknamed Silver, reveals the truth about Mark the Pillow.

At a concert that Patty, Grant, and Sarabeth attend, Patty, who is given to black moods, shows signs of being under terrible stress. During intermission, she breaks down and confesses to Sarabeth that she is being sexually abused by her uncle and that her mother does not believe her. Grant and Sarabeth try to get assistance, even going to the school library in an abortive attempt to find written advice. When another attack occurs, Patty vows she will not return to her uncle's home. Sarabeth takes her to the trailer and after telling her mother Patty's story, begs that the young girl be allowed to stay. Patty's mother is summoned but she steadfastly protects her brother until Patty jumps out of a trailer window, breaking a bone in her foot. Only then, with her daughter at her feet in agony, is Patty's mother able to accept the truth.

Patty stays with the Silvers until her mother can find a job and a new home. It is not an easy time for any of them: three people in a tiny trailer (not to mention Tobias and his catch of the day) and Patty still suffering bouts of depression and uncertainty. However, after a month, Patty's mother is able to take her daughter to a new home. Prompted by the mutual outrage of all Patty's close friends, Asa tells her father, Judge Goronkian, of the attacks and a criminal charge is brought against Patty's uncle.

In spite of many attempts at building a friendship with Mark, including a date in which there was a real kiss, Sarabeth finds that he is attracted to someone else. Anyway, there are lots of other boys around and, in addition to her mother, she now has some new friends to rely on.

**Thematic Material**

In this novel, a sensitive, outgoing young girl faces both economic barriers and difficult social adjustments and through overcoming them finds friendship and achieves a degree of maturity. The story shows that wealth and position do not necessarily guarantee happiness and security. The power of love and the inner strength it brings are well depicted in Sarabeth's relationship with her mother. The effects of divorce and the important role fathers play in the maturation of young girls are interestingly portrayed. Sexual abuse and its consequences are realistically but tastefully depicted. Many scenes reproduce authentically the giddiness, insecurities, and interests of young teenage girls. Other important themes are friendship, poverty, snobbery, and boy-girl relationships.

**Book Talk Material**

An introduction to Sarabeth and her situation on entering junior high school should interest readers. Some important passages are: poverty in the Silver household (pp. 1–5); Sarabeth dreams of a friendship with

Grant (pp. 20–27); Sarabeth cleans the neighbor's trailer and her mother's reaction (pp. 67–72); the reconciliation (pp. 75–82); and Patty tells about her Uncle Paul (pp. 161–69).

## Additional Selections

Thirteen-year-old Dora loves her stepmother but finds that she is fearful for the future of her father's second marriage when he is openly attracted to another woman in C. S. Adler's *If You Need Me* (Macmillan, 1988, $12.95).

In Eve Bunting's *Is Anybody There?* (Harper, 1988, $13.95; pap., $2.75), Marcus, a latchkey child, believes someone has been coming into the house while he and his mother are away.

In Kathy Kennedy Tapp's *The Sacred Circle of the Hula Hoop* (McElderry, 1989, $13.95), Robin's older sister attempts suicide because of the emotional problems resulting from childhood molestation.

A high school sophomore gradually comes to accept the trauma of his sexual abuse by a school doctor in John McLean's *Mac* (Houghton, 1987, $12.95; pap., Avon, $2.95; condensed in *Seniorplots*, Bowker, 1989, pp. 18–21).

Katie and her mother are forced to live with cranky Aunt Rose in *Landing on Marvin Gardens* (Bantam, 1989, $13.95) by Rona S. Zable.

Prin learns that her next door neighbor, fifteen-year-old Mary Faith, is being brutally abused by her father in Katherine Martin's *Night Riding* (Knopf, 1989, $12.95).

A nonfiction introduction to the topic of child abuse in the United States today is given in William Check's *Child Abuse* (Chelsea House, 1989, $18.95).

## About the Book
*Book Report,* November 1988, p. 485.
*Booklist,* November 1, 1988, p. 485.
*Center for Children's Books Bulletin,* November 1988, p. 79.
*Kirkus Reviews,* September 1988, p. 1326.
*School Library Journal,* November 1988, p. 127.
*VOYA,* February 1989, p. 287.
See also *Book Review Index,* 1988, p. 539, and 1989, p. 541.

## About the Author
Chevalier, Tracy, ed., *Twentieth-Century Children's Writers* (3rd ed.). St. James, 1989, pp. 651–52.

Commire, Anne, ed., *Something about the Author.* Gale, 1992, Vol. 67, pp. 131–35.
Holtze, Sally Holmes, *Presenting Norma Fox Mazer.* Twayne, 1987; pap., Dell, 1986.
Holtze, Sally Holmes, ed., *Fifth Book of Junior Authors and Illustrators.* Wilson, 1983, pp. 204–5.
Metzger, Linda, ed., *Contemporary Authors* (New Revision Series). Gale, 1984, Vol. 12, pp. 309–10.
Sarkissian, Adele, ed., *Something about the Author: Autobiography Series.* Gale, 1986, Vol. 1, pp. 185–202.
Senick, Gerard J., ed., *Children's Literature Review.* Gale, 1991, Vol. 23, pp. 214–34.

---

**Myers, Walter Dean.** *Scorpions*
Harper, 1988, $12.89 (0-06-024365-1); pap., $2.95 (0-06-447066-0)

---

Although Walter Dean Myers was born in West Virginia, he spent most of his youth in Harlem and has never lost touch with the environment that helped shape his character. Harlem is the setting for this story and for many of his other books, including his first novel for young adults, *Fast Sam, Cool Clyde, and Stuff* (Penguin, 1975, $12.95; pap., $3.95), which first appeared in 1975, and his story of a black youth who hopes to escape from Harlem through basketball, *Hoops* (Delacorte, 1981, $13.95; pap., Dell, $2.95; condensed in *Juniorplots 3*, Bowker, 1987, pp. 249–53). Perhaps his most famous novel is *Fallen Angels* (Scholastic, 1988, $12.95; pap., $3.95; condensed in *Seniorplots*, Bowker, 1989, pp. 143–47), the harrowing story of a young black soldier in Vietnam. *Scorpions* is read and enjoyed by youngsters in grades 6 through 9.

**Plot Summary**

Only three of the five members of the Hicks family are living in their tiny walk-up apartment in Harlem. They are Mama, who holds the family together by cleaning for white folks; Jamal, her twelve-year-old son who is struggling through seventh grade; and his appropriately named eight-year-old sister, Sassy, who is now in third grade. The two missing members of the household are Jevon Hicks, the father, a somewhat shiftless heavy drinker who has difficulty holding a job but nevertheless visits the family occasionally to deliver lectures on the necessity of hard work and having a sense of responsibility—two lessons he himself has never mastered—and Randy, the eighteen-year-old son who is now serving time in an upstate prison for committing an armed robbery during which a man was shot and killed. There were two others involved in the crime, Mack, who was then only fifteen, and another underage boy. Because he was of age, Randy received the heaviest sentence, fifteen to twenty years with the possibility of parole after seven. Mama is desolate about her son but is unable to collect the $2,000 necessary for an appeal.

After one of her prison visits, Mama returns late at night and tells Jamal that his brother has suggested that he visit Mack, who has just been released on parole. In every way Mack is bad news. He is a crackhead and wino whose brain is so addled that he often is completely out of it. At one time, however, he was the second in command of the Scorpions, a street gang once led by Randy. The Scorpions, now without an official leader, consist of several fourteen- to sixteen-year-old dropouts who make their living as drug runners for the narcotics bosses in Harlem.

The next day, Jamal spends an average day at school being hassled by his teachers and the principal, Mr. Davidson, and being needled by the class bully, Dwayne Parsons, who is almost fourteen and is bigger and meaner than anyone else in Jamal's class. After school, Jamal usually hangs out with his best friend, Tito Cruz. There are really only three people on this earth that Jamal cares about: his mother, Sassy (in spite of her mischief and big mouth), and Tito, the young Puerto Rican his age who lives with his grandmother, Abuela. Tito admires his friend Jamal to the point of adoration and will do anything to maintain their friendship.

Jamal asks Tito to accompany him to the crackhouse where Mack hangs out. There, Mack tells Jamal that his brother wants Jamal to become leader of the Scorpions. In this way, Jamal will be able to make the money necessary for Randy's appeal. The boy is disturbed at this thought and tries to dismiss it, but Mack is persistent and promises that when they meet again in two days he will give Jamal something that will help him gain confidence—a gun.

Without giving any details, Jamal reports this "accidental" meeting with Mack to his mother, who gives him a stern warning never to see him again, but Jamal is confused and feels that for his mother's sake he should try to help his older brother secure an appeal.

The next day, Dwayne continues to harass Jamal, who stands up to him even though Dwayne is much bigger and more powerful. After school they fight but are separated by two passing postmen. They plan to continue the fight later.

As promised, Mack meets Jamal. After telling the young boy that he must become chief of the Scorpions, he gives Jamal a shiny silver pistol. Along with Tito, the two walk to the abandoned firehouse that the Scorpions use as headquarters. There, they meet the members of the gang, including Angel and Indian, the two who appear to be most opposed to Jamal. When Jamal shows them the gun, they are impressed, but no final action on his leadership is taken.

That evening, the Hickses are visited by their father, who once more lectures Jamal on facing up to his responsibilities in the household. The next day Jamal takes the gun to school. Dwayne corners him in an abandoned storeroom and during the ensuing fight, Jamal pulls out the gun and threatens him. Dwayne is vanquished, but Jamal knows that if Dwayne tells Mr. Davidson he will be expelled and perhaps turned over to the police. After school, Jamal gives the gun to Tito for safekeeping.

As expected, Jamal is called to Mr. Davidson's office the following morning, where he is confronted by both Dwayne and his mother. Jamal lies about having a gun and, as it is his word against Dwayne's, the principal dismisses both of them but sends word via Jamal that his mother must come to school immediately for a conference.

At home, there is more bad news. Randy has been knifed during a fight in the prison and is in serious condition. The Reverend Biggs visits and the family prays for his recovery. Now Jamal is further torn between helping his brother by working with the Scorpions and getting rid of the gun and trying to lead a straight life.

There are further complications when Tito's grandmother, a sweet, trusting woman, finds the gun and is so distraught that she orders her grandson out of the house. Jamal is able to intercede on his friend's behalf and once more takes possession of the pistol. In the midst of this turmoil, there is a quiet moment when the two friends visit Grant's Tomb. Jamal has brought along his sketch pad, and as the two try to sort out their troubles, Jamal draws a beautiful likeness of his friend.

Events reach a climax when Jamal arranges a meeting with Angel and Indian in a neigborhood park for late the next night. He plans to renounce his claim to be head of the Scorpions if they will help raise money for his brother's defense. When Tito and Jamal reach the rendezvous spot, Jamal gives the gun to his friend for safekeeping and orders him to remain in the shadows out of trouble. Indian and Angel arrive high on liquor and drugs. Instead of listening to Jamal, they begin attacking him unmercifully. While he is lying on the ground bleeding, Angel approaches knife in hand. Suddenly pistol shots are heard and both Angel and Indian fall to the ground. At a terrible price, Tito has saved his friend's life.

The boys flee and dispose of the gun in a dumpster. The next day Jamal learns that Angel is dead and that Indian is seriously wounded. Because he had drugs on him when the police found him Indian will face criminal charges when he recovers. For some reason, Mack, who was in the park at the time, tells people that he was responsible for the shootings. It would seem, therefore, that Tito is in the clear. However, the young boy's conscience torments him. He refuses to see Jamal, stops eating, and causes his grandmother so much grief that finally he tells her the truth. She calls the police. There is a hearing and, though charges are dismissed, it is decided that Tito must go to Puerto Rico to live with his father. The two boys meet for the last time. With both their friendship and their lives in tatters, Jamal gives Tito the sketch he made only a few days before. The boys hug one another and part.

**Thematic Material**

This novel realistically portrays everyday life in Harlem and the ever-present, corrosive effects of poverty on its inhabitants. Specifically, it is the story of a young boy, not yet a teenager, facing social pressures and shouldering responsibilities that would confound most adults. The pistol represents access to the power that Jamal lacks, a power that is transitory, illegal, and inevitably destructive. Although the Hicks family is characterized as embodying love and decent moral values, it crumbles under the grip of the violence, crime, and pervasive drug culture of the inner city. The friendship between Jamal and the gentle Tito is touchingly portrayed. Other subjects include family loyalties, the destructive power of drugs, the schools' inability to fight these social problems, gang violence, and courage.

**Book Talk Material**

Here are some passages that could be used to introduce the book: Jamal waits for Mama to return from visiting Randy in prison (pp. 3–7); a typical day at school (pp. 16–22); Tito and Jamal first visit Mack (pp. 36–44); Jamal tells his mother about this visit and they discuss the parole money (pp. 49–54). A trip to a boat basin by Jamal and Tito (pp. 60–65) illustrates the nature of their friendship; Jamal's first fight with Dwayne is described on pp. 67–70.

### Additional Selections

Life becomes very complicated for Carl Davis, a bright black youngster, when he goes to South Carolina to live with his grandmother in Rosa Guy's *The Ups and Downs of Carl Davis III* (Delacorte, 1989, $13.95).

A young black basketball player forms a friendship with a white teammate in Bruce Brooks's *The Moves Make the Man* (Harper, 1984, $13.70; pap., $2.75; condensed in *Juniorplots 3*, Bowker, 1987, pp. 235–38).

Willie, a black boy growing up in Brooklyn, has learning problems and is helped by a neighbor's niece from the West Indies in Kay Brown's *Willy's Summer Dream* (Harcourt, 1989, $13.95).

Foster brothers—one white and the other a Navaho youth—gradually grow apart in A. E. Cannon's *The Shadow Brothers* (Delacorte, 1990, $14.95).

Rosa Guy has created a sympathetic black hero in Imamu Jones, the central character in several adventure-mysteries including *And I Heard a Bird Sing* (Delacorte, 1987, $14.95), about a strange death in a wealthy white family.

Homeless Benno and his friends take over an abandoned building and create their own community in Felice Holman's *Secret City, U. S. A.* (Scribner, 1990, $13.95).

In *Pickle and Price* (Scribner, 1990, $13.95) by Pieter Van Raven, Pickle, a thirteen-year-old farm boy, and a twenty-year-old inner-city black named Price travel across country in a rusty old truck.

In Fran Leeper Buss's *Journey of the Sparrows* (Dutton, 1991, $14.95), members of a family of Hispanics who have entered the country illegally try to find work in Chicago.

### About the Book

Book Report, November 1988, p. 36.
Booklist, September 1, 1988, p. 82.
Center for Children's Books Bulletin, July 1988, p. 235.
Horn Book, July 1988, p. 504.
Kirkus Reviews, May 15, 1988, p. 764.
School Library Journal, September 1988, p. 201.
VOYA, August 1988, p. 133.
Wilson Library Bulletin, April 1989, p. 94.
See also Book Review Digest, 1988, p. 1235; and Book Review Index, 1988, p. 587; 1989, p. 590; and 1990, p. 584.

**About the Author**

Chevalier, Tracy, ed., *Twentieth-Century Children's Writers* (3rd ed.). St. James, 1989, pp. 707–8.
Commire, Anne, ed., *Something about the Author.* Gale, 1982, Vol. 27, p. 153; updated 1985, Vol. 41, pp. 152–55.
Evory, Ann, ed., *Contemporary Authors* (First Revision). Gale, 1978, Vols. 33–36, pp. 592–93.
Holtze, Sally Holmes, ed., *Fifth Book of Junior Authors and Illustrators.* Wilson, 1983, pp. 225–26.
Kinsman, Clare D., ed., *Contemporary Authors* (First Revision). Gale, 1973, Vols. 33–36, p. 638.
Metzger, Linda, and Straub, Deborah A., eds., *Contemporary Authors* (New Revision Series). Gale, 1987, Vol. 20, pp. 325–30.
Sarkissian, Adele, ed., *Something about the Author: Autobiography Series.* Gale, 1986, Vol. 2, pp. 143–56.
Senick, Gerard J., ed., *Children's Literature Review.* Gale, 1982, Vol. 4, pp. 155–60.
Senick, Gerard J., ed., *Children's Literature Review.* Gale, 1989, Vol. 16, pp. 134–44.

---

**Newton, Suzanne.**   *I Will Call It Georgie's Blues*
Puffin, 1990, pap., $3.95 (0-14-034536-1)

---

In her young adult novels, Suzanne Newton reveals a penetrating knowledge of the concerns and interests of adolescents. Perhaps some of this insight comes from her years as a high school English teacher. After reading *Georgie's Blues*, youngsters will certainly want to read more by this North Carolinian. *An End to Perfect* (pap., Penguin, 1986, $3.95) and its sequel *A Palace Between* (Viking, 1986, $12.95) tell the story of two girls, Dorjo and Arden, and their embattled friendship. Like the present novel, these books appeal to readers in grades 6 through 9. *Georgie's Blues* is told in the first person by Neal Sloan and takes place over a period of about three weeks.

**Plot Summary**

To residents of the small North Carolina river town of Gideon, and particularly the parishioners of the local Baptist church, the family of the Reverend Richard E. Sloan is a model of respectability, contentment, and gentleness. Appearances, in this case, are definitely deceiving. Actually their life is drab, restrictive, and totally dominated by the tyrannical, rigid Reverend Sloan, who, although he has been preaching in Gideon for sixteen years, is still insecure and fearful that the slightest indiscretion by his family will cost him his parish. His wife, forty-one-year-old Lou, is sixteen years his junior. She married him when she was young and impressionable and has since become worn down by the continual scrimping, the overbearing attitude of her husband, and the fact that she must always present a happy face to the public. There are three children. The oldest is eighteen-year-old Aileen, a senior in high school. Recently she has become increasingly rebellious at home and displays her growing defiance by neglecting her school work and dating the school's deadbeat and hood, nineteen-year-old Pete Cauthin. The youngest and most pathetic is seven-year-old Georgie, who is close to finishing the second grade. He is a frail, sensitive, disturbed youngster, who mistakenly believes that it is because of his failings and shortcomings that his father never shows him the love or understanding he needs. In the middle is the peacemaker, fifteen-year-old Neal. One of the reasons that Neal appears impervious to his father's oppression is his escape valve, the piano. Two years ago an attractive blond woman, Mrs. Jeanette Talbot, moved into town from Chicago and began giving piano lessons. Since then, in exchange for performing her household chores, Neal has been receiving piano lessons. However, fearful that he will be branded a sissy, he has told no one and has also sworn Mrs. T., as he calls her, to secrecy. Mrs. Talbot is sophisticated and understanding and realizes that Neal has great potential as a jazz pianist. She has allowed him free access to her home to practice and the two have become fast friends. Neal has also made a copy of his father's church key so that he can use the piano there.

When his mother forbids him to visit Mrs. Talbot as often as he wants, Neal, for the first time, lashes out against this unfair authority. He refuses to mow the grass at the church unless he is paid for it. Despite his father's stern disapproval, Neal tells the church custodian, Mr. Mac-Nally, of his decision and then experiences a combination of guilt and liberation.

One Saturday on his way to Mrs. T.'s, Neal stops for a sandwich at the local general store. The proprietor, Mr. Bailey, tells him that Georgie has been buying items on credit with promises to pay from future allowances. Continuing his walk by the river, Neal is hailed by the much disliked Pete Cauthin, who offers him a ride in his rowboat. When he learns where Neal is going, Pete makes such rude remarks about Mrs. Talbot that Neal attacks him and overturns the boat. Both are soaked and the ink in Neal's music notebook becomes so smudged that he cannot decipher some of his own precious compositions.

News arrives that Aileen will not graduate because of her English grades. This, coupled with her increased acts of defiance, leads to a terrible confrontation in which her father forbids her to leave the house except to go to school and church. But Aileen continues to sneak out at night to meet Pete.

One Sunday after church Georgie and Neal walk down by the river and meet with an old fisherman, Captain Perry, who has befriended Georgie. On their way home, Georgie tells Neal that he is certain that he is not really his parents' child, but that he is some sort of changeling and will be rejected when their real son appears. Neal is so disturbed by his brother's mental condition that he asks his mother to seek professional help. Neal learns to his amazement that his mother is already aware of Georgie's increasing withdrawal and has begun consulting a local doctor. Neal tries to spend more time with his little brother but Georgie often acts peculiarly. One day, for example, he disappears suddenly for several minutes when Neal is walking him to school.

Pete Cauthin steals an English composition of Neal's on Thelonious Monk and submits it as his own. The deception is discovered and both are sent to the office of the principal, Mr. Thompson. Later Pete picks a fight with Neal and once more they are sent to see Mr. Thompson. This time the principal demands that the parents come in to talk about the situation. The next day, Neal is dismayed when his father fails to defend his son in front of the principal but asks only that he not be blamed for any aspect of Neal's behavior. For Neal, this is the final break.

The custodian catches Neal practicing piano in the church and when the custodian comes to the house later, Neal is afraid that his father will learn about his secret. But the visit is about a more serious matter. The custodian tells Reverend Sloan that someone in town has been spreading rumors that he is emotionally unbalanced and will soon lose his church. Sloan becomes so upset at these accusations that even Neal feels a slight twinge of pity. The family sets out to find the person who began this smear campaign.

It is Mr. Bailey who tells Neal that Georgie's innocent stories about his home life began the rumors. Mr. Sloan finds this out and verbally assaults the pathetic youngster so viciously that Neal intervenes and is slapped across the face. Neal rescues Georgie and puts him to bed. The next morning, the family discovers that Georgie has disappeared. The family and such neighbors as Mrs. Talbot start a frantic search. All the obvious river haunts are checked, including Captain Perry's home. Nothing. Suddenly, Neal remembers how Georgie disappeared so quickly on the way to school. He retraces his steps and finds a dense thicket of vines that cover a chicken coop. Inside, Georgie is hiding, surrounded by the cache of supplies, such as canned soup, that he had secretly bought from Mr. Bailey. The boy is in a catatonic state. Neal scoops him up and takes him home, where arrangements are hastily made to take him to a hospital. For the first time, Neal notices, his father is showing genuine concern for his family.

Later that night, Neal goes to the church to play the piano. Throughout the day's traumatic events, a new tune has been haunting his thoughts. As he elaborates and improvises on it, he decides he will call it "Georgie's Blues." Suddenly he realizes he is not alone. He stops playing and turns around to find a small group of people at the back of the church, led by Mrs. T. Some are crying, others are smiling, but all are applauding.

**Thematic Material**

This novel explores complex family relationships in which exterior appearances hide ugly realities. The need for love and understanding to cement human ties is shown as are the frightful consequences when youngsters are denied them. The struggle between parental authority and adolescent needs is graphically portrayed. Other themes in this novel are religious hypocrisy, brotherly love, friendship, and the power of music.

**Book Talk Material**

Some interesting passages that could be used to introduce this book are: conflicts at the Sloans' dinner table (pp. 14–17); background on Mrs. Talbot and Neal's secret (pp. 23–27); a Sunday School lesson about obligations to one's family (pp. 34–38); the quarrel in the boat (pp. 57–61); Mom talks about being a preacher's wife (pp. 73–75); and Georgie tells Neal that he is a changeling (pp. 86–88).

**Additional Selections**

Eleven-year-old Rob feels the world has turned against him until he finds refuge on Pratt's Island in John Rowe Townsend's English novel, *Rob's Place* (Lothrop, Lee & Shepard, 1988, $12.95).

In *Is That You, Miss Blue?* (Harper, 1975, $12.89; pap., $2.95; condensed in *More Juniorplots*, Bowker, 1977, pp. 35–37) by M. E. Kerr, one of the leading characters is a P.K. (preacher's kid)—and unhappy with the designation.

Shelley learns about the comfort and narrowness of small-town life in Caroline B. Cooney's *Family Reunion* (Bantam, 1989, $13.95; pap., $2.95).

The daughter of the only black family in a small town is the victim of prejudice in Ouida Sebestyen's *Words by Heart* (Little, Brown, 1979, $13.95; pap., Bantam, $2.95).

Teenage Samantha is devastated when her new baby brother is killed in a home accident in Mary K. Pershall's *You Take the High Road* (Dial, 1990, $14.95).

Because his father is away often, a sixteen-year-old boy has been raised by an overly protective mother in Cynthia D. Grant's *Keep Laughing* (Atheneum, 1991, $14.95).

After his sister dies tragically, seven-year-old Sam begins acting strangely in Victor Kelleher's *Del-Del* (Walker, 1992, $16.95).

Addie is the target of her mother's rage after the family divorce in Natalie Honeycutt's disturbing *Ask Me Something Easy* (Orchard, 1991, $13.95).

**About the Book**
*Booklist,* September 15, 1983, p. 160.
*Center for Children's Books Bulletin,* November 1983, p. 55.
*Horn Book,* February 1984, p. 63.
*Kirkus Reviews,* September 1, 1983, p. J 177.
*New York Times Book Review,* November 13, 1983, p. 40.
*School Library Journal,* October 1983, p. 172.
*VOYA,* June 1984, p. 96.
See also *Book Review Digest,* 1984, p. 1129; and *Book Review Index,* 1984, p. 521.

**About the Author**
Commire, Anne, ed., *Something about the Author.* Gale, 1973, Vol. 5, pp. 140–41.
Holtze, Sally Holmes, ed., *Sixth Book of Junior Authors and Illustrators.* Wilson, 1989, pp. 208–9.
Metzger, Linda, ed., *Contemporary Authors* (New Revision Series). Gale, 1985, Vol. 14, pp. 353–54.
Ward, Martha, ed., *Authors of Books for Young People* (3rd ed.). Scarecrow, 1990, p. 526.

**Peck, Richard.**  *Those Summer Girls I Never Met*
Delacorte, 1988, $14.95 (0-440-50054-0); pap., Dell, $3.50 (0-440-98809-8)

Richard Peck has written over a dozen quality young adult novels since his first, *Don't Look and It Won't Hurt* (o.p.), was published in 1972. One distinctive characteristic of his work is that many of his central characters are male. Some fine examples are the present novel and two earlier works, *Father Figure* (pap., Dell, 1988, $2.95) and *Remembering the Good Times* (Delacorte, 1985, $14.95; pap., Dell, $3.25; condensed in *Juniorplots 3*, Bowker, 1987, pp. 90–94). Another important characteristic is that the element of change is important in each of these books. As Peck said in an interview in *School Library Journal* (June 1990, p. 40), "Every young adult novel must be a chronicle of change. You've got to take a step forward or it doesn't work." This is true of the glib narrator of *Those Summer Girls I Never Met*, who finds a new dimension in family relationships during the two-week ocean cruise that is the subject of the novel. The book is enjoyed by readers in grades 7 through 10.

**Plot Summary**

Drew Wingate and his friend Bates Morthland have great plans for the summer after their sophomore year in high school. They involve dating girls, reaching age sixteen, dating girls, getting their driver's licenses, and dating girls. Alas, for Drew, these plans are not to be realized. An invitation comes from his grandmother in Florida for Drew and his bratty fourteen-year-old sister, Stephanie, to accompany her on a Baltic cruise. Connie Carlson, their grandmother, is something of an unknown quantity to the youngsters. Drew remembers seeing her briefly five years ago at the time their father left the family. To the millions of her aging fans, however, she is a legend. At the height of her career during the 1940s, she was one of the country's most famous band singers and is still remembered fondly by that generation, including Bates's father, a latter-day yuppie, who has a collection of her records. Connie continues to perform occasionally, including this engagement on board ship, for which she will receive free passage for herself and her two grandchildren. Connie has never been close to her daughter, the product of a short, failed marriage during World War II. Drew's mother, who now works as a legal secretary to supplement the income from her alimony, spent most of her childhood in private schools while Connie was on tour. Drew and particularly Steph are unenthusiastic about spending two weeks on a ship with 800 elderly retirees. Reluctantly, they board the airplane that will take them to London and their ship, the *Regal Voyager*. After a tiring but uneventful flight, they arrive at the Clarence Hotel, where they are scheduled to spend the night prior to boarding the ship. Steph creates pandemonium when she causes a blackout by blowing fuses with her American-voltage hairdryer. In the morning she realizes with horror that, the night before, she packed all her clothes in the trunk that is now being taken to the dock. Quick-thinking Drew borrows a spare uniform from the tour director and Steph, looking more like a walking tent than a passenger, is accompanied by a smiling brother when they get on the bus that will take them to the ship.

On board, Steph is further dismayed to learn that she will be sharing her grandmother's cabin. It is already filled with wigs, makeup trays, and closets of clothes, but in spite of violent protests, she has no choice but to move in. With the help of their steward, Strovos, Drew and Steph find the way to the ship's nightclub, the Adriatic Room, where they see Connie rehearsing for her first show. Though sixty-four, she is still a petite, glamorous woman. Both the youngsters are instantly won over by her warmth and charm and are mesmerized that evening by her delivery and ability to hold an audience in rapture.

The next day Connie begins to relax because her only other working commitment is to entertain on Gala Night, the last night at sea. During their first meal with the cruise staff and other entertainers, Drew is bowled over by a vision of loveliness at their table. She is Holly, the dance instructor. Almost before he is asked, he accepts an invitation to attend her classes. Later that day, after stumbling through something that is supposed to be the cha-cha-cha, Drew talks with this red-haired beauty. At one point, as though reading his soon-to-be-sixteen mind, she says, "Twenty-two, last March." Steph also settles in and finds a friend in Melanie Krebs, a girl her age who is traveling with her parents, a couple from Florida. The first stop is Copenhagen, where Drew accompanies Connie to a radio interview. Later the two join the Krebs and Steph for an evening at Tivoli. The next day, Connie asks Drew to take the band's drunken piano player, a seventy-year-old boozer from New York named Shep Bailey, to the men's sauna to sober up before the evening performance. The man is pathetic, a has-been with a terrible drinking problem who was hired for the cruise only because his old friend Connie knew he was desperate for work.

Having accomplished his mission, Drew moves on to the next part of the health area and, completely nude, sinks into the Jacuzzi to relax. The door opens and Holly, in a swimsuit, enters and joins him in the whirlpool. Too late, Drew realizes the whirlpool is coed. Speechless with embarrassment, and hoping that he is covered by the swirling waters, he waits out a seeming eternity. Suddenly a loud whistle announces a drill. Having no other alternative, he springs out of the tub and heads for the door. Sounds of Holly's laughter follow him to the locker room.

While touring pre-glasnost Leningrad, the Krebs seem unduly agitated. At a park, Drew notices that they meet an old lady and talk furtively with her. Connie later learns that the woman is Mrs. Krebs's mother, who for political reasons has been under close observance by the secret police. This hoped-for brief meeting was planned months in advance and was the sole reason for their taking the cruise.

In Helsinki, Drew is taken to lunch by Holly and her three gorgeous colleagues, Sandi, Helga, and Jean, in the dining room of Stockmann's, the large department store. After lunch, much to Drew's delight, the four girls take part in a fashion show, which includes modeling the latest in bikinis. Meanwhile, Shep uses the time in port to tie one on. Drew and Holly find him drunk in a dockside bar and drag him aboard moments before sailing time. Connie realizes that Shep must be placed in the ship's hospital and flown back to America as soon as they reach the next port, Stockholm. She makes an amazing confession to Drew. She and Shep were married briefly when Shep was in the service during World War II. Shep is the boy's grandfather.

In Stockholm, Drew and Connie visit an unconscious Shep before he is taken off the ship. Later, by himself, Drew engages in some unenthusiastic sightseeing.

It is Costume Night on board ship. Drew joins his four girlfriends in putting on a skit in which each represents a different kind of railroad car. Calling themselves the Tivoli Trolley, they are so successful, they win the first prize, a bottle of champagne. Later that night a tearful Steph visits Drew in his stateroom. She unburdens herself, telling him a secret: Connie has cancer. The reason she wears wigs is to hide the baldness caused by chemotherapy. She has also shown Steph the scars from a mastectomy performed in the spring. Although Connie gallantly claims she has been cured, Steph, who accompanied her to a cancer clinic in Stockholm, is certain that this is not true. Perhaps this explains the unexpected invitation to join her on the cruise. The two are desolate at the possibility of losing the wonderful Connie, whom, in this short time, they have grown to love.

The next two days pass in a blur for Drew, who succumbs to a combined case of sunburn and seasickness. After forty-eight hours in his stateroom, Steph drags Drew on deck where he is greeted by a mass of shipboard friends. A four-tiered cake is brought in and everyone, including the ringleader, Connie, extends best wishes to him. Suddenly Drew realizes that it is his sixteenth birthday.

The following night is Gala Night, the last night at sea and time for Connie to give her second concert. If possible, it is more successful than the first. Both Drew and Steph are lost in admiration and love for this woman, but this triumph is filled with sadness when they think of tomorrow and the parting that might be forever.

**Thematic Material**

During the interview quoted above, the author, when speaking of the book, says it "is really a story about how two teenagers who can think of no use for a grandparent are suddenly thrust into her presence and therefore see their past and their future in her." Though told with glib insouciance by the teenage narrator, the touching moments showing family love and the sorrow of loss are also well depicted. In several episodes there is an excellent portrayal of the humor and agony of teenage infatuations. Reacting to new people, new emotions, and new situations produces change and a step toward maturity for both youngsters. Information about the Big Band era and the songs of the 1940s is nicely integrated into the plot, as is the atmosphere of life on a cruise ship.

**Book Talk Material**

The contrast between Drew's original summer plans and those that take their place could be used to introduce the novel. Specific passages are: Drew's mother talks about the trip and Connie (pp. 8–12); Mr. Morthland talks about Connie (pp. 20–25); Steph blows fuses with the hairdryer (pp. 35–38) and has no clothes to board the ship (pp. 42–56); Drew meets his grandmother (pp. 53–56) and gets caught in the Jacuzzi (pp. 102–6).

**Additional Selections**

In A. E. Cannon's first novel, *Cal Cameron by Day, Spiderman by Night* (Delacorte, 1988, $13.95; pap., Dell, $3.25), a popular high school quarterback befriends a new girl and endangers his social status.

A high school senior finds amazing parallels between the romance of two friends and that of his dead parents in David Gifaldi's *Yours Till Forever* (Lippincott, 1989, $11.95).

Danielle's life changes dramatically when her mother wins the lottery in Gloria Miklowitz's *Suddenly Super Rich* (Bantam, 1989, $13.95).

In alternating chapters, two sixteen-year-olds in San Francisco tell about their lives and dramatic meeting in Marilyn Sachs's *Circles* (Dutton, 1991, $14.95).

When, in an act of defiance, Philip Malloy does not stand for the national anthem, he becomes the center of a national controversy in Avi's *Nothing but the Truth* (Orchard, 1991, $14.95).

Sixteen-year-old Gina Gari, a bored, spoiled girl, wins a trip to Italy in a yo-yo contest in *Shoot for the Moon* (Crown, 1992, $15) by Norma Howe.

Huey is failing senior English, dating two girls at the same time, and trying to help catch a poacher in this novel by Nancy J. Hopper about an overextended teenager, *The Interrupted Education of Huey B.* (Lodestar, 1991, $14.95).

**About the Book**
*Book Report*, November 1988, p. 37.
*Booklist*, October 1, 1988, p. 259.
*Horn Book*, January 1989, p. 79.
*Kirkus Reviews*, August 15, 1988, p. 1246.
*School Library Journal*, February 1989, p. 84.
See also *Book Review Digest*, 1989, pp. 1297–98; and *Book Review Index*, 1988, p. 636, and 1989, p. 640.

**About the Author**
Chevalier, Tracy, ed., *Twentieth-Century Children's Writers* (3rd ed.). St. James, 1989, pp. 768–69.
Commire, Anne, ed., *Something about the Author*. Gale, 1980, Vol. 18, pp. 242–44; updated 1989, Vol. 55, pp. 126–38.
Gallo, Donald, *Presenting Richard Peck*. Twayne, 1989.
Garrett, Agnes, and McCue, Helga P., eds., *Authors and Artists for Young Adults*. Gale, 1989, Vol. 1, pp. 215–30.
Holtze, Sally Holmes, ed., *Fifth Book of Junior Authors and Illustrators*. Wilson, 1983, pp. 238–40.

Kirkpatrick, D. L., ed., *Twentieth-Century Children's Writers* (2nd ed.). St. Martin's, 1983, pp. 610–11.
Locher, Frances C., ed., *Contemporary Authors*. Gale, 1980, Vols. 85–88, pp. 458–59.
Metzger, Linda, ed., *Contemporary Authors* (New Revision Series). Gale, 1987, Vol. 19, pp. 366–70.
Sarkissian, Adele, ed., *Something about the Author: Autobiography Series*. Gale, 1986, Vol. 2, pp. 175–86.
Senick, Gerard J., ed., *Children's Literature Review*. Gale, 1988, Vol. 15, pp. 146–65.

---

**Rochman, Hazel.**   *Somehow Tenderness Survives: Stories of Southern Africa*
Harper, 1988, $13.00 (0-06-025022-4); pap., $3.25 (0-06-447063-6)

---

This collection of ten short stories explores various aspects of life in South Africa in the past half century. The authors represent a "Who's Who" of contemporary South African writers and include Doris Lessing, Nadine Gordimer, and Dan Jacobson. This fascinating and disturbing anthology is intended for better readers in junior and senior high school.

**Plot Summary**

This book contains ten stories, some autobiographical, by southern African writers of different races. They speak simply and eloquently of the horror that is life under apartheid.

"Crackling Day," by Peter Abrahams, tells of a young black boy from Johannesburg, newly arrived at the rural home of his aunt and uncle. He and his friend Andries are sent off one Wednesday, crackling day, on a long trek in the cold for a square of pig's rind, their daily meat. On their return they are confronted by three white boys. Andries warns the newcomer to run, but he stands and fights. That evening the white *baas* comes with the three bullies and tells the uncle that his nephew must be taught how to act. The uncle is obliged to beat the boy, which he does.

"The Old Chief Mshlanga," by Doris Lessing, shows how the practice of apartheid restricts the lives of white as well as black South Africans. A young white girl, called Nkosikaas, or chieftainess, is taught to regard blacks almost as playthings, but she learns respect and tolerance for another culture from the old chief Mshlanga. Yet when one day when she ventures into the chief's land, she realizes how the policies of her country will keep them apart forever, will prevent their friendship forever.

"A Day in the Country," by Dan Jacobson, is a story in which everybody loses. A Jewish family, out for a Sunday drive, passes a group of Afrikaners tormenting a small black child. When the family and the Afrikaners later meet in anger, the guilt on both sides forces them to forget about the black child in their effort not to ruffle the feathers of the other.

The "Country Lovers," by Nadine Gordimer, are Paulus, a white boy, and Thebedi, a black girl. She marries a young black, Njabulo, but soon after gives birth to a very light child. When Paulus returns home and learns of the birth, he tells Thebedi that she must give the baby to somone; "I feel like killing myself," he says. Soon after, the child dies. Paulus is charged with murder but acquitted. Thebedi says of the incident, "It was a thing of our childhood."

Zoe Wicomb's "When the Train Comes" addresses the loneliness and self-hatred that surround a teenage girl of mixed race. Frieda waits with her father for the train that will take her to a superior education in an all-white school—but she knows that the case, won in the courts, that opened the prestigious school to nonwhites, will not save her from a life without love or friendship, without a place in the world.

"The Toilet," by Geina Mhlope, tells of a young black girl whose only moments of privacy can be found in a public toilet. She lives illegally with her maidservant sister in a white section of town. She must leave her sister's room very early each morning so the white family does not see her. She spends the time before reporting to her own job in the privacy of a public toilet where she can get out of the cold and write poetry. Then one day she finds the door of the toilet locked. She no longer has even that small space to call her own.

"The Road to Alexandra," by Mark Mathabane, is a detailed description, through the eyes of a young black child, of the night during "Operation Cleanup Month," when black policemen comb the Alexandra ghetto in search of blacks who have "violated" the law. Such infringements may be late payment of the poll tax or living in town illegally. The child describes his terror as he is beaten by the policemen until they find his father and take him away for two months at hard labor for an out-of-order passbook.

Nadine Gordimer's "A Chip of Glass Ruby" tells of a traditional Indian woman who spends her evenings printing illegal pamphlets to aid the cause of black South Africans, much to the bewilderment, and unrecognized admiration, of her husband.

In "A Farm at Raraba," by Ernst Havemann, a young Afrikaner soldier on border patrol talks through the night with a wounded black guerrilla whom he aids. In the morning they part and go back to their business of killing and torture.

Violence, suffering, and rebellion are just part of daily life for a township resident in "It's Quiet Now," by Geina Mhlope.

**Thematic Material**

There is violence in these ten stories, as well as love and compassion, acceptance, fear, rebellion, dignity, and tenderness. But there is no laughter. Above all, in their simple realism these tales eloquently depict the true cruelty of racism and prejudice and show that the lives of both oppressor and oppressed are crushed, twisted, and held captive by a system that forces one to be master, another to be slave.

**Book Talk Material**

Use the following questions to prompt a discussion of the ways in which racism and discrimination, in this case the policies of apartheid, cripple the lives of both whites and blacks. What does Aunt Liza mean in "Crackling Day," when she tells her nephew after the beating that "it hurt him," meaning Uncle Sam (p. 18). Why did the two groups in "A Day in the Country" go out of their way to avoid confrontation over the black boy's torment (pp. 42–47)? Is the girl in "When the Train Comes" happy about going off to school (pp. 61–76)? If not, why not? What is the attitude of the narrator in "It's Quiet Now" about the violence in the township (pp. 135–37)? What accounts for that reaction?

**Additional Selections**

Judith Bentley's *Archbishop Tutu of South Africa* (Enslow, 1988, $16.95) tells about the life of this distinguished crusader for peace in South Africa.

Race relations in South Africa are explored from the standpoint of a teenage Jewish girl growing up in the early 1960s in Margaret Sacks's novel *Beyond Safe Boundaries* (Lodestar, 1989, $13.95).

Two recent nonfiction accounts give a good introduction to South Africa and race relations there: Jonathan Paton's *The Land and People of*

*South Africa* (Lippincott, 1989, $14.95), and K. C. Tessendorf's *Along the Road to Soweto: A Racial History of South Africa* (Atheneum, 1989, $14.95).

Young blacks protest their forced removal to new barren lands in *Chain of Fire* (Lippincott, 1990, $12.95), a brutal novel by South African author Beverley Naidoo. This is a sequel to *Journey to Jo'burg* (Harper, 1988, $3.50).

*Waiting for the Rain* (Orchard, 1987, $12.95; pap., Bantam, $2.95; condensed in *Seniorplots*, Bowker, 1989, pp. 136–37) by Sheila Gordon describes the tragedy of apartheid through the doomed friendship of a white boy and a black boy in South Africa.

A young black boy supports his pregnant mother and his brothers and sisters by selling newspapers in modern South Africa in Maretha Maartens's *Paper Bird* (Clarion, 1991, $13.95).

**About the Book**
*Book Report*, May 1989, p. 60.
*Booklist*, August 1988, p. 1915.
*Center for Children's Books Bulletin*, September 1988, p. 1155.
*Horn Book*, March 1989, p. 220.
*Kirkus Reviews*, August 1988, p. 1155.
*New York Times Book Review*, November 17, 1988, p. 36.
*School Library Journal*, December 1988, p. 8.
*VOYA*, December 1988, p. 254, and October 1989, p. 201.
*Wilson Library Bulletin*, January 1989, p. 94, and September 1989, p. 13.
See also *Book Review Digest*, 1989, p. 1590; and *Book Review Index*, 1988, p. 694, and 1989, p. 699.

---

**Spinelli, Jerry.** *Maniac Magee*
Little, Brown, 1990, $13.95 (0-316-80722-2)

---

Jerry Spinelli's first books for young readers appeared in the early 1980s with such titles as *Space Station Seventh Grade* (Little, Brown, 1982, $14.95; pap., Dell, $2.95), the story of Jason Herkimer and his adolescent problems with pimples, girls, and puberty. His problems with sex continue into the ninth grade in the sequel *Jason and Marceline* (Little, Brown, 1986, $12.95; pap., Dell, $3.50). The author's knack for realistically re-creating the irreverent vocabulary and concerns of today's young people is again evidenced in *Maniac Magee*, but here this material is handled with greater depth and scope. The hero of this novel is a pint-size contemporary version of Pecos Bill or Paul Bunyan with one important difference: Although Maniac's story is set within a tall-tale framework, at its center is the reality of today's social concerns. This novel won both the 1990 Boston Globe–Horn Book Award and the Newbery Medal. Most of the novel takes place in a small town in southeastern Pennsylvania and covers a period of about one year. It is enjoyed by both girls and boys in grades 5 through 8.

**Plot Summary**

At age three, Jeffrey Lionel Magee (he was later nicknamed "Maniac" by people who witnessed his amazing feats) was orphaned when the trolley on which his parents were passengers left the tracks of the Schuylkill River trestle and plunged into the water. For the next eight years he lived with an ever-quarreling couple, Aunt Dot and Uncle Dan, until one day, unable to take it any longer, he ran away.

Now, one year later, he suddenly appears on the streets of Two Mills, a small Pennsylvania town just across the river from where he was born. Two Mills is divided geographically and emotionally by rampant racism. The blacks live in the East End and the whites, or fishbellies, in the West End. The dividing line is the uncrossable Hector Street.

Unaware of this division, Maniac wanders aimlessly from one area to another. In the black neighborhood, he meets a high-spirited girl named Amanda Beale, who grudgingly lends him one of her precious reading books. It is on the white side of town, however, that Maniac performs his most-talked about feats and is given his nickname. First, he outshines even James "Hands" Down in a high school football practice; next, he shows fantastic courage by entering the dreaded Finsterwald property to rescue a youngster who was there as a result of a cruel practical joke. His most important accomplishment occurs during his appearance at a Little League game when he scores several home runs at the expense of the hitherto invulnerable pitcher, John McNab. Maniac is even able to score with a bunt when John pitches a frog instead of a ball. However, Magee still does not have a home. Sometimes he eats meals with the Pickwells, a family so large they often don't realize they have a guest, and sometimes in the evenings he climbs the fence at the zoo and sleeps in the lean-to in the buffalo enclosure.

Seeking revenge for his humiliating baseball defeat, John McNab and his street gang, known as the Cobras, chase Maniac, who innocently seeks refuge in East End. Here he is confronted by a big black bully named

Mars Bar Thompson but fortunately is rescued by Amanda, who is as anxious to save her precious book as she is to help Maniac. Amanda invites Maniac to her home and here he instantly becomes a part of the family. The Beale family so adores him, even the younger children Hester and Lester, that they invite him to stay.

His reputation in town increases when he is able to untie the fabled Cobble's Knot, a mass of tangled rope the size of a volleyball that has defied hundreds of attempts to undo it. His reward is a year's supply of pizza, a food to which Maniac is unfortunately allergic.

His stay with the Beales is cut short when racist threats by black extremists in the neighborhood make him fearful for the safety of the Beales. Regretfully, he leaves and moves back to the zoo.

There he is found by an old park hand named Grayson, who moves Maniac into the equipment room at the back of the bandstand. Grayson tells an enthralled Maniac about his career as a pitcher in the minor leagues, of such glories as striking out a young Willie Mays, and of the tragedy of his eventual discharge. They become such close friends that Grayson gives up his room at the YMCA and moves in with Maniac. One day the old man asks Maniac if he will help him learn to read and so, every day after working in the park, Maniac gives instruction from old books, like *The Little Engine That Could,* purchased from the discard pile at the local library. Their little home is the scene of wonderful feasts at Thanksgiving and Christmas. At the latter, Grayson gives Maniac a box of his favorite candy, Krimpets, and Maniac gives Grayson a hand-printed book he has written called *The Man Who Struck Out Willie Mays.*

Just before New Year, Grayson dies suddenly and Maniac is again without a home. Once more he begins wandering and one night takes shelter from the bitter cold in one of the cabins at Valley Forge that are replicas of the army shelters used during the Revolutionary War. In a neighboring shelter, he encounters two scruffy young brothers, Russell and Piper, who are runaways. Maniac persuades them to go back to their home in Two Mills. He accompanies them and finds himself in one of the dirtiest, roach-ridden hovels imaginable. Here, Maniac meets the boys' older brother, Giant John McNab, the once-ace pitcher whom he had humiliated at Little League months before, and the father, George McNab, a filthy redneck who is so obsessed with racial hate that he is building a mortar bunker in his living room in case the blacks cross Hector Street. In spite of these obvious inconveniences, Maniac stays with the McNabs to be sure that Russell and Piper remain in school. In order to accomplish this, he bribes the boys by performing a series of physical feats that again enhance his reputation. One such exploit involves entering the East End, where once again he encounters Mars Bar. To settle their old dispute, they engage in a road race. When Maniac wins, Mars Bar not only declares a truce but even extends the hand of friendship. Maniac reciprocates by inviting the black boy to the McNabs for Piper's birthday party. When father George and John's gang, the Cobras, arrive, Maniac realizes his mistake and manages to escape with Mars Bar before violence erupts.

Once again, Maniac is on his own living with the buffalo. One day he again encounters Mars Bar. Together they wander toward the trestle where Maniac's parents were killed. There they see a stranded Russell McNab, who has wandered halfway out on the trestle and is now motionless with fright. Maniac is so traumatized by his memories that he walks away, leaving Mars Bar to effect a rescue.

In spite of Mars Bar's entreaties to come home with him, Maniac continues to stay at the zoo until one day forceful Amanda Beale accompanies Mars Bar. She demands that he give up this unhealthy way of life and come back to live with the Beales. Maniac capitulates, secretly overjoyed that somebody wanted him enough to give him a permanent home.

**Thematic Material**

Although this story uses many features of the tall tale, these elements not only amuse but also soften the poignant story of a vulnerable young boy looking for a home, family, and security. This is also a good-natured spoof of some of our folktales and myths (e.g., the variation of the Gordian knot story). Maniac is, in some respects, a present-day Candide, unable and unwilling to believe the ugly aspects of reality. Three of the contemporary problems that are addressed in this story are racial prejudice, homelessness, and illiteracy. In spite of the seriousness of these themes, this is a hopeful book, one in which optimism, innocence, and positive values prevail. The importance of getting to know one another as individuals in order to combat bigotry and misunderstandings is stressed. Other subjects dealt with are baseball, friendship, survival, and various kinds of family life.

**Book Talk Material**

How Jeffrey Lionel became known as Maniac can provide a fine introduction to the book. Important episodes include: Maniac leaves Aunt

Dot and Uncle Dan (pp. 5–7); he meets Amanda Beale (pp. 10–13) and saves a child from the Finsterwald backyard (pp. 16–19); the Little League game with John McNab as pitcher (pp. 22–27); Maniac first encounters Mars Bar and is invited to Amanda's house (pp. 33–40); and untying Cobble's Knot (pp. 70–73).

**Additional Selections**

Thirteen-year-old Jamie and her older brother, Luke, are driving cross-country when they pick up an unusual hitchhiker, an elderly man with a passion for gambling, in Stephen Mooser's *The Hitchhiking Vampire* (Delacorte, 1989, $13.95; pap., Dell, $3.25).

In Paul B. Janeczko's book of poems *Brickyard Summer* (Orchard, 1989, $13.95), a boyhood in a small town is celebrated.

Faith Futterman is fearful she is losing status with her sixth-grade group in Phyllis Shalant's *The Transformation of Faith Futterman* (Dutton, 1990, $12.95).

Newly adopted, Rocky forms a friendship with a rumpled artist named Mick who is designing a monument for the town's war dead in *The Momument* (Delacorte, 1991, $15) by Gary Paulsen.

Henry schemes with his pen pal Lesley to bring together Henry's eccentric mother and Lesley's rich father with matrimony as the objective in Janice Marriott's hilarious *Letters to Lesley* (Knopf, 1991, $7.99; pap., $3.50).

Thomas finds that he is gradually getting to like his fellow seventh-grader Elaine when they are paired in a class biography project in Mark Geller's *The Strange Case of the Reluctant Partners* (Harper, 1990, $13.95).

Two misfits, a twenty-year-old punk artist, Angie, and a bullied eleven-year-old boy find temporary happiness in their friendship in Robin Klein's *Came Back to Show You I Could Fly* (Viking, 1990, $11.95).

**About the Book**
*Booklist*, June 1, 1990, p. 1902.
*Horn Book*, May 1990, p. 340.
*Horn Book Guide*, January 1990, p. 250.
*Kirkus Reviews*, May 1, 1990, p. 655.
*New York Times Book Review*, April 21, 1991, p. 33.
*School Library Journal*, June 1990, p. 138.
See also *Book Review Digest*, 1990, pp. 1738–39; and *Book Review Index*, 1990, p. 769, and 1991, p. 856.

**About the Author**

Commire, Anne, ed., *Something about the Author.* Gale, 1985, Vol. 39, p. 198.
Holtze, Sally Holmes, ed., *Sixth Book of Junior Authors and Illustrators.* Wilson, 1989, pp. 284–85.
May, Hal, ed., *Contemporary Authors.* Gale, 1984, Vol. 111, p. 435.

---

**Voigt, Cynthia.**  *Seventeen against the Dealer*
Atheneum, 1989, $13.95 (0-689-31497-3)

---

In this, the last of the Tillerman cycle, Dicey, now twenty-one, decides to earn her living by building boats in Maryland. Dicey and her three homeless younger siblings first made their appearance in *Homecoming* (Atheneum, 1981, $14.95; condensed in *Juniorplots 3*, Bowker, 1987, pp. 110–13). In that novel, Dicey, then thirteen, shepherds her abandoned brood from Connecticut to their maternal grandmother's home on the coast of Maryland. This series, which features individual books on other members of Dicey's family, is enjoyed by readers in both junior and (to a lesser extent) senior high school.

**Plot Summary**

Dicey Tillerman is a boat builder. At least, that is what she is going to be, what she has always wanted to be. Dicey has a one-track mind about her life's goal. She will build sailboats for those who can truly appreciate the craftsmanship in a slender, well-built wooden boat as it moves across the water.

Although boatbuilding is what Dicey most wants to do, it must also earn her a living. That will not be easy in her small Maryland town, but life hasn't been easy for the Tillermans for a long time. It wasn't easy to take over the care of her brothers and sister after their mother abandoned them. It wasn't easy to persuade Gram to take them all in. Yet Dicey did both, and now they live in relative peace with Gram. James has a full scholarship to Yale. Sammy dreams of a summer tennis camp they can't possibly afford. Maybeth worries about passing tests.

And Dicey? All she dreams about is her goal. She has to work hard, plan carefully, be cautious with money, and ignore anything that tries to get in her way. That includes the suggestion of Jeff Greene, whom Dicey loves, that they marry now, before he finishes college.

The trick is to keep her mind firmly on the goal. Ken Forbeck offers her a good price on wood because he has no place to store it; that will reduce her bank account by $590, but it's a good buy. She turns down an offer from Claude Shorter, who rents her the boatbuilding shop. He hasn't got time to finish an order for thirty rowboats and wants Dicey to do it for him, but Claude does shoddy work, and Dicey doesn't want to waste her time. She does get an offer to build a boat for a Mr. Hobart; he gives her a check for $500 now, with delivery expected in April. This will be the first boat Dicey has built on her own.

Then, fate intervenes. Dicey's shop is burglarized; her expensive tools are stolen, and she has no insurance. Replacing the tools will just about wipe her out. She refuses Jeff's offer to buy them for her—Tillermans don't borrow money. Dicey revises her plan. She accepts Claude's offer to finish the rowboats and works extra hours every day so she can stay in business and still finish Mr. Hobart's boat.

Dicey throws herself into her work, desperate to maintain her hard schedule. She doesn't have time to help Sammy and Maybeth as they study for exams; she rarely has time to return Jeff's phone calls and it's hard to stay awake when he does come around. And there isn't time to worry about the fact that Gram's cold seems to linger.

Then one morning while she is at work, a ray of sunshine appears at the shop in the form of Cisco, a drifter with thick, dark hair streaked with gray, faded jeans, and laughing eyes. Dicey doesn't want him around and doesn't want to hear his endless talk, but he keeps coming back, even helping her work in exchange for staying at the shop. Before long she welcomes his presence and his conversation. One day, he cautions Dicey with the words to an old song: "Never hit seventeen, when you play against the dealer, for you know the odds won't ride with you." She begins to like and to trust Cisco.

Dicey throws herself into work harder than ever, even though the world around her doesn't seem to be going so well. When she tries to call Jeff now, he usually isn't in. Mr. Hobart changes his mind about ordering a boat from her and she can't do anything but return the $500 because they didn't have a written contract. Gram gets very sick. When a doctor is finally called in, he tries to tell Dicey that sometimes being so independent just isn't a good idea. It's right to call for outside help when you need it.

When it looks like Gram is going to recover, Dicey returns to the shop, where Cisco has been working pretty much on his own. She asks him to deposit a check for her, a part payment from Claude Shorter for the work on the rowboats. She never sees Cisco again after that. He is gone; as is her money.

It's hard for Dicey to tell the family because she feels so ashamed of herself. She does tell them, however, and then decides that she will finish the work on Claude's rowboats, and then give up the shop because she can't afford it.

She has one more thing to do. She goes to see Jeff. "I want to marry you," she tells him. "I don't have to be a boatbuilder."

Jeff tells Dicey in a voice as cold as moonlight that she doesn't have to choose. "You dropped out of college," he says, "but you never even considered that there might be another way—like apprentice programs. And you say you want to marry me and that you don't have to be a boatbuilder all in one breath, as though that's what I wanted."

During their conversation, Dicey finally understands something that has been in the back of her mind for some time now. You don't get any guarantees in life; everything is a risk. Trusting someone is a risk. Taking a chance is a risk. Still, Dicey knows that she doesn't need a guarantee; she just needs a chance—just the chance to take a chance.

Dicey and Jeff will marry in June after his graduation. In the meantime, while he has his studying and his school, she has a boat to build.

### Thematic Material

This novel quietly explores human values and the development of character. Dicey is depicted as a young woman who is fiercely independent and stubborn in her single-minded pursuit of her goal. It is as though she regards softness or reliance on others as a sign of weakness. Her inner strength and pride at keeping her family together are well drawn, as is her struggle to overcome the pain she feels over what she regards as failure.

### Book Talk Material

The booktalker might trace Dicey's development through her conversations with other characters. See: Dicey and Jeff discuss sex and love (pp. 6–7); Dicey and Mr. Hobart talk about building the boat (pp. 32–34); Dicey meets Cisco for the first time (pp. 61–69); they discuss gambling, marriage, and family (pp. 102–10); Dicey tells her family that the money is gone, and she makes a decision (pp. 167–70).

**Additional Selections**

Peter D. Sieruta's *Heartbeats and Other Stories* (Harper, 1989, $12.95) contains nine stories about today's teenagers at school, at home, with friends, and in love.

When Gracie's mother sinks into depression and her stepfather's business fails, Gracie must assume new responsibilities in A. E. Cannon's *Amazing Grace* (Delacorte, 1991, $15).

Cab's mother remarries and the young girl is sent to Washeo, a Pittsburgh neighborhood, to spend the summer with the grandmother she has never met in *Checking on the Moon* (Orchard, 1991, $14.95) by Jenny Davis.

In Harry Mazer's novel *Someone's Mother Is Missing* (Delacorte, 1990, $14.95), Lisa's mother has a breakdown after her husband dies and she abandons teenager Lisa and her younger sister.

Beth longs for independence from her poor home where she is the oldest of eight children in *Send No Blessings* (Atheneum, 1990, $13.95) by Phyllis Reynolds Naylor.

Casey learns that the wolf of her dreams is actually a fugitive terrorist in Gillian Cross's *Wolf* (Holiday, 1991, $13.95).

Half English, half Noutka Indian, Annette Broadhead confronts an alien culture when she receives a scholarship to an English-style academy in Margaret Robinson's *A Woman of Her Tribe* (Scribner, 1990, $13.90).

**About the Book**
*Book Report*, September 1989, p. 45.
*Booklist*, March 15, 1989, p. 276.
*Center for Children's Books Bulletin*, April 1989, p. 209.
*Horn Book*, July 1989, p. 492.
*Kirkus Reviews*, February 1989, p. 103.
*School Library Journal*, February 1989, p. 103.
*VOYA*, April 1989, p. 33.
*Wilson Library Bulletin*, November 1989, p. 12.
See also *Book Review Digest*, 1989, p. 1715; and *Book Review Index*, 1989, p. 848, and 1990, p. 839.

**About the Author**
Chevalier, Tracy, ed., *Twentieth-Century Children's Writers* (3rd ed.). St. James, 1989, pp. 1004–5.
Commire, Anne, ed., *Something about the Author*. Gale, 1983, Vol. 33, p. 226.
Holtze, Sally Holmes, ed., *Fifth Book of Junior Authors and Illustrators*. Wilson, 1983, pp. 320–21.

Locher, Frances C., ed., *Contemporary Authors*. Gale, 1982, Vol. 106, p. 508.
Metzger, Linda, ed., *Contemporary Authors* (New Revision Series). Gale, 1986, Vol. 18, p. 468.
Senick, Gerard J., ed., *Children's Literature Review*. Gale, 1987, Vol. 13, pp. 223–41.

---

**Wersba, Barbara.** *Just Be Gorgeous*
Harper, 1988, $11.89 (0-06-026359-8); pap., Dell, $3.25 (0-440-20810-6)

---

*Just Be Gorgeous* is one of three novels about Manhattan teenager Heidi Rosenbloom. In it and its first sequel, *Wonderful Me* (Harper, 1989, $12.95; pap., Dell, $3.50), she is in conflict with a mother and a father who, respectively, want her to be beautiful and talented. In the third installment, *The Farewell Kid* (Harper, 1990, $12.95), she has graduated from her disliked private school and is in love with Harvey Beaumont III. They make passionate love and find happiness until his mother, an anti-Semite, intervenes. These books are both humorous and insightful and are suited to mature readers in junior and senior high school.

**Plot Summary**

This is a warm, funny, tender, bittersweet story of two misfits, even if one doesn't recognize that fact. Heidi Rosenbloom, age sixteen, considers her life and herself a mess. Her parents are divorced. She lives with her mother on Manhattan's Upper East Side. She attends private school, has a dumpy shape, and her best friend has moved to California. Heidi's mother seems to exist only for shopping at Bloomingdale's or urging her daughter to go to beauty salons. She is forever buying Heidi frilly clothes, but what Heidi likes to wear is a man's overcoat purchased at a thrift shop. To Heidi, her mother is seeing someone else everytime she looks at her.

Heidi's father, whom she sees often since he lives downtown in the Village, doesn't regard Heidi as a beauty, but rather looks on her as an Einstein. He truly expects her to be going to Radcliffe. Heidi is sure she hasn't got the qualifications for that either.

Heidi isn't sure who she is or what she wants to do. She loves dogs but doesn't know if she could qualify as a vet; perhaps she'll just be a dog walker or maybe a bicycle messenger.

On a day when Heidi is most depressed, her life changes. As she waits in line in front of a Broadway theater to pick up tickets as a Christmas present for her mother, she watches a young man with bleached blond hair dancing on the sidewalk for money. On an impulse, she gives him $5. Heidi is so entranced with his dancing that she asks if she can buy him some coffee when he is finished dancing.

Over coffee, Heidi learns that the young man's stage name is Jeffrey. He lives in an abandoned building in Manhattan; he is from the Midwest; he is an orphan; he wants more than anything in the world to get into the theater as a dancer; and, oh yes, he is gay.

Heidi is fascinated and totally enchanted. She and Jeffrey become fast friends. He takes her to see his abandoned building and she is shocked at the conditions in which some people must live. They meet nearly every day in front of whatever theater he has chosen for his dancing. Sometimes she goes with him when he tries out for a bit part, which he never gets.

Heidi has found a friend. She asks Jeffrey to dinner at her apartment. Her mother is delighted that her daughter is finally interested in a boy— until she sees Jeffrey, who arrives with his bleached hair and wearing a woman's fur jacket. Mrs. Rosenbloom tells Heidi not to see him anymore, an order she ignores.

Despite the fact that Jeffrey talks very openly about being gay and answers any questions Heidi has about his life-style, Heidi falls in love with him. Jeffrey becomes her whole life, which has suddenly taken on a purpose. At Christmas time, she takes out the $400 she has been saving and gives it to him so that he can spend a week in a real hotel room instead of the abandoned building. Jeffrey is touched, but he gives the money back to her.

When Mrs. Rosenbloom begins going to her friend's home in Connecticut and staying overnight on Fridays, Heidi invites Jeffrey to the apartment so that he can have a bath and sleep in a real bed at least once a week. Jeffrey seems unaware of Heidi's love for him, but he tells her repeatedly that she must have faith in herself, that whatever she is going to become is already there inside of her, and there is not one thing in the world she can't do if she puts her mind to it. He tells her that she is an original.

More than anything, Heidi wants to help Jeffrey get into show business. She enlists the aid of her music and drama teacher at school, who has had some limited success on Broadway. Miss Margolis agrees to accompany Heidi one day to see Jeffrey dancing on the street. Later she tells Heidi that although her friend is a very good dancer, he's "nothing special." He lacks that magic something that will make him stand out from all the rest. Heidi is crushed by this news at first, then defiant. Perhaps Jeffrey is just too young yet; he needs more practice.

As they are sitting in the park one day, a small dog takes a liking to Heidi. She knows instantly that it is a stray and decides to take it home. Jeffrey warns her to go to the vet first for shots, which she does. Her mother is most unhappy at the arrival of the dog but when she protests, Heidi tells here that she has to have the dog because she needs someone to love her. Her mother is shocked and hurt. "No one has ever loved a child as much as I love you," she tells her—and suddenly Heidi understands that, even with the trouble they have communicating, it is true. Her mother really does love her, and her father too. For the first time she fells compassion for her parents, if only she could bring herself to express it.

One day Jeffrey calls and asks her to meet him. He has fantastic news. The news turns out to be that two friends of his have decided to try their luck out in Hollywood, and Jeffrey is going along. Perhaps he can break into television more easily than Broadway.

Heidi is devastated at first as Jeffrey prepares to leave and then becomes angry at his flippant attitude. Hasn't their friendship meant anything to him at all? She thinks he will just walk out of her life as though they have never known each other. However, as she says good-bye to Jeffrey while he and his friends pack the car for their trip, he suddenly begins to cry. "I don't want to go. I don't want to leave you," he tells her. Now Heidi understands. She knows that his flippant behavior is his way of breaking away, and she knows he must go because Jeffrey is a dreamer and has to keep trying to catch that brass ring.

Jeffrey never writes, of course, and Heidi realizes she has fallen in love with the wrong person. But it's all right now because she also knows that everything Jeffrey told her she was is true.

**Thematic Material**

This is a love story, in a way, of two misfits, an unattractive teenager whose parents both want her to be what she is not, and a young gay boy with a single-minded dream. Both are touching and believable and likable, and their friendship warms the heart.

**Book Talk Material**

Heidi's relationship with her parents and with Jeffrey can open discussions of how the teenage years are often a time of ups and downs and back-and-forth emotions. See: Heidi and her mother argue over her father and "the coat" (pp. 13–16); Heidi meets her father for dinner (pp. 19–26); Heidi meets Jeffrey (pp. 41–49); and Heidi talks to Jeffrey about herself (pp. 61–66).

**Additional Selections**

Grace is an unhappy, overweight fifteen-year-old who receives help from a sympathetic gym teacher in *Monday I Love You* (Harper, 1988, $11.95) by Constance C. Greene.

At his London ballet school, Jamie thinks he finds true love in Jeane Ure's *You Win Some, You Lose Some* (Delacorte, 1986, $14.95; pap., Dell, $2.95).

Sixteen-year-old Becky Seville has a hopeless crush on John, who lives across the street, in Joyce Sweeney's *The Dream Collector* (Delacorte, 1989, $14.95).

For mature readers, suggest Francesca Lia Black's *Weetzie Bat* (Harper, 1989, $12.95; pap., $3.50) in which a young girl and her gay boyfriend, Dirk, set up house together. There is also a sequel, *Witch Baby* (Harper, 1991, $13.95).

Fourteen-year-old Alice Lonner enters the dazzling world of modeling and develops a crush on a thirty-one-year-old photographer in Erika Tamar's *High Cheekbones* (Viking, 1990, $12.95).

Summer resident Jenny tries to form a friendship with the handsome boy next door but is rebuffed in Karin Mango's *Just for the Summer* (Harper, 1990, $13.95).

In this very humorous novel, *The Book of the Banshee* (Little, Brown, 1992, $13.95) by Anne Fine, Will Flowers tells how his sister turned from a model, angel-like individual into a teenage banshee.

**About the Book**

*Booklist*, September 1, 1988, p. 69.
*Kirkus Reviews*, September 15, 1988, p. 144.
*School Library Journal*, November 1988, p. 133.
*VOYA*, December 1988, p. 244.
See also *Book Review Index*, 1988, p. 859, and 1989, p. 870.

**About the Author**

Chevalier, Tracy, ed., *Twentieth-Century Children's Writers* (3rd ed.). St. James, 1989, pp. 1025–26.
Commire, Anne, ed., *Something about the Author*. Gale, 1990, Vol. 58, pp. 179–87.
de Montreville, Doris, and Hill, Donna, eds., *Third Book of Junior Authors and Illustrators*. Wilson, 1972, pp. 298–99.
Garrett, Agnes, and McCue, Helga P., eds., *Authors and Artists for Young Adults*. Gale, 1989, Vol. 2, pp. 235–43.
Kirkpatrick, D. L., ed., *Twentieth-Century Children's Writers* (2nd ed.). St. Martin's, 1983, pp. 811–12.
Metzger, Linda, and Straub, Deborah A., eds., *Contemporary Authors* (New Revision Series). Gale, 1986, Vol. 16, pp. 430–31.
Sarkissian, Adele, ed., *Something about the Author: Autobiography Series*. Gale, 1986, Vol. 2, pp. 293–304.
Senick, Gerard J., ed., *Children's Literature Review*. Gale, 1976, Vol. 3, pp. 213–20.
Ward, Martha, ed., *Authors of Books for Young People* (3rd ed.). Scarecrow, 1990, p. 743.

---

**Zindel, Paul.**   *A Begonia for Miss Applebaum*

Harper, 1989, lib. bdg. $12.89 (0-06-026877-8); pap., Bantam, $3.50 (0-553-28765-6)

---

In his novels for young adults, Paul Zindel often deals with the theme of teenagers' forming symbiotic attachments to vulnerable—often ill—adults. This situation forms the basis of his first novel, award-winning *The Pigman* (Harper, 1968, $13.89) in which two teenage misfits—a girl and a boy—befriend a lonely old man, Mr. Pignatti. *A Begonia for Miss Applebaum* explores a similar situation. In this case two unconventional teens take a favorite teacher who is dying of cancer under their wings. These two novels are read and enjoyed by both junior and senior high school students.

**Plot Summary**

At the outset of this novel, Henry and Zelda assure the reader that, even though something terrible has happened, they never meant to hurt Miss Applebaum.

At age fifteen, Zelda Einnob and Henry Maximilian Ledniz are New York City high school students. They are bright, studious, streetwise. Although they have families—Zelda's parents are a normal-appearing guidance counselor and a librarian; Henry says his psychoanalyst mother and college professor father are berserk—what they really have is each other. Zelda and Henry are best friends and confidants. They share their thoughts and feelings about life and death, their jokes, fears, and tears. They also share their admiration for Miss Applebaum, a sixty-two-year-old dynamo and their favorite teacher, who opens up wonders to them far beyond the laws of science.

On the first day of school this September, Zelda and Henry race to the lab to sign up once again as Miss Applebaum's assistants. To their great dismay, they learn that the unthinkable has come to pass—she has *retired*. What could school possibly be like without Miss Applebaum, who wore a black homburg hat on days when she wanted to feel "special" and once taught a nature class by hanging seventy cocoons from the classroom windows, which eventually turned into about seven million grasshoppers jumping all over their desks?

Because Miss Applebaum is the most special teacher Zelda or Henry ever had, they don't take her retirement lightly. Henry suggests visiting her apartment near Central Park and bringing her a begonia plant. Miss Applebaum loves anything living, and at $2.98, a begonia is more afford-able than roses.

Miss Applebaum is surprised and delighted to see them. Zelda and Henry are, to say the least, surprised and delighted at her apartment. As Zelda recalls, at first it looked like a dense jungle, a startling laboratory, a library, and a storage room all rolled into one, but then she and Henry begin to see that the room actually has rhyme and reason to it, just like Miss Applebaum. It contains the strangest scientific equipment they have ever seen—a giant atom model, a large model of an ear, barometers, microscopes—a crazy, wonderful laboratory.

As delighted as Zelda and Henry are with Miss Applebaum's apart-ment, they are not delighted to discover the real reason for her retire-ment. She is ill, apparently very ill; indeed, Zelda's mother later says that their beloved teacher is terminally ill with cancer.

Shocked though they are, Zelda and Henry have little time at first to deal with this news, for Miss Applebaum seems to have no time at all to deal with it. She whisks her two students off to such places as the roller coaster in Central Park. Long-time, you-can't-sell-me-the-Brooklyn-Bridge New Yorkers, both Zelda and Henry know there is no roller coaster in Central Park—until Miss Applebaum shows them the great sloping lawn by the fountain, where to their amazement and shrieking laughter the citywise youngsters find themselves rolling over and over downhill on Miss Applebaum's Central Park roller coaster.

The teenagers begin to spend as much of their free time as possible with Miss Applebaum. There are marvelous, eye-opening trips to the museum. Every outing with her is a new learning experience, a new adventure. It's as though she isn't ill at all. Zelda and Henry can't understand it, but she does not seem to be aware of her condition.

Yet it is obvious to them that their teacher is growing worse. Frightened by the prospect of her death and even more frightened by the prospect of death itself, the teenagers decide that they must discuss Miss Applebaum's illness outright with her. Together they will find the right doctor, a second opinion, and surely a cure. In a touching scene, they tell the older woman of their fears.

"I know, my sweet children," is Miss Applebaum's calm reply.

But Zelda and Henry are not satisfied with their teacher's acceptance. They are also not satisfied with the treatment she gets from her doctor, who is, they reason, only a general practitioner. They insist that Miss Applebaum needs a specialist in cancer, an oncologist, and they talk her into a second opinion.

It is not until Miss Applebaum is put into the hospital for testing and chemotherapy that Zelda and Henry realize the enormity of their mistake. The first time they see her in a stark white hospital gown with a small bandage on her neck, she bursts into tears. "They cut me," she tells them. Henry realizes then that they should have left things as they were. What they have done is not going to help Miss Applebaum at all. Miss Applebaum was dealing with cancer in her own way. Now all three of them must squarely confront her illness, and her impending death. The teenagers also must confront Bernice, Miss Applebaum's niece, who calls them stupid, hateful children.

"She could have lived her last days in peace," Bernice says. "You had to give her hope! Well, don't you see what you've done!"

Miss Applebaum endures forty-five days of treatment for cancer, during which time she never stops teaching her two prize pupils. But they know the end is near. When the hospital treatment is over, Zelda and Henry take her in a wheelchair through Central Park on their way to her apartment, where, after putting her affairs in order, she soon dies. Her last words are "Bury me in the park."

Zelda and Henry honor their beloved teacher's request. They wheel her body to the park and bury her in a trench. Miss Applebaum will stay in her beloved Central Park, and Zelda and Henry, on a beautiful spring day, will bring her a begonia once more.

**Thematic Material**

This book is, above all, the familiar but always heartwarming story of the influence that a caring teacher can have on young minds and characters. Miss Applebaum is portrayed as a slightly unusual, a bit-off-the-wall, wonderfully imaginative woman who imparts bits of knowledge as though she were passing out gumdrops to eager hands. The book is also about death. It deals sensitively with the issue of one adult facing her own impending death and with the way in which two young people attempt to run from not only the death of someone they love, but the very idea of death itself. Another important theme is friendship, in this case the close friendship of two young people who find that they can face a turbulent society in a large city as long as they have each other. In and around these serious themes is the author's constant thread of humor, which keeps the subject matter from getting too heavy even at the most solemn of times.

**Book Talk Material**

The key themes in this sensitive novel are the influence of an imaginative teacher and how humans of any age deal with death. See: Zelda and Henry get their first look at Miss Applebaum's living room (pp. 24–26); the Central Park "roller coaster" (pp. 57–59); the trip to the museum (pp. 97–106); and the most challenging exam (pp. 114–16). See also: Zelda's fears about dying (pp. 87–88); Zelda and Henry tell Miss Applebaum what they know (pp. 106–7); the teenagers realize what they have done (pp. 136–39); and Miss Applebaum's death (pp. 175–76).

**Additional Selections**

Annie hopes that taking care of a ten-year-old boy during the summer will help erase the pain of her parents' divorce in Gloria Whelan's *The Secret Keeper* (Knopf, 1990, $12.95; pap., $3.50).

There are nine short stories about teenagers facing life's problems in Peter D. Sieruta's *Heartbeats and Other Stories* (Harper, 1989, $12.95).

A boy finds it difficult adjusting to his father's death and acquiring a stepfather in Michael Morpurgo's *Mr. Nobody's Eyes* (Viking, 1990, $12.95), a novel set in post–World War II England.

A thirteen-year-old girl is embarrassed about her family's tenement home and her non-English-speaking Russian Jewish mother in Fran Weissenberg's *The Streets Are Paved with Gold* (pap., Harbinger, 1990, $5.95).

All sorts of human relationships are explored in the stories written by Cynthia Rylant in *A Couple of Kooks and Other Stories about Love* (Orchard, 1990, $13.95).

In the Bronx of 1948, a lonely girl reaches out for the friendship of popular Jean but finds that the girl has a mean streak in Jan Slepian's *Risk n' Roses* (Philomel, 1990, $14.95).

Al Capsella has trouble with a weird assortment of eccentric adults in J. Clarke's humorous *The Heroic Life of Al Capsella* (Holt, 1990, $14.95) and its equally funny sequel, *Al Capsella and the Watchdogs* (Holt, 1991, $14.95).

**About the Book**
*Book Report*, November 1989, p. 48.
*Booklist*, March 15, 1989, p. 1276.
*Center for Children's Books Bulletin*, April 1989, p. 212.
*Horn Book*, April 1, 1989, p. 380.
*Kirkus Reviews*, April 1989, p. 556.
*School Library Journal*, April 1989, p. 122.
*VOYA*, June 1989, p. 109.
*Wilson Library Journal*, September 1989, p. 3, and October 1989, p. 107.
See also *Book Review Digest*, 1989, pp. 1841–42; and *Book Review Index*, 1989, p. 910, and 1990, p. 900.

**About the Author**
Chevalier, Tracy, ed., *Twentieth-Century Children's Writers* (3rd ed.). St. James, 1989, pp. 1078–79.
Commire, Anne, ed., *Something about the Author*. Gale, 1979, Vol. 16, pp. 283–90; updated, 1990, Vol. 58, pp. 198–210.
Estes, Glenn E., ed., *American Writers for Children since 1960: Fiction* (Dictionary of Literary Biography: Vol. 52). Gale, 1986, pp. 405–10.
Garrett, Agnes, and McCue, Helga P., eds., *Authors and Artists for Young Adults*. Gale, 1989, Vol. 2, pp. 245–61.
Holtze, Sally Holmes, ed., *Fifth Book of Junior Authors and Illustrators*. Wilson, 1983, pp. 243–44.
Kirkpatrick, D. L., ed., *Twentieth-Century Children's Writers* (2nd ed.). St. Martin's, 1983, pp. 853–54.
Locher, Frances C., ed., *Contemporary Authors*. Gale, 1978, Vols. 73–76, p. 659.
Senick, Gerard J., ed., *Children's Literature Review*. Gale, 1978, Vol. 3, pp. 244–54.
Ward, Martha, ed., *Authors of Books for Young People* (3rd ed.). Scarecrow, 1990, p. 779.

# 2

---

# Adventure and Mystery Stories

T EENAGE readers, like their adult counterparts, enjoy escapist literature involving mysteries and tales of adventure. In this section, there are thirteen exciting, suspenseful stories, two of which were written about one hundred years ago but still hold readers enthralled. The others are by contemporary authors, each of whom scores high in quality writing and reader satisfaction.

---

**Aiken, Joan.**   *The Teeth of the Gale*
HarperCollins, 1988, $14.89 (0-06-020045-6)

---

This novel is a sequel to the author's earlier action suspense books *Go Saddle the Sea* (o.p.) and *Bridle the Wind* (Delacorte, 1983, $14.95). Each of the three can be read separately and each is narrated by Felix de Cabezada y Brooke. In this, the third in the series, again set in nineteenth-century Spain, Felix is eighteen and on the trail of three children who have been kidnapped. Once more the author combines the political issues of the day with an exciting personal narration. Although the narrative is complete and leaves no loose ends, the inconclusive last sentence of the book would hint at more to come. These novels are intended for a junior high school audience.

**Plot Summary**

Set against the violent revolutionary backdrop of Spain in the 1820s, this is the story of the only surviving heir of a Spanish count and an English duke. Eighteen-year-old Felix de Cabezada y Brooke is now in Salamanca studying law. He receives an urgent message that his ailing and beloved grandfather, Don Francisco, has requested his immediate return to his home in Villaverde. The message is delivered by Pedro, who has long been in the employ of his grandfather and whom Felix has known for many years.

The two young men set out for Villaverde. Pedro knows only that Don Francisco sent for his grandson after he received a letter from the Reverend Mother of a convent in Bilbao. Felix's heart skips a beat when he hears this, for Juana Esparza, the young woman Felix loves, is preparing to take her vows as a nun.

At Villaverde, Don Francisco tells Felix that the Reverend Mother has asked the young man's aid. It seems that a cousin of Juana Esparza, Conchita de la Trava, is in distress. Her husband, Manuel de la Trava, is said to be mad, and he has escaped from prison and kidnapped their children, vowing that he will never return them. Conchita and Juana are given permission to travel to Jaca to find someone to help them secure the release of the children, but they need an escort. Will Felix oblige?

Some years before, young Felix had escorted the lovely Juana Esparza across the Pyrenees and into the safekeeping of her uncle—and fallen in love with her. A series of tragedies in her family have caused her to enter the convent. Felix agrees to escort the young lady again and Felix and Pedro set out on the journey to Bilbao. It takes a week to reach the convent where the Reverend Mother, whom Felix instantly dislikes, interrogates him as though he were before the Inquisition. Finally, he sees his beloved Juana and realizes that his feelings for her are as strong as ever. He finds, however, that Conchita is a self-willed, spoiled young woman. She questions him about his background and the fact that he carries an English title. He explains that his father, now dead, was an English officer serving in the French wars and that his grandfather, still alive in England, has an English title. Conchita also shows Felix pictures of the three children who have been kidnapped, nine-year-old Nico, eight-year-old Luisa, and the baby, four-year-old Pilar.

The group sets out for Berdun, the home of Don Ignacio, brother to Manuel de la Trava. Felix overhears a conversation in the house about Manuel's madness. If Manuel were to be judged mad, the family estates would go to Don Ignacio, whom Felix instantly distrusts.

Before the journey can continue the next day, their horses are poisoned. While waiting for the animals to recover, Felix and Pedro set off to see if they can discover the hiding place of Manuel de la Trava. In the little mountain village of Santa Cruz de la Seros, they meet the young political writer and foe of the government, Jose de Larra. He says that he would like to help his friend Manuel and the two children. Felix says there are three children, which confuses de Larra, who is sure that Manuel spoke only of two.

The journey resumes with the two women. Pedro, who has gone on ahead, meets them at a prearranged spot. With the aid of de Larra, he has found Don Manuel's hiding place. He is high up the mountain in a ruined castle called Castille de Acher. He communicates by lowering notes in a basket. De Larra offers to help Manuel escape into France with the three children, but Manuel tells him that there are only two children.

How very strange, Felix thinks. What has become of the third child?

Felix decides to see if he can talk to Manuel. As they take the women to a safe spot, they meet Don Amador de Castanos, a "fat man" whom Felix and Pedro saw with a young child on their trip to Villaverde. Now they find out that the young child with Don Amador is actually Conchita's daughter Pilar, the third child. But she is the child of Conchita and her lover, Don Amador. If this were known, it would spoil the picture of Conchita as the bereaved mother and wronged wife, so she must have little Pilar on hand when the other two children are rescued so that it will appear that all were kidnapped in the first place.

Felix does manage to meet Don Manuel and everything seems to fall into place. Young Felix realizes that Don Manuel is not mad at all; he took his children because he loved them and wanted them away from Conchita. He left Pilar behind because she was not his child. But Conchita, who did not want it to be known that Pilar had been fathered by her lover, had instructed Don Amador to keep Pilar out of sight until the other two children could be rescued and Manuel could be disposed of, thereby giving Conchita the inheritance.

Don Manuel refuses to give up the children and Don Amador tells Felix that a company of soldiers will be sent to bombard the castle. If the children are hurt, so be it. That will be on Don Manuel's head.

Don Manuel considers escape, but he cannot take the children with him. He asks that Juana leave the convent and pledge herself to care for his children, and she agrees to do so. However, tragedy strikes when Luisa dies from poisoned glue on the pages of a book, which was transferred from her fingers to her mouth. The book was sent by Conchita and meant for Don Manuel. The little boy, Nico, does not die from ingesting the poison, but he becomes very ill.

Manuel and Conchita meet face to face at the castle, and in an accident, she falls over the wall and is killed. Manuel must leave the country at once to escape imprisonment.

So begins a journey back to the convent to try to save the life of little Nico. During the trip, Pedro is shot and Felix rendered unconscious by the forces of Don Ignacio. Don Amador is killed, but Felix manages to free Juana and the children and they find a doctor to try to save Nico's life.

Once again Felix is called to Villaverde, where his grandfather is now very ill. He tells the old man what has happened, that Don Manuel has escaped, that one of the children and Conchita and her lover are dead. Felix also tells his grandfather that he will return to the convent and ask permission to pay his addresses to Senorita Esparza. The old man gives his permission happily.

In time Felix and Juana are married, with the two children—Nico has now recovered—and Pedro in attendance. Very soon after the ceremony they begin their trip back to Villaverde, where Felix hopes to see the happiness on his grandfather's face. Alas, that final happiness is not permitted.

**Thematic Material**

This is an old-fashioned novel of a turbulent time in the history of Spain, when the country was desperately poor and in a state of upheaval. The one historical character in the story is de Larra, who actually was a Liberal journalist during this period. Felix is a dashing young hero and Juana an independent, high-spirited young woman who is his match. The intrigues of treachery in the high seats of government add to the excitement of this adventure, which is somewhat reminiscent of swash-bucklers of many years past.

**Book Talk Material**

Felix has many adventures that should be of interest to readers. See: the terrible meal at the inn (pp. 20–21); Felix and Pedro first meet the spoiled child, Pilar (pp. 24–29); two travelers meet their deaths on the road (pp. 42–43); Felix is interrogated by the Reverend Mother (pp. 67–72); and the fight with the bears (pp. 173–76).

**Additional Selections**

A teenage girl saves a half-drowned man on the beach and finds he is a member of the sealskin-wearing tribe, the Rigi, who has come to help her in this folktale-like fantasy by Betsy James, *Long Night Dance* (Dutton, 1989, $12.95).

In Elizabethan England, a Jewish family illegally practices its faith in Pamela Melnikoff's *Riots & Players* (Bedrick, 1989, $9.95).

When Chad and his family rent an old brownstone in Manhattan, they are visited by the residents of over a hundred years before in Richard Peck's *Voices after Midnight* (Delacorte, 1989, $14.95; pap., Dell, $3.50).

Birle has a series of adventures, including being captured by pirates, when she accompanies a runaway in Cynthia Voigt's *On Fortune's Wheel* (Atheneum, 1990, $15.95).

A youngster joins the abolitionist band of John Brown to help slaves reach freedom in Patrice Beatty's *Jawhawker* (Morrow, 1991, $13.95).

In Michael Bedard's *Redwork*, Cass is both intrigued and frightened by his new landlord, the mysterious Mr. Magus (Atheneum, 1990, $15.95).

Julie moves back in time to experience murders, shipwrecks, and romance in this time-travel novel by Deborah Lisson, *The Devil's Own* (Holiday, 1991, $13.95).

**About the Book**

*Booklist*, September 15, 1988, p. 152.
*Center for Children's Books Bulletin*, November 1988, p. 63.
*Horn Book*, November 1988, p. 786.
*Kirkus Reviews*, September 1, 1988, p. 786.
*School Library Journal*, November 1988, p. 124.
*VOYA*, December 1988, p. 233.
See also *Book Review Digest*, 1989, p. 20; and *Book Review Index*, 1988, p. 11, and 1989, p. 11.

**About the Author**

Block, Ann, and Riley, Carolyn, eds., *Children's Literature Review*. Gale, 1976, Vol. 1, pp. 1–9.
Chevalier, Tracy, ed., *Twentieth-Century Children's Writers* (3rd ed.). St. James, 1989, pp. 9–11.
Commire, Anne, ed., *Something about the Author*. Gale, 1983, Vol. 30, pp. 28–33.
de Montreville, Doris, and Hill, Donna, eds., *Third Book of Junior Authors*. Wilson, 1972, pp. 4–5.
Garrett, Agnes, and McCue, Helga P., eds., *Authors and Artists for Young Adults*. Gale, 1989, Vol. 1, pp. 1–14.
Kirkpatrick, D. L., ed., *Twentieth-Century Children's Writers* (2nd ed.). St. Martin's, 1983, pp. 16–17.
Sarkissian, Adele, ed., *Something about the Author: Autobiography Series*. Gale, 1986, Vol. 1, pp. 17–37.
Senick, Gerard J., ed., *Children's Literature Review*. Gale, 1990, Vol. 19, pp. 1–19.
Straub, Deborah A., ed., *Contemporary Authors* (New Revision Series). Gale, 1988, Vol. 23, pp. 3–5.
Ward, Martha, ed., *Authors of Books for Young People* (3rd ed.). Scarecrow, 1990, p. 6.

**Banks, Lynne Reid.** *Melusine*
HarperCollins, 1989, $12.95 (0-06-020394-3); pap., $3.95 (0-06-447054-7)

Lynne Reid Banks is perhaps best known for her fantasy "Indian" series for younger readers (e.g., *The Indian in the Cupboard* [Doubleday, 1985, $15.95; pap., Avon, $3.50]). *Melusine* combines fantasy with overtones of realism. In this Gothic mystery that includes such standard incidents as violent midnight storms, both myths and fairy tales are drawn upon to tell a contemporary story of sexual abuse mixed with fantasy based on legend. It is read by both junior and senior high school students.

**Plot Summary**

Roger and his family are on holiday from their home in England. The family consists of his mother and father and his mostly pain-in-the-neck twin sisters, Emma and Polly. They enjoy a stay in Paris and, as the story opens, have rented a car and are driving into the French countryside for a two-week stay at the Chateau de Bois-Serpe.

It is not an auspicious beginning for Roger, crammed as he is between his two boring sisters in the back seat of the car. When he spies a huge question mark painted on one of the barns they pass, he begins to think that there is a question mark over the whole area they are going to—or over their whole holiday.

At first it seems as though Roger may be right. Although their own quarters are large and beautifully furnished, except for his small room, the rest of the Chateau de Bois-Serpe, isolated and spooky looking, is run-down and decrepit. The only two inhabitants are the proprietor, the hostile Monsieur Serpe, and his daughter, Melusine, who is about Roger's age. Monsieur Serpe tells them that he has another daughter, but she no longer lives at home.

With some difficulty, Roger begins to make friends with Melusine. She speaks little English and seems shy, but she does allow him to help her with milking the goat herd. Not long after they arrive, Roger is disturbed by two things: Melusine tells him emphatically never to go near the chateau tower, and one day by accident he sees the young girl sitting on her father's lap. It looks as though he is trying to kiss her and she is struggling. Later, after a conversation with his own father about what he has witnessed, Roger entertains the horrifying possibility that Melusine is enduring sexual abuse from her father.

One day while the family is visiting the small village nearby, Roger sees Melusine watching two local street entertainers. One of them is playing Eastern music, and Melusine begins to sway to it. Roger's father comments that Melusine does a snake dance better than a snake.

As their stay lengthens and Roger's interest in Melusine grows, he becomes convinced that at times some other being is sharing his small room with him. He awakens one night in a panic, feeling something heavy across his feet. He screams and wakens his family who try to convince him that it is a nightmare. But Roger knows it is not.

When the family decides to take a day trip to visit the canals, Roger gets permission for Melusine to go with them. She, Roger, and Polly take a boat and become separated from his parents and Emma. Polly has an accident and falls into the water. Roger seems paralyzed and unable to save her. When he looks for Melusine, she too is gone. Suddenly, when Roger is sure his sister is lost, she appears—it seems to him she is thrust back up out of the water—unhurt. Melusine also reappears, but her clothes are dry.

After this incident, Roger becomes convinced that the strange girl Melusine, to whom he is so attracted, has other-worldly powers. He believes she can turn herself into a snake. Indeed, one night he finds in his bed the long body of a reptile. But how can he tell anyone that he believes he has a friend who is able to change her body into that of a snake?

Roger and his father discover what seems to be a passageway that might lead to the forbidden tower. Together one night they decide to explore it. They end up in a small room that looks as though it is preserved as a shrine. Two candles flank a coffin.

Before Roger and his father can examine this eerie sight further, Monsieur Serpe appears at the doorway with a gun in his hands. Roger is sure they will be killed. Monsieur Serpe fires the gun. It goes off with a deafening roar, but strangely enough, misses them both. In terror, Roger watches as an unseen force seems to attack the Frenchman. "Don't kill him!" Roger tries to cry out to Melusine, convinced that the girl is there. But the unseen force causes the man to fall, and he dies.

It takes some time to straighten out the father's mysterious death with the police. Roger learns that the tower room with the coffin held the body of Melusine's long dead sister. She had apparently committed suicide, a victim of the same abuse that Melusine has had to endure. Melusine herself has disappeared.

Roger and his family must return to England, but the boy does not want to leave without finding Melusine. The lawyer in charge of the estate says that he will take care of matters and claims that the girl, in fear, has merely run off somewhere to hide. The lawyer says he will ask Melusine's uncle in Canada to care for her.

Roger does not believe the lawyer and begins to hunt for Melusine himself, eventually finding her hiding place near the goats. He convinces his family that they cannot leave this young girl alone and afraid, especially after the terrible abuse she has endured.

It is decided Roger's father and the twins will return to England, and Roger and his mother and Melusine will follow as soon as the necessary arrangements have been made. Melusine will stay with them for a time, until she can go to her uncle in Canada. However, when Roger, Melusine, and his mother leave the chateau, Roger's mother loses control of the rented car and crashes right into the huge question mark that Roger had noticed painted on a barn at the beginning of their holiday. He later learns that the question mark, far from something sinister, was once part of a cigarette advertisement. More importantly, Melusine has once again disappeared.

Back in England, Roger cannot get over the disappearance of his friend. Finally, his family convinces him to see a counselor. In time he feels confident enough to tell the counselor that Melusine is able to change herself into a snake. The counselor's reaction is to recommend a psychiatrist. Roger confides his beliefs to his mother. She understands his torment and agrees to return to France to look for the girl.

Roger and his parents go back to France. Directed only by his feelings, Roger leads them to the chateau, where they find Melusine living in the great ballroom. She has taken all the furniture that she could drag from the quarters they had stayed in to make the ballroom beautiful once again, as it had apparently been long, long ago.

She greets Roger with joy and asks for his help.

"My help with what?" Roger asks.

Melusine wants him to help her move a table into the ballroom. Roger realizes that young Melusine will need a lot more help than he can give her at the moment, but he laughs and says yes. Together, Roger and Melusine force open the huge front doors of the Chateau de Bois-Serpe, letting in the fresh air for perhaps the first time in a hundred years.

**Thematic Material**

This is a well-written, fast-paced mystery that involves mythology, supernatural powers, and abuse. The almost run-of-the-mill wholesomeness of this English family is nicely contrasted with the sinister air that surrounds Melusine and her father. Young Roger's feelings toward Melusine are believable as he tries to sort out his concern for her welfare and his attraction to her. The young boy's relationships with his parents are well drawn, and there are enough chills here to keep the mystery fan entranced.

**Book Talk Material**

The family's arrival at the chateau will serve as a good introduction to this intriguing tale (see pp. 6–12). Mystery fans will especially be interested in Roger's growing suspicions about the chateau and Melusine; see: the first eerie feeling in his room (p. 48); Melusine dances to the snake music (pp. 57–59); Roger sees Melusine sitting on her father's lap (pp. 72–73); and he first feels the weight across his legs in bed at night (pp. 75–78).

**Additional Selections**

To escape the Japanese invasion of China, a disguised father and son travel to Tibet, where they encounter a Yeti tribe in Michael Morpurgo's *King of the Cloud Forest* (Viking, 1988, $11.95).

Life in the desert area of present-day Pakistan as seen through the eyes of a twelve-year-old girl already promised in marriage is the subject of *Shabanu, Daughter of the Win* by Suzanne F. Staples (Knopf, 1989, $13.95).

An Arab teenager is drawn into a web of terrorism and espionage in contemporary Damascus in *A Hand Full of Stars* (Dutton, 1990, $14.95) by Rafik Schami.

During World War II in a French village close to the Spanish border, young Jo becomes involved in smuggling Jews to freedom in Michael Morpurgo's *Waiting for Anya* (Viking, 1991, $12.95).

Politics, starvation, and terror mix in Minfong Ho's novel about the 1970s revolution in Thailand, *Rice without Rain* (Lothrop, Lee & Shepard, 1990, $11.95).

In *Split Image* by Michael French (Bantam, 1990, $14.95), Garrett discovers that his father is really a spy for North Korea.

A childhood in war-torn Korea is described in Sook Choi's *Year of Impossible Goodbyes* (Houghton, 1991, $13.95).

In the British thriller *Hairline Cracks* (Dutton, 1990, $14.95) by John Robert Taylor, Sam investigates the kidnapping of his mother.

**About the Book**
*Booklist*, October 1, 1989, p. 273.
*Center for Children's Books Bulletin*, September 1989, p. 1.
*Horn Book*, September 1989, p. 626.
*Horn Book Guide*, July 1989, p. 76.
*Kirkus Reviews*, July 15, 1989, p. 1071.
*School Library Journal*, November 1989, p. 124.
*VOYA*, February 1990, p. 340.
See also *Book Review Digest*, 1989, p. 1508; and *Book Review Index*, 1989, p. 684.

**About the Author**
Chevalier, Tracy, ed., *Twentieth-Century Children's Writers* (3rd ed.). St. James, 1989, pp. 56–58.
Commire, Anne, ed., *Something about the Author*. Gale, 1981, Vol. 22, pp. 208–9.
Holtze, Sally Holmes, ed., *Sixth Book of Junior Authors and Illustrators*. Wilson, 1989, pp. 23–24.
Kirkpatrick, D. L., ed., *Twentieth-Century Children's Writers* (2nd ed.). St. Martin's, 1983, pp. 651–52 (listed under Reid).
Straub, Deborah A., ed., *Contemporary Authors* (New Revision Series). Gale, 1988, Vol. 22, pp. 381–82.
Ward, Martha, ed., *Authors of Books for Young People* (3rd ed.). Scarecrow, 1990, p. 36.

---

**Bennett, Jay.** *The Haunted One*
Watts, 1987, $12.95 (0-531-15059-3); pap., Fawcett, $2.95 (0-449-70314-2)

---

With *The Haunted One*, Jay Bennett continues his output of fast-paced, suspenseful murder mysteries begun years ago with *Deathman, Do Not Follow Me* (pap., Scholastic, 1986, $2.50), the story of a young man pursued by art forgers after he accidentally discovers a fake Van Gogh. Two other recent novels are *Coverup* (Orchard, 1988, $12.95) and *The Dark Corridor* (Orchard, 1988, $12.95; pap., Fawcett, $3.50). All are enjoyed by readers in both junior and senior high school.

**Plot Summary**

Eighteen-year-old Paul Barrett has the world by the tail. It is summer-time, and this championship swimmer has landed a fine job as a life-guard on the New Jersey shore. He will graduate from high school in February. From there he goes to Syracuse University in upstate New York on a full athletic scholarship. As the summer begins, he is confi-dent, content, and happy.

This is Paul's first job as a full-time lifeguard. On his first day, his chief, Joe Carson, impresses on him the importance of the job and the seriousness of the responsibility. Carson assigns Paul to a fairly deserted stretch of the beach. The young man feels a certain pride at being accepted as one of Carson's boys, known as among the best of the life-guard teams along the East Coast.

The warm, sunny days of summer pass by. Paul does his job well. He is alert and serious and he manages a few routine rescues; they sound dramatic, but Paul knows they are all part of the job. Nevertheless, he feels a certain pride in his ability. Joe Carson stops by to praise him in a fatherly way. Paul likes that.

Occasionally, a couple of Paul's school friends come to the beach. Some of them smoke grass. Paul takes a few puffs now and again. How-ever, smoking grass really isn't his life-style. He just does it to be sociable, although he has the uneasy feeling that by doing so, he is betraying Joe Carson's trust in him.

Then one day a young woman appears on the beach. She looks to Paul like a goddess, with golden hair and a dancer's body. Day after day, she reads her book in the late afternoon sun, then walks out into the water and swims with powerful strokes. Paul is fascinated by her.

One early evening, when it is time for him to climb down from his lifeguard perch, Paul summons up the courage to speak to her. Her name is Jody Miller and she is a dancer, at the famed Lincoln Center in New York City. She dances ballet and has the promise of a great career. These days at the beach are vacation for her; she is staying at a motel nearby.

Paul Barrett falls totally, hopelessly in love with this beautiful girl—so much so that at the end of one day, he forgets to check in from his shift. Joe Carson finds him, just sitting on his lifeguard stand, staring out into the darkness. Of course, Paul doesn't tell Joe that he has been thinking about the goddess, but Joe is disturbed at Paul's lack of attention. This has not happened before, and Paul promises that it will not occur again.

To Paul's amazement, beautiful and talented Jody Miller seems to care for him too. Still, the day after he kisses her for the first time, Jody unexpectedly returns to New York City. She leaves a note for Paul at the motel saying that she has been called back for some unscheduled rehearsals but will return at the end of the week if possible. If she can't, she will see him sometime the following week.

Paul fears, however, that he will never see her again. The days, now near the end of summer, seem endless as he waits for her return. Then it seems as though fate takes over in a deliberate attempt to hurt him. It is the last day of the season and his last day as a lifeguard. No one is on the beach or in the water this drizzly, chilly afternoon.

Convinced that no one will come, and certainly not Jody, Paul decides to pass the boring time by smoking a little grass. Lulled into complacency, he thinks he hears someone calling to him. By the time he actually recognizes Jody's voice calling out in distress, it is too late. Although he does finally respond and swims desperately to save her, Jody drowns.

Paul later learns that Jody had asked another lifeguard up the beach if he were on duty so that she could swim to him and surprise him. Everyone, including Joe Carson, assures Paul that he did all he could to save her. Paul lives alone with his guilt, knowing that he was not at his best, knowing that he was not alert. When Carson finds the remains of Paul's cigarette on the beach, he knows it too.

Strangely enough, life goes on almost as before. Paul returns to school. His friends find him a little quieter, and his mother grows concerned about him. He denies any problem, but, looking into a mirror, Paul can see the haunted look in his own eyes.

Wherever he goes, whatever he does, the image of Jody Miller is before him. Then one day his mother tells him that a young woman has called him three times from the motel; she left her name—Jody Miller. In anger and shock, he calls the motel and learns that, indeed, a young woman named Jody Miller is registered, in the same room that Jody rented before. Paul begins to wonder if he is losing his mind.

One day when Paul is home alone, the woman calls him, and he is convinced that it is, indeed, Jody's voice. How could this be? She tells him that she loves him and wants to see him that evening, near the Ferris wheel. Paul knows that he is haunted by the girl's memory, but he goes to the meeting anyway. When he reaches the Ferris wheel, he sees Jody sitting in one of the seats high above him. They talk. She sends him off to a man named Morgan, who tells Paul that a girl called Jody paid him to let her sit up in the Ferris wheel.

Paul needs to talk to someone, and he confides in Joan, a girl he has dated. He tells her that he has spoken to and seen the dead Jody Miller. He confesses to Joan how much he loved Jody and that it is his fault that she is dead. Joan says that somehow, someone is playing a horrible trick on him.

Distraught, Paul returns to the beach, where he contemplates swimming out into the ocean and finding peace in his own way. Joe Carson finds him there and confesses that after Jody Miller's death, he sent a harsh report about Paul's part in the drowning to Jody's twin sister. Carson tells Paul that the twin is now almost insane with grief.

Paul waits on the beach, knowing she will come. And she does. Jody's twin tells Paul that Jody loved him and that he is responsible for her death. Jody would have become a great ballerina, the twin says, but Paul destroyed it all. Then she takes a gun from her purse. Paul tells her to kill him if that will bring her rest—but it won't, he asserts, for like him she will forever be haunted.

Paul reaches out and takes the gun. He holds Jody's twin sister close against him for a moment and then watches as she disappears into the darkness.

### Thematic Material

This is a taut and suspenseful story with overtones of melancholy and an air of the supernatural. The relationship between Paul and Jody Miller takes on an almost mystical quality. Paul is presented as a likable, self-assured young man who is confident of his future and content with his world. But he becomes totally captivated by this somewhat secretive young woman. His descent into a life forever haunted by his mistake is touched with sadness. The lesson of Paul's dereliction of duty may be harsh but will not be lost on the reader.

### Book Talk Material

The key to understanding the haunting of one young man lies in his character (see pp. 20–22, 25–28). Readers will also be interested in Paul's feelings about Jody Miller from the very beginning of their relationship (see pp. 31–41, 49–51, 53–58).

## Additional Selections

A young girl's world falls apart when her father is arrested for a twenty-year-old crime involving espionage in Robert Hawks's *This Stranger, My Father* (Houghton, 1988, $13.95).

April and her family are pursued by a vicious killer and must go into the witness protection program in Lois Duncan's *Don't Look behind You* (Delacorte, 1989, $14.95; pap., Dell, $3.50).

Nick realizes the terrible accidents happening to him are part of a fiendish plot in Willo Davis Roberts's *Nightmare* (Atheneum, 1989, $13.95).

For a younger audience, use the Sebastian books by James Howe. In a recent title, *Dew Drop Dead* (Atheneum, 1990, $13.95), Sebastian and his friends discover a corpse in a room in an abandoned inn.

In Frances A. Miller's *The Truth Trap* (pap., Fawcett, 1984, $3.95), a fifteen-year-old boy must prove he is not guilty of murder. Followed by *Aren't You the One Who . . . ?* (Macmillan, 1984, $14.95; pap., Fawcett, $3.50).

Bia, a Thai exchange student, reveals a mysterious past in William Sleator's *The Spirit House* (Dutton, 1991, $13.95).

In Julian F. Thompson's *The Grounding of Group 6* (pap., Avon, 1983, $3.50; condensed in *Juniorplots 3*, Bowker, 1987, pp. 152–56), some misfits at a country school discover a plot to destroy them.

### About the Book

*Book Report,* March 1988, p. 33.
*Kirkus Reviews,* September 14, 1987, p. 1388.
*School Library Journal,* November 1987, p. 112.
*VOYA,* February 1986, p. 277.
See also *Book Review Index,* 1987, p. 62.

### About the Author

Bowden, Jane A., ed., *Contemporary Authors.* Gale, 1978, Vols. 69–72, p. 62.
Commire, Anne, ed., *Something about the Author.* Gale, 1985, Vol. 41, pp. 36–37.
Evory, Ann, ed., *Contemporary Authors* (New Revision Series). Gale, 1984, Vol. 11, pp. 52–53.
Holtze, Sally Holmes, ed., *Sixth Book of Junior Authors and Illustrators.* Wilson, 1989, pp. 28–29.
Sarkissian, Adele, ed., *Something about the Author: Autobiography Series.* Gale, 1987, Vol. 4, pp. 75–91.
Ward, Martha, ed., *Authors of Books for Young People* (3rd ed.). Scarecrow, 1990, p. 55.

---

**Duncan, Lois.** *The Twisted Window*
Delacorte, 1987, $14.95 (0-385-29566-9); pap., Dell, $3.50 (0-385-29566-9)

---

In 1992, Lois Duncan won the fourth annual Margaret A. Edwards Award for her lasting contributions to young adult literature. One of the seven novels cited in the award was *The Twisted Window.* Award winning is not new to this much-honored novelist who is particularly noted for her spine-tingling mysteries. Some of them use elements of the supernatural, as in *Locked in Time* (Little, Brown, 1985, $12.95; pap., Dell, $3.50; condensed in *Juniorplots 3*, Bowker, 1987, pp. 125–29); others, like the present novel and *Killing Mr. Griffin* (Little, Brown, 1987, $14.95; pap., Dell, $3.50) are more firmly grounded in reality. This novel employs two points of view, those of the heroine, Tracy, and her newfound friend, Brad. The action takes place over approximately one week. This novel is enjoyed by young readers in both junior and senior high school.

**Plot Summary**

Seventeen-year-old Tracy Lloyd, a junior at Winfield High School, and her friend Gina Scarpelli one day become aware in the school cafeteria that a handsome young man neither has seen before is staring intently at them. He introduces himself as Brad Johnson and soon makes it clear that his interest lies only with Tracy. He asks her if he might get in touch with her that evening at her home. Tracy, who is both flattered and intrigued by this attention, tells him that she lives with her aunt and uncle, Cory and Irene Stevenson. On her way home from school, she is convinced that someone is following her and as she reaches her home she sees a car speeding away.

Tracy's life has been marred by tragedy. For three years she had lived alone with her mother after her parents, both New York actors, were divorced. However, a few months ago her mother was murdered by a mugger outside their Brooklyn Heights apartment. Since then Tracy has lived with the loving but overly protective Stevensons in Winfield, Texas. Although outwardly she is trying to adjust to her new home and surroundings, she is still in a vulnerable state since her mother's death and is filled with resentment toward her father, whom she incorrectly believes pays more attention to his successful motion picture career than to her well-being.

That evening, Brad arrives and the two go for a walk. He confesses that in his anxiety he had followed Tracy home earlier that day and further explains that he has traveled to Winfield from Albuquerque during his school's spring break to effect a special mission. Shortly after his father died of a heart attack while he and Brad were camping in the family's isolated mountain cabin, his mother married Gavin Brummer. They had one daughter, Mindy, but the marriage ended in divorce, with Brad's mother gaining custody. Four months ago, Gavin visited them in Albuquerque and kidnapped his two-and-a-half-year-old daughter. Knowing that Gavin has a sister living in Winfield, Brad believes he has relocated here with Mindy. He is determined to find his sister and bring her back home. Knowing there would be opposition to this unusual rescue operation, he told his mother and his best friend Jamie Hanson that he was spending the week at the mountain retreat. Fearful of being recognized by his former stepfather, he visited the local high school looking for an innocent, attractive girl to act as his accomplice and found in Tracy the person he believes can help him. The young girl has some misgivings but is so moved by Brad's story that she agrees.

The next day after school, Tracy goes with Brad to an apartment complex, the Continental Arms, where, according to the telephone directory, a Mr. Brummer lives. Using the excuse that she is a new tenant and needs to use a telephone, she gains access to the Brummer apartment and is greeted by Brummer's apartment mate, Jim Tyler. While Tyler is on the phone she secretly explores the apartment and in one of the bedrooms sees a photograph that matches the one of Mindy that Brad carries in his wallet. She also overhears Jim tell a friend that his roommate will be having dinner that evening at the home of his sister and brother-in-law, Doug and Sally Carver.

When darkness falls, Brad and Tracy find the Carver house and, peering through a kitchen window, see the Carvers seated with a young girl and Gavin around the dining table. Brad is ecstatic that he has found Mindy.

To gain access to the young girl, Tracy calls the Carvers and offers her services as a baby-sitter. The Carvers, who refer to the child as Cricket, think they are in luck because that evening they have theater plans and their regular sitter has just called in sick. After the couple leave, Brad joins Tracy and they rouse a sleeping Mindy. Unfortunately for them, Mr. Carver, who has forgotten the tickets, returns before they can make their escape. Brad rushes to his car and returns with a shotgun. Carver is locked in a closet at gunpoint and the two, with a protesting Mindy, flee in Brad's car. Tracy, fearful of facing the Stevensons after all she has done, agrees to accompany Brad to Albuquerque.

When changing the child's clothes in the car, she notices that Mindy does not have the scars from a childhood accident that Brad had once mentioned. Her suspicions are further aroused when the child stoutly refuses to answer to any name other than Julianne or her nickname Cricket.

Brad drives all night. In the morning, when they are just two hours from their destination, he allows Tracy to take the wheel while he sleeps. On the car radio, she hears an emergency news bulletin that sends terror into her heart: Three-year old Julianne Carver has been kidnapped by her baby-sitter, Tracy Lloyd, and an unidentified accomplice. Warrants have been issued for their arrest. In a panic, Tracy excuses herself when they stop for breakfast and calls Brad's mother. Mrs. Brummer is stupefied at the news and immediately sends Brad's lifelong buddy, Jamie, to the restaurant to intercede. However, unknown to Tracy, Brad sees her make the telephone call, and, sensing danger, drives off with Cricket.

When Jamie arrives, Tracy is amazed to see that Brad's dearest friend is actually a girl who looks so much like herself that she now realizes why Brad chose her as a helper. Jamie obviously loves Brad deeply and tells Tracy something of his troubled past. He blamed himself for his father's death in the cabin and was slowing sinking into mental confusion when, four months ago, he accidentally ran over and killed his young sister, Mindy. After that he sank into deeper despondency until, unable to accept the ghastly truth, his tortured brain fabricated the kidnapping story.

Jamie is convinced that he has gone to the mountain shack, his favorite haunt when troubled. While Tracy enters the cabin from behind to rescue Cricket, Jamie approaches the front of the cabin where Brad is sitting alone on the steps. After a tense confrontational scene, Brad surrenders to Jamie and, sinking to his knees, says quietly that he now accepts the truth of his sister's death. Inside the cabin, Tracy comforts a frightened Cricket with promises of an early return to her parents.

**Thematic Material**

This page-turning novel combines elements of breathtaking suspense with an exploration of the meaning of reality. Both Brad with his twisted view of the past and Tracy in feeling rejected by her father are seeing reality as through a distorting window. Various aspects of family ties and devotion, as well as the nature of guilt, are depicted in this mystery story.

## Book Talk Material

Some interesting passages are: Brad chooses Tracy to be his accomplice (pp. 2–11); he follows her home (pp. 15–18); Brad tells why he is in Winfield (pp. 33–37); Tracy at the Continental Arms (pp. 49–56); and outside the Carvers' kitchen (pp. 61–66).

## Additional Selections

An eighteen-year-old boy suspects a police cover-up in the investigation of a fatal accident in Todd Strasser's *The Accident* (Delacorte, 1988, $14.95; pap., Dell, $3.25).

Meredith's beloved uncle is kidnapped by Middle East terrorists in the thrilling spy story *The Delphic Choice* (Four Winds, 1989, $13.95) by Norma Johnston.

Alison gradually assumes the identity of Camilla, the dead daughter of fabulously rich Mrs. Considine in the suspenseful Gothic entitled *The Bewitching of Alison Allbright* (Viking, 1989, $17.95; pap., Puffin, $3.95) by Alan Davidson.

Jane wonders if she is the missing child snatched from her family years ago in Caroline B. Cooney's *The Face on the Milk Carton* (Bantam, 1990, $14.95; pap., $3.50).

The sudden disappearance of brother Michael takes a toll on Jody and the rest of her family in *The Year without Michael* (Bantam, 1987, $13.95; pap., $2.95) by Susan Beth Pfeffer.

When Rachel's young brother is kidnapped and she feels no one is working on the case properly, she sets out to solve the mystery in Jean Thesman's *Rachel Chance* (Houghton, 1990, $13.95).

Though short on self-esteem, Liz Raffery, with her boyfriend, somehow solves some puzzling mysteries in a series of novels by Joan Lowery Nixon including *The Dark and Deadly Pool* (Delacorte, 1987, $14.95) and *The Weekend Was Murder* (Delacorte, 1992, $15).

## About the Book

*Book Report,* January 1988, p. 32.
*Booklist,* September 1, 1987, p. 54.
*Center for Children's Books Bulletin,* July 1987, p. 205.
*Kirkus Reviews,* June 1, 1987, p. 855.

*School Library Journal,* September 1987, p. 178.
*VOYA,* October 1987, p. 200.
See also *Book Review Digest,* 1988, p. 477; and *Book Review Index,* 1987, p. 212, and 1988, p. 228.

**About the Author**
Chevalier, Tracy, ed., *Twentieth-Century Children's Writers* (3rd ed.). St. James, 1989, pp. 302–4.
Commire, Anne, ed., *Something about the Author.* Gale, 1971, Vol. 1, p. 13; updated 1984, Vol. 36, pp. 67–72.
Duncan, Lois, *Chapters: My Growth as a Writer.* Little, Brown, 1982.
Evory, Ann, ed., *Contemporary Authors* (New Revision Series). Gale, 1980, Vol. 2, p. 189.
Holtze, Sally Holmes, ed., *Fifth Book of Junior Authors and Illustrators.* Wilson, 1983, pp. 106–7.
Kirkpatrick, D. L., ed., *Twentieth-Century Children's Writers* (2nd ed.). St. Martin's, 1983, pp. 252–54.
Sarkissian, Adele, ed., *Something about the Author: Autobiography Series.* Gale, 1986, Vol. 2, pp. 67–79.
Straub, Deborah A., ed., *Contemporary Authors* (New Revision Series). Gale, 1988, Vol. 23, pp. 129–31.
Ward, Martha, ed., *Authors of Books for Young People* (3rd ed.). Scarecrow, 1990, p. 198.

---

**Hall, Lynn.** *A Killing Freeze*
Morrow, 1988, $11.95 (0-688-07867-2)

---

Lynn Hall is a prolific writer of books for young people, including humorous fantasies involving Dagmar Schultz (e.g., *Dagmar Schultz and the Angel Edna* [Macmillan, 1989, $11.95]) and many excellent animal stories such as *Danger Dog* (Macmillan, 1986, $12.95), about futile efforts to retrain an attack dog, and *Danza!* (Macmillan, 1981, $12.95), about Paul's love of horses, particularly the stallion Danza. She also writes mysteries, such as this title and *Murder at the Spaniel Show* (Macmillan, 1988, $12.95). All of these titles are suitable for junior high school readers.

**Plot Summary**
Clarie lives in Harmon Falls, a small cold spot in Minnesota. Her friends in high school may be looking forward to college to get away from their dinky town where nothing happens, but not Clarie. The life

she lives in the oddball house that she and her father built is exactly what she wants it to be.

Clarie and her dad live alone. Her mother ran off soon after Clarie's birth, and her dad, at the time just seventeen years old and still in high school, got three jobs and managed with difficulty to build a life for himself and his daughter. Now her father has a snowmobile and bike business and Clarie helps him when she isn't in school.

The highlight of the year for them both, and for the town, is the Winter Fest—four days of fun and sports competitions. It was her dad's idea, he runs it, and over the past ten years it has come to mean a lot to Harmon Falls. It certainly means a lot to Clarie and her dad, for it brings in neighbors and tourists and the money that allows them to live the kind of life they enjoy.

This year, however, the Winter Fest is threatened; unthinkable events are taking place in Harmon Falls. First, Clarie discovers the body of their neighbor, Mrs. Arnling, a widow who writes children's books. She is frozen out in the snow. It looks as though she has been hit on the head. Was it an accident? Could it be murder?

Clarie and the sheriff, Keith Dittmer, sort through Mrs. Arnling's belongings in search of a clue. They come upon correspondence between Mrs. Arnling and one Richard Moline, an illustrator who was apparently annoying the author, pushing her to use his illustrations in her books. Clarie wonders if Moline could be so unbalanced as to commit murder.

That suspicion is answered soon enough. The town is shocked by another tragedy, and this time there is no doubt—it *is* murder. The body of Richard Moline is found, stabbed and frozen in a block of ice intended for the ice sculpture contest. If he killed Mrs. Arnling, who killed him? And why?

The sheriff brings up the possibility that Moline did not kill Mrs. Arnling at all. Perhaps some other person killed them both.

A new mystery crops up when Clarie finds a family portrait of Mrs. Arnling and her dead husband with a small child standing between them. The child appears to be a boy and his face, although fuzzy in the photograph, looks somehow familiar to Clarie. She is puzzled as Mrs. Arnling has never mentioned any children. Clarie also finds a letter addressed to "Mama," threatening to "kill myself and you, too."

Mrs. Arnling's death and the murder of Richard Moline have turned the small friendly Minnesota town into a community of fear and suspicion. Will this be the end of the Winter Fest? For the first time that Clarie can remember, her father insists on locking their door at night. Try as she may, Clarie cannot identify the face of the little boy in the photograph, even though she is more and more certain that she has seen that face somewhere.

The Winter Fest goes on while the sheriff searches for answers and the town looks over its collective shoulder. One day Clarie is frightened to discover that she can't reach Bernie Rodas by phone. Bernie is supposed to be in charge of one of the Winter Fest races, but she doesn't show up. Finally, with great relief, Clarie discovers that Bernie has only overslept. Clarie thinks that, like the whole town, she is getting jumpy over nothing.

On the final day of the fest, Clarie attends the dogsled races, trying not to think about the murders. As she watches one of the families, she sees a little girl whom a few days earlier she had mistaken for a little boy. In a flash it occurs to her! The little boy in the photograph with Mrs. Arnling, the face that looked familiar, might not be a little boy at all; at that age, boys are sometimes mistaken for girls, and vice versa. Now Clarie tries to put a girl's face on the child in the photograph—and light dawns.

Clarie races to the sheriff's office, only to find that he has gone to the Arnling house. Without thinking, Clarie takes her father's truck and heads out after him. When she arrives, the sheriff's car is not there, but another car blocks the driveway.

Out steps Bernie Rodas. "This is my mother's house," Bernie tells her. "Did you know that?" Bernie attacks Clarie as a huge icicle falls from the roof. Clarie picks it up to use as protection, and another answer flashes into her mind. Mrs. Arnling was not murdered at all; it was an accident. A huge icicle must have fallen from the roof and struck her head. By the time she was found, the icicle had melted.

Clarie distracts Bernie long enough for the sheriff and her father to rescue her and provide some answers. Mrs. Arnling was indeed killed in a freak accident when an icicle fell from the roof, but Bernie thought Moline was the killer and so she killed him. Bernie, it turns out, was not Mrs. Arnling's daughter, but a foster child the Arnlings had cared for years earlier. She had proved to be a youngster with a serious problem; although she worshiped Mrs. Arnling, she was impossible to handle. The authorities felt she had a criminal mentality. Mrs. Arnling's husband's death was officially considered an accident, but Mrs. Arnling was not sure that Bernie hadn't been responsible, and so she had returned the child to state care. Years later, Bernie came back to town unrecognized. She never bothered Mrs. Arnling but continued to worship her from afar, until she mistakenly believed that her foster mother had been killed by Richard Moline.

Clarie's father says: "Just think of all the sorrow that could have been avoided if only someone had loved that little baby."

Clarie thinks of her own good fortune, and she and her dad look at each other in relief and love.

**Thematic Material**

Murder and mystery come together nicely in this fast-paced, tightly written story that uses Winter Fest in a small north country town as an unusual backdrop. Clarie is presented as a happy young girl who does not quite fit the mold of giggly adolescence but exhibits an enviable independence and a self-reliant spirit. The relationship between father and daughter is warmly drawn and presented as a healthy picture of how love and understanding can build a single parent and child into a well-adjusted family unit.

**Book Talk Material**

Life in the cold north country can serve as a good introduction to this tale of murder and mystery in Minnesota. See: troubles with the Winter Fest (pp. 2–4); Dad and Clarie build the house (pp. 11–12); the ice blocks in the park (pp. 33–35). Several passages point up the relationship between Clarie and her father (pp. 4–5); after Mrs. Arnling's death (pp. 23–24); they talk about being careful (pp. 38–43).

**Additional Selections**

In *Trick or Treat* (pap., Scholastic, 1989, $2.75) by Richie Tankersley Cuslick, Martha uncovers strange happenings related to a murder in the house where she lives.

On a camping trip, Matt, an overweight boy, and his friend Parker find a body floating face down in the water in *The Dead Man in Indian Creek* (Clarion, 1990, $13.95) by Mary Downing Hahn.

In a park late one night, Zoe meets a silver-haired boy who is a member of the undead, a vampire, in Annette Curtis Klanse's *The Silver Kiss* (Delacorte, 1990, $14.95).

Phineas and his sister are determined to find out who is trying to steal the mummy in the collection of Egyptian antiquities in their father's care in Cynthia Voigt's *The Vandemark Mummy* (Atheneum, 1991, $14.95).

When Brad tries to shield a hit-and-run driver who is a friend, he risks losing his girlfriend in Jay Bennett's suspenseful mystery *Coverup* (Watts, 1991, $13.90).

Kate unravels the mystery behind her father's death in Phillipa Pearce's *The Way to Sattin Shore* (Greenwillow, 1983, $10.50).

A boy who witnesses a murder is targeted as the next victim in Willo Davis Roberts's *The View from the Cherry Tree* (Macmillan, 1975, $14.95; pap., $3.95).

**About the Book**

*Book Report,* January 1989, p. 36.
*Booklist,* April 1988, p. 1914.
*Center for Children's Books Bulletin,* October 1988, p. 37.
*Kirkus Reviews,* September 1, 1988, p. 1322.
*School Library Journal,* September 1988, p. 198.
*VOYA,* December 1988, p. 238.
See also *Book Review Index,* 1988, p. 337, and 1989, p. 343.

**About the Author**

Chevalier, Tracy, ed., *Twentieth-Century Children's Writers* (3rd ed.). St. James, 1989, pp. 420–22.
Commire, Anne, ed., *Something about the Author.* Gale, 1987, Vol. 47, pp. 97–104.
Holtze, Sally Holmes, ed., *Sixth Book of Junior Authors and Illustrators.* Wilson, 1989, pp. 145–47.
Kirkpatrick, D. L., ed., *Twentieth-Century Children's Writers* (2nd ed.). St. Martin's, 1983, pp. 351–52.
May, Hal, and Straub, Deborah A., eds., *Contemporary Authors* (New Revision Series). Gale, 1989, Vol. 25, pp. 178–79.
Sarkissian, Adele, ed., *Something about the Author: Autobiography Series.* Gale, 1987, Vol. 4, pp. 181–96.
Ward, Martha, ed., *Authors of Books for Young People* (3rd ed.). Scarecrow, 1990, p. 301.

---

**Hamilton, Virginia.**   *The House of Dies Drear*
Macmillan, 1984, $15.95 (0-02-742500-2); pap., $3.95 (0-02-043520-7)

**Hamilton, Virginia.**   *The Mystery of Drear House*
Greenwillow, 1987, $13.95 (0-688-04026-8); pap., Macmillan, $3.95 (0-02-043480-4)

---

Since beginning to write children's books in 1967, Virginia Hamilton has produced an astonishing total of nearly thirty titles and has won many major awards in the field of children's literature, including the 1975 Newbery Medal, Boston Globe–Horn Book, and National Book Award for *M. C. Higgins, the Great* (Macmillan, 1974, $14.95; pap., $3.95; condensed in *More Juniorplots*, Bowker, 1977, pp. 195–99). She is the granddaughter of a fugitive slave who traveled with his mother via the Underground Railroad from Virginia to Jamestown, Ohio. The author continues to live in the part of Ohio where there is a house like Dies Drear and where there are secret rooms and tunnels used as waystations on the railroad. These novels are suitable for readers in grades 6 through 10.

**Plot Summary**

In the first book of this two-volume chronicle of Drear House, thirteen-year-old Thomas Small and his family leave their home in North Carolina and head for a new life in Ohio. They say good-bye to Great-grandmother Jeffers, who does not want to leave her Blue Ridge Mountain home. Thomas's father has a new teaching job in a small Ohio college town and they are to live in a huge old house on the edge of town. Only Mr. Small has seen the house, and Thomas is a little apprehensive about moving in. His father has told him that the place was once a stop on the Underground Railroad and that the original owner, the long-dead abolitionist Dies Eddington Drear, helped slaves to escape north. It is said that the owner and two slaves had been murdered in the house one night, but that a third slave had escaped.

A chill passes over Thomas when he first sees the huge house of Dies Drear, looming gray and formless on the side of a hill. Thomas is certain that the house is haunted, but his mother and father, and the very young twin boys, Billy and Buster, seem to take their new home in stride, especially when they discover that the old caretaker, taciturn Mr. Pluto, has arranged their furniture in the huge rooms, apparently trying to make their arrival comfortable. Even so, he is most unfriendly.

Thomas meets their new neighbors, young Pesty Darrow, who is adopted, and her aloof brother, Macky, who is slightly older than Thomas. Their father and brothers are not friendly, perhaps because for years they have been certain that a treasure to which they lay claim is buried somewhere around the Drear house.

Only a short while after their arrival, Thomas uncovers one of the secret tunnels that was used to aid the runaway slaves. He is both intrigued and frightened by these mysterious passages. The very night of their arrival, eerie things begin to happen. Ghosts walk. Walls move. Thomas's father discovers strange triangles above the bedroom door. What do they signify?

After church on Sunday, the family returns to find that someone has broken into the house and practically destroyed the kitchen. When Thomas and his father go in search of Mr. Pluto, they accidentally discover the spacious underground cave that is the caretaker's secret. It is filled with tapestries and carpets, Indian crafts of all kinds, glassware, silks and embroidered materials, jewelry, and chains of gold. It represents one hundred years of buying and selling, and elderly Mr. Pluto is its caretaker. In ill health and afraid that the Darrows will take his trove, Mr. Pluto has been trying to keep the cave secret.

With the help of Mr. Pluto's actor son, the Smalls and Pesty Darrow devise a plan. The Darrows are lured to the property at night and are frightened by the appearance of the ghosts of dead slaves. Figuring that their shame at being so tricked will keep them from trying to interfere with the Smalls any longer, Thomas and his family agree to keep the cave treasure a secret for the time it will take to inventory everything before turning it over to a foundation. This should take as long as the elderly Mr. Pluto lives.

In book two, *The Mystery of Drear House,* it is now eight months later. The inventory is still going on; Pesty Darrow spends a lot of time with the Smalls; Thomas and Macky Darrow are forming a tentative friendship, although the elder Darrows are aloof and angry, still looking for the treasure.

Thomas's great-grandmother has consented to come and live with the family, so Thomas and his father drive back to North Carolina to get her. After their return, Thomas comes upon another secret tunnel in the house. Pesty Darrow knew about this one but told no one because it leads from one of the bedrooms in Drear house right to the Darrows' own home. In fact, Pesty and her mother use the tunnel at times. Pesty's mother suffers from a mental illness and has periods of not being lucid. She likes to go and sit in one of the underground rooms where the children of slaves slept, and Pesty does not want anyone to stop her mother's harmless wanderings.

Mr. Small now realizes that his plan to keep the great treasures of the underground room a secret is not feasible. It is a cherished history of a people and should be on display. But how can he let the secret out without bringing harm to old Mr. Pluto? Perhaps the Darrows' claim to the treasure might be verified.

Mr. Small comes up with a brilliant plan. With Pesty's help, the Darrows are lured to the great cave with all its treasures, but just as they are gasping with delight at having found what they had sought, they are astonished to find not only newspaper reporters but also Pesty herself and Mrs. Darrow waiting for them. Thomas's father reasoned that if the cave is no longer a secret and if everyone knows that *both* Mr. Pluto and Mrs. Darrow herself have had a part in the discovery, then the Darrows cannot confiscate the treasures for themselves, as Mr. Pluto feared they would.

The Darrows are outraged at first, but what can they do? Over the next few days, the Smalls find themselves the object of much attention in the small town. The foundation will take over the treasures of the cave and a museum will be established to honor the memory of the many slaves who fled through these mysterious tunnels and those who aided them. Mrs. Darrow and Mr. Pluto are given a reward of $10,000 each for finding the treasure. The mystery of the triangles found by Mr. Small on their arrival is solved: They turn out to be a very clever code for instructing runaway slaves on safe routes to freedom.

Perhaps life will now become more normal in this strange old Drear house. It is decided that there is room in the rambling structure for elderly Mr. Pluto. And it looks as though, with a little work, Thomas will have a friend in Macky Darrow.

On Thanksgiving the unthinkable occurs. The Darrows are invited to the Drear house for dinner with the Smalls, and they actually accept. Thomas isn't quite sure yet how much the Darrows can be trusted and how far this friendship will go, but it's a start.

**Thematic Material**

This gripping mystery story and its sequel are filled with sinister-appearing people, a dark, foreboding old house, moving panel walls, secret tunnels, and a fabulous hidden treasure. There is good, fast-paced suspense as ghosts appear and danger seems to lurk in every corner. Thomas is presented as an average, likable teenager with a good sense of curiosity but very normal fears as well. The family relationships are warm and true, especially the fondness and respect between Great-grandmother and Thomas. These two books also present a story of conflicting loyalties and friendships.

**Book Talk Material**

Young readers will be intrigued with the descriptions of the house, its strange tunnels and moving walls that surprise the unwary visitor. In *The House of Dies Drear*, see: Thomas first sees the house of Dies Drear (pp. 30–33); Thomas finds the rock stairway (pp. 53–58); Thomas meets the demon (pp. 78–82); Thomas refuses to spend the night in his new bedroom (pp. 99–106); and Mr. Small and Thomas see the great room of treasure for the first time (pp. 182–95). In *The Mystery of Drear House*, see: Thomas runs from the Indian maiden (pp. 14–16); they show Great-grandmother the kitchen wall that rises (pp. 33–35); Thomas first meets Mrs. Darrow (pp. 74–82); and Thomas and Great-grandmother explore the decorated room (pp. 83–93).

**Additional Selections**

The ghost of a slave who was murdered a century ago seeks the aid of a contemporary youngster to solve the mystery of his death in Avi's *Something Upstairs: A Tale of Ghosts* (Orchard, 1988, $11.95; pap., Avon, $2.95).

Andy and Kat, twelve-year-old twins, encounter the ghost of a nine-year-old boy who wants revenge for a crime committed a century ago in Eloise Jarvis McGraw's *The Trouble with Jacob* (McElderry, 1988, $14.95).

In Joyce Hansen's novel *Which Way Freedom* (Walker, 1986, $12.95), former slaves help Union soldiers during the Civil War.

On a Virginia farm during 1855, two unhappy girls, one a black slave and the other a white orphan, escape together in *Steal Away* (Orchard, 1991, $14.95) by Jennifer Armstrong.

In the *Underground Railroad* (Watts, 1991, $12.40), Sharon Cosner discusses antislavery groups, the important conductors and depots, and some of the most dramatic rescues.

A twelve-year-old blind boy forms a friendship with someone he later realizes is a ghost in Nicholas Wilde's *Into the Dark* (Scholastic, 1990, $12.95).

The saga of the black Logan family and their struggles for justice have been part of many of Mildred D. Taylor's novels, including *Let the Circle Be Unbroken* (Dial, 1981, $14.95; pap., Bantam, $2.95; condensed in *Juniorplots 3*, Bowker, 1987, pp. 226–30) and *The Road to Memphis* (Dial, 1990, $14.95).

**About the Book:** *House of Dies Drear*
*Horn Book,* October 1968, p. 563.
*Library Journal,* December 15, 1968.
*New York Times Book Review,* October 13, 1968, p. 26.
See also *Book Review Index,* 1968, pp. 555–56.

**About the Book:** *Mystery of Drear House*
*Book Report,* September 1987, p. 38.
*Booklist,* January 15, 1987, p. 1601.
*Center for Children's Books Bulletin,* May 1987, p. 168.
*Horn Book,* September 1987, p. 617.
*Kirkus Reviews,* May 1, 1986, p. 379.
*School Library Journal,* January 1987, p. 96.
*VOYA,* August 1987, p. 120.
See also *Book Review Digest,* 1987, pp. 728–29; and *Book Review Index,* 1987, p. 301.

**About the Author**
Block, Ann, and Riley, Carolyn, eds., *Children's Literature Review.* Gale, 1976, Vol. 1, pp. 103–7.
Chevalier, Tracy, ed., *Twentieth-Century Children's Writers* (3rd ed.). St. James, 1989, pp. 442–44.
Commire, Anne, ed., *Something about the Author.* Gale, 1973, Vol. 4, pp. 97–99; updated 1989, Vol. 56, pp. 60–70.
de Montreville, Doris, and Crawford, Elizabeth D., eds., *Fourth Book of Junior Authors and Illustrators.* Wilson, 1978, pp. 162–64.
Estes, Glenn E., ed., *American Writers for Children since 1960: Fiction* (Dictionary of Literary Biography: Vol. 52). Gale, 1986, pp. 174–84.
Garrett, Agnes, and McCue, Helga P., eds., *Authors and Artists for Young Adults.* Gale, 1989, Vol. 2, pp. 53–64.
Kirkpatrick, D. L., ed., *Twentieth-Century Children's Writers* (2nd ed.). St. Martin's, 1983, pp. 353–54.
Metzger, Linda, and Straub, Deborah A., eds., *Contemporary Authors* (New Revision Series). Gale, 1987, Vol. 20, pp. 207–12.
Nasso, Christine, ed., *Contemporary Authors* (First Revision). Gale, 1977, Vols. 25–28, p. 299.
Senick, Gerard J., ed., *Children's Literature Review.* Gale, 1986, Vol. 11, pp. 94–95.
Ward, Martha, ed., *Authors of Books for Young People* (3rd ed.). Scarecrow, 1990, p. 527.

## London, Jack. *White Fang*
Scholastic, 1986, pap., $2.75 (0-8049-0030-2)

Jack London (1876–1916) lived the life of a sailor, loafer, and adventurer. In addition to traveling the continental United States as a hobo, he followed the trail of the Gold Rush to the Klondike when he was only twenty-one. His most popular early novel was *The Call of the Wild,* published in 1903, about Buck, a sled dog. Two years later *White Fang* appeared. During his lifetime London wrote thirty-three books, only a handful of which have survived. Both *White Fang* and *The Call of the Wild* were written for adults, but now they are also read by both junior and senior high school students.

### Plot Summary

This is the classic story of White Fang, a wolf dog that is gradually domesticated.

White Fang was born in the savage, frozen Northland Wild, the one little gray cub of the litter. His mother is She-wolf, his father old One Eye. White Fang spends his first months with his two brothers and two sisters. He grows strong and resourceful and curious.

Hs is not yet full grown when he meets humans for the first time. The Indians recognize his mother as a dog who was lost the year before and they realize that the cub's father was a wolf. Since his fangs are white and there is much fight in him, they name him White Fang.

There is a great deal for White Fang to learn about human ways as he and his mother become part of the Indian village. Then one terrible day, the half-grown cub is separated from his mother to settle a debt between two men and he becomes the property of the cruel owner known as Gray Beaver. White Fang not only learns the ways of humans but becomes dependent on them for his survival.

As he reaches full growth, White Fang is strong and quick and clever. By the time he is five years old, he is an adept and vicious fighter. That summer he and Gray Beaver reach Fort Yukon, where White Fang encounters his first white men. The wolf dog gains a reputation as a fierce and formidable opponent. A white man who has long lived in the region, one of the hardy breed who call themselves Sour-doughs, is named Beauty Smith. This ugly, harsh fellow takes a great liking to White Fang, admiring his fighting ability. Gray Beaver at first refuses to sell him at any price. But when the price comes to bottles instead of dollars, Gray Beaver is more amenable. Eventually, Beauty Smith becomes his new master and never was there a more vicious, cruel one.

Chained at the rear of the fort, White Fang now becomes a fiend, for Beauty Smith wants to ensure that the wolf dog will remain the most feared fighter in the area. White Fang learns to hate with all his being.

As time passes, White Fang gains a reputation as the most vicious fighter in the land. He has earned the title of "the Fighting Wolf." He even bests a full-grown lynx in a match. In what becomes his final fight, however, White Fang nearly loses his life to a ferocious bulldog. When Beauty Smith sees that his fighter is about to lose for the first time, in his rage he begins to beat White Fang. Out of the crowd steps a newcomer, who smashes Beauty Smith full in the face. When the newcomer, Weldon Scott, is able to pry the dogs apart, he gives Beauty Smith money and takes White Fang from him.

In the months that follow, Scott tries to tame White Fang, although his friends tell him that it is hopeless. After White Fang bites Scott's hand one day, he is nearly destroyed, but Scott sees the intelligence in the animal's eyes and will not have him harmed.

Slowly, so slowly, White Fang's old life and reign of hate begin to fade. Scott understands the terrible injustices that have been done to White Fang and vows to redeem humankind in the animal's eyes. Little by little he gains the wolf dog's trust and even begins, cautiously, to pet him. White Fang grows to love this petting even though he continues to growl all through it. Scott senses that the growl contains a thread of contentment too.

As time passes, White Fang grows to know love for the first time. He is now too mature, too set in his ways to be demonstrative to this man; he will never run to meet him, for instance. But he is always there, waiting at a distance.

Late one spring Scott disappears and White Fang is filled with anxiety. He becomes ill, and a letter is sent to Scott, who is off on a mining trip, telling him that White Fang may die. Scott returns, and White Fang wags his tail. With Scott's return, White Fang's recovery is rapid.

In due time Scott must leave the north country and return to his home in California. He decides that he cannot take White Fang with him, that the wolf dog would not fit in with his homelife. But when the time comes to leave, Scott looks into the animal's eyes and knows he cannot part with him.

White Fang, somewhat bewildered at first, becomes a part of the Scott home in California. He even allows all the members of the household, including the children, to pet him, although Weldon Scott remains his special person. White Fang has much to learn, including how to get along with the other dogs of the house, especially Collie, who never gives him a moment's peace.

Although the family tolerates White Fang, they do not fully trust him—after all, he is at least part wolf. Then one day White Fang accompanies Scott when he goes horseback riding. Scott is thrown, breaking his leg. He tells White Fang to go home. The animal understands the meaning of home and returns to the house, where he terrifies Scott's wife by ripping at her dress. She screams until she realizes that the dog is trying to tell her something. Then White Fang begins to bark and leads the family to Scott. After this event, White Fang is a true hero to all.

He becomes even more of a hero when he attacks an escaped convict who is breaking into the Scott household. But the brave wolf dog is gravely wounded, shot by the convict and suffering broken ribs and a broken leg as well. The Scotts call in the best medical help, but the outcome is not promising. The doctors say White Fang must be nursed as they would nurse a sick child. And that is exactly what the Scott household does.

It is a long recovery, but finally the last bandage is removed and a shaky, emaciated White Fang stands tottering and swaying. The family gives him a new name. They call him "Blessed Wolf."

A procession of the Scott family and White Fang slowly moves out into the yard. There in the doorway of the stables is Collie, a half-dozen pudgy puppies playing about her.

What is this, White Fang thinks? One puppy runs in front of him and licks his face. Not really knowing why, White Fang licks the puppy's face, too.

There are pleased cries and much hand-clapping from the family, but by now White Fang is tired from all the commotion. He lies down and lets the puppies climb over him, much to Collie's disgust. There rests the great White Fang, with half-shut, patient eyes, drowsing in the sun.

**Thematic Material**

This is a truly classic dog story that recounts a unique relationship between man and animal. It is filled with love and dignity, bravery and honor, tragedy and cruelty, and a strong and enduring bond of love and

friendship. Readers of all ages cannot help but be moved by this enduring, inspiring story of one animal's greatness and one man's goodness.

### Book Talk Material

The feelings and thoughts of White Fang are the focal point of this
riveting adventure story. (There are numerous editions of this classic;
therefore, passages are indicated here by chapter rather than page number.) See: the early years of the gray cub (part two, chapter 3); the cub
learns to fight (part two, chapter 5); the young wolf dog meets the
Indians for the first time (part three, chapter 1); and White Fang loses
his mother (part three, chapter 2).

### Additional Selections

When her father is injured, a young Inuit girl must face the challenging Iditarod dog race alone in Scott O'Dell's *Black Star, Bright Dawn*
(Houghton, 1988, $14.95; pap., Fawcett, $3.50).

Matthew and his Eskimo friend, Kanak, set out in the Arctic to find
Matthew's father in *Frozen Fire* (McElderry, 1977, $12.95) by James
Houston.

In Harry Mazer's *Snowbound* (pap., Dell, 1975, $2.95), Tony and a
hitchhiker brave a terrible blizzard when his car is wrecked.

Past and present merge for young Russel when he, with his grandfather's help, runs an Arctic sled dog team in Gary Paulsen's *Dogsong*
(Bradbury, 1985, $11.95; pap., Puffin, $3.95).

When Sox's beloved German shepherd is kidnapped, he tracks him to
the thieves' hideout in Lynn Hall's *The Tormentors* (Harcourt, 1990,
$14.95).

When his father refuses to let him keep an orphaned bear cub, Josh,
with the cub, family dog, and some supplies, heads into the mountains
on his brother's motorcycle in *Rescue Josh McGuire* (Hyperion, 1991,
$14.95) by Ben Mikaelson.

Three animals—two dogs and a cat—make a lonely trek through Canadian wilderness to their home in Sheila Burnford's *Incredible Journey*
(Little, Brown, 1961, $14.95; condensed in *Juniorplots*, Bowker, 1967, pp.
155–57).

### About the Author

Commire, Anne, ed., *Something about the Author*. Gale, 1980, Vol. 18, pp. 195–
214.

Kunitz, Stanley, and Haycraft, Howard, eds., *The Junior Book of Authors* (2nd ed.). Wilson, 1951, pp. 843–45.

Ward, Martha, ed., *Authors of Books for Young People* (3rd ed.). Scarecrow, 1990, p. 446.

General encyclopedias and standard literary reference works contain information on Jack London.

---

**Nixon, Joan Lowery.**   *A Candidate for Murder*
Delacorte, 1991, $14.95 (0-385-30257-6)

---

Joan Lowery Nixon is one of the most prolific writers for young readers with an impressive array of titles in print that represent a number of genres intended for readers of different ages. For teenagers, she is best known for her many action-filled mysteries, including her Edgar Allan Poe Award–winning *The Kidnapping of Christina Lattimore* (pap., Dell, 1980, $3.25). Other popular titles include *The Stalker* (Delacorte, 1988, $14.95) and *The Séance* (pap., Dell, 1981, $2.95; condensed in *Juniorplots 3*, Bowker, 1987, pp. 141–45). They are enjoyed by readers in grades 6 through 10.

**Plot Summary**

Wealthy oilman Charles Amberson announces his intention to run for governor of Texas. Although she first greets the news with pride, his only child, sixteen-year-old Cary (short for Caroline Jane), soon realizes that life is not going to be quite the same. A few days after the announcement, Cary inadvertently overhears a conversation between two unknown men at a country club party. Although she does not grasp the significance of the conversation or even remember much of what they said, she is aware that the men realize she has overheard them. For no reason she can define, this makes Cary feel uneasy.

The first hint of trouble comes the very next day when Cary is driving away from her girlfriend's house. Convinced that she is being followed, Cary drives to a busy shopping center and calls her father. He arrives with their new handyman, butler, and chauffeur, Dexter Kline, whom Cary vaguely distrusts. Her father dismisses the idea that someone has tailed her and assures her that being in the public eye attracts all kinds of curiosity seekers.

That night Cary receives a late-night phone call from a woman who obviously has had too much to drink. She tells Cary: "If they think you don't know nothin' you'll be all right." Cary tells her parents about this and her father admits that he has also had weird calls at work, but he still attributes such happenings to the strange things that occur when people run for public office. Cary isn't so sure.

The next day when Cary's father drives her to Gormley Academy, where Cary is a senior, he tells her that he feels strongly that he must try to oust Governor Milco, whose bank accounts, says her father, are growing at the people's expense. On the way they are detoured by an accident; part of the new state highway has collapsed. Reporters at the scene record her father's statement that he and his staff are compiling evidence to show that the present administration has been devious in its handling of contracting bids, the result being accidents of the kind they have just witnessed.

Cary decides to do some volunteer work at her father's campaign office and asks her boyfriend, Justin, to join her. He is reluctant to do so at first because he doesn't want to declare his support for her father. Soon after, there is a break-in at the campaign office. The police think it's the work of kids, but Cary worries that all these incidents are connected.

Cary receives another call from the strange woman, whose name she learns is Nora. This time the woman is sober. She tells Cary that she doesn't want her to get hurt; then the line goes dead. Cary determines to find out Nora's identity.

Back in the campaign office, Cary meets a new volunteer, Francine, a political science major in college, and she is interviewed by Sally Jo Wilson of *The Dallas Gazette*. It is Sally Jo who reminds Cary that if her father's campaign is successful, she and her mother will be moving to Austin, away from her mother's law practice, away from Cary's school and friends. This thought, coupled with the snide jokes about her father's wealth and political motives that she begins to hear on television and among her friends, including Justin, makes Cary take a new and deeper look at the difficulties of running for public office.

One night Cary realizes she has left her purse at the campaign office. When she returns for it, she runs into Francine, who has obviously been going through files, although she denies any wrongdoing.

Another night Cary, Justin, and some friends go to a dance. Cary thinks she sees Francine there, but why would she be at a school dance?

On the way home the four teenagers are stopped by police, who search the car and find some drugs. Cary realizes that someone has planted the drugs in order to disgrace her father.

The story gets out, but testing proves that Cary and her friends are innocent. The next incident involves a break-in at the Amberson home; Cary's father thinks it's just a burglary attempt, but Cary is suspicious. Nothing, however, seems to be missing.

In a conversation with reporter Sally Jo, Cary tries to remember the talk she overheard between the two men at the country club. She is certain now that one of the men was Ben Cragmore, of the construction company that is involved with the present governor. The other man had a scratchy voice, and they were talking about a problem that had been taken care of. Cary thinks that the name of the man who they said was causing the problem was Bill, or Phil, or perhaps Gil. She can't remember for sure, and asks Sally Jo to see if she can come up with any information. Sally Jo finds out that the man with the scratchy voice works for the present governor, Milco; his name is John Lamotta.

Some time later at school, Cindy, a friend of Cary's, borrows her raincoat and is deliberately run down in the street. Cary realizes that the hit-and-run driver was after her. Luckily, Cindy only has a broken leg. Cary does not tell her parents what she suspects, but she learns from her father that he now has solid information about the governor and how he is lining his pockets with construction kickbacks.

That night Cary's parents go to a political barbecue, and Cary is startled when Dexter Kline enters her bedroom. He tells her that he heard a noise and was checking it out—he didn't know she was at home. She doesn't know whether to believe him or not. Velma, the housekeeper, tells Cary that Sally Jo dropped off an envelope for her. Cary wonders if Dexter was looking for it.

She opens the envelope and learns that, indeed, the man she had heard talking to Ben Cragmore that night at the country club was John Lamotta. A girl in a photograph with him is identified as Francine Lamotta: Francine Smith is actually John Lamotta's daughter. Cary also learns that Ben Cragmore's family includes a mother-in-law—Nora Broussard. Nora—the drunken woman on the phone.

Cary calls Justin and asks him to take her to see Nora. She does not find her but leaves a message with a neighbor and is awakened in the night by a phone call from a slurry-voiced Nora, who will only say that Cary is in trouble. She also says, "Maybe Herb Gillian wouldn't have been so quick to want to blow the whistle. . . . He shouldn't have said anything. Poor Gil. Poor Gil." With horror, Cary realizes that what she overheard Cragmore and Lamotta discussing that night at the country club was murder!

In the morning, Cary tells her parents about Nora's phone call and they realize that someone may indeed be trying to kill her. The police arrive, but find no proof that Herb Gillian has been murdered or that Cragmore and Lamotta were involved in his disappearance.

A banquet is held that night, attended by Cary's parents, Justin, and Cary. They are all on edge. Cary meets Sally Jo and tells here what Nora said. As she recounts the story, another snatch of conversation from the country club comes back to her. She tells Sally Jo, "Lamotta said because of Gil's big mouth, he's up a creek. Then he laughed. I think the police will find Gillian's body buried in the creek bed near where they're building the freeway."

Suddenly, Sally Jo and Cary are confronted by a strange waiter. He pulls a gun and motions them to a deserted area. When a waitress appears behind him, Cary calls for help, but the waitress turns out to be Francine. Cary and Sally Jo fight their attackers and manage to knock the gun out of the man's hand. Cary screams for help, and the first person she sees is Dexter Kline, and behind him, her father!

It turns out that Dexter Kline is actually a bodyguard. Her parents didn't want to tell her, to make her more nervous, but it looks as though Cary has uncovered the mystery. Cragmore and Lamotta were after her because they realized she had overheard their conversation about killing Gillian, who was onto their kickback schemes.

Going home with Justin that night, Cary realizes that if, indeed, her father becomes governor, she and Justin will be parting. He will probably soon be dating other people. Come to think of it, she'd probably begin dating other people, too.

**Thematic Material**

This is a nicely paced, on-the-edge-of-your-seat mystery with the modern involvement of big-time politics and construction kickbacks. Cary is perhaps a bit more savvy and courageous in the ways of unraveling mysteries than most sixteen-year-olds, but she is a believable and appealing heroine, and the picture of a family that is both wealthy and in politics, yet decent and close, is refreshingly drawn.

**Book Talk Material**

The first hints of things going wrong can serve as a good introduction to this swiftly moving mystery. See: Cary overhears the conversation at the country club and realizes that she has been recognized (pp. 2–7); Cary thinks she is being followed and calls her father (pp. 11–17); the first phone call from Nora (pp. 17–18); and Cary hears the scratchy voice again (pp. 37–38).

**Additional Selections**

Fifteen stories—some scary, some humorous—are found in *Werewolves* (Harper, 1983, $13.95), a collection edited by Jane Volen and Martin H. Greenberg.

Is missing teen star Dory West a victim of a serial killer? Amateur sleuth Carter Colburn tries her best to find out in Diana Shaw's *Gone Hollywood* (Little, Brown, 1988, $12.95).

Seventeen-year-old Lauren refuses to believe that her friend is guilty of child murders in the suspenseful *Show Me the Evidence* (Bradbury, 1989, $10.95; pap., Avon, $2.95) by Alane Ferguson.

When Robbie takes a lawn-mowing job at the Swinton estate, she discovers fifty tanks filled with piranhas and a tantalizing mystery in Barry Faville's *Stanley's Aquarium* (Oxford Univ. Pr., 1990, $14.95).

The dreams of teenager Rose tell her where a serial killer is burying the bodies in Patricia Windsor's chilling *The Christmas Killer* (Scholastic, 1991, $13.95).

In Liza Ketchum Murrow's *Fire in the Heart* (pap., Troll, 1989, $2.95), a teenager sets out to uncover the details of her mother's death ten years before.

Mayra takes a job as a companion to a strange old woman and finds her life suddenly in danger in *The Sleepwalker* (pap., Pocket, 1990, $2.95) by P. L. Stine.

**About the Book**

*Book Report,* January 1991, p. 47.
*Booklist,* November 15, 1990, p. 672.
*Center for Children's Books Bulletin,* February 1991, p. 151.
*Kirkus Reviews,* May 15, 1991, p. 398.
*School Library Journal,* May 1991, p. 216.
*VOYA,* February 1991, p. 355.
See also *Book Review Digest,* 1991 pp. 1378–9; and *Book Review Index,* 1991 p. 671.

**About the Author**

Chevalier, Tracy, ed., *Twentieth-Century Children's Writers* (3rd ed.). St. James, 1989, pp. 723–24.

Commire, Anne, ed., *Something about the Author*. Gale, 1976, Vol. 8, pp. 143–44; updated 1986, Vol. 44, pp. 131–39.

Ethridge, James M., ed., *Contemporary Authors* (First Revision). Gale, 1965, Vols. 11–12, p. 297.

Evory, Ann, ed., *Contemporary Authors* (New Revision Series). Gale, 1982, Vol. 7, pp. 363–64.

Holtze, Sally Holmes, ed., *Fifth Book of Junior Authors and Illustrators*. Wilson, 1983, p. 230.

Kinsman, Clare D., ed., *Contemporary Authors* (First Revision). Gale, 1974, Vols. 9–12, pp. 678–79.

Senick, Gerard J., ed., *Children's Literature Review*. Gale, 1991, Vol. 24, pp. 131–54.

Straub, Deborah A., ed., *Contemporary Authors* (New Revision Series). Gale, 1985, Vol. 24, pp. 344–45.

---

**Paulsen, Gary.** *The Voyage of the Frog*
Watts, 1989, $12.95 (0-531-08405-1)

---

Gary Paulsen's writing forte is the outdoor survival and adventure novel. Typical of these is *Dogsong* (Bradbury, 1985, $11.95; pap., Penguin, $3.95), in which an Eskimo youth faces hardship and danger when he ventures by dogsled alone into the wilderness. *The Voyage of the Frog* is also a survival story of a fourteen-year-old boy's ordeal at sea alone on a twenty-two-foot sailboat. The story is told in short choppy sentences, as in the style of Ernest Hemingway. There are plenty of nautical terms for authenticity and many cliff-hanging chapter endings to supply suspense. This book is recommended particularly to readers in grades 6 through 8.

**Plot Summary**

For most of his fourteen years, David Alspeth has known two very special delights: his life-loving Uncle Owen and Owen's twenty-two-foot sailboat, the *Frog*. David's happiest times have been casting off from the marina at Ventura, California, north of Los Angeles, and spending long hours sailing with his uncle. Uncle Owen has taught him love and respect for the sea and for the *Frog*.

In an unbelievably short time, David's life changes dramatically. From his hospital bed where he lies dying from an incredibly fast-growng tumor, his uncle tells David that he is leaving the *Frog* to him. In return, he asks a favor. Owen will be cremated, and he asks that David take his ashes out to sea in the *Frog* alone and when he can no longer see land, to scatter the ashes on the water.

Beloved Uncle Owen dies on the last day of David's eighth-grade classes. Now David stands on the deck of the *Frog* in the California sun carrying the small urn that is all he has left of his uncle. David is thinking that he is fourteen years old and he owns his own sailboat and he would give everything, all that he is, not to have it.

As he cries silently, an idea comes to him. David has told his parents that he will spend the night on the *Frog* and sail out in the morning to honor Uncle Owen's request. He decides instead to make the journey now, in the late afternoon. It will be a perfect night for a sail and this was Owen's favorite time to be at sea.

Everything is, as usual, in order on the sailboat, and David sails for Owen's last trip in a perfect twenty-knot wind. Although he realizes that he really should check the weather—the *Frog* has no radio gear except a cheap transistor battery-powered receiver that rarely works—the sky seems clear and the wind steady. David figures that he will sail a line due west into the Pacific until morning, then he will scatter the ashes of his beloved uncle and return home.

As the wind fills the sails of the *Frog* and the setting sun casts a reddish gold beam on the water, David thinks of it as a golden path for Uncle Owen, and he follows the path into the night.

David spends the dark hours following his course and thinking of his uncle. By nine the next morning, still in clear skies, he can see no land, no other boat, nothing to indicate that he is anything but alone on the ocean. Reluctantly, David takes the urn, uncovers it, and scatters the gray ashes over the water.

Now David wants nothing more than to get away from this sad memory. As he attempts to turn the *Frog* about to head home, a strand of nylon from one of the sails catches on the front hatch. David has to climb up on the cabin to unhook it, and this small act saves his life: As he stands on the forward hatch, he can see two to three miles in the distance, and he notices that the swells of the ocean waves look strange, as though they have been cut off at the top. What could cause that, he wonders.

The answer comes in a flash—wind. It is obviously a freakish wind, stronger than anything David has ever seen. If he had not noticed it and the sails were all up when the wind hit, the *Frog* would sink in seconds.

David scrambles to get the sails down. A terrible wind strikes the *Frog* with the force of a sledgehammer and David is hit on the top of the head by the fifty-pound wooden boom.

When he regains consciousness, the *Frog* is taking water and seems in danger of going down. The inside of the boat looks as though it has been turned upside down. David has no idea how long he has been lying there or what he can do to save himself. He may be hundreds of miles from home, all alone on the sea, with little water or food. He is alone. He is terrified. Still, frightened as he is, the words and the teachings of his uncle subconsciously come back to him. All the things Owen had taught him about the sea start to return. The first thing he must do is get the water out of the *Frog*. This takes hours with a small hand pump. He finds his drinking water and food supply. It is night again now, and he is beginning to get things in order when he hears a horrible scraping sound. To his absolute terror, he realizes that the boat is being attacked by sharks. Steady, steady, he tells himself, remembering that his uncle used to say that knowledge is everything. Why would the sharks be after him, personally? Then David remembers reading that sharks may hit or attack flashing lights or movement in the sea, and he realizes that what the sharks are really attacking is the path of moonlight bouncing off the hull of the *Frog*. The attacks go on for a few more hours, and then stop— the sharks swim away.

Calmer now, David puts the cabin to rights, tends his wounds with salt water, rations his food and water, and tries to figure out where he is. For the first time in his life he senses what the homeless and hungry must endure.

Another day passes and, in darkness again, an oil tanker appears. He has been found! Instead of rescuing him, however, the tanker nearly collides with the tiny sailboat. David helplessly watches the tanker sail off into the darkness, and he knows real hate for the ship.

Night passes, another day, another night. David has no idea of the exact time, although he does start to make entries in the ship's log. His spirits lift when the wind picks up and he thinks he is headed in the right direction for the California coast. As the winds push the little sailboat ever faster, David runs into a school of killer whales, who stay with him until morning in what seems a friendly fashion.

Finally, magically, there before him is land. Yet there are no lights, no signs of civilization. Where is he? David stays about two miles from shore trying to figure out where he is. Finally, he reasons that he must be off the coast of Baja California, the long Mexican peninsula south of the California border.

Another storm comes up, but David and the *Frog* are ready this time. Just before dusk an old coastal freighter appears. The captain shouts from the bridge, asking if David is the kid from Ventura that everyone has been searching for. The captain tells David that he is about 250 miles south of San Diego; the freighter will have him home in a few days.

There is one problem, of course. David will have to abandon the *Frog*. The old freighter has no equipment to lift it aboard and it will only break up if they attempt to tow it.

David thinks of the past few days, and his memories. He thinks of what he has gone through, what he has done as "captain" of the *Frog*. No, he tells the freighter captain, he'll stay with *his* ship.

The captain protests, telling David that the return trip will take him two to three weeks. What if there is bad weather?

"I got here with her and I'm going home with her," David says. "That's it."

"I'd do the same," the freighter captain tells him.

David asks the captain to radio his parents that he is alive and well and will be sailing home. The freighter furnishes him with fresh water and food, and the old ship chugs off into the dusk.

David is alone once more. The wind is coming up, the *Frog* is headed home, and David has some sailing to do.

**Thematic Material**

This is a satisfying, exciting adventure at sea that manages fast-paced action even though most of the book lacks conversation and describes only the thoughts and deeds of one person. David is presented as a thoughtful but average fourteen-year-old who learns to use his head in times of crisis and to rely on the knowledge that he has gained, in this case mainly from a beloved uncle who impressed on him that knowledge, all knowledge, is important. David's life is saved because he *thinks*, an important lesson, and his pride in his accomplishments, his decision to sail home alone and save the *Frog*, will be understandable to all readers.

**Book Talk Material**

Two main aspects of David's character are especially important to understanding this story. One is David's feeling for his uncle; see: David visits Owen in the hospital (pp. 4–6); the ghost of Owen is on the *Frog* (p.

8); and the decision to sail at night (pp. 14–15). The other is what David has learned from his uncle and how he begins to use his head to save his life at sea; see: Uncle Owen talks about study (pp. 24–25); David realizes a strange wind is coming (pp. 34–38); the decision not to panic (pp. 50–54); and fighting down the terror of the shark attack (pp. 60–66).

## Additional Selections

In Colin Thiele's *Shadow Shark* (Harper, 1988, $13.95), two Australian youngsters outsmart a huge shark but are marooned on a lonely island.

Sam must live off the land when he decides to leave New York City and rough it on his grandfather's undeveloped land upstate in Jean Craighead George's *My Side of the Mountain* (Dutton, 1988, $14.95; pap., $4.95). This story is continued in *On the Far Side of the Mountain* (Dutton, 1990, $14.95).

After a plane crash, three young people conquer their fears to find their way home in Marilyn Halvorson's *Hold On, Geronimo* (Delacorte, 1988, $14.95; pap., Dell, $2.95).

In Depression America, two orphans run away and practice survival skills on Pelican Island, Florida, in *Angels of the Swamp* (Walker, 1991, $15.95) by Dorothy Whittaker.

Teenager Joe Rogers finds himself alone in the wilderness after the plane he stowed away on is destroyed in Walt Morey's *Death Walk* (Blue Heron, 1991, $13.95).

Michael's reunion with his father backfires when he spends a summer with him white-water rafting in Colorado in Marion Dane Bauer's *Face to Face* (Clarion, 1991, $13.95).

When Chris's father and the pilot of their plane are both injured in a crash, Chris must learn the ways of survival in the plains of Serengeti in Eric Campbell's *The Place of Lions* (Harcourt, 1991, $15.95).

## About the Book

*Book Report*, September 1989, p. 43.
*Booklist*, March 1, 1989, p. 6.
*Center for Children's Books Bulletin*, January 1989, p. 131.
*Horn Book*, March 1989, p. 219.
*School Library Journal*, January 1989, p. 94.
*VOYA*, February 1989, p. 288.
*Wilson Library Bulletin*, September 1989, p. 15.
See also *Book Review Digest*, 1989, pp. 1290–91; and *Book Review Index*, 1989, p. 638.

**About the Author**

Chevalier, Tracy, ed., *Twentieth-Century Children's Writers* (3rd ed.). St. James, 1989, pp. 763–65.
Commire, Anne, ed., *Something about the Author*. Gale, 1981, Vol. 22, pp. 192–93; updated 1989, Vol. 54, pp. 76–82.
Garrett, Agnes, and McCue, Helga P., eds., *Authors and Artists for Young Adults*. Gale, 1989, Vol. 2, pp. 165–73.
Holtze, Sally Holmes, ed., *Sixth Book of Junior Authors and Illustrators*. Wilson, 1989, pp. 219–20.
Senick, Gerard J., ed., *Children's Literature Review*. Gale, 1990, Vol. 19, pp. 167–78.
Ward, Martha, ed., *Authors of Books for Young People* (3rd ed.). Scarecrow, 1990, p. 553.

**Petersen, P. J.** *Going for the Big One*
Delacorte, 1986, $14.95 (0-385-29453-0); pap., Dell, $2.95 (0-440-93158-4)

P. J. Petersen has established a fine reputation for writing action novels for junior high readers. Some, like this one, are survival stories that take place in the outdoors. Others use the familiar setting of high schools. One of these is the story of how a substitute teacher persuades a group of junior high boys to help rehabilitate an incorrigible delinquent named Arnold Norberry. Whether they are successful is the plot of *Would You Settle for Improbable?* (pap., Dell, 1981, $2.50; condensed in *Juniorplots 3*, Bowker, 1987, pp. 94–98). A sequel is *Here's to the Sophomores* (Delacorte, 1984, $14.95). All of these stories are enjoyed by readers in grades 6 through 9.

**Plot Summary**

Since their mother died some years ago, life for the three Bates children has been a series of stepmothers and boarding houses caused by the erratic behavior and harebrained schemes of their well-meaning father, the misnamed Lucky Bates. His latest misguided act is leaving the youngsters in the care of his new bride, Grace, in their rented home in northern California while he seeks his fortune in the gold mines of Alaska.

Unfortunately this plan is not to Grace's liking, and one day the children return from a movie to find Grace gone and the house stripped of all food and furniture. All that is left is their personal belongings, including their camping gear, and an apologetic note from Grace with a $20 bill.

The three youngsters are different in age and temperament. The oldest is Annie, sixteen, the rock of the family. She is kind, resourceful, and idealistic. Next comes Dave, fifteen. He is a somewhat troubled boy, outwardly a klutz who is a constant complainer but inside an insecure teenager filled with resentment and feelings of rejection. Last there is thirteen-year-old Jeff, implike both in appearance and behavior, always making bad jokes and writing supposedly humorous poetry.

During their first night alone, Dave, in a misguided effort to help, steals a television set from a nearby house and is caught by the police. Annie persuades their elderly, infirm neighbor, Mrs. Locke to act as their grandmother at the police station so that they can secure Dave's release. It works, but back home the three realize that without parents they cannot successfully cope with the hearing on Dave's case scheduled the following week. Not only will Dave face a sentence in a reform school but Annie and Jeff could be sent to foster homes. Their only solution is to flee.

It is now mid-July and the weather is good, so they decide to hike to White Bar, a camping ground some thirty miles away in the shadow of the High Sierras where they had stayed two summers before with their father. Annie writes to Lucky explaining their situation; they pack their camping gear; and the following morning they leave with plans to stay at White Bar until they hear from their father.

Thirty-six hours later they arrive at the campground and establish contact at the local post office/general store run by a man named Darby. However, they are spotted two days later by the deputy who arrested Dave. When he abandons his police car to give chase on foot, Annie takes the car and through frantic horn-blowing and some reckless driving manages to distract the policeman sufficiently so that all three escape.

With the police on their trail, they must change their plans. Jeff is sent to the local store to question Darby about places for hiking in the vicinity. They decide on Alder Creek, a small town on the other side of the closest mountain. Darby warns Jeff that it is a difficult, dangerous climb, but the three youngsters know they have no alternative. They post another letter to their father, buy more provisions and a map with the last of their money, and set off on the run once again.

During their first night out, the peacefulness of their campsite is shattered by the sound of gunshots. Within minutes, a bearded young man staggers out of the darkness and begs for help. He is bleeding profusely from a wound in the shoulder. He identifies himself as Cracker and tells the frightened teenagers that his two camping buddies became hostile after he won a poker game and shot him when he tried to leave.

They hide Cracker under Jeff's sleeping bag minutes before his two pursuers appear. One of them explains that they are searching for his brother, who is psychotic and has turned nasty. Annie lies and says that the man had passed by their campfire some fifteen minutes ago but did not stop. When they leave, Cracker rouses himself and, displaying a huge roll of money, offers Dave $50 if he will go to the campers' cabin and retrieve the first aid kit so that his wound can be dressed.

At the cabin, Jeff, who has volunteered to accompany Dave, discovers that he is small enough to enter via a small back window. Unfortunately, while he is still inside one of the campers returns. With first aid kit in hand, Jeff hides under the living room table until the camper enters the bedroom and then he makes a successful dash for freedom through the open front door.

Back at camp Annie tends to Cracker's wound, and when it is time to start out again, Cracker begs to be allowed to accompany them. At first they all refuse but when Cracker promises to give them $500, the combination of Dave's greed, Annie's compassion, and Cracker's display of his long-barreled revolver changes their minds. All four set out.

Jeff, who is acting as advance scout, encounters one of Cracker's pursuers. Through a clever ruse and some judicious lying, he manages to convince the man that Cracker is traveling in the opposite direction.

After several days of hiking made particularly arduous and slow because Cracker has difficulty keeping up, they hit the snow line. Dave almost loses his life when the snow on which he is walking caves in. Only Annie's quick thinking saves him.

With their supplies running low, their feet blistered, and their faces sunburned, Annie's optimism and Jeff's feeble jokes keep them going. Finally they scale the summit and reach the timberline on the other side of the mountain.

When they are only a few days from their goal, Cracker reveals the truth about himself. He and his companions were actually drug dealers who managed several marijuana farms in the mountain canyons and also owned a stash of cocaine worth about $100,000. Cracker stole the coke, which he still has in his pack. All three youngsters are horrified by the news, but later that night when the others are asleep, Cracker draws Dave aside and, with the promise of making him a partner on the sale of the cocaine, persuades him to "go for the big one" and steal the few remaining provisions and the camping gear and leave with him.

As soon as Cracker is convinced that he is close to Alder Creek and civilization, he turns on Dave, ties him up, and leaves him to die of starvation and exposure. Luckily, Annie and Jeff follow the same path and are able to rescue their now half-conscious brother. Although relations between them are strained, the ever-forgiving Annie readily accepts Dave back into the family fold and persuades Jeff to do the same.

Using a makeshift spear, Jeff is able to kill a deer for food, and later that night Dave redeems himself by using the same stick to frighten off a marauding bear intent on stealing the carcass. For the first time Dave feels a sense of self-worth.

With renewed strength, they set out again and, to their dismay, catch up with an exhausted, disgruntled Cracker. Again, but this time at gunpoint, he tries to persuade Dave to be his partner. Dave feigns acquiescence, but when Cracker's back is turned he jumps him and grabs the gun. Dave has at last proven himself a hero. A jubilant Annie scatters the stash of cocaine to the four winds. After removing the bullets from the pistol, Dave gives it back to Cracker. A terrifying moment occurs when Cracker, claiming he has reloaded the pistol from a secret cache of bullets, aims the gun at Annie and gets ready to shoot. It is a ruse. He has no bullets, and, defeated, Cracker wanders off into the woods.

Within hours the youngsters reach Alder Creek and there, waiting for them, is their father. Lucky promises to reform and even though his children are skeptical they know that whatever happens they have proven that in the future they can survive together.

**Thematic Material**

This is essentially a story of high adventure and dark villainy that contains a series of scenes filled with suspense and excitement. It is also a story of courage, resourcefulness, and resilience in the face of hardships caused by both man and nature. Wilderness survival is an important subject as is the evil caused by the illicit drug trade. Sibling loyalty and the tragedy of abandonment are well portrayed. The transformation of Dave into a worthy, needed member of the family is well handled and his journey to feelings of self-worth through several courageous acts is convincingly drawn. Annie's inner strength and pride along with her determination to keep the family together regardless of the sacrifices involved make her a most appealing heroine.

**Book Talk Material**

This book contains so many exciting moments that it will not be difficult to find many suitable for reading aloud or retelling. Some are: the youngsters discover that Grace has abandoned them (pp. 4–6); with the help of Mrs. Locke, Annie and Jeff save Dave from jail (pp. 11–16); Annie distracts the deputy who is chasing Dave (pp. 27–31); Jeff gets supplies and directions from Darby at the store (pp. 36–42); Cracker enters their lives (pp. 50–57); and Jeff retrieves the first aid kit from the cabin (pp. 59–65).

**Additional Selections**

A fifteen-year-old boy travels alone more than 100 miles to bring back wild horses for a rodeo during 1932 in Florida in Robert Newton Peck's *The Horse Hunters* (Random, 1988, $15.95).

In 1935, while visiting his grandmother in Wyoming, Alex meets Kid Curry, an outlaw, and together they rob a bank in Warwick Downing's *Kid Curry's Last Ride* (Orchard, 1989, $12.95).

A fourteen-year-old boy must decide whether to become a shark fisherman like the rest of his family or return to school in Jean Craighead George's *Shark beneath the Reef* (Harper, 1989, $11.95; pap., $3.50).

A young teenager with only a hatchet survives in a Canadian wilderness in *Hatchet* by Gary Paulsen (Bradbury, 1987, $12.95; pap., Puffin, $3.95; condensed in *Seniorplots*, Bowker, 1989, pp. 227–31).

In Carolyn Meyer's *Wild Rover* (McElderry, 1989, $13.95), an escaped convict and his arrogant teenage daughter travel together while hiding from the police.

*Flight #116 Is Down* (Scholastic, 1992, $13.95) by Caroline B. Cooney is an exciting page-turner about rescue operations on a downed 747.

Two boys team up with Lucinda and Randolph, who are really bank robbers, in Harvey Watson's hilarious *Bob War and Poke* (Houghton, 1991, $13.95).

**About the Book**
*Center for Children's Books Bulletin*, September 1986, p. 16.
*School Library Journal*, September 1986, p. 146.

*VOYA,* June 1986, p. 82.
See also *Book Review Digest,* 1987, p. 1469; and *Book Review Index,* 1986, p. 573.

**About the Author**
Commire, Anne, ed., *Something about the Author.* Gale, 1986, Vol. 43, p. 186.
Commire, Anne, ed., *Something about the Author.* Gale, 1987, Vol. 48, pp. 179–81.
Holtze, Sally Holmes, ed., *Sixth Book of Junior Authors and Illustrators.* Wilson, 1989, pp. 221–22.
May, Hal, ed., *Contemporary Authors.* Gale, 1985, Vol. 112, p. 395.

---

**Scoppettone, Sandra.** *Playing Murder*
Harper, 1985, lib. bdg. $12.89 (0-06-025284-7); pap., $2.75 (0-06-447046-6)

---

Sandra Scoppettone has dealt with some weighty subjects in her young adult novels. For example, she was one of the first to explore teenage male homosexuality in the tragic *Trying Hard to Hear You* (Harper, 1974, $13.89; pap., Alyson, $7.95; condensed in *More Juniorplots,* Bowker, 1977, pp. 169–72) and in *The Late Great Me* (pap., Bantam, $3.50) the heroine is a young alcoholic. In contrast, *Playing Murder* is an old-fashioned, conventional whodunit featuring a group of youthful suspects. It is told in the first person by Anna Parker and, apart from flashbacks, takes place over a period of a few days on an island in Maine. It will be enjoyed by mystery fans, particularly girls, in both junior and senior high school.

**Plot Summary**
Seventeen-year-old Anna Parker is dismayed when she learns that she and her family—Mom, Dad, twin brother Bill, and eleven-year-old sister Kate—will be moving permanently at the end of the current school year from their home in Maplewood, New Jersey, to Blue Haven Island off the coast of Maine. It will mean being deprived of spending her senior year at Columbia High as well as leaving all her friends, including her steady, Tony Nardone. The cause of this upheaval is her brother Bill. As children the two were very close, but recently they have grown apart, chiefly because Bill has been plagued with teenage inferiority anxieties compounded by the fact that he is only five foot four. A few months ago he was found guilty of stealing $300 from Columbia, money earmarked

for new football uniforms. Their father, who is a teacher at Columbia, now thinks that it is best for the entire family to move and start over, and Mom, a mystery story writer, agrees. The family has bought an outdoor seafood restaurant on Blue Haven from the Cunninghams, who have promised to help them with the takeover. Mr. Cunningham was forced to sell because he is suffering from an incurable brain tumor and wants to live his last days in peace.

After the Parkers arrive and settle into their spacious new house, they visit the restaurant and find that they have inherited a group of wonderful helpers, most of them young members of the Cunningham family. There is the oldest brother—tall, blond, and incredibly handsome Kirk—who has returned from his freshman year at college; his seventeen-year-old brother, Larry; and two sisters, sixteen-year-old Nicki, and twelve-year-old April. As well, there is Kirk's best friend Dick Beal and Charlotte Coombs, Kirk's steady girlfriend. Although he doesn't work for the restaurant, Watson Hayden, an eighteen-year-old lobsterman, is also part of the gang. Within a few days Anna, Bill, and Kate are accepted as part of the group. Anna finds that she is very much attracted to Kirk, who encourages these feelings in spite of Charlotte's obvious jealousy.

On nights when they are not working, the gang plays a game in the woods called "Murder," a variation on hide-and-seek, in which one member of the group is supposedly killed by another and an appointed detective must find the guilty party. One night someone decides to play for keeps. During the game, Kirk gets Anna alone and, declaring his love, kisses her passionately. They separate, and one minute later he is found dead, his own knife in his back.

The young people are in a state of disbelief and shock when they report the murder to the police. Parents are summoned and it is midnight before Anna, numb with grief, enters her bedroom. Her closet door slowly opens and Tony steps out. He has quit his summer job to visit Anna on Blue Haven. Under Anna's insistent questioning, he admits that, earlier in the evening, he had been in the woods when Kirk was killed. Unwilling to cause her parents more alarm, Anna conceals him in the attic for the night.

The next morning, the Parkers are visited by a Columbo-like detective, Harvard Smolley, who questions both Bill and Anna separately about the murder. When she thinks it is safe, Anna returns to the attic and finds that Tony has mysteriously disappeared.

Later that day she and Bill meet with Dick Beal and lobsterman Watson to hold a postmortem. It is a time for confession: Anna tells them about Tony but leaves out the fact that he was in the woods, and Bill talks about the theft that has caused his family misery. They all wonder if one of the night before's game players—Anna and Bill Parker, Larry and Nicki Cunningham, Dick, Watson, or Charlotte—could have murdered Kirk. Anna mentally adds an eighth possibility: Tony. When she praises their dead friend, Dick and Watson exchange glances that seem to signify that they know more about Kirk than they wish to reveal. At Kirk's funeral, Anna is amazed at how impassive all of his friends are while she can't seem to control her sobs. Could this be more than simply Down East reserve?

That evening, Tony reappears. To avoid embarrassment for Anna, he had stolen out of the attic. He has now found a job and decided to spend the summer on the island. He kisses Anna and admits that he was jealous of Kirk when he saw them together in the woods. Suddenly she feels uneasy with him.

Bill's fingerprints are discovered on the murder weapon and, though he is released later, he spends the night in the local jail and undergoes close questioning by Harvard Smolley, who has somehow found out that he was responsible for the theft in New Jersey.

This adversity brings Anna closer to her brother, who tells her that he had indeed borrowed Kirk's knife on the night of the killing but that he was not guilty of murder. To clear her brother's name, Anna decides to do some sleuthing on her own, like her mother's fictional detective, Libby Crawford.

She begins questioning each suspect while recording all her findings and observations in a small notebook. From these interviews a picture of Kirk emerges that is far from that of the gallant, dashing gentleman she believed him to be. From Charlotte, she finds out that Kirk continually lied to her, took advantage of her feelings for him, and fooled around with other girls. He had forced his sister Nicki to pose for nude pictures, which he later sold at college. He stole Watson's girlfriend, Charlotte, from him. After coercing his brother, Larry, into selling pot at the restaurant, he was now blackmailing him into pushing cocaine. Even Dick was becoming increasingly alienated because of his best friend's criminal behavior. It now appears that everyone had a motive for killing Kirk, including Tony.

Anna deliberately baits the killer by telling everyone that she has uncovered important evidence and recorded it in her notebook. Unfortunately, it works. While she is in the woods, someone creeps up behind her, hits her on the head, and steals the notebook. However, as she sinks to the ground and into unconsciousness, she touches her assailant's legs and realizes that he is wearing the type of waders that lobstermen wear.

Anna is now convinced that Watson is the murderer. She drives alone to his isolated shack in search of the incriminating notebook. Her search is interrupted by the arrival of Dick. It was in fact Dick who murdered Kirk, to stop his once-adored friend from sinking further into depravity. And it was Dick who told Smolley about Bill's past and later deliberately wore fisherman's waders to confuse Anna before he attacked her. Now he plans to kill her in Watson's shack so that Watson will be accused of both murders. As his gloved hands reach her throat, Anna grabs a hammer from a toolbox on the floor and knocks him unconscious. She has solved the murder, but almost at the cost of her own life.

**Thematic Material**

This is a fast-paced, suspenseful, often chilling murder mystery that gains immediacy and realism by being told in the first person. Anna is a courageous, resourceful heroine and the changing relationship between brother and sister is well depicted. The author has also captured the atmosphere of New England and Maine's life-style.

**Book Talk Material**

A description of the game "Murder" should interest mystery fans. Some specific incidents that will pique interest are: introductory atmosphere (pp. 1–2); Anna describes the game to Smolley (pp. 62–64); Tony frightens Anna and she hides him in the attic (pp. 26–31); the game as it was played the night Kirk was killed (pp. 136–39); and Anna reviews the list of suspects (pp. 140–44).

**Additional Selections**

In Sonia Levitin's *Incident at Loring Groves* (Dial, 1988, $14.95; pap., Fawcett, $2.95), two friends find a classmate murdered after a party during which drugs were used.

In Elizabeth Levy's thriller *Cold as Ice* (pap., Avon, 1989, $2.95), Kelly tries to help solve the mystery of who is attacking two young ice-skating stars.

Marti is convinced that her friend Barry did not commit suicide but was murdered, and she sets out to prove it in Joan Lowery Nixon's *Secret Silent Screams* (Delacorte, 1988, $14.95; pap., Dell, $3.25).

In Patricia Windsor's *The Hero* (Delacorte, 1988, $14.95; pap., Dell, $3.25), a supposedly kindly doctor is intent on controlling the world through using a young boy's gift of ESP.

During a high school scavenger hunt, one of the players falls from a rock and goes into a coma. Jenny wonders if it is an accident in Carol Ellis's *My Secret Admirer* (pap., Scholastic, 1989, $2.95).

In Mary Towne's *Paul's Game* (Delacorte, 1983, $13.95), Paul, through telepathy, exerts a sinister influence over Julie.

The blanks in Melanie's stage pistol turn out to be murderously real in *Last Act* (pap., Pocket, 1988, $2.75) by Christopher Pike.

**About the Book**
*Center for Children's Books Bulletin,* May 1985, p. 113.
*Kirkus Reviews,* May 15, 1985, p. J44.
*School Library Journal,* May 1985, p. 111.
*VOYA,* June 1985, p. 135.
See also *Book Review Digest,* 1986, pp. 1437–38; and *Book Review Index,* 1985, p. 550.

**About the Author**
Commire, Anne, ed., *Something about the Author.* Gale, 1976, Vol. 9, p. 162.
Harte, Barbara, and Riley, Carolyn, eds., *Contemporary Authors* (First Revision). Gale, 1969, Vols. 5–8, p. 1023.
Holtze, Sally Holmes, ed., *Fifth Book of Junior Authors and Illustrators.* Wilson, 1983, pp. 277–79.
Ward, Martha, ed., *Authors of Books for Young People* (3rd ed.). Scarecrow, 1990, p. 632.

---

**Verne, Jules.**   *Around the World in Eighty Days*
Bantam, 1984, pap., $2.95 (0-553-21356-3)

---

Many people associate the writings of the Frenchman Jules Verne (1828–1905) with the pioneer days of science fiction. It is true that most of his novels, beginning with *A Voyage to the Center of the Earth* (1964) and continuing with such classics as *20,000 Leagues under the Sea* (1970) and its sequel, *The Mysterious Island* (1985), are science fiction, but Verne was also fascinated with geographical discovery and travel. These interests are displayed in his rollicking adventure *Around the World in Eighty Days* (1873), which many consider to be his most lasting and entertaining book. Today a trip around the world can be accomplished in a matter of hours, but contemporary readers might have to be reminded that in 1872, the year of Phileas Fogg's odyssey, traversing the globe in only eighty days was considered almost impossible. This novel is enjoyed by readers in junior high and up.

**Plot Summary**

Even his fellow members of the ultraconservative Reform Club in London have labeled Phileas Fogg an eccentric because of his solitary and taciturn behavior. Friendless, without family, but of independent means, Fogg, a man in his forties, is a slave to punctuality, silence, routine, reading the newspapers, and playing whist. Change rarely rears its ugly head in the life of Phileas Fogg, but a disturbing incident has recently forced him to advertise for a new male servant. The incident in question involved receiving his shaving water at eighty-four degrees Fahrenheit instead of the prescribed eighty-six. The new servant is Passepartout, a young Frenchman of about thirty who has in the past been a circus rider, an itinerant singer, a fireman, and a gymnast.

As Passepartout moves in, Fogg leaves for his club, where members are involved in two topics of conversation. The first concerns a daring bank robbery in which £55,000 were stolen; the second is an item in the *Daily Telegraph* claiming that with uncanny luck and a flawless travel schedule, it is now possible to travel around the world in eighty days. All believe that such a tight timetable is impossible, leaving no allowance for probable delays. Fogg is the sole dissenter. He is so adamant in his belief that such a trip is possible that he wagers £20,000 (half his fortune) that he will appear at the club, having accomplished this feat, in exactly eighty days, at 8:45 P.M. on December 21, 1872.

That evening, he and Passepartout leave London by rail on the first stage of their journey, to Brindisi in Italy where they will catch the steamer *Mongolia,* whose destination is Bombay via Suez.

In Suez, a British detective, Mr. Fix, has been following both stories—the robbery and the wager—in the newspapers. After seeing Fogg when the boat docks and making comparisons with descriptions of the robber, he becomes convinced that they are the same person and applies to headquarters in London for a warrant to arrest Fogg in Bombay. Fix then boards the *Mongolia.*

Because of propitious weather conditions, the ship arrives in Bombay two days ahead of schedule. There, Passepartout runs afoul of a group of Parsee priests when he innocently enters their sacred temple. They report him to the police, but he and Fogg leave by train for Calcutta before charges can be made. Fix, still without his arrest warrant, continues to follow them.

Midway on this trip, an unforeseen delay occurs. Contrary to published reports, there is a stretch of fifty miles without railroad. Fogg solves the problem by buying an elephant and hiring a guide. Along the way, they pass a funeral procession of Brahmins who are taking the body of an aged prince to a sacred pagoda for cremation. Unfortunately, the wife of the prince, whom the travelers see is a beautiful young woman, is, by custom, to be burned alive with her husband in a religious rite known as a suttee. She is obviously terrified and our intrepid travelers vow that in spite of the delay, they will save her. Passepartout secretly mounts the pyre and when the smoke ascends, he rises. The natives, thinking that the prince has been resurrected, flee in terror. The servant carries the princess to safety and the party hurriedly continues its journey.

In Bombay, thanks to delaying tactics by Fix, Passepartout is arrested for his breach of sacred rites in Bombay. Fogg is able to post bail before they miss their ship for Singapore and Hong Kong. Aouda, the princess whom they saved, asks to accompany them to Hong Kong, where she believes she has a rich uncle. However, when they arrive there, she discovers he has moved to London. Phileas Fogg persuades her to travel with them to their final destination. Passepartout notices that his master is becoming unusually attentive to the needs of the attractive young woman.

Further misadventures delay the travelers. The dogged Fix, trying to prevent their departure from Hong Kong until the elusive arrest warrant arrives, drugs Passepartout while he is on his way to give his master the revised departure time of their ship, the *Carnatic*. Miraculously, a dazed Passepartout boards the ship on time but the others are forced to hire a pilot boat and risk death during a violent storm at sea in order to intercept the steamer they are to take to San Francisco.

During each segment of the trip, unforeseen delays occur, often because of the schemes of Fix. But using his imagination and the ingenious application of various modes of transportation, Fogg manages to surmount these obstacles and keep the travelers fairly close to schedule.

While they are crossing the Great Plains of America, their train is attacked by Indians. Passepartout saves them by stopping the runaway train at a U.S. Army fort, but in the ensuing confusion he is captured by the Sioux. Fogg effects a rescue, but this causes yet another delay. However, by traveling at high speed across the snow on a sled equipped with sails, they catch up with the train.

A crushing blow is suffered in New York when they arrive forty-five minutes after their boat has left for Liverpool. Fogg hires a trading vessel, the *Henrietta*, and they set off across the Atlantic. Because Fogg demands that they travel at full speed, all the fuel is consumed before they reach Liverpool. Fogg then buys the boat from the captain and orders that all the wood on the ship—furniture, decks, runways—be used to feed the furnaces. They arrive on the morning of the eightieth day in time to make the train to London and victory.

It is then that Fix plays his trump card and produces the arrest warrant. After a few hours of bureaucratic delays, Fogg is eventually cleared of the charges. It is too late—he arrives in London at 8:50.

Outwardly unruffled, Fogg is nevertheless dejected and discouraged when he returns to his quarters. The next day brings consolation however, when Aouda agrees to marry him. While Passepartout is out making arrangements for the wedding, he makes a marvelous discovery: Because the travelers had passed the international date line during the trip without changing their calendars, it is now only the eightieth day since their departure. Promptly at 8:45 P.M. that evening, Phileas Fogg enters the Reform Club to claim his winnings.

**Thematic Material**

The author describes each country, city, and national landmark that Phileas Fogg and his friends encounter so vividly and with such detail that this becomes not only an exciting adventure story but also an authentic travelogue of the world 100 years ago. Verne gives a wealth of historical and geographical background information that fascinates today's readers as it has generations of readers interested in their world, past and present. Through both the central and some peripheral characters, the author pokes gentle fun at the stereotypic national traits of the English, French, and Americans. Above all, this is a wild and woolly adventure story filled with tongue-in-cheek humor, wild coincidences, subtle ironies, and cliff-hanging suspense.

**Book Talk Material**

Perhaps some readers have seen the successful motion picture that was made of this classic. For others it is necessary to explain a little about the way people traveled 100 years ago and therefore how revolutionary and dangerous an eighty-day global trip would have been in 1872. There are many specific passages that can be used but because many editions of this title are currently available, each with different pagination, we give only chapter numbers: Phileas Fogg is introduced and he hires Passepartout (chaps. 1 and 2); the robbery is discussed and Fogg accepts the wager at the Reform Club (chap. 3); Fix and his mission are introduced (end of chap. 5 and chap. 6); Aouda is rescued (end of chap. 12 and chap. 13); and Fix drugs Passepartout in Hong Kong (chap. 19).

**Additional Selections**

Would-be travelers will enjoy the many adventures in exotic places experienced by teenager Vesper Holly and her bumbling guardian Brinnie in Lloyd Alexander's *The Illyrian Adventure* (Dutton, 1986, $12.99; pap., Dell, $2.50), *The El Dorado Adventure* (Dutton, 1987, $12.95; pap., Dell, $3.25; condensed in *Seniorplots*, Bowker, 1989, pp. 212–16), and *The Jedera Adventure* (Dutton, 1989, $12.95; pap., Dell, $3.50).

Chris Cooper and his family move to Florida Keys in search of buried treasure in Todd Strasser's *Beyond the Reef* (Delacorte, 1989, $14.95; pap., Dell, $3.50).

Seventeen-year-old Nick finds that his working colleague in present-day California is illegally hunting for stolen buried treasure from Sir Francis Drake's sunken ship in Welwyn Wilton Katz's *Whalesinger* (Mc-Elderry, 1991, $13.95).

In *The Dark Canoe* (Houghton, 1968, $13.95) by Scott O'Dell, sixteen-year-old Nathan finds adventure and tragedy on the high seas in the late nineteenth century.

In *Great Tales of Action and Adventure* (pap., Dell, 1978, $2.75), edited by George Bennett, there is an excellent collection of fast-moving stories by such masters as Jack London and Arthur Conan Doyle.

Erich Kastner's classic *The Little Man* (pap., Avon, 1980, $1.95) is an adventure story for young readers about a two-inch-high boy who is kidnapped.

In Theresa Nelson's *Devil Storm* (Orchard, 1987, $12.95), Walter and his family rely on an old tramp during the terrible hurricane that hit Galveston in 1900.

**About the Author**

Commire, Anne, ed., *Something about the Author*. Gale, 1980, Vol. 21, pp. 178–93.
Kunitz, Stanley, and Colby, Vineta, eds., *European Authors, 1000–1900*. Wilson, 1967, pp. 959–61.
Kunitz, Stanley, and Haycraft, Howard, eds., *The Junior Book of Authors* (2nd ed.). Wilson, 1951, pp. 959–60.
General encyclopedias and standard literary reference works also contain information on Jules Verne.

# 3

# Science Fiction and Fantasy

ONCE considered a genre relegated largely to pulp magazines, the worlds of science fiction and fantasy writing have now joined the mainstream of literature. In this section there are twelve novels, some of which are the questing tales characteristic of fantasies while others deal with the future worlds found in science fiction.

---

**Alexander, Lloyd.** *The Remarkable Journey of Prince Jen*
Dutton, 1991, $14.95 (0-525-44826-8)

---

Reminiscent of the author's earlier Prydain cycle, this novel again brings Lloyd Alexander back to full-bodied fantasy, a genre he temporarily abandoned to write the series of exciting Vesper Holly "Adventure" novels (e.g., *The Illyrian Adventure*). In Prince Jen, the author has created an impulsive, clever, pampered young man who gains experience and maturity through a series of adversities while seeking the knowledge that a neighboring king can impart. This journey from innocence to experience uses a Chinese setting with elements from South European and Oriental folklore. This adventure is suitable for readers in grades 6 through 9.

**Plot Summary**
King T'ai of the Kingdom of T'ang is convinced by Master Wu that he should see the remarkable kingdom of T'ien-kuo, presided over by the most noble of rulers, where all thrive in harmony and happiness. The king wants to see how this is accomplished, but he is too weak to make the long journey. So his naive but well-meaning son, Prince Jen, volunteers to go in his place, accompanied by his unwilling and irreverent servant, Mafoo.
Master Wu instructs Prince Jen to bring along six gifts: an iron sword,

a leather saddle, a wooden flute, a bronze bowl, a sandalwood paint box, and a kite. Both the prince and Mafoo think old Master Wu is off his rocker, but they set out for T'ien-kuo with the six humble gifts.

It isn't long before the entourage, led by General Li Kwang, runs into trouble. They come upon an old man in a river and try unsuccessfully to rescue him. Finally, the prince wades into the water and pulls out Master Fu. Prince Jen agrees to escort the old man to his home, even though it is far out of their way.

In short order, Jen manages to lose the saddle that was to be a gift and to lose General Li Kwang and his men when they are turned into stone. One bright spot, however, is the addition of Voyaging Moon to their party. The young prince is immediately fascinated by this flute girl and gives her the flute that he carries as a gift—just as a loan while they journey—for she plays it in a most enchanting manner. Voyaging Moon warns that they may run into the dreaded bandit, Natha Yellow Scarf, who roams the countryside. Indeed they soon do, and he takes the sword, which was to be a gift, from the prince. Jen is lucky to escape with his life and those of his remaining travelers. Natha Yellow Scarf finds the sword to be magical—it slices anything it touches in two.

Misfortune follows on misfortune as young Prince Jen learns about life and living from the assorted characters he meets on the long journey. He discovers that the bandit stole not only his sword but also the papers he carries identifying him as the prince.

On the trail, Jen, Voyaging Moon, and Mafoo are nearly robbed by Moxa, the Mad Robber, who agrees to accompany them. Then they run into the magistrate Fat-choy, who refuses to believe that Jen is the prince because he has no papers. In fact, Fat-choy beats the prince, who must be rescued by his companions.

Once more on the trail, they come upon Master Shu, an old man who is wearing a cangue—a wooden collar bolted around the neck of those sentenced for crimes. Anyone who removes it is sentenced to death. Jen and his travelers remove it anyway after they learn that Master Shu was condemned by Fat-choy.

In time Jen and his group reach the River Lo, which they must cross. By this time Jen realizes that he loves the flute girl, Voyaging Moon, and that she loves him too. However, disaster once again strikes the travelers as their boat is capsized when they try to cross the river. Jen is separated from Voyaging Moon and everyone else.

While Voyaging Moon makes her way to an inn called the Golden

Grasshopper, where she earns money for a time by playing the flute, Prince Jen goes in search of her and his companions. He gives up his resolve to reach the legendary court of T'ien-kuo, for life without Voyaging Moon means nothing to him.

Many more trials await the young prince and one by one the rest of the gifts he has been carrying are lost or given away. He gives the kite to a young girl who is in a comalike state. The magical kite brings her back to life enabling her to fly like an eagle.

Soon after Jen gives the bowl to a beggar, Master Chu, he learns that the beggar has been arrested for stealing it. Jen goes to the magistrate to explain that the bowl was his, only to find that the magistrate is Fat-choy, who decides to put Prince Jen in the cangue for his lifetime.

Jen wanders far and long as he tries to work out how to release himself from the collar. Through the long winter, Jen learns many lessons—to sleep sitting up, to lap water like an animal, to walk half bent. Finally, Jen wanders into a town where, unbelievably, he is reunited with Mafoo and Moxa.

Moxa shatters the dreaded wooden collar. Mafoo tells Jen that news has reached them of his father's death. Prince Jen is now King of T'ang, but without identification, who will believe him? The three set off for the capital of Ch-ang-an, searching for Voyaging Moon on the way.

Near the city they meet Plum Blossom, mother of the child to whom Jen gave the magic kite. She tells the prince that the child flew away with the kite and has not returned, but that surely she is happy with her new life. Then, to Jen's great astonishment and delight, there stands Voyaging Moon, who had been traveling with Plum Blossom.

Voyaging Moon tells Prince Jen that she was with his father when he died and she told the old king of their journeys and of their betrothal. The king gave them his blessing. Now, however, bandit Natha Yellow Scarf has taken over the capital and proclaimed himself King of T'ang. What is worse, in order to spend a few hours with Jen, Voyaging Moon has promised Natha that she will marry him.

Prince Jen enters the village square to face the dreaded Natha. Guards seize him and drag him before the bandit to be executed. But as the executioner raises his sword, the crowd lets out a gasp—the tall stone statues in the square have come to life. They are Li Kwang and his warriors, the spell broken!

As Li Kwang moves to help Jen and the others, a great eagle sweeps out of the sky. It is the child, Fragrance of Orchid, and the magic kite.

She has also come to rescue Jen, even though she knows that once her feet touch the ground, she will never fly again.

In a marvelously wild skirmish, the bandit Natha is vanquished forever. Later, in the great Hall of Audience, Jen is amazed to recover all of the six gifts lost in his journey—all but the flute, still in the hands of Voyaging Moon. Jen says she must not return it; it was hers, always, from the first.

King Jen and Voyaging Moon marry and rule their kingdom in peace and harmony for many long years. They raise many sons and daughters. As the years pass, King Jen frets that he never fulfilled the promise he made to his father of journeying to the Kingdom of T'ien-kuo to uncover the secrets of good and benevolent rule. So he and Voyaging Moon decide to set out alone. This time they will go empty-handed.

Scarcely a day out on the journey, they meet an old man—Master Hu, Jen's beloved teacher as a child, who vanished from the palace many, many years before. When King Jen tells Master Hu of their intention, the old man says, "Have I not taught you to avoid useless pursuits and the pointless waste of time? If indeed the Kingdom of T'ien-kuo exists, it is any place you make it to be. Why seek what you have already found?"

Why indeed? Voyaging Moon takes the arm of her beloved Jen. "Come home," she says. "If, that is, we ever truly left it."

### Thematical Material

This delightful fantasy speaks of honor and truth and discovering the true meaning of life. It is also about courage, self-doubt, love, and pride. Through it all the author weaves authentic details of Chinese life and culture. Young Prince Jen grows from a naive, well-meaning young man into a person of depth and honor and courage and decency. The characters around him are also filled with breezy humor as they try to aid the prince in his danger-filled, impossible journey.

### Book Talk Material

A number of humorous incidents can serve as an excellent introduction to this delightful fantasy. See: Jen volunteers himself and Mafoo (pp. 6–8); Master Wu chooses the gifts (pp. 11–12); Jen rescues Master Fu (pp. 18–26); they meet the Mad Robber (pp. 84–92); and Master Hu's guidance (pp. 110–20).

**Additional Selections**

In Grace Chetwin's *The Riddle of the Rune* (Bradbury, 1987, $14.95; pap., Dell, $3.50), young Gom sets out with a mysterious stone around his neck to find his mother and in *The Crystal Stair* (Bradbury, 1988, $14.95; pap., Dell, $3.50), he is temporarily reunited with his mother before setting out in search of a wizard to teach him magic. An earlier title in this series is *Gom on Windy Mountain* (Lothrop, Lee & Shepard, 1986, $12.95; pap., Dell, $3.50) and a later one, *The Starstone* (Bradbury, 1989, $14.95).

A young girl, Periwinkle, whose father drowned in the sea, decides to disrupt the Sea Queen's magic in *The Changeling Sea* (Atheneum, 1988, $12.95) by Patricia A. McKillip.

In Marie Goodwin's time-travel fantasy *Where the Towers Pierce the Sky* (Four Winds, 1989, $13.95), a thirteen-year-old girl goes back in time to 1429 when Jeanne d'Arc is leading an attack on the British.

A female acrobat and a charlatan join forces to destroy the Red King and his powers of darkness in *The Red King* (Dial, 1990, $13.95) by Victor Kelleher.

Llyndreth sets out on a dangerous journey to find her brother, who is fighting goblins, in Pat Zettner's *The Shadow Warrior* (Atheneum, 1990, $13.95).

An apprentice goldsmith, fifteen-year-old Aracco, tries to find the legendary city of Terenger with its streets lined with gold in *Goldclimbers* by Nancy Luenn (Atheneum, 1991, $13.95).

Zan continues a quest against the Trickster Legend in *Colors of the Dreamweaver's Loom* (Houghton, 1989, $14.95) and in *The Feast of the Trickster* (Houghton, 1991, $14.95), both by Beth Hilgartner.

**About the Book**
*Booklist*, December 1991, p. 696.
*Center for Children's Books Bulletin*, November 1991, p. 55.
*Horn Book*, March 1991, p. 200.
*Kirkus Reviews*, September 15, 1991, p. 1219.
*School Library Journal*, December 1991, p. 113.
*VOYA*, February 1991, p. 378.
See also *Book Review Digest*, 1987, pp. 24, 26; and *Book Review Index*, 1987, p. 13.

**About the Author**
Chevalier, Tracy, ed., *Twentieth-Century Children's Writers* (3rd ed.). St. James, 1989, pp. 16–18.

Commire, Anne, ed., *Something about the Author*. Gale, 1972, Vol. 3, pp. 7–9; updated 1982, Vol. 49, pp. 21–35.

de Montreville, Doris, and Hill, Donna, eds., *Third Book of Junior Authors*. Wilson, 1972, pp. 6–7.

Estes, Glenn E., ed., *American Writers for Children since 1960: Fiction* (Dictionary of Literary Biography: Vol. 52). Gale, 1986, pp. 3–21.

Ethridge, James M., ed., *Contemporary Authors* (First Revision). Gale, 1967, Vols. 1–4, p. 17.

Senick, Gerard J., ed., *Children's Literature Review*. Gale, 1983, Vol. 5, pp. 13–26.

Straub, Deborah A., ed., *Contemporary Authors* (New Revision Series). Gale, 1988, Vol. 24, pp. 7–10.

Ward, Martha, ed., *Authors of Books for Young People* (3rd ed.). Scarecrow, 1990, p. 9.

**Bell, Clare.** *Ratha's Creature*
Atheneum, 1983, $11.95 (0-689-50262-1)

This is the beginning of a fantasy trilogy about a band of intelligent cats. In this, the first book, and the second, *Clan Ground* (pap., Dell, 1987, $2.95), the central character, Ratha, becomes leader of the pack after harnessing fire. In the final volume, *Ratha and Thistle-Chaser* (McElderry, 1990, $14.95), she leads her clan in search of water to a land near the ocean and here she confronts Thistle-Chaser, the daughter she abandoned as a cub. The outcast daughter has been befriended by Seamares, who are later captured by Ratha and her group. Thistle-Chaser frees them and meets her mother in a final dramatic confrontation. These thought-provoking novels are enjoyed by better readers in junior and senior high school.

**Plot Summary**

In this tale of discovery, rebellion, and exile set some 25 million years ago, the creatures of earth are undergoing profound change. Ratha is part of the Named, a band of intelligent wild cats who are related to the ancient sabertooth. The Named have a society of laws and leaders that is based on herding forest animals. Their enemy is the Un-Named, a wild band that lacks the laws and intelligence of the Named. Yet the wild band is pushing the Named ever closer to extinction.

Ratha, a yearling, is being trained as a herder under the watchful eye of Thakur Torn-Claw. But the clan leader, Meoran, whom many feel does not have the qualifications for the job, will no longer allow she-cubs to be trained as herders and he keeps a watchful eye lest Ratha disgrace herself and the clan.

Ratha spots one of the Un-Named attacking the herd and she fights him. To her great surprise, the attacker speaks to her. (Ratha and the others have been taught that the Un-Named cannot speak.) When she questions Thakur about this strange occurrence, he refuses to answer her questions.

Besides the threat of the Un-Named, the clan of the Named must constantly be alert for fires that often sweep the herds, sometimes caused by lightning. One such fire sweeps the meadow, and as Ratha tries to protect her herds, she is plunged into a stream, from which Thakur rescues her. To regain her strength, Ratha stays behind with Thakur as the clan moves ahead in search of food and safety. During this period she learns that Thakur's sire was an Un-Named and that his brother runs with the Un-Named clan.

On their journey to rejoin the herd, Ratha must coax Thakur across still smoldering logs, which he fears, as do all members of the clan. Ratha suddenly looks on these still-burning twigs as Red Tongue, a fire-animal. As she would at other prey, she leaps at Red Tongue and sinks her teeth into it. The branch breaks off, falls into the dirt, and dies. Ratha realizes she has tamed the Red Tongue.

Ratha tells her friend Fessran what she did and Fessran is impressed, comparing Ratha's feats favorably with those of Meoran, the clan leader. Thakur warns that Meoran would rip her throat if he heard such words.

Meoran does learn of Ratha's accomplishment with the Red Tongue. For her boldness, for doing what none of the other Named could do, Ratha is banished from the clan, for Meoran feels threatened by her power. Ratha asks Thakur to accompany her, but he refuses, saying the clan leader will not harm her because Meoran needs the knowledge of old Thakur in order to rule.

When Ratha leaves the clan, Fessran goes too. Ratha carries a torch of the Red Tongue in her mouth. But when she slips into a stream, the torch dies. Ratha tells Fessran to go back to the clan and tell Meoran that she killed the Red Tongue and drove Ratha away. Fessran will then be spared.

Alone, Ratha turns from the clan and runs toward the horizon. When she captures something to eat it is taken from her by a young male, whom she calls scavenger and Un-Named dung-eater. So begins her association with Bonechewer, who chides Ratha on her poor hunting skills and shows her where to find fresh water.

Ratha, against her better judgment, travels with Bonechewer, who shows her the ways and skills of the Un-Named. Through the days of summer, Ratha and Bonechewer work hard to keep their bellies full. Ratha learns many things. She learns that among both the Named and the Un-Named, for instance, there are those who speak, such as Bonechewer, and those who are witless and cannot. She also learns from Bonechewer that the Un-Named will now no longer kill just for food as before. They will go after the Named. When Ratha asks why, Bonechewer answers that he doesn't know but perhaps it is because Meoran now grazes the Named on land once held by the Un-Named—or perhaps because the winter has been hard and all are hungry, or because there are now too many of the Un-Named to feed by hunting alone.

When it is time, Ratha and Bonechewer mate. More months pass, and four cubs are born, a female and three brothers. With the birth of the cubs, Ratha begins to feel that perhaps it is time for change. She will found a new clan to take the place of the old. She can teach the Un-Named as well so that they can keep their own herds and need no longer live by raiding.

Time passes as Ratha and Bonechewer tend the cubs. As spring turns to summer, they both must acknowledge the fact that their cubs will never speak; they are of the witless number. In her rage, Ratha, who now knows that Bonechewer is the brother of Thakur, asks why their cubs should lack wit. Such a thing does not make sense, says Bonechewer, but he feared that it might be true. Once before he had had cubs, but that time with a female who was Un-Named. This time he thought it would be different. Ratha cannot be consoled and suggests that they leave the cubs to starve, but Bonechewer says he will keep them, for he will not mate again.

Ratha wanders on like a leaf blown by the wind, having no clan and no ties. One midsummer's day, to her great surprise, she stumbles on a cat with the face of Bonechewer but with eyes of green. It is Thakur! He tells Ratha that just a few of the clan are left. Meoran is still the leader for he is strong and they need his strength, even though he has not the wit to lead. Thakur begs Ratha to return, for they need her intelligence.

When Ratha and Meoran confront each other, she tries to control her feelings for the leader. She promises to obey him in order to return to the clan but Meoran says that he can see in her eyes that she once challenged him with the Red Tongue. She would never forget that Meoran had bowed before that power. Ratha acknowledges his words and tells the remaining clan that it is not Meoran who has made her an outcast, but Ratha herself. "Take care of your people, Meoran," she says and leaves.

Ratha makes a den by herself. Time passes and one morning she finds Thakur waiting there. He says he will come and see her when he can get away and as summer turns into fall Thakur brings her stories of the loss of more clan members.

One night during a fierce storm, Ratha realizes that the Red Tongue has returned. Her friend Fessran suddenly appears at her den, telling her that through Meoran's stupidity, another cub has been lost. Ratha and the Red Tongue must return to lead them or they will all die. Ratha refuses and Fessran asks if Ratha is afraid to take up the creature again. "It never was my creature," Ratha replies. Still, to show that she does not fear the Red Tongue, Ratha picks up a glowing stick. Together the two friends return to the clan grounds carrying the Red Tongue. In the ensuing fight between Meoran and Ratha, the burning shaft that Ratha carries is jammed into Meoran's throat. He dies trying to reach the stream.

Thakur tells Ratha that she must now be the leader. "No," she cries. "The way of the Red Tongue is madness." It may be madness, Thakur tells her, but it is also life. Ratha holds the flame aloft. "This is my creature," she tells the clan. "It shall be yours as well. I will teach you to keep it and feed it, for it must never be allowed to die. You shall be called the Named no longer. Now you are the People of the Red Tongue."

And so the People of the Red Tongue learn to guard the fire day and night, keeping away their enemies. Ratha tries not to think that out in the darkness Bonechewer could be wandering with her cubs. She tries not to think that even with the Red Tongue, her people are too few to stand against those wandering around them in the blackness.

When the Un-Named do surge forward out of the darkness, Ratha and her Red Tongue bearers go to fight them. The Un-Named flee before their power. When the fight is over, Thakur takes Ratha to one of the wounded Un-Named who has asked for her. It is Bonechewer. He tells her that the cubs all left him and that they have become savage killers. Bonechewer dies. Ratha feels great sorrow and tells Thakur, "A clan leader should not bawl like a cub."

"No one was watching," is Thakur's gentle reply.

Ratha knows she will take no mate until the memories of Bonechewer are soothed and healed. It will not be an easy path she has chosen, but with Thakur beside her as a wise and comforting friend, she will challenge what is still unknown, for she is Ratha, tamer of the Red Tongue and leader of her people.

**Thematic Material**

This is an interesting, exciting science fiction novel that intermingles the instincts of the animal world with the emotions of the human species. Ratha remains true to her animal instincts, yet there is often conflict between those instincts and her intelligence in this fast-paced adventure that is both tragic and hopeful.

**Book Talk Material**

The maturing of Ratha into the leader of the clan can serve as a good introduction to this thoughtful science fiction tale. See: Ratha and Thakur make a kill (pp. 4–10); Ratha meets an Un-Named who speaks (pp. 23–24); Ratha tames the Red Tongue (pp. 56–68); Ratha kills the creature and leaves the clan (pp. 93–101).

**Additional Selections**

James travels in a future world of a fossilized dump patrolled by vicious rats and giant seagulls in Peter Dickinson's *A Box of Nothing* (Delacorte, 1988, $14.95).

In Shirley Rousseau Murphy's *Nightpool* (Harper, 1985, $11.89; pap., $2.95; condensed in *Seniorplots*, Bowker, 1989, pp. 203–7), the beautiful dragon Seastrider becomes bonded to young Teb, later Prince Tebriel. Their struggle against the dark forces that threaten the world is continued in *The Ivory Lyre* (pap., Harper, 1988, $3.25) and *The Dragonbards* (Harper, 1988, $14.95; pap., $3.50).

As seen through the eyes of a dog, Patricia Wrightson's novel set in Australia, *Moon-Dark* (McElderry, 1988, $13.95), tells how settlers in a remote area upset the balance of nature.

Masklin, a gnomelike creature, shoulders the responsibility of saving his community from extinction in Terry Pratchett's *Truckers* (Delacorte, 1990, $14.95).

Twelve-year-old Miranda and her catlike friend from another world travel through time and space to fight the Charmer in Marilyn Singer's *Charmed* (Atheneum, 1990, $14.75).

On a shell-selling expedition to Sydney, Australia, Riko is aghast when a shell collector discovers that she lives in an underwater world in Ruth Park's *My Sister Sif* (Viking, 1991, $12.95).

**About the Book**
*Booklist,* May 15, 1983, p. 956.
*Center for Children's Books Bulletin,* July 1983, p. 202.
*School Library Journal,* September 1983, p. 130.
See also *Book Review Index,* 1983, p. 51.

---

**Brooks, Bruce.** *No Kidding*
HarperCollins, 1989, $13.95 (0-06-020723-X); pap., $3.50 (0-06-447051-2)

---

Bruce Brooks's first book for young adults was *The Moves Make the Man* (Harper, 1984, $14.89; pap., $2.95; condensed in *Juniorplots 3*, Bowker, 1987, pp. 235–38), the story of a friendship between two very different boys, one black and one white, who are both interested in basketball. His next, *Midnight Hour Encores* (Harper, 1986, $13.95; pap., $3.50; condensed in *Seniorplots,* Bowker, 1989, pp. 45–49), tells of a girl's cross-country odyssey in search of a mother who deserted her at birth. The present novel moves into the future and describes a bleak society that has lost its way and sunk into alcoholism. The story spans six days and is told in a series of terse objective vignettes using a staccato, sparse style reminiscent of Hemingway. It is a challenging, disturbing novel that will be read by better readers in junior and senior high.

**Plot Summary**
In the mid-twenty-first century, life in the United States is far from utopian. Many scientific marvels have proven to have disastrous long-term effects on humankind. For example, prolonged exposure to emissions from cathode-ray tubes used in television sets and other electronic inventions has brought sterility to large segments of the population. Though these devices are now banned, the birth rate has plummeted so that married couples are clamoring to adopt any available child. The environment has also suffered, with many species, including the whale, now extinct. To escape their bleak, joyless existence, millions have

turned to alcohol. The latest statistics show that 69 percent of the population is classified as alcoholic.

With 50 percent of the people in some form of treatment program, this has become the second largest business enterprise in the nation, led only by the post office. Soberlife, funded jointly by the government and the private sector, is the major network of rehabilitation centers. The plague of alcoholism has affected every aspect of American life. A new fundamentalist religious group, known as the Steemers, is preaching a doctrine of hate, claiming that people who drink are evil and that their alcoholism is actually a punishment for past and present sins. Some established churches have also made unusual adjustments to this crisis by forming congregations restricted only to children of alcoholics. With most of the adults incapacitated, the government has passed a series of laws giving children decision-making powers hitherto held only by adults. The school system also reflects these social problems. Most public schools are classified AO for Alcoholic Offspring because they devote large sections of the curriculum to alcohol studies; others, run by the Steemers, brainwash their students with doctrines of hate and prejudice, while still others, including some private schools, are classified non-AO because they teach only the conventional subjects to children of nonalcoholics.

Sam's ten-year-old brother, Oliver, attends a private non-AO school in their home city of Washington, D.C. For the past year, Ollie has been living in a foster home with the childless Mr. and Mrs. Bigelow. Sam is only fourteen but, like many other children growing up in this society, he has had to assume adult responsibilities. After their father left home to become a missionary, the boys' mother turned to alcohol, and, although she managed to hide this from Ollie, Sam was so aware of her self-destructive behavior that he had her committed to Soberlife. Since that time—a year and a half ago—besides working full time in a printing plant owned by the benevolent Mr. Culpepper, he has devoted every spare moment to checking on his mother's progress and making sure that Ollie is well cared for. He was the one who a year ago chose the middle-class Bigelows as the stable foster parents his brother needed and, since then, he has guided their every decision concerning the boy's welfare. Somehow, in his welter of duties and anxieties, Sam has never had time himself for the childhood that he now knows is gone.

It is Sunday, and during the coming week many important events will take place in Sam's life. At his own bidding, his mother is to be released from Soberlife and, because the year's probation period for Ollie's adoption ends on Friday, he must decide whether his brother should remain with the Bigelows. During his Sunday visit with them, the couple make it clear that they love Ollie and want complete custody, but Sam is secretly hoping that his mother will be sufficiently recovered so that they will be able to become a family again. He has made careful plans for her return, renting a small, tastefully furnished room for her, buying a small wardrobe of new clothes, and securing her a job as a salesperson in a boutique.

His mother arrives on Tuesday. She is a realistic, caring woman who sincerely tries to establish contact with this son who seems so old and staid for his years. To Sam's amazement, she seems reluctant to see Ollie and postpones their first meeting until Friday.

Later that day, Sam encounters Archie, a recovering alcoholic who works at the printing plant. He is roaring drunk and falls, breaking his nose. Sam first helps him into a "sober bar," where he is fed coffee laced with an emetic to cause vomiting; then he takes him to a treatment center where he will dry out and get medical attention.

The Bigelows are becoming increasingly concerned over the number of evenings Ollie has been spending away from home at soccer and band practice. Ollie is not only a fine goalie but also plays a mean saxophone. He is also a lonely, sensitive boy who, though Sam has hidden the truth from him, inwardly knows his mother is an alcoholic. Secretly, at night, he is attending a church for children of alcoholics and getting guidance from its pastor, Prior Jack Marloe.

Friday comes and Sam takes Ollie to the boutique to be reunited with his mother. The store is in complete disarray—their mother, in a drunken state, has run amok and thrown a mannequin through the front window. The boys follow her to her room, where Ollie becomes so agitated that he flings his saxophone at her. Sam sends the boy back to the Bigelows and confronts his mother, demanding to know why she has gone back to alcohol. Suddenly he realizes that she is not drunk and that the bottle before her contains only soda. Why this hoax? His mother explains that this was her way of convincing Sam that Ollie must remain with the Bigelows to get the attention and love he needs. In the meantime, she has other plans. She and Sam will move in together so that she can give him the childhood he has been denied.

**Thematic Material**

This thought-provoking novel portrays a disturbing future where unrestrained selfishness and misplaced faith in technology have produced a sterile society that has retreated from reality into alcohol and drugs. However, while there is a strong anti-alcohol message here, this is far from being a temperance tract. It also shows how misplaced and distorted human values can lead to aberrations in both religion and education. The importance of the family unit in providing security and stability is stressed. The guilt and confusion that children of alcoholics face is also well portrayed. Other themes include the development of responsibility, sibling love, mother-son relations, the importance for young people of having time to develop naturally, and the destructive effects of deception on children.

**Book Talk Material**

Explaining the title in reference to Sam's lost childhood and displaying the dust jacket will help introduce the plot. Some interesting episodes are: the Bigelows discuss Sam's visit (pp. 3–12); Sam goes to Soberlife to arrange for his mother's release (pp. 25–33); Sam talks to an old man about life in Washington (pp. 34–42); Sam's mother comes home (pp. 57–61); and Sam helps Archie (pp. 130–40).

**Additional Selections**

Judith Gorog's *Three Dreams and a Nightmare* (Philomel, 1988, $13.95) is a collection of short stories that combine the macabre and the fantastic.

Barney is befriended by a fellow loner named Snowy Cobb and introduced to the remains of an Indian civilization whose members were only inches tall in Rosemary Wells's *Through the Hidden Door* (Dial, 1987, $14.95; pap., Scholastic, $2.95).

The Earth is computer-ruled and on a path to destruction in Deborah Moniton's suspenseful science fiction novel, *Children of Time* (Dial, 1989, $14.95).

What starts as a computer-simulation game for some unemployed teenagers in the year 2154 becomes frighteningly real in Monica Hughes's *Invitation to the Game* (Simon & Schuster, 1991, $14).

In the twenty-first century, food is so scarce that seventeen-year-old Laddie is sent to a work camp in Thomas Baird's *Smart Rats* (Harper, 1990, $14.95).

In Laurence Yep's *Sweetwater* (pap., Harper, 1975, $2.95), Tyree wants to keep Earth's traditional values on his new planet.

Two youngsters and their teacher are involved in a revolt against an alien race in H. M. Hoover's *The Delikon* (pap., Puffin, 1986, $3.95).

SCIENCE FICTION AND FANTASY · 197

**About the Book**
*Booklist,* March 15, 1989, p. 1274.
*Center for Children's Books Bulletin,* June 1989, p. 124.
*Horn Book,* July 1989, p. 486.
*Kirkus Reviews,* March 1, 1989, p. 375.
*New York Times Book Review,* June 25, 1989, p. 30.
*School Library Journal,* March 1989, p. 198.
*VOYA,* August 1989, p. 155.
See also *Book Review Digest,* 1989, p. 203; and *Book Review Index,* 1989, p. 107.


**About the Author**
Commire, Anne, ed., *Something about the Author.* Gale, 1988, Vol. 53, p. 7.
Holtze, Sally Holmes, ed., *Sixth Book of Junior Authors and Illustrators.* Wilson, 1989, pp. 43–44.
Senick, Gerard J., ed., *Children's Literature Review.* Gale, 1991, Vol. 25, pp. 16–26.


**Christopher, John.** *When the Tripods Came*
Dutton, 1988, $12.95 (0-525-44397-5); pap., Collier, $3.95 (0-02-042575-9)

In the first of the Tripods Trilogy (also called the White Mountains trilogy), *The White Mountains* (Macmillan, 1967, $13.95; pap., $3.95), three boys in the twenty-first century try to escape both the domination of malevolent machines known as the Tripods and the coming-of-age operation known as Capping that will destroy their self-will by traveling to isolated mountains in a land once known as Switzerland where a band of humans still live a free life. From there, a guerrilla warfare is launched that inevitably leads to the defeat of the Tripods. This forms the exciting subject matter of the other two books in this series, *The City of Gold and Lead* (Macmillan, 1967, $12.95; pap., $3.95) and *The Pool of Fire* (Macmillan, 1968, $12.95; pap., $3.95).

Although this series has been read extensively during the twenty-five-plus years it has been in print, its popularity rose spectacularly after a British television series based on these books was shown a few years ago in the United States. This novel, set in contemporary England, is a prequel to the White Mountains series and tells of the first appearances of the Tripods, how they came to dominate the earth, and of the formation of the resistance movement. It is a first-person narrative told by Laurie

Cordray, the young hero of this novel. It is popular with readers in grades 6 through 10.

**Plot Summary**

Fourteen-year-old Laurie (short for Laurence) Cordray and his friend Andy take the wrong turn during a camping expedition on the moors of Dorset and are forced to spend the night in a deserted shed. About five in the morning, they are awakened by a series of loud explosions. From the window of the hut, they see something unbelievable—a giant hemispherical capsule with three mechanical legs has landed on a nearby farm. Using huge tentacles that issue from the underside of its body, it destroys the farmhouse and takes its terrorized occupant aboard. Airplanes from the Royal Air Force attack and destroy this marauder from outer space.

Two other landings take place that night. In Russia rockets destroy the mysterious intruder, and in the United States the capsule self-destructs after a period on the ground. It becomes obvious, particularly after the body of the farmer is found with his brain neatly dissected, that these unmanned space vehicles, now known as Tripods, have come to Earth on an intelligence-gathering expedition.

For a time, Laurie and Andy are celebrities in the media and at school, where even their gruff physics teacher "Wild Bill" Hockey wants any insider information they can provide.

Laurie lives in a small English town in Dorsetshire only miles inland from the English Channel. His mother left him and his father some years ago. Pa, a real estate agent, remarried and now has a seven-year-old daughter, Angela, by his second wife, a Swiss woman named Ilse. All four live with Pa's feisty mother, an antiques dealer whom everybody calls Martha. Ilse's parents, the Ardakers, who are affectionately called Swigramp and Swigram, live in Switzerland in a former guesthouse on the outskirts of a small town close to Interlaken. Before Ilse can assimilate her stepson's unusual experience, she is summoned home because her beloved father has had a severe heart attack. Laurie and Angela are left under the care of Martha and Pa.

All of Britain, indeed the world, is abuzz with speculation about the Tripods. A half-animated/half-real-life television show about them, called *The Trippy Show*, becomes an international sensation, though in Laurie's household only Angela is a fan. Within weeks, it becomes apparent that this show is casting a sinister influence over its viewers, now known as Trippies. Even normally placid Angela becomes violent when she learns that Laurie has neglected to tape one of the shows. She attacks him physically and leaves the house intent on joining one of the Trippy communes that have grown up around the country. Her father forcibly drags her back into the house where, through hypnosis administered by their family doctor, Dr. Monmouth, she is exorcised of these mind-controlling influences.

Millions of others are not so fortunate and soon the rallying cry of "Hail the Tripod" and echoes of brainwashing slogans about peace and harmony for humankind are heard everywhere. Several teachers at Laurie's school, including "Wild Bill," have Tripped. When Andy's mother leaves to join a commune, he comes to live with the Cordrays. During the next invasion, the Tripods distribute "Caps," rubber helmets equipped with electronic devices, which induce slavish compliance to the Tripods' will.

One day when Laurie is alone in the house, his very wealthy Uncle Ian and his teenage son, Nathanael, arrive. Soon Laurie realizes this is not a social call. Both have become Tripod fanatics and they have brought four Caps to turn the Cordrays into converts. The two pin Laurie to the floor and are about to Cap him when Martha arrives, brandishing her revolver.

This incident, coupled with a national situation comparable to civil war, forces Pa to make a grim assessment of their future. All avenues of communication, including the news media and the airlines, are under the control of the Trippies, who have cut off information from outside England. Under Pa's leadership, the family, with Andy, decide to escape on their yacht, the *Edelweiss*, to the Channel Island of Guernsey, where Martha owns some property. After a rough crossing, they are greeted in port by the dockmaster, who shouts "Hail the Tripods." Realizing that they cannot stay, they plan to get to Switzerland and reunite with Ilse. Pa disconnects the electronic device in the Caps left behind by Uncle Ian and they all don this disguise. Martha sells some of her jewelry and the five are grudgingly allowed to buy airplane tickets to London. In midair, Pa uses Martha's pistol to hijack the plane and directs the pilot to land in Geneva.

Laurie and family are joyfully reunited with Ilse along with Swigram and Swigramp, although everyone realizes the old man is failing fast and that Tripod invasion is imminent.

The invasion comes within a few weeks and there are mass Cappings of the Swiss people, including the residents of Fernohr, the little town near Ilse's home. Andy is captured and held for Capping. When Laurie is also captured in an abortive rescue mission, Pa engineers a daring escape. That night Swigramp dies and the family, now joined by a faithful farmhand named Yone and a young village boy, Rudi, flees into the mountains and takes refuge in an unused train tunnel where they can take advantage of the supplies left in a nearby abandoned ski resort. As the winter passes, they are joined by a few others who tell them that the Tripods are replacing the mind-controlling Cap with a permanent steel plate that cannot be removed. Eventually a small resistance movement is formed with Pa as its leader. Their first act of defiance is to destroy a reconnoitering Tripod by causing an avalanche that buries it. This signifies the beginning of a war of liberation against the Tripods that may take generations.

**Thematic Material**

Although this is basically a thrilling science fiction adventure, it portrays an evil that is found in contemporary life in totalitarian regimes and sometimes in religious cults—the tyranny of brainwashing and mind control. This novel describes both the frightening effects of such control and the accompanying struggle people endure to remain free. Laurie is an average teenager who through adversity rises to acts of daring and courage. This is also a story of friendship, and one that explores the bonds of family and the meaning of freedom.

**Book Talk Material**

Some thrilling episodes that can be used are: Andy and Laurie witness the landing of the first Tripod (pp. 1–11); Angela overreacts when Laurie forgets to tape the Trippy show (pp. 29–34); Angela is hypnotized by Dr. Monmouth (pp. 39–44); Laurie is almost Capped by Uncle Ian and Nathanael (pp. 55–61); and the flight to Guernsey (pp. 78–84).

**Additional Selections**

The celebrated author of adult science fiction Poul Anderson has written an exciting adventure for young readers, *The Year of the Ransom* (Walker, 1988, $15.95) that hopscotches over centuries in a pursuit involving the treasure of conquistador Francisco Pizarro.

Seventeen-year-old James and friend Robert travel from Mexico to

Missouri as North America is in the grip of an approaching ice age in Gary L. Blackwood's *The Dying Sun* (Atheneum, 1989, $13.95).

Earth is the only stumbling block left for an invincible race that plans to control the universe in Tom McGowen's *The Magical Fellowship* (Lodestar, 1991, $14.95).

Laddie, a seventeen-year-old boy, fights to save himself and his family in 2016 when the earth can no longer support its population in Thomas Baird's *Smart Rats* (Harper, 1990, $14.95).

There are two stories in Jean Karl's *Strange Tomorrow* (Dutton, 1985, $12.95; pap., Dell, $2.95), one about survivors after a holocaust on earth and the other about building a new society.

Cat, a young boy of sixteen, survives by his wits in the twenty-fifth century on the planet Ardatte in Joan D. Vinge's *Psion* (Delacorte, 1982, $12.95; pap., Dell, $2.95; condensed in *Juniorplots 3*, Bowker, 1987, pp. 202–5).

In Pamela Sargent's *Earthseed* (pap., Harper, 1987, $2.75; condensed in *Juniorplots 3*, Bowker, 1987, pp. 194–98), Zoheret and her companions prepare to populate a new planet.

**About the Book**
*Booklist,* July 1988, p. 1832.
*Center for Children's Books Bulletin,* July 1988, p. 224.
*Horn Book,* September 1988, p. 625.
*Kirkus Reviews,* April 15, 1988, p. 615.
*School Library Journal,* August 1988, p. 92.
*VOYA,* August 1988, p. 138.
See also *Book Review Digest,* 1989, pp. 289–90; and *Book Review Index,* 1988, p. 152.

**About the Author**
Chevalier, Tracy, ed., *Twentieth-Century Children's Writers* (3rd ed.). St. James, 1989, pp. 195–96.
Commire, Anne, ed., *Something about the Author.* Gale, 1987, Vol. 47, pp. 216–20 (under Samuel Youd).
de Montreville, Doris, and Crawford, Elizabeth D., eds., *Fourth Book of Junior Authors and Illustrators.* Wilson, 1978, pp. 78–79.
Kirkpatrick, D. L., ed., *Twentieth-Century Children's Writers* (2nd ed.). St. Martin's, 1983, pp. 170–71.
Locher, Frances C., ed., *Contemporary Authors.* Gale, 1979, Vols. 77–80, pp. 617–18 (under Samuel Youd).
Riley, Carolyn, ed., *Children's Literature Review.* Gale, 1976, Vol. 2, pp. 37–44.

**Conford, Ellen.**  *Genie with the Light Blue Hair*
Scholastic, 1989, $14.95 (0-553-05806-1); pap., $3.50 (0-553-28484-3)

This is one of more than twenty books that Ellen Conford has written for young people. They are characterized by fast-moving plots, likable characters, familiar situations, and a generous amount of humor. They always have a central positive theme with which youngsters can identify. For example, Carrie Wasserman, the heroine of *Dear Lovey Hart, I Am Desperate* (Little, Brown, 1975, $14.95; pap., Scholastic, $2.95) and its sequel, *We Interrupt This Semester for an Important Bulletin* (Little, Brown, 1989, $14.95; pap., Scholastic, $2.95; condensed in *Juniorplots 3*, Bowker, 1987, pp. 20–23), learns that with privilege comes responsibility. In *Seven Days to a Brand New Me* (Little, Brown, 1981, $14.95; pap., Scholastic, $2.95), Maddy learns that in spite of following Dr. Dudley's program that supposedly will turn her into a teenage vamp, she is better being her original self. Jean Warren, the central character in *Genie*, learns valuable lessons from the amazing adventures she has with Arthur, the blue-haired genie. This easily read tale is enjoyed by young people in grades 6 through 9.

**Plot Summary**

Jean Warren is spending her fifteenth birthday in her comfortable suburban home with her family: Mom and Dad; younger brother Richie; and Aunt Jean and Uncle Rocky. Jean is a quiet, shy girl who is so intimidated by the size of her high school, Hungerford High, where she is a freshman, that she has been unable to meet new people and instead relies entirely on the friendship of Lynn Shoemaker, whom she has known since sixth grade.

Her aunt and uncle give Jean a most unusual birthday present, which they purchased from "Unique Antiques." It is a teapot-shaped lamp that contains a blue candle. Later that night Jean is reading in her bedroom during an electrical storm when the lights fail and the room is plunged into darkness. She lights the lamp and suddenly the room is filled with light and a strange blue smoke. From out of the smoke appears a man with light blue hair who is dressed like a character from the *Arabian Nights* with a turban, curled slippers, and pantaloons. His face, however, seems familiar and Jean realizes he is a Groucho Marx look-alike. He introduces himself as Arthur, a genie who has not worked in thirty-three years and is now waiting to fulfill any of Jean's wishes. In disbelief, she asks for a boyfriend and suddenly a young man appears. After asking Arthur to get rid of him, she asks that her overheated room be cooled. "Okey-dokey," says Arthur and the room is filled with snow. Jean, realizing that you must be specific with genies, asks that the snow be exchanged for an air conditioner and one appears in her window.

The next morning, Jean wakes up convinced she has had a most unusual dream. Not so. The air conditioner is still there. Before the family can see it, she hastily summons Arthur to remove it.

That day at school, Lynn is invited to have lunch with Tiffany Tupperman, the most popular, sophisticated, and richest girl at Hungerford High. Jean tags along but is so overawed and tongue-tied that once again she is a social washout. Back home, she tells Arthur, "I want to be Tiffany Tupperman." In an instant she is driving Tiffany's Trans Am with her handsome boyfriend, Ned Bayer, beside her. They park and begin deep kissing, a new and decidedly distasteful experience for Jean. Back at the Tuppermans', Jean looks in the mirror and realizes she really is Tiffany. The next day at school, the novelty of having a new identity soon wears off, and a frightened and anxious Jean leaves school at lunch time to go home to the lamp and deliverance. Her house is locked so she breaks in through a basement window—only to be confronted by Richie, who is home sick from school. Not knowing who this stranger is, he threatens to call the police. Luckily Jean is able to sneak into her room and have Arthur transform her before disaster strikes.

Jean tells Lynn about Arthur. Lynn asks her to use Arthur's power to fulfill her secret wish, to be a winning contestant on the "Name That Person" television show. Anxious to please her friend, Jean summons Arthur and within seconds after his familiar "okey-dokey," the two girls are partners in a television studio facing an audience and a jovial master of ceremonies. Unfortunately, there has been a misunderstanding; the show is actually "Name That Poison." Again Jean is able to effect a rescue via Arthur, who also obligingly makes Lynn forget the whole experience.

When Mom washes the lamp and soaks both the candle and the wick, Jean is afraid she has lost Arthur forever. But judicious use of her hair dryer enables her to dry the lamp and relight it. This time, Jean requests that she be loved by her heartthrob, her English teacher, Mr. Kellogg. Within an "okey-dokey," she is dancing with Mr. Kellogg in the school gym at a Valentine's Day dance. Unfortunately he calls her Penelope, the name of his beloved daughter—once more, a fiasco. There are further complications, when Jean-Penelope discovers that the Warrens have returned the lamp to Unique Antiques and exchanged it for a rare edition of *Huckleberry Finn*. Luckily her Aunt Jean repurchased it and Arthur again is called on to effect a rescue.

So far, Jean's identity exchanges have all been catastrophic, but she gives Arthur one more chance. She wants to be a modern, best-selling author. In her new identity she becomes Jillian Farquahar. She discovers that Ms. Farquahar may be rich and famous but her fame rests on writing a smutty series called Heartbreak High for young adults. She again makes a wish that Arthur return her to being simple Jean Warren.

When Arthur accidentally calls her Jean Roxbury, Jean realizes that her blue-haired genie really belongs to her aunt. She returns the lamp to Aunt Jean, actually glad to be rid of the temptation and confusion it has caused her.

The next day at school she feels so happy to be plain, uncomplicated Jean Warren again that she begins smiling and talking with her fellow students. She is amazed at the reaction. Even gorgeous Ned Bayer returns her greeting. She is so overcome at how everyone is suddenly friendly that she suspects Arthur's magic is at work. She calls Aunt Jean, who assures her it is not so. By being friendly and outgoing, Jean has created her own magic.

**Thematic Material**

During this lighthearted fantasy, Jean learns the valuable lesson that happiness comes from getting outside oneself and caring for others. She also learns the truth behind the "grass is always greener" adage and the fact that one must come to a stage of self-acceptance to find contentment. Many teenage concerns are touched on, such as the need for group status, coping with feelings of insecurity, problems in being accepted by one's peers, and dealing with crushes on favorite teachers. Jean is a plausible and likable heroine who, like many girls her age, suffers from a lack of self-confidence in confronting the problems of growing up. However, it is probably literal-minded Arthur and his ever-cheerful "okey-dokey" who will remain longest with the reader.

**Book Talk Material**

After one describes Jean's gift and its powers, prospective readers could be asked what their first wish might be if they had a genie at their command. Some interesting passages are: Arthur's first appearance (pp.

7–17) and Jean's first wishes (pp. 17–22); Jean's life as Tiffany Tupperman (pp. 32–42); the "Name That Poison" show (pp. 57–67); and drying the lamp and wishing to be loved by Mr. Kellogg (pp. 74–79).

## Additional Selections

Frankie Stein obtains some unknown genetic material and soon finds herself tending to a growing monster in Vivien Alcock's *The Monster Garden* (Delacorte, 1988, $13.95; pap., Dell, $2.95).

A magic charm leads to Stanley's fulfilling his secret ambition to be a wheeler-dealer in his high school in Bill Brittain's comic novel *The Fantastic Freshman* (Harper, 1988, $12.98; pap., $3.25).

Two young humans and four ghosts form the Ghost Squad and together appear in an extensive series in which they solve many mysteries, such as the unmasking of a murderer in *The Ghost Squad and the Menace of Malevs* (Dutton, 1988, $12.95) by E. W. Hildick.

When Miranda tries out her magic love potion, she conjures up a with-it ghost in Herma Silverstein's *Mad, Mad Monday* (Lodestar, 1988, $12.95; pap., Archway, $2.50).

Joanna accidentally masters a way to make herself invisible in Dorothy Morrison's *Vanishing Act* (Atheneum, 1989, $13.95).

In Margaret Buffie's *The Haunting of Frances Rain* (Scholastic, 1989, $13.95; pap., $2.95), Lizzie finds a pair of magical spectacles that take her into the past.

In the third part of a series by Lynn Hall, *Dagmar Shultz and the Angel Edna* (Scribner, 1989, $11.95), thirteen-year-old Dagmar from New Berlin, Iowa, meets her guardian angel.

## About the Book

*Book Report*, September 1989, p. 39.
*Booklist*, February 15, 1989, p. 1000.
*Center for Children's Books Bulletin*, February 1989, p. 145.
*Horn Book*, March 1989, p. 215.
*Kirkus Reviews*, January 1, 1989, p. 47.
*New York Times Book Review*, August 6, 1989, p. 29.
*School Library Journal*, February 1989, p. 100.
*VOYA*, April 1989, p. 26.
See also *Book Review Digest*, 1989, p. 322; and *Book Review Index*, 1989, p. 171.

## About the Author

Chevalier, Tracy, ed., *Twentieth-Century Children's Writers* (3rd ed.). St. James, 1989, pp. 228–29.

Commire, Anne, ed., *Something about the Author*. Gale, 1974, Vol. 6, pp. 48–49.
Evory, Ann, ed., *Contemporary Authors* (First Revision). Gale, 1978, Vols. 33–36, pp. 203–4.
Holtze, Sally Holmes, ed., *Fifth Book of Junior Authors and Illustrators*. Wilson, 1983, pp. 82–83.
Metzger, Linda, ed., *Contemporary Authors* (New Revision Series). Gale, 1984, Vol. 13, p. 117.
Senick, Gerard J., ed., *Children's Literature Review*. Gale, 1986, Vol. 10, pp. 87–100.
Ward, Martha, ed., *Authors of Books for Young People* (3rd ed.). Scarecrow, 1990, p. 143.

---

**Dickinson, Peter.** *Eva*

Delacorte, 1989, $14.95 (0-385-29702-5); pap., Dell, $3.50 (0-440-20766-5)

---

In the world of contemporary English literature, Peter Dickinson has a dual personality because he writes both highly acclaimed adult thriller-fantasies and equally exciting books for young adults. In the former genre, his novel *The Poison Oracle* (o.p.) is an *Eva* in reverse. This mystery involves a scientist who is able to teach a chimpanzee to communicate with humans. Among his many books for junior high readers are the famous Changes Trilogy, an exciting fantasy series that chronicles the dire results of the accidental unearthing of the bones of Merlin the Magician. The individual titles are *The Devil's Children*, *Heartease*, and *The Weathermonger* (pap., Dell, $2.95 each). *Eva* is set in the unspecified future and covers a period of slightly more than two years—from Eva's awakening after an operation to her finding refuge on the island of St. Hilaire. There is a brief epilogue that takes place some twenty years later. Each chapter begins with a few stream-of-consciousness lines that express Eva's inner feelings. Better readers in grades 7 through 12 find this novel intriguing.

**Plot Summary**

Eva's first stirrings of consciousness after the operation involve hearing the sound of her mother's voice explaining that the chimpanzees had got loose in the car after the picnic, causing a terrible accident in which her parents had escaped unharmed but she had suffered terrible injuries. She also learns that the doctors plan to gradually reduce the drug-induced paralysis that has immobilized her entire body. First they allow

Eva to open her eyes and view the world beyond her hospital bed through a large overhead mirror. She sees in the distance the thousands of buildings where the half-billion people in her megalopolis live and work. In a few days she is allowed to move her left hand and manipulate a typewriter-like keyboard that not only produces the human words she wishes to speak but also can change emphasis and expression at command. For amusement, she uses the mirror to watch various zones on the shaper, a sophisticated descendant of television that immerses one in three-dimensional environments. She is, however, unable to erase a growing feeling of unease caused by the seeming strangeness of her body. Her hand feels smaller than before and, on looking downward, she is aware that she has no nose. Distraught, she begs that the overhead mirror be focused on her face and sees the face of Kelly, a young female chimpanzee that lived in her father's Chimpanzee Pool.

Eva's father is Dr. Dan Adamson, director of primate zoology and manager of the International Chimpanzee Pool, a complex of steel jungles that houses primates for observation and experimentation. Eva grew up in such close contact with chimpanzees that she is able to understand their thoughts and language. The outside world, however, has little respect for nature. Gradually the forests and other natural habitats have been destroyed to supply humans with material wealth. All of the large animals, such as elephants, have disappeared and there remain only a few isolated areas on earth with normal foliage and the remnants of wildlife. Humans' only experience of extinct natural phenomena comes through manufactured tapes played on the shaper. In order to save Eva's life, humans have committed the ultimate assault on the animal kingdom: transplanting a human brain into the body of a chimpanzee.

Adjusting to being in the body of a chimpanzee causes Eva some problems, but gradually her new body takes over and she begins walking in a knuckling fashion as well as climbing and swinging from objects like a true chimp. She gets to know the many medical assistants in the hospital, including the leader of the project, Dr. Joan Pradesh, a specialist in neuron memory.

Eva learns that her many operations and lengthy stay in the hospital (almost eight months) have been sponsored jointly by a shaper company, called SMI, and World Fruit, producers of the popular Honeybear drink. To help pay these expenses she will be required to appear on shaper programs and commercials. For the first of these she is dressed in a pair of overalls with a butterfly design created by her mother on the left pocket. The host is a condescending talk-show veteran named Dirk Ellan. At the end of a demeaning interview, Eva gets her revenge by grabbing Mr. Ellan and planting a loud kiss on his cheek.

When she returns home from the hospital, Eva's life becomes a media nightmare. The doorbell rings incessantly and their apartment building is continually filled with reporters and shaper cameras. In desperation, Dr. Adamson signs a long-term exclusive rights contract with SMI and World Fruit that will allow some privacy for Eva and some additional grants for his financially pressed pool. But Eva is not happy. She feels humiliated being forced to do shaper commercials with a group of chimpanzees for whom she feels both empathy and pity. School is unsatisfying and her bodyguard, Cormac, is a nuisance. Only Grog (Giorgio) Kennedy, the son of her volatile shaper director Mimi Venturi, seems to understand her misery and loneliness.

After a fiery argument with her parents, Eva is allowed to visit the pool alone. Here she first watches the activities of the chimps, then, in time, begins communicating with them through voice and gesture. Finally the group accepts her, albeit tentatively, as a member. For the first time in months, she is at peace with herself and life around her. Of all the chimps, she becomes particularly intrigued with a young male named Sniff, who though a loner seems more intelligent than the rest. Grog becomes aware of these visits and, convinced that Eva will be happy only with her fellow chimps, tries to devise a plan to transport Eva and her friends to one of the few remaining natural environments left on earth.

Two further brain transplants by Dr. Pradesh fail and Eva is so outraged at this useless exploitation of animal life that, using her language keyboard, she publicly denounces her surgeon during a shaper press conference. She tears to shreds her overalls with the embroidered butterfly, the symbol of her dwindling contact with humankind, before running offstage.

Animal rights activists, many of whom are either ego-tripping or seeking financial rewards, begin to support Eva. Their logo becomes a butterfly torn in two. Grog hatches a plan to take advantage of the situation. He persuades SMI and World Fruit to transport Eva and twenty other chimps to St. Hilaire, a deserted island off the coast of Madagascar that was once owned by World Fruit. There they will be photographed living at one with nature, thus assuaging the consciences of all concerned. Secretly, however, Eva and Grog hope that she and some of the chimps will be able to escape and stay behind when the party leaves.

As planned, Eva and her friends, including Sniff, arrive at St. Hilaire and are placed in a large compound surrounded by an electrified fence. Hidden cameras are placed on surrounding hills and Eva periodically visits the media crews and her father, who has accompanied the expedition.

A fierce typhoon hits the island and the electric current is broken. Eva uses this opportunity to assemble two females, their two babies, and Sniff. Together they make a perilous escape from the compound into the neighboring mountains, narrowly escaping being swept away in the swollen rivers and being killed by falling tree branches.

When the typhoon subsides and news of the escape spreads, Eva becomes the object of another media event. The sky above their hiding place is filled with airships and helicopters eager to spot their quarry. The activists, including Grog, also appear in an airship bearing the broken butterfly symbol and the message "The World's on Your Side, Eva." SMI and World Fruit, fearful of adverse publicity, capitulate. At a conference that Eva attends on the island, an agreement is reached that all the chimps in the pool will be allowed to live on the island provided that shaper crews will be allowed in occasionally for filming. Eva and her friends have triumphed.

In an epilogue that takes place twenty years later, Eva lies dying of old age surrounded by her children and other members of the chimpanzee colony. A group of scientists from the pool arrive on one of their periodic visits. The news from the outside is discouraging. Many humans, unable to cope with the rampant nihilism in the world, are committing mass suicide. Eva's reply, using the antiquated keyboard of her youth, is only that she and her group are grateful to be left alone to live by nature's laws. When the humans depart, her followers carry her on a litter that she has constructed into the woods, where one by one they touch a part of her body as a farewell gesture.

### Thematic Material

With flawless detail, the author has created a nightmarish future world governed by greed, ambition, and selfishness. Central to this decline is the growing exploitation of all forms of life by humans intent only on immediate gratification of needs. Humans are depicted as unable to see outside themselves or realize that humanity is only part of a larger natural world. As the epilogue points out, the inevitable consequence of this egocentrism is nihilism and eventual self-destruction. The dehumanizing effects of technology, the dangers of mass media unleashed without control, and the increasing decline of ethics and respect for human dignity form other important themes. The reader not only learns a great deal about the life-styles of chimpanzees but also learns to admire their behavior and respect for each other. The rights of animals and the consequences of ecological indifference are also well-developed themes. The reader will also empathize with the courageous Eva and her struggle to find peace in two conflicting worlds.

**Book Talk Material**

An explanation of the unusual operation Eva has undergone should interest young readers. Specific passages are: Eva awakes (pp. 5–10); Eva sees herself in the mirror (pp. 14–17); with the help of Robbo, a physiotherapist, she tries to use her new body (pp. 33–38); the shaper interview with Dirk Ellan (pp. 49–53); Eva gets permission to visit the pool (pp. 84–86); and her first visit with the chimpanzees (pp. 89–95).

**Additional Selections**

Thirteen-year-old Laurel is fearful that her father, a parapsychologist, will exploit her amazing psychic gifts in his experiments in Wilanne Schneider Belden's *Mind-Find* (Harcourt, 1987, $14.95). Another recommended novel by this author is *Mind-Hold* (Harcourt, 1987, $14.95), about the adventures of a young girl with the power of extrasensory perception and her brothers.

In a world almost completely unpopulated because of pollution and nuclear accidents, two teenagers discover one another in Caroline Macdonald's *The Lake at the End of the World* (Dial, 1989, $12.95).

After a nuclear war, a woman scientist and her daughter survive with the help of a pack of wolves in Whitley Strieber's *Wolf of Shadows* (Knopf, 1985, $9.95).

Willow is convinced that she lived before as a girl in ancient Egypt in this novel about reincarnation, *Sisters, Long Ago* (Dutton, 1990, $13.95) by Peg Kehret.

In *2041* (Delacorte, 1991, $16), Jane Yolen has selected twelve short stories by important science fiction writers that depict a vision of life on earth fifty years from now.

Ann Burton thinks she is the only person alive after the nuclear holocaust, but to her dismay she learns otherwise in Robert C. O'Brien's *Z for*

*Zachariah* (Atheneum, 1974, $13.95; pap., $3.95; condensed in *More Juniorplots*, Bowker, 1977, pp. 37–40).

In Louise Lawrence's *Andra* (Harper, 1991, $14.95), a part of the brain of a seventeen-year-old boy, who died in 1987, is grafted into Andra's brain 2,000 years later.

**About the Book**
*Book Report*, May 1989, p. 43.
*Booklist*, May 1, 1989, p. 1546.
*Center for Children's Books Bulletin*, May 1989, p. 220.
*Horn Book*, July 1989, p. 487.
*Kirkus Reviews*, February 1, 1989, p. 207.
*New York Times Book Review*, October 8, 1989, p. 34.
*School Library Journal*, April 1989, p. 118.
*VOYA*, June 1989, p. 115.
See also *Book Review Digest*, 1989, pp. 404–5; and *Book Review Index*, 1989, p. 212.

**About the Author**
Chevalier, Tracy, ed., *Twentieth-Century Children's Writers* (3rd ed.). St. James, 1989, pp. 287–89.
Commire, Anne, ed., *Something about the Author*. Gale, 1990, Vol. 62, pp. 23–32.
de Montreville, Doris, and Crawford, Elizabeth D., eds., *Fourth Book of Junior Authors and Illustrators*. Wilson, 1978, pp. 117–18.
Kinsman, Clare D., *Contemporary Authors* (First Revision). Gale, 1974, Vols. 41–44, p. 162.
Kirkpatrick, D. L., ed., *Twentieth-Century Children's Writers* (2nd ed.). St. Martin's, 1983, pp. 243–45.
Ward, Martha, ed., *Authors of Books for Young People* (3rd ed.). Scarecrow, 1990, pp. 184–85.

---

**Forrester, John.** *Bestiary Mountain*
Bradbury, 1985, $11.95 (0-02-735530-6)

---

John Forrester's trilogy on the struggle between the Round Beast of Old Earth and the Forbidden Beast of Luna begins with *Bestiary Mountain*, continues in *The Secret of the Round Beast* (Macmillan, 1986, $13.95; pap., Harper, $2.75), and concludes in *The Forbidden Beast* (Macmillan, 1988, $12.95; pap., Harper, $3.50). All three deal with a universe peopled by descendants of those who fled Earth. In *Bestiary Mountain,* four teenagers from the moon battle a group of human-animal hybrids to find the geneticist of Old Earth. This series is intended for junior high readers.

**Plot Summary**

This opening volume of the Bestiary Trilogy begins more than a century after the chemical wars of the 2130s have destroyed civilization and wrapped Old Earth in poisonous clouds. Humankind now lives on Luna, their existence controlled by the Overones. Such things as feelings for plants and animals must be watched closely, a result of the wars that came after genetic engineering had given minds and hands to animals. Now the last remaining plant and animal species are kept in zoos lest they ever rise again.

All life is strictly watched and controlled. The sixteen-year-old twins, Tamara and Drewyn Langstrom, are well aware of this. Drewyn will soon graduate from Spaceforce training and be sent to far moonside for two years of right-think instruction. He has qualified to become an officer and he will spend his life flying and fighting laser wars. Tamara will be enrolled in the guardian school, separate from the "ordinary" boys and girls and destined to become a political ruler. Tamara and Drewyn are closely watched but so far they have been able to keep secret their meetings with their outlaw father, Ryland Langstrom, living on lunar orbiting Island V. Dr. Langstrom has told the twins of his plans for all of them to return to Old Earth, even though the Overones claim nothing can be alive on the abandoned planet. However, fifteen years earlier, the twins' mother, Tava, left her husband and children for the journey to Earth to study and keep alive the animals and human-animal hybrids. No one knows if she survived the journey.

Plans for the proposed trip to Earth are hastily triggered by the Overones' discovery that Tamara and her boyfriend, Jaric, have been exchanging secret and forbidden messages. They decide to leave immediately, but Tamara insists that Jaric and her dormpound-mate, Saraj, accompany them. The Overones try to stop them and Dr. Langstrom is captured. The twins, with Jaric and Saraj, must take off without him.

As the four head for Earth, the twins notice changes in Jaric, probably the result of his interrogations by the Overones. They also discover the startling fact that Saraj is not human at all, but a robot. This is especially disturbing to Drewyn, who loves her. It would have been even more disturbing if the twins realized that Saraj was programmed to spy on them.

After days of space travel, the foursome lands on the abandoned planet Earth, where they discover that the air is breathable. Their first trial is an attack by hungry wolves that surround the spaceship. Their landing has also been noticed by Gorid Malcolm Hawxhurst, who had escaped from the moon ten years before. His work is the antithesis of the work of the twins' mother. She wants to preserve the Earth's old species; Gorid wants to create new types to hunt and kill.

Gorid heads to Bestiary Mountain, where Dr. Tava Langstrom lives and works in the company of Kana, half human, half cat. Kana is guardian of Bestiary Mountain and of Tava, living in a lonely world with no other of his kind and growing more restless because he depends more and more on her friendship and love.

Gorid tells Tava that her children have landed on Earth but in his territory. He will spare them if she turns over to him her laboratories and her work, including her masterpiece Kana, as well as the key to the chamber of the Round Beast, where Tava goes to be restored in spirit.

Tava decides it is time to think like a warrior. If she succeeds in rescuing her children and destroying Gorid, the animals will have Old Earth back again—and who knows where evolution might go this time.

In a fight with one of Gorid's creatures, Saraj is badly wounded, but the four are rescued by Tava and Kana flying in a 200-year-old helicopter. Tava is overjoyed to see her children and takes all of them back to Bestiary Mountain. There the twins learn that Tava and Kana run the mountain stronghold with the help of a master computer and the Round Beast. They are told that Tava has spent these fifteen years trying to produce breeding pairs of all the animals whose cells she and the twins' father had stored. She created Kana out of a lynx and growth hormone, even though it was forbidden to mix human genes with other species. Tava is aware of the strength of the bond between Kana and herself, although the notion is unsettling to her.

Because Saraj is badly wounded, she is taken into the chamber of the Round Beast. As she rests in darkness, she hears a warm voice comforting her. The Round Beast tells her to call up the image of the Overone designer that created her. The Overone tells her to keep watching, although Saraj declares that she loves Tamara and Drewyn and will not spy on them.

While Saraj is in the chamber of the Round Beast, Kana is guarding the restless Jaric. Increasingly unhappy because Saraj is learning the secrets of the Round Beast when Tava has never allowed him in that presence, Kana confides in Jaric and shows him a small transmitter that he has hidden in the mountain. Gorid had said, "Stay up on that mountain as long as you can stand it, Kana, but when you're ready for a real life—an interesting life—hit the code, that's all you've got to do." Kana had never believed he would do it, but now he is convinced that Tava no longer needs him, that she has her human children, that his dream of a new life with her is over. All he need do, Gorid told him, is to hit the code.

In the meantime, walking slowly on the mountain are Tava and the twins. She speaks of their life together on Bestiary Mountain and the contributions they all can make to her work. She says that she realizes how lonely life has been for Kana, but with the twins here, they will all have a new future.

Let us go and talk to Kana now, Tava tells them. I want all of you to know the whole story of the Round Beast—how he came to be, how he creates himself now, and the future he sees for us all.

So ends the first volume of the Bestiary Trilogy.

**Thematic Material**

This is a serious look at some of the concerns voiced about advances in genetic engineering and about mind control. The author looks at some interesting questions. What is Tava's responsibility toward the creature Kana, whom she has created? How can Drewyn deal with his feelings of love for Saraj, whom he now knows to be a robot?

**Book Talk Material**

The feelings of Kana, half human, half cat, make a provocative introduction to this science fiction adventure (see pp. 2–4; 100–3). Also of interest are the controls imposed by the Overones: see the attitudes toward plants and animals (pp. 6–7); Tamara is questioned about an illegal transmission (pp. 23–24); and Saraj meets her designer (pp. 44–49).

**Additional Selections**

In *Exiles of ColSec* by Douglas Hill (pap., Bantam, 1986, $2.95), six teenagers survive the crash of their spaceship. Two sequels are *The Caves of Klydor* (pap., Bantam, 1987, $2.95) and *Colsec Rebellion* (pap., Bantam, 1989, $2.95).

A fantasy trilogy popular with readers is the Darkangel series by Meredith Ann Pierce involving Aeriel and her former darkangel friend's plot to overthrow the evil White Witch Oriencor. The last in this series is *The Pearl of the Soul of the World* (Little, Brown, 1990, $15.95).

In *Beyond the Labyrinth* (Orchard, 1990, $14.95) by Gillian Rubinstein, a fourteen-year-old misfit and his friend Vicky meet an extraterrestrial who has come to Australia to find the ancient natives.

On planet Ceti, Maya and a teenage friend set out to unravel the mystery of the sudden disappearance of some children in *The Face of Ceti* (Houghton, 1991, $14.95) by Mary Caraker.

In Monica Hughes's *The Keeper of the Isis Light* (Macmillan, 1981, $11.95), a sixteen-year-old girl's lonely existence on the planet Isis comes to an end when settlers arrive.

Lissa joins an institute monitoring messages from outer space in George Zebrowski's *The Stars Will Speak* (pap., Harper, 1987, $2.95).

Earth is dominated by creatures from another planet who believe in mind over emotions in John Rowe Townsend's *The Creatures* (Harper, 1980, $12.95).

**About the Book**
*Booklist,* November 15, 1985, p. 482.
*Center for Children's Books Bulletin,* January 1986, p. 85.
*School Library Journal,* January 1986, p. 73.
*VOYA,* April 1986, p. 40.
See also *Book Review Digest,* 1986, p. 538; and *Book Review Index,* 1985, p. 212, and 1986, p. 254.

---

**Gilmore, Kate.**  *Enter Three Witches*
Houghton, 1990, $13.95 (0-395-50213-6); pap., Scholastic, $3.95 (0-590-44494-8)

---

Kate Gilmore has combined magic and first love in this story of Bren a boy who is beset with problems from two groups of three witches. At home there are genuine witches—his mother, grandmother, and a boarder—and at school there are three theatrical witches from the school production of *Macbeth* for which he is doing the lighting. Both sets bring problems for Bren and laughter for the readers in this satisfactory blend of the real and the fantastic, which is enjoyed by readers in grades 6 through 10.

**Plot Summary**

Teenager Bren West admits that, on the whole, his life isn't bad. True, his mother and father are separated, but they are on friendly terms and he sees his father often. Bren attends a small private school, which he likes, on the west side of Manhattan, New York City. His best friend is Eli, unless you count Bren's dog, Shadow, a Newfoundland of heroic proportions and a champion Frisbee player. Bren lives in a somewhat shabby but comfortable building not far from Central Park, with his mother, Miranda West; his grandmother, Rose; the formidable Louise LaReine, who rents the basement apartment; and a Siamese cat called Luna. Unconventional, perhaps, but not all that unusual or disturbing, except, of course, for the fact that his mother, Miranda, is a witch. So is his grandmother—and the basement tenant practices black magic all day.

Bren has long known that his mother is a witch, just as he knows that her gift, so to speak, is the cause of his parents' separation. Although his father and mother still love each other, his father admits that he finally just got tired of spells and of toads and pythons turning up in odd places and at unexpected moments. Such things have never really bothered Bren, who has always found the antics of his mother and grandmother somewhat amusing. For instance, he has never really been distressed by the fact that his mother can make him hear her summoning him in his head. It is somewhat disconcerting, but it has never been a problem—until now.

For now Bren has met *the* girl. She is a thin wisp named Erika, who dances like a dream and has been cast as one of the witches in the fall school production of *Macbeth*. Suddenly, Bren becomes very interested in joining Eli, who is in charge of lighting for the production. Erika seems to be interested in Bren, too, but soon becomes puzzled by his lack of enthusiasm about talking about his home life or inviting her to his house. Yet, Bren reasons, how can you invite a girl home when your mother might be doing a little conjuring and summoning in her studio tower? His problem is not helped when his mother asks him to snitch a frog from his biology lab because she needs it to whip up a special spell for someone.

The road to love proves bumpy but Bren makes some progress, inviting Erika to accompany him to Greenwich Village for the annual Halloween parade spectacle. Erika is fairly new to New York, having arrived recently with her wealthy and busy father, whom she seldom sees. The two teenagers lose themselves in the fun of the spectacle until—to Bren's horror—there marching down the street in the midst of the paraders comes a lone, dignified figure dressed from head to toe in a black robe adorned by a girdle of golden serpents. No one in the crowd can doubt that she is a genuine witch, even Erika. But Bren sees only that this preposterous figure is his mother. He is horrified. Without thinking, he darts off into the crowd, leaving Erika lost and angry.

Bren's attempts to explain his weird behavior to Erika fall on closed ears. However, one day while Erika is walking past some shops in the city, she sees an advertisement for crystal ball readings and recognizes the address of the fortune-teller (Rose) as Bren's. She goes to the house and "gets a reading" from Bren's grandmother and then meets his mother. Now Erika understand's Bren's peculiar behavior, and she is enchanted, figuratively speaking. During the meeting, Bren's mother asks Erika to get her three seats in the balcony for the opening night of *Macbeth*. Erika says she can't because the balcony is closed and will be unused that night. Miranda tells her just to dance and say her lines; she will take care of the rest.

Bren returns home and groans at the sight of Erika with his family, but she assures him that it is all amazing and wonderful. "Did you think I was some kind of nitwit who wanted everything to be like a TV cereal commercial?" she asks.

Before the opening night of *Macbeth*, Bren discovers that his father is "seeing someone." He meets the woman, named Alia, and recognizes what his father has not: that she, too, is a witch. Bren reasons that his father must be attracted subconsciously to witches. It appears that the confrontation between his mother and Alia, which Bren feared at the opening night of *Macbeth*, will not take place because Alia is ill.

The opening night performance is fantastic—in fact, it might be said to be somewhat out of this world. The whole production is spectacular. The tempest roars and the air crackles with blue light. To Bren, it is as though the entire lighting has been taken out of his hands. When the director compliments Erika on her performance, she says, "I didn't do anything. It just happened . . . and it scared me out of my wits."

Later Erika confesses to Bren, "It was almost as if someone or something was working on the play in a supernatural way. I know this sounds far-fetched. I don't suppose it's even the kind of thing she could do, but well, you know what I'm thinking." Indeed, Bren does know. It looks like mother was just being—mother.

At the party after the performance, Alia arrives unexpectedly and the two witches meet. Bren helps his father to see the truth, and his father agrees that he really should make a choice or there will never be any peace. His choice is Miranda. It looks as though the West family will be reunited again, and if not normal, life may be at least a little more conventional.

Alia, however, does not take defeat so easily and Bren sees that a test of wills between two witches is coming up. When Alia is about to attack his mother with a strange shaft of wood, Bren saves the day and earns a witch's curse in so doing. Bren laughs off the curse, reasoning that he has his mother on his side.

He also has Erika on his side, and that's the best of all.

### Thematical Material

This is a tale of witchcraft set in modern-day life in a modern-day city and touched with humor. The characters are believable, as is Bren's acceptance of the fact that his mother and grandmother are witches. He reacts to his household in the same way another teenager might react to the fact that one of his parents might, on occasion, drink too much. Bren comes off as a likable young man going through the agonies of first love, with an added twist. Bren's relationships with his mother and father are nicely and realistically drawn.

### Book Talk Material

The humor in this tale stems from the unusual "witch activities" that go on in an otherwise conventional setting. See: Bren's father comes to dinner (pp. 8–15); Miranda tries a little conjuring but lacks a frog (pp. 30–33); Miranda and the basement tenant fiddle with recipes (pp. 54–56); Bren's father tells him about the night he brought his business associates home to dinner (pp. 61–63); and Miranda summons Bren "in his head" at a most inopportune time (pp. 73–74).

### Additional Selections

In a haunted house, a young teenager encounters the ghost of a Puritan girl wrongfully hanged as a witch in Gilbert B. Cross's *Witch across Time* (Atheneum, 1990, $14.95).

After her parents' death, Anthea resents having to live with messy relatives and cope with visits from her grandfather's ghost in Margaret Mahy's *Dangerous Spaces* (Viking, 1991, $12.95). Kate must become a witch to save her brother in *The Changeover*, a taut supernatural thriller by the same author (Atheneum, 1984, $12.95; pap., Scholastic, $2.95; condensed in *Juniorplots 3*, Bowker, 1987, pp. 132–37).

Behind-the-scenes tension and trauma in a local amateur theater presentation are recalled by a teenage member of the cast in the English novel *Happy Endings* (Harcourt, 1991, $14.95) by Adele Geras.

In *The Dog Days of Arthur Cane* (Holiday, 1976, $13.95) by T. Ernesto Bethancourt, Arthur literally leads a dog's life.

A beautiful girl who is really a witch demands her lover's life in Louise Lawrence's *The Earth Witch* (Harper, 1981, $12.89).

In Diane Duane's *So You Want to Be a Wizard* (Delacorte, 1982, $14.95; pap., Dell, $2.95), Nita and another wizard in training embark on a journey.

**About the Book**
*Booklist*, May 15, 1990, p. 1446.
*Center for the Children's Books Bulletin*, May 1990, p. 159.
*Horn Book*, January 1990, p. 255.
*Kirkus Reviews*, May 1, 1990, p. 341.
*School Library Journal*, April 1990, p. 139.
*VOYA*, April 1990, p. 29.
See also *Book Review Digest*, 1990, p. 669; and *Book Review Index*, 1990, p. 301.

---

**Heinlein, Robert A.**   *Tunnel in the Sky*
Macmillan, 1988, $15.95 (0-684-18916-X)

---

In addition to his prize-winning adult novels, Robert A. Heinlein wrote twelve science fiction tales for young adults. Another of his young adult titles recently reissued by Scribner is the 1957 *Citizen of the Galaxy* (1987, $14.95; condensed in *Juniorplots*, Bowker, 1967, pp. 160–62). It tells about Thorby's search for justice and the identity of his parents in a group of outer planets known as the Nine Worlds. The hero of *Tunnel in the Sky*, first published in 1955, is Rod Walker, a young man who is transported to an uninhabited planet as part of a survival course. Both novels are enjoyed by junior and senior high school readers.

**Plot Summary**
In a time somewhere in the future, Rod Walker and his classmates travel to other planets as twentieth-century people once traveled to other

countries. As the story opens, Rod is getting ready for his final exam. He, his classmates, and strangers from other schools will be transported, one at a time, to a planet that is uninhabited. In order to pass this exam, they must survive for a period of from two to ten days, until they are recalled to the exit gate.

Rod is taking this test to qualify to study for an Outlands profession in college. He wants to be an explorer, like his instructor Doctor Matson, even though Matson tells Rod not to take this course. The professor feels Rod is too romantic, not practical enough to survive. Annoyed, Rod insists on going ahead.

When Rod goes home the night before the test, he finds that his sister Helen, ten years older and an assault captain in the Amazons, is home on a rare visit. He learns from her that their father has a degenerative disease from which he will surely die. His parents are opting for an out-of-time jump, leaving this world for a twenty-year period, which will seem like two weeks to them, in the hope that during that period a cure for his condition will be found. Helen also gives Rod her pet knife, Lady Macbeth, to take on his solo test.

Rod is transported to a place with earthlike gravity. Almost at once he sees an animal that looks very much like a lion, except that it seems about eight times larger than any lion he has ever seen. After he has survived for what he reckons to be at least an earth day, he becomes aware that he is being followed. He finds an area in which to rest; when he wakes up he realizes he has been hit over the head. His knife, his water, all his survival gear, everything except the shorts he is wearing is gone—everything except Helen's Lady Macbeth, hidden in a bandage.

Soon after, Rod meets another youngster, Jack Daudet, also on a survival test. They decide to team up and make their way to a cave Jack has found. Rod tells Jack that he thinks they are not on another planet at all, but instead on Earth. In fact, he thinks they are in Africa or South America. Jack says no, the stars in the sky are not the stars of Earth. He convinces Rod that they are on Mars. They are also convinced that they have missed the recall and are stranded on the planet.

Rod and Jack set out to see if they can find others and come upon Jimmy Throxton, who is in a comalike state. They nurse him back to health. When Jimmy is himself again, he informs a startled Rod that his pal Jack is a girl: Jacqueline Marie Daudet.

After that shock, the threesome begins the task of surviving in this strange place. Soon they run into two others, Bob Baxter and Carmen

Garcia. They burn a smoke signal to call in any other recruits who may still be roaming around. Pretty soon the cave is so crowded that they have to have girls' and boys' dormitories.

Now comes the hard work of keeping this large group together and surviving in this strange land. They find that they must hold elections to establish authority, and they must have laws to keep chaos to a minimum. Rod loses the election for mayor. The winner, Grant Cowper, soon has an official duty to perform—two group members wish to marry.

The next order of business is to draw up a constitution, but this soon degenerates into a squabble among different factions, some saying they have too many laws already.

Time passes in their strange land. Others marry, buildings are constructed, babies are born. In short, these young people set up their own civilization, called Cowperstown, and after Grant Cowper's death, Rod becomes the leader.

The ups and downs of this civilization continue until the day that members of the group are out scouting with Rod for a new location. Suddenly they see a stranger in coveralls and shoes. Rod turns to face an open gate and a long, closed corridor. They have been found by the Emigration Control Service. Rod is furious when given orders for their return to the life they have left. He intends to stay and he can't believe it when one by one members of the group begin to drift back.

When Rod meets his sister Helen and instructor Matson, he tells them he will not go back. He is happy with the new civilization they have built. Matson tells him that he knows it will be difficult for him to return, but that if he refuses to come back he must stay forever. If he returns, he will have to wear a boy's shoes again, but he will learn a lot that he does not yet know. Matson tells him that he realizes adolescents are neither adult nor child and that Rod has been leading the life of a leader. Still, it might pay for Rod to go back and learn.

Rod is not persuaded, until Helen tells him that their parents are back, their father cured. He decides to go home.

As Rod suspected and as Matson told him, it is very difficult to return to the life of a boy when he has been the leader of the civilization.

**Thematic Material**

This is a fast-paced science fiction adventure with the familiar theme of young people thrown into situations with which they must cope or be destroyed. All the facets and frustrations of adult civilization turn up when these teenagers try to construct a society of their own.

**Book Talk Material**

Some oddities of this future life make a good introduction to this science fiction tale. See: Rod goes home after school (pp. 13–25); the work of Dr. Ramsbotham (pp. 28–31); Rod and Helen talk about their parents and the survival test (pp. 39–46); and the survival test begins (pp. 56–70).

**Additional Selections**

The recent installment in Anne McCaffrey's hugely successful series, *Dragonsdown* (Ballantine, 1988, $18.95; pap., $4.95) tells the story of the early colonization of this earthlike planet. In *Juniorplots 3* (Bowker, 1987, pp. 178–81), there is a condensation of this author's earlier *Dragonsong* (Atheneum, 1976, $15.95; pap., Bantam, $3.50).

Three people from different times and places work together in the time-travel tale *Collidescope* (Bradbury, 1990, $14.95) by Grace Chetwin.

Twelve intriguing stories from Isaac Asimov's *Science Fiction Magazine* have been collected in *Why I Left Harry's All-Night Hamburgers* (Delacorte, 1990, $14.95), edited by Sheila Williams and Charles Ardai.

Kate and her astrophysicist grandfather try frantically to stop our sun by traveling to a distant star in *Heartlight* by T. A. Barron (Philomel, 1990, $15.95), a thoughtful science fiction adventure.

The two young sisters of Melne find that theirs is not the only colony on their planet in Lucy Cullyford Babbitt's *Children of the Maker* (Farrar, 1988, $13.95).

In Andre Norton's *The Time Traders* (pap., Ace, 1974, $1.95), Ross Murdock becomes part of an experiment that takes him through several levels of time.

Steve discovers that he and his friends are actually aliens from another world in Bernal C. Payne's *Experiment in Terror* (Houghton, 1987, $13.95).

**About the Author**

Chevalier, Tracy, ed., *Twentieth-Century Children's Writers* (3rd ed.). St. James, 1989, pp. 441–42.

Commire, Anne, ed., *Something about the Author*. Gale, 1976, Vol. 9, pp. 102–3.

Fuller, Muriel, ed., *More Junior Authors*. Wilson, 1963, pp. 109–10.

Kirkpatrick, D. L., ed., *Twentieth-Century Children's Writers* (2nd ed.). St. Martin's, 1983, pp. 367–68.
Metzger, Linda, and Straub, Deborah A., eds., *Contemporary Authors* (New Revision Series). Gale, 1987, Vol. 20, pp. 220–25.
Ward, Martha, ed., *Authors of Books for Young People* (3rd ed.). Scarecrow, 1990, p. 322.

---

**Jones, Diana Wynne.** *Castle in the Air*
Greenwillow, 1990, $12.95 (0-688-09686-7)

---

Although this book is labeled a sequel to *Howl's Moving Castle* (Greenwillow, 1986, $12.95; condensed in *Juniorplots 3*, Bowker, 1987, pp. 170–71), it can be read quite independently of the first volume. Two of the characters from the first book, Sophie and the Wizard Howl, do make an appearance late in the second, but a knowledge of their former adventures is not necessary. *Castle in the Air* is the story of Abdullah, his pursuit of lady love Flower-in-the-Night, and the constant help he receives from a tired but loyal magic carpet. This book is a charming mixture of magic, humor, adventure, and romance and is enjoyed by readers in both junior and senior high school.

**Plot Summary**

Far away in the Sultanates of Rashpuht in the city of Zanzib lives a young carpet merchant named Abdullah. He was not left much money when his father died, only enough to buy a modest carpet booth in the northwest corner of the bazaar. The rest of the money went to the relatives of his father's first wife, none of whom Abdullah likes very much, especially as they visit him and annoy him at least once a month.

Abdullah's father left him only a small fortune because he was disappointed in his son. Abdullah is not sure why, but it has something to do with a prophecy made at his birth. A handsome and rather good young man, Abdullah is given to daydreams. In most of them he is the long-lost son of a great prince.

One day a tall, rather dirty-looking man stops at Abdullah's booth and offers to sell him a worn-looking piece of carpet for an astounding price. The stranger says the carpet is magic. Abdullah has heard all this before, but nonetheless, when the man demonstrates that the carpet does indeed rise two feet in the air at his command, they settle on a price.

That night Abdullah goes to sleep on the carpet. He wakes to find himself still on the carpet in the most beautiful garden he has ever seen. He is sure he is dreaming, but no matter because he meets the most beautiful girl, Princess Flower-in-the-Night. She thinks Abdullah is a girl, too, because he is wearing a nightshirt and because she has never seen a man besides her father, who keeps her in virtual isolation and has betrothed her to the ugly Prince of Ochinstan. Abdullah, who gives the princess the impression that he too is a prince, promises to return the next night bringing her pictures of men so she can see that there are many different kinds.

Abdullah returns the next night on his carpet and convinces the princess that men do come in different varieties. She in turn says she will ask her father to let her marry Abdullah instead of the ugly Prince of Ochinstan. Abdullah doesn't mind at all, but he doesn't think her father will agree to such a proposal, especially when he finds out his true background.

Abdullah begins to have trouble with the magic carpet—it does not always do his bidding. Convinced that he can only be reunited with Flower-in-the-Night when he goes to sleep, he sells his best carpets so that he will have a small fortune to take to her—he thinks that by the next meeting she will have figured out a way for them to marry. By now Abdullah has realized that he is truly in love with the princess.

When Abdullah meets his princess once more and tells her to jump on the carpet beside him, a mighty creature, the flying djinn, drops out of the sky and grabs her. The carpet refuses his command to follow her.

Before Abdullah can recover from his grief, he is taken prisoner and brought before the sultan, father of Flower-in-the-Night, who wishes to know what Abdullah has done with his daughter. Before the sultan can kill him, Abdullah inadvertently admits that he and the princess did not have time to marry before she was abducted. This very much excites the sultan, who says that a prophecy at his daughter's birth said she would marry the first man she saw apart from her father, which is why he brought her up as he did. Now Abdullah must be spared to fulfill the prophecy—at least until he gets the princess back, for one must not fight a prophecy. Then the sultan can kill Abdullah.

Abdullah manages to summon up the magic carpet and escape. Unfortunately, he lands in the desert practically in the arms of the world-famous bandit, the matchless Kabul Aqba. To save his life, Abdullah convinces the bandit that he is a magician and that the bottle one of his men has found contains a genie. And lo and behold, it does.

With a little luck and the help of the carpet and the genie, Abdullah manages to escape misfortune once again. He does have a little trouble with the genie, however, who insists he can grant only one wish fulfillment a day. When Abdullah asks to be transported to the side of his bride-to-be, the genie replies that he can't because she is nowhere on earth.

That means she must be in the realm of the djinns, reasons Abdullah. So Abdullah convinces the genie to transport him to the nearest person who can help him find Flower-in-the-Night. What he finds is an old soldier who looks like a ruffian. Instead of getting help from the soldier, Abdullah has to help the soldier by saving him from ambush.

This quite unlikely pair, along with the genie, team up to find the princess, Abdullah having enlisted the aid of the soldier by promising him the hand of a princess for himself. Along the way they meet a cat. Abdullah is not fond of cats, although the soldier is, but this cat has an interesting habit of turning itself into a great beast whenever it is crossed. With this in mind, Abdullah consents to the cat's accompanying them, and she is called Midnight.

Through some very tricky and merry adventures, Abdullah and the soldier and Midnight meet up with Hasruel, brother to the djinn who stole Flower-in-the-Night. It was Hasruel who, almost as a cruel joke, sold the magic carpet to Abdullah in the first place because he knew about the strange prophecy at Abdullah's birth: It merely said that Abdullah would rise above the rest.

Hasruel's brother, Dalzel, is a cruel djinn who has Hasruel under his power and has ordered him to steal every princess in the world, since Dalzel is about to marry. Flower-in-the-Night must be in his cruel clutches.

Once in Dalzel's floating palace, Abdullah and the soldier do find an astounding number of princesses, including the lovely Flower-in-the-Night. They all conspire to break the spell that the cruel Dalzel has over his brother. When they succeed and Hasruel is about to send his brother away, out of his sight forever for his meanness, Dalzel breaks down and cries because he is going to be so lonely. Enter Abdullah's two fat nieces, the only members of his family left behind when the rest left to escape the wrath of Flower-in-the-Night's father. Wonder of wonders, Dalzel is enchanted with both of them! The loneliness problem is solved!

That is not all. The soldier turns out to be Prince Justin; he was enchanted, too. Now he will marry Princess Beatrice.

The wedding of the prince and princess and Abdullah and Flower-in-the-Night is quite a grand affair. (She knew all the time that he was not really a prince.) Although the sultan gives them land to build a palace in the Chipping Valley, they actually build rather a modest house with a thatched roof—and the most beautiful gardens in the world.

**Thematic Material**

A delightfully wacky fantasy filled with prophecies that are fulfilled, tantalizing twists and turns, magic carpets and lovely princesses, and all manner of surprises. An action-packed, fun-filled, humorous, impossible adventure on a grand scale.

**Book Talk Material**

A number of amusing incidents will make a delightful introduction to this charming fantasy. See: Abdullah meets the seller of the magic carpet (pp. 4–10); Abdullah and the princess discuss whether he is a woman (pp. 12–16); Abdullah tries to get the carpet to fly (pp. 21–23); the prophecy is read (pp. 31–38); Abdullah becomes the sultan's prisoner (pp. 42–47).

**Additional Selections**

The four friends introduced in *The Blade of the Poisoner* (McElderry, 1987, $13.95; pap., Bantam, $2.95) set out to rescue the wizard that has been imprisoned by an evil demon in *Master of Fiends* (McElderry, 1987, $13.95), both by Douglas Hill.

Wizard Merlin's dreams while he is buried alive under a huge stone form the basis for nine unusual stories set in Arthurian times in Peter Dickinson's *Merlin Dreams* (Delacorte, 1988, $19.95).

An old woman and a mean-spirited gnome fight it out in a remote Australian farmhouse in Patricia Wrightson's *A Little Fear* (McElderry, 1983, $12.95; pap., Puffin, $3.95).

In James Cross Giblin's *The Truth about Unicorns* (Harper, 1991, $14.95), there is a collection of legend and lore about this mythical beast as recorded in Western history.

The half-human Percinet comes to the rescue of Graciosa when her father marries the evil Lady Eglantine in Josepha Sherman's *Childe of Fairie, Childe of Earth* (Walker, 1992, $14.95).

Louise Cooper's romantic fantasy *The Sleep of Stone* (Atheneum, 1991, $14.95) tells of the doomed love Ghysla feels for the prince. Princess Cimorene would rather take lessons in fencing and juggling than dancing and embroidery in Patricia C. Wrede's playful *Dealing with Dragons* (Harcourt, 1990, $15.95).

### About the Book

*Book Report,* September 1991, p. 49.
*Booklist,* May 15, 1991, p. 1503.
*Center for Children's Books Bulletin,* February 1991, p. 206.
*Horn Book,* May 1991, p. 206.
*Kirkus Reviews,* February 15, 1991, p. 249.
*School Library Journal,* April 1991, p. 141.
See also *Book Review Digest,* 1991, pp. 967–68; and *Book Review Index,* 1991, p. 471.

### About the Author

Commire, Anne, ed., *Something about the Author.* Gale, 1976, Vol. 9, pp. 116–18.
Evory, Ann, ed., *Contemporary Authors* (New Revision Series). Gale, 1981, Vol. 4, pp. 336–37.
Holtze, Sally Holmes, ed., *Fifth Book of Junior Authors and Illustrators.* Wilson, 1983, pp. 166–67.
May, Hal, and Lesniak, James G., eds., *Contemporary Authors.* Gale, 1989, Vol. 26, pp. 184–86.
Nakamura, Joyce, *Something about the Author: Autobiography Series.* Gale, 1989, Vol. 7, pp. 155–70.
Senick, Gerard J., ed., *Children's Literature Review.* Gale, 1991, Vol. 23, pp. 177–98.

---

**L'Engle, Madeleine.** *An Acceptable Time*
Farrar, 1989, $16.00 (0-374-30027-5); pap., Dell, $3.95 (0-440-20814-9)

---

This novel is both a continuation of the author's earlier Time Trilogy and a sequel to another novel about Polly O'Keefe. As a continuation, it complements novels like *A Wrinkle in Time* (Farrar, 1962, $15.95; pap., Dell, $3.50; condensed in *Juniorplots,* Bowker, 1967, pp. 188–90), in which Polly's mother, the then twelve-year-old Meg Murry, and her friend Calvin O'Keefe, her future father, first travel in time. It is also a sequel to *A House Like a Lotus* (Farrar, 1984, $16.95; pap., Dell, $3.50;

condensed in *Seniorplots*, Bowker, 1989, pp. 73–77), in which Polly, the central character, first meets Zachary Gray. This novel is somewhat more introspective and meditative than others by this author but it will be enjoyed by loyal L'Engle fans in both junior and senior high school.

**Plot Summary**

Red-headed, attractive Polly O'Keefe has been sent north from her parents' isolated island home off the coast of South Carolina to live in rural Connecticut with her grandparents, the eminent scientists Kate and Alex Murry, where she will complete high school. The Murrys live in a large rambling house complete with a small indoor swimming pool and an adjoining outbuilding that is used as a laboratory. It is late October and the extensive woods surrounding the house are alive with the colors of a New England autumn. One day, while walking in these woods, Polly is surprised to see by an ancient oak a young man dressed in a white tunic, with his dog. Suddenly they both disappear. Polly is alone for only a few moments before she is confronted by Zachary Gray, whom she had met the summer before in Athens, Greece. Zachary is an attractive, charming young college student who has been spoiled by immense family wealth and is inclined to be self-centered and shallow. He explains that he is involved in an internship semester with a law firm in nearby Hartford and has tracked Polly down to resume their friendship. They happen on a large black snake sunning itself. Zachary is terrified until Polly explains it is harmless and that it has already been nicknamed Louise the Larger by her grandmother, who saw it some days before. Polly takes Zachary to meet her grandparents and finds that they are entertaining two old friends from the neighborhood, Dr. Louise Colubra and her brother, Bishop Nason (Nase) Colubra. Both are widowed and now live together in a nearby farmhouse. Talk centers on the many ancient stones found on the Murry property inscribed with the Ogam script of primitive Celtic tribes that lived in the area about 3,000 years ago.

That evening, while swimming alone in the pool, Polly sees a young girl her age outside peering in. In her strange dress—a soft leather tunic and leggings—she appears to be from another era. Polly begins talking to her, but the girl is frightened and disappears into the night.

In the woods again the next day, Polly feels an unusual earth tremor and suddenly finds that she is in a different time period. The beautiful young girl from the night before approaches her and introduces herself as Anaral, a druid of the tribe known as the People of the Wind. She explains that their leader is peace-loving Karralys, the man whom Polly had seen the day before with his dog. He had arrived three years before, accompanied by a flaxen-haired warrior named Tav from a land across the ocean known as Britain. Both have assumed leadership roles in the tribe, Karralys as the chief religious leader and healer and Tav as the head of the warriors. Somehow, Polly has passed through a time gate, into an era 3,000 years before. She is surprised to see a very twentieth-century Band-Aid on one of Anaral's fingers. Anaral explains that Bishop Colubra visits the tribe and took her through the time threshold to see Dr. Louise after she cut her finger. Polly gathers that the good bishop has had many contacts with these people, even to the point of teaching them English, and Anaral tells Polly that she has been sent to them to fulfill some unknown purpose. After walking through the tribe's village on the banks of a lake, Polly finds herself back in the familiar woods of her grandparents.

Through conversations with the bishop, Polly learns more about this strange time-traveling phenomenon. It appears that the Murrys' home was built on grounds sacred to the druids of the People of the Wind and it was there, in their root cellar, that Nase was first transported into this distant time. Since then he has visited often, learned the Ogam language, and become a respected member of the tribe. However, complete freedom of passage is not possible, and sometimes he must wait weeks before the time gate opens as it did for Polly. He explains further that this time of year, around All Hallows' Eve, the druid festival of Samhain, it is particularly easy to enter for those the tribe wants to see. The bishop gives Polly his notebooks on Ogam to introduce her to the language.

Polly is fascinated by these occurrences and this ancient civilization but her grandparents are extremely apprehensive and caution Polly to stay out of the woods and resist any contact.

Zachary visits once more and confides in Polly his terrible secret. He has been diagnosed as having a degenerative heart disease and has only, at most, two years to live. He is terrified of death and is unable to accept what the doctors think is inevitable. Polly promises to speak to Dr. Louise about this but inwardly realizes it seems hopeless.

On different occasions, her three friends from the Ogam world come to visit. On one occasion, Tav comes; on another, Karralys; and on a third occasion, at the swimming pool, she is again transported back in time. She learns through these meetings that the tribe is threatened by a neighboring group called the People Across the Lake, who have experienced months of drought and are conducting raids on the People of the Wind in search of food and animals.

When Polly tells Zachary about her travels in time, he begs her to let him visit the People of the Wind, hoping that the legendary druid magic might help him overcome his physical problems. Reluctantly, she accompanies him through the time threshold. Within minutes of arriving at Karralys's village, they are engulfed in violence when the People Across the Lake attack. Polly is almost kidnapped but suddenly Louise the Larger slithers into view. The attackers flee in disarray, believing that the snake, whom they hold sacred, has been called up by this mysterious redheaded goddess. The bishop arrives to bring Polly and Zachary back to the present but, when they are unable to find the time gate, they realize that they are trapped, at least temporarily, in the past.

Two wounded raiders, Klep and Brown Earth, were left behind when their colleagues fled. Brown Earth secretly persuades Zachary to help him escape and accompany him across the lake, where, he maintains, a powerful medicine man in the tribe will heal him. Zachary agrees, but when he arrives at the village of the People Across the Lake, their leader, Tynak, denies him treatment until he brings the goddess Polly to their village. The next night, accompanied by warriors, he helps abduct Polly, who soon realizes that she is intended as a human sacrifice to bring rain to the drought-ridden area. With the guidance of Og, Karralys's dog, who has followed her to the village, she is able to escape and swim across the lake to safety. However, once there, she is striken with pangs of guilt because of abandoning Zachary, and with the help of Tav, Anaral, and Cub, a young healer in the tribe, she—along with Klep, who has vowed to bring peace to the warring tribes—returns to Tynak's village.

This time, she is taken prisoner by Tynak's men and is told that unless rain comes, she will be sacrificed two nights later during the festival of the full moon. Zachary is too preoccupied with his own condition to offer any help.

The fateful night arrives. Polly is being led to her execution when shouts of terror arise from the tribesmen. A war canoe from across the lake has arrived, carrying Karralys and Og, and in the prow Bishop Colubra, holding Louise the Larger aloft. Simultaneously, a torrential rain begins falling. Polly is released and Karralys and Tynak begin negotiating a peace treaty between the tribes. Zachary is so filled with remorse at his indifference toward Polly that he begs for death, but in an act of forgiveness and expiation, the medicine men from both tribes, along with Bishop Colubra and Polly, spread their hands over his heart in an act of healing. Back at the village, the three time travelers bid their friends good-bye, and accompanied by Og, return to the present and the arms of the welcoming Murrys and Dr. Louise.

### Thematic Material

This is a novel that explores the mysteries of the fourth dimension and the continuum of time. It also explores the eternal aspects of such qualities as truth and love (at one point in the novel, Bishop Colubra says, "Truth is eternal. Knowledge is changeable."). The similarities in purposes and beliefs found in various religions of the world are explored. Zachary's redemption illustrates the power of love to effect change and transcend the boundaries of time and space. The nature of healing and courage and the mysteries of science form important secondary themes.

### Book Talk Material

References to time travel and the author's earlier works will serve as a good introduction to this work. Some interesting passages are: Polly first sees Karralys and later Zachary and Louise the Larger are first introduced (pp. 3–12); Anaral comes to the swimming pool (pp. 27–29); Polly's first visit to the People of the Wind (pp. 43–53); her grandparents warn her against time travel (pp. 64–66); and two other journeys into the past (pp. 94–100 and 149–56).

### Additional Selections

H. M. Hoover, in *The Dawn Palace* (Dutton, 1988, $15.95), retells the story of Jason and Medea, a tale of romance, bloodshed, and violence.

At a Passover Seder, a twelve-year-old Jewish girl is transported in time to Poland during the Holocaust in Jane Yolen's *The Devil's Arithmetic* (Viking, 1988, $12.95; pap., Puffin, $3.95).

In Patricia Wrightson's *Balyet* (McElderry, 1989, $12.95), a fourteen-year-old Australian girl encounters the ghost of an aboriginal girl who has been working in the outback for a thousand years.

A high school junior wonders if the mysterious young man she meets at the pond is really a ghost in Jean Thesman's *Appointment with a Stranger* (Houghton, 1989, $13.95).

In ancient Scotland, rebellious Caitlin tries to learn the secret druid ways in Margaret J. Anderson's *The Druid's Gift* (Knopf, 1989, $13.95).

A walk in the woods brings Zan into an alternate world where she begins a dangerous quest in Beth Hilgartner's *Colors in the Dreamweaver's Loom* (Houghton, 1989, $14.95). Such subjects as the origin of life and the universe and the compatibility of religion and science are discussed in *Science and Religion: Opposing Viewpoints* (Greenhaven, 1988, $15.95), edited by Janelle Rohr.

**About the Book**
*Book Report,* May 1990, p. 47.
*Booklist,* January 1, 1990, p. 902.
*Center for Children's Books Bulletin,* December 1989, p. 87.
*Horn Book Guide,* July 1989, p. 84.
*New York Times Book Review,* March 25, 1990, p. 29.
*School Library Journal,* January 1990, p. 120.
*VOYA,* April 1990, p. 38.
See also *Book Review Digest,* 1990, pp. 1071–72; and *Book Review Index,* 1990, p. 481.

**About the Author**
Block, Ann, and Riley, Carolyn, eds., *Children's Literature Review.* Gale, 1976, Vol. 1, pp. 129–34.
Chevalier, Tracy, ed., *Twentieth-Century Children's Writers* (3rd ed.). St. James, 1989, pp. 571–73.
Commire, Anne, ed., *Something about the Author.* Gale, 1971, Vol. 1, pp. 141–42; updated 1982, Vol. 27, pp. 131–40.
Estes, Glenn E., ed., *American Writers for Children since 1960: Fiction* (Dictionary of Literary Biography: Vol. 52). Gale, 1986, pp. 241–49.
Ethridge, James M., ed., *Contemporary Authors* (First Revision). Gale, 1967, Vols. 1–4, pp. 582–83.
Evory, Ann, ed., *Contemporary Authors* (New Revision Series). Gale, 1981, Vol. 3, pp. 331–32.
Fuller, Muriel, ed., *More Junior Authors.* Wilson, 1963, pp. 137–38.
Garrett, Agnes, and McCue, Helga P., eds., *Authors and Artists for Young Adults.* Gale, 1989, Vol. 1, pp. 115–28.
Gonzales, Doreen, *Madeleine L'Engle: Author of "A Wrinkle in Time."* Dillon, 1991.
Kirkpatrick, D. L., ed., *Twentieth-Century Children's Writers* (2nd ed.). St. Martin's, 1983, pp. 467–69.
Senick, Gerard J., ed., *Children's Literature Review.* Gale, 1988, Vol. 14, pp. 132–57.
Straub, Deborah A., ed., *Contemporary Authors* (New Revision Series). Gale, 1987, Vol. 21, pp. 240–43.
Ward, Martha, ed., *Authors of Books for Young People* (3rd ed.). Scarecrow, 1990, p. 427.

**Sleator, William.** *The Duplicate*
Dutton, 1988, $12.95 (0-525-44390-8); pap., Bantam, $2.95 (0-553-28634-X)

In *The Duplicate*, the author explores the situation that results when a boy discovers a machine enabling him to clone himself. This is typical of the subjects handled by Sleator in which established scientific theories are applied in situations where conditions become extreme and uncontrollable. Other popular titles with similar themes by this author are: *Singularity* (Dutton, 1985, $12.95; pap., Bantam, $2.95; condensed in *Seniorplots*, Bowker, 1989, pp. 186–89), about twins who discover a playhouse where time proceeds at an alarmingly fast pace, and *House of Stairs* (Dutton, 1985, $14.95; pap., Puffin, $3.95; condensed in *More Juniorplots*, Bowker, 1977, pp. 43–46), in which the limits of human conditioning experiments are explored. These novels are popular with youngsters in grades 7 through 10 and older reluctant readers.

**Plot Summary**

For sixteen-year-old David, it is the impossible dream come true—at least at first. Annoyed because he has to join his parents in a visit to his grandmother when he really wants to be over at Angela's house, he takes to the beach to grumble about his plight. There he discovers the strangest object he has ever seen—a small, boxlike contraption with a lever and the words *Spee-Dee-Dupe* across the top.

Before David's astonished eyes, a gull jumps on the lever and seems to reproduce itself. Can this be what David suspects it is? He takes the box home to experiment. After some unsuccessful tries with inanimate objects, he uses his goldfish. It works. Now he has two goldfish swimming in the tank in his room. Does he dare try it on himself? He does, and another boy, who looks exactly like David, is suddenly in his room. Surely this is the answer to all David's problems. For instance, now he can go see Angela and send the duplicate off to Grandma's.

Almost from the start, however, there is trouble in paradise. First of all, David does not count on the fact that the duplicate thinks *David* is the duplicate. Since the duplicate is an exact copy of David, he thinks like him too, so the duplicate insists that *he*, not David, go to see Angela tonight. The problem is solved with a coin toss, which the duplicate wins, but that problem is just the beginning.

Only *one* David can go to school, of course, or to band practice, or to see Angela for that matter. Only *one* David can go down to breakfast or to dinner with his parents. Does the other starve? How are they going to explain to David's mother why he suddenly has twice as much laundry?

What seemed such a wonderful discovery in the beginning is starting to look just a little less so. Instead of making life easier and more fun, having an exact copy of himself—David later learns that the word for this is "bifurcation"—is making life more stressful and complicated. The most troubling aspect is the duplicate himself. He looks like David, to be sure, and he acts like him and he thinks like him, but perhaps the duplicate is just a shade different, a little nastier perhaps, a bit more devious.

When they run into too many complications with school and home and Angela, the duplicate shows David a secret hideout he has discovered. One of them can stay safely in the abandoned World War II army watchtower with a sleeping bag and some food. David hates the hideout and is afraid to stay there, but the duplicate convinces him that it is the solution to their predicament. He even takes the Spee-Dee-Dupe to the hideout for safekeeping.

Perhaps things will work out after all. Just as David is starting to relax back in his room at home, he suddenly notices that one of the goldfish now has a black mark behind his gills that wasn't there before. This fish is acting in a rather strange fashion, as though it is going crazy—if fish can go crazy, thinks David. Is the black-marked fish the original or the clone? What does the black mark mean?

When David returns to the watchtower hideout, he is nearly killed by the booby trap that must have been put there by the duplicate. David figures the duplicate is trying to get rid of him—and David has to agree that life would be much better if one of them were gone.

David confronts the duplicate about the booby trap, but the duplicate denies setting it up. He also denies writing on the tower wall the words that David discovers: "Life is hard. Then you die."

As though things are not confusing enough, that night David discovers something even more frightening. One of the goldfish is dead; the one with the black mark is still alive. David searches his own body but finds no black marks. To his shock, he later discovers black marks on the duplicate, which the duplicate seems not to notice. David reasons that the black marks must appear on whatever is the duplicate, the goldfish, for instance, and when that happens the duplicate goes crazy in some way and attempts to kill the other. What does this mean for David and his duplicate?

When David returns to the tower, he is in for another unpleasant surprise. Someone is already there, someone who looks almost exactly like David, but isn't the duplicate. That is, he isn't the original duplicate—Duplicate A. Apparently the duplicate himself tried out the Spee-Dee-Dupe. Now there is Duplicate B as well, and if Duplicate A is almost but just not quite like David, Duplicate B is just a little less so—a really rather unlikable fellow.

When Duplicate B begins to talk about killing Duplicate A to solve their now more complicated problems, David realizes he must come up with a plan. First, he paints fake black marks on his neck and hands. When Duplicate A arrives at the tower, David tries to enlist his aid against Duplicate B. Duplicate B meanwhile goes off to lure Angela to the beach and the deserted tower.

A terrible and confusing struggle occurs when David and the two duplicates and Angela confront each other. In a battle five stories up, Duplicate B pushes Duplicate A from the tower. Then he confronts David, saying David would not have the nerve to kill him. David tells the duplicate that the marks he has painted on are fake, that the duplicate has the real marks and they will eventually kill him. With Angela's help, David prods Duplicate B into a fall from the tower and he too dies.

David and Angela cover the bodies on the deserted beach. Three weeks later the bodies are still undiscovered and David reasons that the bifurcated bodies would have disintegrated by that time. He also thinks that the mysterious Spee-Dee-Dupe must have been made for short-term use; after that the duplicate's built-in self-destruct mechanism takes over. Without a self-destruct mechanism, David thinks, there could be several people in the world running around thinking they are the same person. Why the duplicates go crazy and why Duplicate B was so evil right from the beginning are questions no one can answer, but David feels especially bad about the death of Duplicate A. After all, David was responsible for creating him.

David and Angela decide they must get rid of the Spee-Dee-Dupe in any case. They can't risk trying to destroy it, since they have no idea what it contains, so they rent an outboard motor and sail far out to sea. They weight down the sack and dump the Spee-Dee-Dupe into the ocean. Will someone find it one day? Will someone else make duplicates as David did? What if the Spee-Dee-Dupe has a memory? What if someone tries to use it again and out spring Duplicate David A and B? What if—perhaps it's better not to think about it?

**Thematic Material**

This is a science fiction story that starts off "funny" and quickly turns into anything but. The idea of a clone who will do all the things the individual finds boring is certainly appealing, but from the very start the reader is confronted with the mundane problems of eating and dressing and hiding out that quickly turn a teenager's dream into a nightmare. This fast-paced tale of a likable young man whose crush on a girl turns his life upside down in a most unusual way will bring a smile to readers as well as a chill down the spine.

**Book Talk Material**

Finding the Spee-Dee-Dupe and making the first clones are good introductions to this sci-fi tale; see David finds the Spee-Dee-Dupe on the beach and the first "bifurcation" (pp. 3–5), and a new goldfish and a new David (pp. 6–9). Readers will also be interested in the "everyday" problems that crop up when you have a duplicate person; see sneaking the duplicate upstairs (pp. 18–22); who eats breakfast (pp. 29–32); and David talks to Angela about a conversation he didn't have with her brother (pp. 39–40).

**Additional Selections**

*Hong on the Range* by William F. Wu (Walker, 1989, $17.95) presents an unemployed narrator in this sci-fi spoof set in the American West during a future filled with cyborgs and partly mechanical cattle called "steerites."

Two Irish boys become the captives of a recluse intent on ruling the world in Ellis Dillon's *The Island of Ghosts* (Scribner, 1989, $13.95).

Janna is concerned about the strange power a totem pole wields over the life of her younger sister in Helen K. Passey's *Speak to the Rain* (Atheneum, 1989, $12.95).

There are four interrelated stories about life aboard an orbiting high school in the distant future in Stephen Bowkett's *Frontiersville High* (Gollancz, 1991, $17.95).

A computer game to rescue the kidnapped daughter of King Ulric the Fan becomes real for eighth-grader Arvin Rizalli in Vivian Vande Velde's *User Unfriendly* (Harcourt, 1991, $16.95).

In diary form, a young hero tells of his encounter with a time machine in *Journal of a Teenage Genius* (Greenwillow, 1987, $12.75; pap., Troll, $2.50) by Helen V. Griffith.

In Annabel Johnson's and Edgar Johnson's *The Danger Quotient* (Harper, 1984, $12.89; pap., $2.95; condensed in *Seniorplots*, Bowker, 1989, pp. 177–81) K/C-4, alias Casey, discovers his identity through time travel.

**About the Book**
*Book Report*, May 1991, p. 64.
*Booklist*, December 15, 1990, p. 866.
*Center for Children's Books Bulletin*, June 1985, p. 195.
*Horn Book*, May 1985, p. 320.
*School Library Journal*, August 1985, p. 82.
*VOYA*, April 1991, p. 74.
See also *Book Review Index*, 1991, p. 840.

**About the Author**
Chevalier, Tracy, ed., *Twentieth-Century Children's Writers* (3rd ed.). St. James, 1989, pp. 889–90.
Commire, Anne, ed., *Something about the Author*. Gale, 1972, Vol. 3, pp. 207–8.
Evory, Ann, ed., *Contemporary Authors* (First Revision). Gale, 1978, Vols. 29–32, p. 645.
Holtze, Sally Holmes, ed., *Fifth Book of Junior Authors and Illustrators*. Wilson, 1983, pp. 295–96.
Kinsman, Clare D., ed., *Contemporary Authors* (First Revision). Gale, 1972, Vols. 29–32, p. 585.
Roginski, Jim, ed., *Behind the Covers*. Libraries Unlimited, 1985, pp. 194–205.

# 4

---

# Historical Fiction

EXPLORING history through fiction brings the past to life for readers and helps them appreciate the continuity of time and civilizations. There are seven novels included in this section; four of them deal with various aspects of America's past and the remaining three with British history.

---

**Avi.**  *The True Confessions of Charlotte Doyle*
Orchard, 1990, $14.95 (0-531-05893-X)

---

Avi is a prolific and versatile author of books for young people. In addition to writing fast-paced thrillers like *Wolf Rider* (Bradbury, 1986, $14.95; pap., $2.95; condensed in *Seniorplots,* Bowker, 1989, pp. 232–36) and stories that deal with contemporary social issues like *A Place Called Ugly* (Pantheon, 1981, $8.99), he has a number of excellent historical novels to his credit. Two of these are *The Fighting Ground* (Lippincott, 1987, $12.95; pap., Harper, $3.50), which tells of one eventful day in the life of thirteen-year-old Jonathan when he marches off during the Revolution to fight the British, and *The Man Who Was Poe* (Orchard, 1989, $13.94; pap., Avon, $3.50), an engrossing story set in Providence, Rhode Island, during 1848 when a young boy named Edmund elicits the help of Edgar Allan Poe to find his missing sister. *The True Confessions of Charlotte Doyle,* a Newbery Honor book, is a rousing sea adventure told in the first person and set in the days of the trans-Atlantic sailing ship. It is enjoyed by readers in grades 6 through 9.

### Plot Summary

It is 1832, and after almost eight years in England, the Doyle family is moving back home to Providence, Rhode Island, because Mr. Doyle has received a promotion. Unwilling to take thirteen-year-old Charlotte out of school at midyear, they decide to leave her behind and instead book passage for her two-month trans-Atlantic crossing for the beginning of summer on the brig *Seahawk,* a merchant vessel owned by Mr. Doyle's firm.

At the dock in Liverpool, Charlotte receives several pieces of disquieting news. First, Mr. Grummage, the gruff, unfeeling man designated by Mr. Doyle's company to see Charlotte safely on board, discovers that the two families scheduled to travel with her have mysteriously canceled their bookings, leaving her the lone passenger on the ship. Second, at the mention of the *Seahawk* or the name of its captain, Jaggery, dockhands either refuse outright or are extremely reluctant to help her with her trunk.

Mr. Grummage, who is anxious to be rid of his charge, dismisses Charlotte's fears as nonsense and demands that she board the ship. The second mate, Mr. Keetch, a subservient, unpleasant man, shows her to her ugly, dark, airless cabin. It measures about six feet by four feet and the ceiling is so low that even diminutive Charlotte must stoop continually when inside. Left alone except for the roaches she discovers in her bed, Charlotte is interrupted by the arrival of an ordinary seaman, Barlow, who mysteriously warns her that for her own safety she should not sail on the *Seahawk.* Later she receives another visitor, a kindly old black man, Zachariah. He is the ship's cook and offers her his friendship as well as a small dagger for protection. Hesitantly, she accepts the knife and hides it under her mattress.

During the night, Charlotte vows to leave the ship before it sails the next day, but on awakening discovers she is too late. In the early morning hours they had lifted anchor and were now in the Irish Sea. Her fears are somewhat allayed when later that day she meets Captain Jaggery, a man of patrician looks and bearing, who though extremely severe with the crew seems pleasantly disposed toward Charlotte. When the nine crew members, including Zachariah, are assembled on deck by First Mate Hollybrass, Jaggery seems relieved to learn that a tenth member of the original crew from Providence, Mr. Cranick, has not appeared for the homeward journey.

Charlotte succumbs to a four-day bout of seasickness but on recovery is anxious to become acquainted with the crew and the three officers. She asks Zachariah why she needs the knife and is told that on the trip to England, Jaggery had behaved so cruelly toward the entire crew and in particular toward a seaman named Cranick, whose arm had to be amputated after an unjust flogging, that the crew had signed for the return voyage solely in the hopes of finding an opportunity for revenge.

Charlotte finds it difficult to believe these stories about Captain Jaggery, who, though stern and unyielding, seems only to be doing his duty. During one of their meetings in his cabin, he requests that Charlotte report to him any signs of disquiet or possible preparations for mutiny in the crew. She agrees.

One day Charlotte goes below deck to fetch some clothes from her trunk. While rummaging through the contents, she suddenly feels she is being watched and, spinning around, sees the grinning face of a stranger staring at her from the entrance to the hold. Further suspicions are aroused when she overhears talk of mutiny and discovers a tenth used hammock in the crew's quarters.

Dutifully, she reports this to Captain Jaggery, who arms himself and his two mates, Hollybrass and Keetch, with pistols and muskets and calls the crew on deck. A tenth man appears, a man with only one arm. The mystery of the stowaway is solved: It is Cranick, who demands that Jaggery relinquish command of the ship. The captain's reply is a bullet that kills Cranick. After tossing the body overboard, Jaggery collects weapons the crew had assembled and after choosing Zachariah to be the official scapegoat for the planned mutiny, personally flogs the old man until he lies bleeding and unconscious. Charlotte, now realizing the truth about Jaggery, tries to intervene but is brusquely pushed aside. Later that night, she sees the seamen conduct a religious service on deck and throw a stitched hammock overboard. Zachariah has been buried at sea.

Charlotte is now a soul adrift. Fearful of the hated Jaggery, who distrusts her since her interference at the flogging, she is also shunned by the crew, who believe her to be an informer. In desperation, she discards her dresses and finery and, donning canvas seaman's garments, appears before the crew asking that they accept her as one of them. To test her sincerity, the crew demand that she prove herself by climbing to the top of the royal yard, the highest sail on the mainmast. In spite of terror, dizziness, and nausea, she passes the test. Though she is cheered by the crew, Jaggery, now filled with scorn and hatred for her, forces her to move to the crew's quarters in the forecastle. He venomously begins referring to her as *Mister* Doyle.

A hurricane is predicted and though First Mate Hollybrass suggests a detour to avoid it, Jaggery, intent on making good time to Providence and more profits on his cargo, ignores the first mate's warning and heads into the storm's path. The hurricane's power is much greater than anticipated and the ship is soon enveloped in darkness, thunder, and lightning and is driven by winds that toss it about like a matchstick. At the height of the storm, Jaggery commands Charlotte to climb the foremast to cut the foreyard sail. There she loses her footing but is yanked to safety by another sailor. A flash of lightning reveals his face—it is Zachariah.

During the cleanup after the storm, the body of First Mate Hollybrass is found on the deck. Charlotte's dagger is in his back and he is clutching one of her handkerchiefs. Jaggery conducts a hasty trial and condemns Charlotte to death by hanging within twenty-four hours for the murder.

In the brig, she is visited by Zachariah, who explains that to protect him from Jaggery, the crew had staged the funeral, secretly nursing him back to health in the hold. After Zachariah tells her he had witnessed a quarrel between the captain and his first mate during the storm, they both realize that Jaggery murdered Hollybrass to accomplish two ends: to rid himself of an insubordinate officer and to eliminate his enemy, Charlotte, who could cause trouble in Providence.

Zachariah helps Charlotte escape from the brig but on deck she is confronted by a pistol-brandishing Jaggery. She flees in terror and climbs out onto the bowsprit. Jaggery follows her but loses his balance and falls into the sea.

All aboard decide that once in America, no one will speak of the horrible events on the crossing and that Captain Jaggery's death with be reported as an accident. However, after the boat arrives in Providence, events work out otherwise.

Charlotte is forced to bid a hasty, tearfull farewell to her shipmates, including her beloved Zachariah. On shore, she has serious problems adjusting to the prim, stultifying middle-class life of her family and within a few days of arrival, her somewhat tyrannical father begins demanding to see the log she kept while at sea. Reluctantly, she presents it to him. He is so shocked and disbelieving of its contents that he burns the document and chastises his daughter for having an overactive imagination. Charlotte begins to feel like a prisoner within her own home. Later that week, Charlotte sees a newspaper item reporting that the *Seahawk* is departing for England on September 9. In her room the night of September 8, she puts on her sailor's clothes and climbs out her window and down the trellis. She doesn't stop until she reaches the docks and boards what has become her real home, the *Seahawk*. There she is greeted by an incredulous but delighted Zachariah.

**Thematic Material**

Although this is basically a riveting swashbuckler told at breakneck speed and filled with suspense, nonstop action, and unexpected plot twists, there are other important elements in this novel. The reader witnesses the transformation of a prim, protected, and somewhat prissy young lady into a self-reliant, responsible woman who now understands life's true values. Even the differences in the writing style as her journal progresses reflect these changes. The friendship and sense of devotion that develops between Charlotte and Zachariah are presented logically and not oversentimentalized. Avi has captured an authentic feeling for life at sea during the early nineteenth century, including details of the ship and its construction (a labeled diagram of the *Seahawk* is included). Other themes developed are the importance of friendship and devotion; the danger of accepting first impressions; the need to fight injustice; and tyranny, courage, and the nature of evil.

**Book Talk Material**

The first three pages of the novel (labeled "An Important Warning") foreshadow the thrilling events to come and will capture the interest of most readers. Some other important passages are: Mr. Grummage forces Charlotte onto the *Seahawk* (pp. 7–14); she sees her cabin (pp. 16–18) and meets Zachariah, who gives her the knife (pp. 18–24); Charlotte's first impressions of Captain Jaggery (pp. 27–30); Zachariah explains why she might need the knife (pp. 36–38); Jaggery tells Charlotte about a possible mutiny (pp. 41–48); and Charlotte sees the face while at her trunk (pp. 49–55).

**Additional Selections**

A Southern girl in Civil War Richmond learns some dreadful family secrets in Ann Rinaldi's *The Last Silk Dress* (Holiday, 1988, $15.95; pap., Bantam, $3.50).

During the seventeenth century, two Jewish sisters stow away on different ships to escape their slavish existence in Brazil in Jacqueline Dembar Greene's *Out of Many Waters* (Walker, 1988, $16.95).

During King Philip's War in 1675, a fifteen-year-old girl newly arrived from England lives through an Indian massacre in Winifred Bruce Luhrmann's *Only Brave Tomorrows* (Houghton, 1989, $13.95).

In Idaho country during 1875, a trapper whose wife has died takes in a teenager to care for his six children in Kristiana Gregory's *Jenny of the Tetons* (Harcourt, 1989, $13.95). In 1855, a twelve-year-old boy visits a Shoshoni camp and finds that he cannot leave in *The Legend of Jimmy Spoon* (Harcourt, 1990, $14.95), also by Kristiana Gregory.

A Narraganset Indian boy is a printer's apprentice during Colonial times in a grim tale of exploitation, *Saturnalia* (Harper, 1990, $12.95), by Paul Fleischman.

In *Another Shore* (McElderry, 1988, $15.95) by Nancy Bond, a young girl in present-day Nova Scotia is transported back to 1744 and the Fortress of Louisbourg.

**About the Book**
*Book Report*, May 1991, p. 64.
*Booklist*, September 1, 1990, p. 44.
*Center for Children's Books Bulletin*, December 1990, p. 44.
*Horn Book*, January 1991, p. 65.
*Horn Book Guide*, July 1990, p. 70.
*Kirkus Reviews*, October 1, 1990, p. 1390.
*School Library Journal*, September 1990, p. 221.
*VOYA*, December 1990, p. 275.
*Wilson Library Bulletin*, April 1991, p. 101.
See also *Book Review Digest*, 1991, p. 42; and *Book Review Index*, 1990, p. 37, and 1991, p. 91.

**About the Author**
Bowden, Jane, ed., *Contemporary Authors*. Gale, 1978, Vols. 69–72, pp. 621–22.
Chevalier, Tracy, ed., *Twentieth-Century Children's Writers* (3rd ed.). St. James, 1989, pp. 45–46.
Commire, Anne, ed., *Something about the Author*. Gale, 1978, Vol. 14, pp. 269–70 (under Wortis, Avi).
Holtze, Sally Holmes, ed., *Fifth Book of Junior Authors and Illustrators*. Wilson, 1983, pp. 15–16.
Metzger, Linda, ed., *Contemporary Authors* (New Revision Series). Gale, 1984, Vol. 12, pp. 517–18 (under Wortis, Avi).
Roginski, Jim, ed., *Behind the Covers*. Libraries Unlimited, 1985, pp. 33–42.
Senick, Gerard J., ed., *Children's Literature Review*. Gale, 1991, Vol. 24, pp. 1–15.

**Fleischman, Paul.**   *The Borning Room*
Harper, 1991, $13.89 (0-06-023785-6)

Paul Fleischman is known for both the quality and the variety of his writings for young people. In the field of poetry he is best known for his collections of "poems for two voices," *I Am Phoenix* (Harper, 1985, $11.95; pap., $3.95), lyrical poems about birds, and the 1989 Newbery Medal winner, *Joyful Noise* (Harper, 1988, $12.95), which contains fourteen verses about insects. In the novel *Rear-View Mirrors* (Harper, 1986, $12.95; condensed in *Juniorplots 3*, Bowker, 1987, pp. 45–48), he explores the complicated relationship between a father and daughter in a contemporary setting. His many historical novels include *The Borning Room* and *Saturnalia* (Harper, 1990, $12.95), the story, set in Colonial times, of an Indian boy who is a printer's apprentice. *The Borning Room* is told in a series of six vignettes (with a brief epilogue) spanning a period of about thirty years around the Civil War. Each involves the special room in the Lott household called the "borning room." This brief novel is suitable for readers in grades 6 through 10.

**Plot Summary**

Grandfather Lott moved his family from New Hampshire to Ohio in 1820. On part of the land he cleared for farming, he built, beside a large maple tree, a New England–style home complete with a simple borning room off the kitchen—a place that could be used for dying, for caring for the sick, and for giving birth.

Many years later, granddaughter Georgina Lott is told by her mother Caroline about a young girl's entry into the world in that room. It was January 11, 1851, and in the borning room, Georgina's mother, with the help of a superstitious but very competent German midwife, Mrs. Radtke, brought her into the world. She is now the eighth member of the Lott household, joining Grandfather, a widower, Georgina's mother and father, and their four other children, sons Titus and Spencer and daughters Lucilla and Ada.

The summer of 1859, when Georgina is eight and a half, is proceeding fairly uneventfully. Mother is again pregnant and Georgina's friend Hattie Puckett, age nine, is helpful in explaining that babies grow inside women when they eat melon seeds after marriage. The grown-ups talk about the political problems facing the nation, with the southern states threatening to secede over the issue of slavery. Although Ohio is a free state, it is nevertheless a criminal offense—punishable by a heavy fine and prison term—to help an escaped slave. Georgina's family is sympathetic toward the abolitionist movement and toward the Quakers, who openly disobey the law.

One day when picking berries in the woods, Georgina happens on a middle-aged escaped slave, Cora, cowering in the grass. She has missed connections that would have enabled her to reach Canada. She is crippled from a snake bite and begs Georgina for help. The girl responds by hiding her in the barn and secretly bringing her food. Georgina does not tell her family for fear that, if caught, they too would be charged with harboring a slave. Cora tells Georgina about the incredible cruelty of slavery. She had been used for breeding purposes, sold from one plantation to another, forced in each case to leave her children behind.

The next day, Lucilla, Georgina, and Mama are alone at home when Mama suddenly begins feelings labor pains. Lucilla is sent on foot to fetch Mrs. Radtke, some ten miles away. In the borning room, Mama realizes that something is wrong in the baby's placement. In desperation, Georgina rushes to the barn to get Cora, who carefully massages Mama's belly until the baby is turned around and a safe birth can take place. When the family returns, they are greeted by the yowls of a new baby brother, whom Father names Zeb. The family gives Cora clothing and provisions before she leaves with Father that night to meet a neighboring Quaker who will arrange to smuggle her into Canada. Later, Georgina finds a cornhusk doll made by Cora in the barn. She keeps it as one of her most cherished possessions.

Then it is 1863, and the country is torn apart by civil war. One Sunday, Georgina stays home with Grandfather when the rest of the family goes to church. Although he does not believe in formal religion, he pursues his own devotions every Sabbath. He walks in the woods and, in a sense, worships the greatest creation, the world of nature. When Georgina goes with him she realizes that he is really more religious than many who attend church. She loves this independent, free-thinking man who has always lived for family and justice.

Shortly after, Grandfather suffers a serious stroke and is taken into the borning room. One by one, a parade of churchgoers visit him, including the Methodist minister, Mr. Boole, each hoping that he will convert before death. True to his own beliefs, he resists them all and dies peacefully in his sleep. Father builds a coffin, a grave is dug, and the family gathers silently as Grandfather is buried beside his wife.

By 1885, both Titus and Ada have left the household, but a new member arrives, Father's sister, Aunt Erna. She is a widow who lost both her sons in the Civil War. Mother is in her ninth month of pregnancy and, to keep up with the times, engages the new town doctor, Dr. Roop, who uses the modern drug chloroform in delivering babies. When labor begins, Mother takes to the borning room and Dr. Roop is summoned. Something terrible goes wrong and both mother and baby die, but miraculously a second child, a boy, is born alive.

The months that follow are filled with sorrow and loss for the family. Lucilla's marriage brings some diversion as does caring for the new baby, whom father has named Ellsworth. In 1867, another diversion occurs in the form of visits by Zeb's new teacher, Clement Bock, a charming, loquacious young man with a wonderful sense of humor.

There is a diphtheria epidemic in the area. Many children have died, and Ellsworth is stricken. He is taken to the borning room. Later that day, Mr. Bock arrives with Zeb in his arms. He, too, has the disease. The family begins a twenty-four-hour vigil with Georgina taking command. In spite of constant care, the boys grow worse. In both cases, an ash-gray membrane is growing over their throats and producing slow suffocation. As death approaches, Mr. Bock in desperation suggests a home remedy he remembers from Pennsylvania. Crushed egg shells are forced down the boys' throats. The coughing that results causes the sharp shells to puncture the membranes. Both children recover.

In the spring of 1869, Georgina and Clement Bock marry. In mid-August, almost a year and a half later, Georgina moves into the borning room and Clement is sent to fetch a now ancient Mrs. Radtke. Within hours, Emmaline Bellflower Bock is born.

The cycle of births and deaths continues in the borning room until one day, in 1918, an old and frail Georgina enters it for the last time.

**Thematical Material**

This quiet, poetic novel explores the circle of life from birth to death as it occurs in four generations of a family. From this microcosm of life, readers also view some of the major events of the period from the emancipation movement, through the Civil War, to the fight for women's suffrage in the early twentieth century. The book contains a tender portrait of a loving, close family whose ties are built on affection and trust. Various aspects of religious beliefs are explored. Fascinating historical details of daily life over a century ago are also given. The home borning room as a center where life both begins and ends is no longer a part of contemporary life, but this novel points out the power of such institutions in preserving tradition, memory, and the continuity of life. Other themes and subjects explored are courage, the horrors of slavery, familial devotion, the oneness of humankind, and the great beauty of nature.

**Book Talk Material**

One can use the painting on the dust jacket to point out the uses of the borning room in the households of early settlers. Some specific passages are: the borning room and the birth of Georgina (pp. 3–7); Georgina finds Cora and hides her in the barn (pp. 18–24); Cora helps with the birth of Zeb and is rewarded by the family (pp. 25–33); Georgina shares a Sunday with Grandfather (pp. 35–41); the death of Grandfather (pp. 44–55); and Mr. Bock and Georgina save the two boys from diphtheria.

**Additional Selections**

In alternating chapters, two Australian teenage girls, separated by 300 years of history, tell their stories, connected by gold mining and a nugget with a mysterious inscription, in Maureen Pople's *A Nugget of Gold* (Holt, 1989, $13.95).

In Jan Hudson's *Sweetgrass* (Philomel, 1989, $13.95; pap., Scholastic, $2.95), the life of the Dakota Indians in the 1830s comes alive through the story of a fifteen-year-old girl who is reaching maturity in her tribe.

An eleven-year-old boy experiences the seasons on a northern Minnesota farm in Gary Paulsen's *The Winter Room* (Orchard, 1989, $11.95).

The harsh life of pioneers is described through the experiences of a fourteen-year-old orphan named Maggie Callahan in Robin Moore's *The Bread Sister of Sinking Creek* (Lippincott, 1990, $12.95).

Through the eyes of young Ben Curtis, the reader is introduced to a realistic picture of what the Old West was like in Peter Carter's *Borderlands* (Farrar, 1990, $16.95).

Based on a true story, Sally M. Keehn's *I Am Regina* (Philomel, 1991, $15.95) tells about two sisters who, in 1755, were captured by Indians.

A practical introduction to genealogy for young people interested in tracing family roots is given in Lila Perl's *The Great Ancestor Hunt* (Clarion, 1989, $15.95).

248 · JUNIORPLOTS 4

**About the Book**
*Booklist,* October 1, 1991, p. 328.
*Kirkus Reviews,* August 1, 1991, p. 1009.
*School Library Journal,* September 1991, p. 278.
*VOYA,* December 1991, p. 310.

**About the Author**
Chevalier, Tracy, ed., *Twentieth-Century Children's Writers* (3rd ed.). St. James, 1989, pp. 349–50.
Commire, Anne, ed., *Something about the Author.* Gale, 1983, Vol. 32, p. 71; updated 1985, Vol. 39, pp. 72–73.
Holtze, Sally Holmes, ed., *Fifth Book of Junior Authors and Illustrators.* Wilson, 1983, pp. 114–16.
May, Hal, ed., *Contemporary Authors.* Gale, 1985, Vol. 113, p. 158.
Senick, Gerard J., ed., *Children's Literature Review.* Gale, 1990, Vol. 20, pp. 63–70.
Ward, Martha, ed., *Authors of Books for Young People* (3rd ed.). Scarecrow, 1990, p. 231.

---

**Garfield, Leon.** *The Empty Sleeve*
Delacorte, 1988, $14.95 (0-440-50049-4)

---

Leon Garfield's name is justly famous for his series of robust, rollicking historical novels filled with adventure, wild coincidences, gallant heroes, and often more than a touch of the supernatural. His story-telling gift is reminiscent of Stevenson's in *Treasure Island* and the Dickens of *Oliver Twist.* Garfield's first book for young adults was *Jack Holborn* (o.p.), which was first published in 1965. Since then he has written over a dozen superb novels.

Like most of his books, *The Empty Sleeve* is set in eighteenth-century England and does not flinch at describing the grime and squalor of everyday life during that period. This novel shifts between two settings. The first is the parish of Rotherhithe, part of the borough of Southwark, once known for its commercial dockyards on the south bank of the Thames. The other is the bustling area of Covent Garden in London proper and the neighborhoods around Bow Street and Longacre. The novel is suitable primarily for readers in grades 6 through 10.

**Plot Summary**
One Saturday morning in late January, a sudden violent blizzard cripples the parish of Rotherhithe. Through the blinding storm, Mr. Bagley,

an eccentric, superstitious old ship's carpenter, fights his way to Gannet's ship chandlery to buy a pound of half-inch tacks. He is greeted by a distracted Mr. Gannet and two locals, Mr. Purvis, a seller of wines and spirits, and Mr. Velonty, the local schoolmaster. All three are intent on what is happening in an upstairs room, where Mrs. Gannet is in labor. As the local church bells chime twelve noon, Mrs. Jiffy, a widow helping with the birth, rushes downstairs with news that a baby boy has been born. Mr. Bagley becomes extremely agitated, claiming that a chime child born on a Saturday will see ghosts and have communication with the devil. His dire predictions are cut short by the reappearance of Mrs. Jiffy, announcing the birth of a twin, a second boy. Mr. Bagley becomes so incensed by this news that he must be forcefully thrown out of the chandlery after trying to pour salt into the babies' cradle, an act he believes will exorcise the evil spirits and omens that will surround these children.

Fourteen years have passed and Peter and Paul, as the boys have been named, are now young men. The two are as unalike as chalk and cheese. Peter is a strong, virile, somewhat loutish youngster whose impetuous actions often get him into trouble. Paul is quiet, contemplative, seemingly submissive but often quite devious; he is also clearly the Gannets' favorite. The boys dislike each other intensely. Peter has dreams of finding adventure and wealth in far-off Zanzibar and the China Seas, but at present is preparing to move to Cucumber Alley in Covent Garden, where he is to be apprenticed to a locksmith, Samuel Woodcock, Mr. Velonty's brother-in-law. Before final partings are made, smelly, foreboding Mr. Bagley reappears with a gift for each of the boys: delicately carved ship models in glass bottles. To assert his independence, Paul secretly exchanges models and it is his brother's model that Peter takes with him when he leaves.

Peter is unhappy and lonely in his spartan, severe life as an apprentice. Mr. and Mrs. Woodcock and daughter Maria are cold and inhospitable, and their sarcastic workman, Mr. Shoveller, continually compares Peter unfavorably with the previous apprentice, Thomas Kite, who left to go north a month before. Only Polly, the kitchen girl, shows him any kindness, occasionally visiting him at night with gifts of food.

After church on Sunday, Peter catches a glimpse of the local gentry, Lord and Lady Marriner, who live on Bow Street. He also meets two other Cucumber Alley apprentices, Jay and Dawkins, who tell about Thomas Kite's thriving business "renting" the Woodcocks' duplicate key to the gates of the alley so that apprentices can occasionally enjoy a surreptitious night on the town. Peter promises that he too will be cooperative—he is desperate to accumulate the funds necessary to secure a place on a ship bound for the South Seas and freedom.

The first heist is planned for Friday night. Peter will steal the key and meet the apprentices at the Bedford Head, a local tavern. Unfortunately, Mr. Velonty arrives at the Woodcocks for a dinner visit on Friday and Peter is late for his assignation. Luckily, the boys are still there and the key is delivered. At the tavern, Peter is introduced to Lord Marriner, who takes an unusual interest in him when he learns that Peter is Woodcock's new apprentice. Lord Marriner tells Peter how Woodcock and apprentice Kite had recently spent days in his home changing the locks. When he also mentions that he is a great collector of objects d'art, Peter suggests that he might wish to pay twenty pounds for his model ship. His lordship expresses some interest.

Peter shows Polly the model and, with her keen eyes, she detects the word Paul inscribed on it. Peter is furious but, regardless of ownership, he still hopes to sell it. That night in the locksmith's workroom, apparitions of workmen once involved in constructing buildings in Cucumber Alley appear before a terrified Peter. When they disappear, Peter is confronted with another specter, a black, hooded phantom without a face that beckons to him with an empty sleeve.

In the morning, a shaken and fearful Peter creeps out of bed to retrieve the key, as arranged, from the mouth of the wooden devil over the door of Mr. Stint's neighboring jewelry shop. He sees Lady Marriner leaving the Bible shop across the way. She is paying an early visit to the alley. Meanwhile, back in Rotherhithe, Paul notices that Peter's ship shows damage and appears to be mysteriously disintegrating. Perhaps it means that his brother is in trouble.

Later that day, Peter is sent to deliver a key to Lord Marriner. When the boy mentions seeing Lady Marriner earlier that day in Cucumber Alley, his lordship becomes agitated and requests that six days hence Peter secretly "borrow" another master key from Woodcock. He needs the key to Lady Marriner's jewel box because he plans to buy her a bracelet for their wedding anniversary and wants to place it there as a surprise. Lord Marriner also promises to examine the boy's model ship and gives Peter an advance of one pound.

The phantom appears more frequently as though trying to tell Peter something. Peter thinks it is the ghost of Thomas Kite, but when the former apprentice comes to visit, the boy is baffled and unable to fathom the reason for these visitations.

On the same day that Peter is to meet Lord Marriner, Paul finds that Peter's ship has completely crumbled. Alarmed and worried that switching the models might have caused harm to his brother, Paul leaves Rotherhithe for Cucumber Alley.

When Peter goes to Lord Marriner's with the key and his model, he is immediately fed so much brandy that he becomes impossibly drunk. At this point, Lord Marriner leaves the room and Peter quietly crawls after him. In a terrible shadow play, Peter witnesses Lord Marriner bludgeoning his wife to death with his silver-tipped cane. Marriner returns; thrusts jewelry, part of the broken cane, and the stolen key into Peter's pockets; and begins shouting "thief" and "murderer." Peter escapes into the night, leaving the model behind, and is found by Paul outside the gates of Cucumber Alley. While Peter hides to sober up, Paul takes the keys to return them to Woodcock's before they are discovered to be missing.

Unfortunately, he is discovered by the Woodcock family before he can complete his mission. At this point Lord Marriner arrives at the locksmith's distraught and shouting that his wife has been murdered by the apprentice, Peter Gannet. After he leaves, other tradesmen, who have been awakened by the commotion, come to the locksmith's. One is Mr. Lott, the Bible seller, who belatedly delivers a note to Mr. Woodcock that Lady Marriner left that morning. It is a warning stating that her husband has found out about her love affair with Mr. Woodcock and is planning something horrible involving his apprentice.

When Paul fails to return, Peter, still in a confused state, returns to Lord Marriner's to retrieve the ship model. He confronts his lordship and accuses him of murdering his wife. They run into the streets. Suddenly the phantom appears once more and this time beckons to Lord Marriner. Confused, the man turns and walks into the path of an oncoming horse and cart. He is killed instantly. When Peter looks directly at the phantom, he sees his own face. Like the warnings of the disintegrating ship, these supernatural occurrences have been warnings from his inner self of the consequences of his wrongdoing. He returns to Cucumber Alley to greet a new friend, his brother Paul.

**Thematic Material**

This is essentially an entertaining, melodramatic adventure story, but some novelistic techniques about fine historical writing are displayed.

The past is not glamorized. The picture of London that the author creates is of a city filled with squalor and ugliness but one where positive human values also exist. Sufficient details are given to make the setting lifelike and believable. An eerie mood of impending violence is created on the first page and sustained throughout. The problem of sibling rivalry is explored with a satisfactory resolution and the consequences of greed and wrongdoing and the nature of retribution are also important themes.

**Book Talk Material**

There are a number of suspenseful incidents that could be read or retold after describing a little about the novel's setting. Some are: Mr. Bagley and the birth of the twins (pp. 2–9); the differences between Peter and Paul are established (pp. 13–16); Mr. Bagley gives the boys the ship models and Paul switches them (pp. 22–28); Peter meets the apprentices and discovers how he can make money supplying them with keys (pp. 37–42); Peter meets Lord Marriner at the Bedford Head (pp. 64–66); Peter sees apparitions and the phantom with an empty sleeve for the first time (pp. 79–83).

**Additional Selections**

In Ann Cheetham's *The Pit* (Holt, 1990, $14.95), a young boy in present-day England is drawn back to London during the 1600s when it was stricken by the Great Plague.

In Victorian England, Andrew and Sara help Scotland Yard solve a baffling crime in Robert Newman's *The Case of the Watching Boy* (Macmillan, 1987, $12.95).

Buried treasure and Dickensian derring-do are featured in Bruce Clements's *The Treasure of Plunderell Manor* (Farrar, 1987, $12.95; pap., $3.95), in which a young maid serves a girl who is kept hidden by her wicked aunt and uncle.

*The Writing on the Hearth* (Lerner, 1984, $9.95) by Cynthia Harnett deals with intrigue and witchcraft in fifteenth-century England.

Sally Lockhart finds danger, murder, and love in nineteenth-century London in *The Ruby in the Smoke* by Philip Pullman (Knopf, 1987, $11.95; pap., $2.95; condensed in *Seniorplots*, Bowker, 1989, pp. 147–53).

In eighteenth-century England, Damaris and her friends help a wounded smuggler in Rosemary Sutcliff's *Flame-Colored Taffeta* (Farrar, 1986, $11.95; pap., $3.50).

**About the Book**
*Book Report,* November 1988, p. 34.
*Booklist,* September 15, 1988, p. 158.
*Center for Children's Books Bulletin,* October 1988, p. 35.
*Horn Book,* January 1989, p. 78.
*Kirkus Reviews,* July 1, 1988, p. 972.
*School Library Journal,* October 1988, p. 161.
See also *Book Review Digest,* 1988, p. 615; and *Book Review Index,* 1988, p. 292, and 1989, p. 295.

**About the Author**
Chevalier, Tracy, ed., *Twentieth-Century Children's Writers* (3rd ed.). St. James, 1989, pp. 374–76.
Commire, Anne, ed., *Something about the Author.* Gale, 1983, Vol. 32, pp. 73–79.
de Montreville, Doris, and Crawford, Elizabeth D., eds., *Fourth Book of Junior Authors and Illustrators.* Wilson, 1978, pp. 144–45.
Kinsman, Clare D., *Contemporary Authors* (First Revision). Gale, 1976, Vols. 17–20, p. 268.
Kirkpatrick, D. L., ed., *Twentieth-Century Children's Writers* (2nd ed.). St. Martin's, 1983, pp. 312–14.
Senick, Gerard J., ed., *Children's Literature Review.* Gale, 1990, Vol. 21, pp. 82–122.
Ward, Martha, ed., *Authors of Books for Young People* (3rd ed.). Scarecrow, 1990, p. 259.

---

**Paterson, Katherine.** *Lyddie*
Dutton, 1991, $14.95 (0-525-67338-5)

---

*Lyddie* is the story of a plucky young girl who, unable to pay off the debt on the family farm, goes to work in the textile mills in Lowell, Massachusetts, during the 1840s, where she endures both loneliness and harsh working conditions. This enterprising, feisty young heroine is reminiscent of another Paterson heroine who overcame adverse conditions and achieved self-reliance. She is Louise, the central character in the Newbery Medal-winning *Jacob Have I Loved* (Harper, 1988, $12.95; pap., $3.95; condensed in *Juniorplots 3,* Bowker, 1987, pp. 85–90). Both novels are enjoyed by junior and senior high school readers.

**Plot Summary**
It is November 1843, and Lyddie will always remember this as the year of the bear. Her father took off for parts unknown some years before,

and with Mama and her brother Charles, she has tried to keep their debt-ridden Vermont farm together and provide a home for the two youngest, Agnes and Rachel. However, now a bear gets into the cabin and nearly scares them to death before he wrecks the place and then lumbers off. This proves too much for Mama's frail mental state and, declaring that the end is near, she insists on leaving with the two young ones for the home of her sister and her end-of-the-world-shouting husband.

Lyddie refuses to go. She and Charles will stay and keep the farm going until her father returns.

By dint of backbreaking work, Lyddie and Charlie make it through the Vermont winter, but in the spring Mama writes to tell them that she has hired them out—Lyddie to work at Cutler's tavern, Charlie to the mill—to help pay the farm's debts.

At the tavern, Lyddie feels she is no better than a slave, but at least Charlie has been taken in by a family that seems to love and want him. Lyddie decides that she cannot endure this life any longer and sets out for the mill town of Lowell, Massachusetts, where she applies for a job in the factory. At least there she can earn a wage and be free.

Lyddie *is* free, in a manner of speaking. The hours are unbearably long, the work tedious, hard, and dirty, the pay unbelievably small. She must live in a crowded boarding house with several other factory girls. Her days are filled with the incessant booming noises of the mill and her nights echo with the coughs of the mill girls, who stand all day long in the lint-filled air. But exhausted as she is, Lyddie holds the dream of paying off the debts and, with Charlie, going back to their Vermont farm.

Lyddie becomes friendly with the radical Diana, who urges the girls to sign a petition for better working conditions. Although Lyddie doesn't sign, through Diana's influence she becomes interested in bettering her reading and writing skills.

Lyddie begins to save her money, but her dream of returning to the farm slips further away when she learns that the farm is to be sold to pay off the debts. She also realizes that Charlie has a home now with a family that loves him and wants him to go to school. He is better off where he is.

Word comes to Lyddie that young Agnes has died. Then Mama becomes ill and is put in an institution. After Mama's death, Lyddie returns to Lowell with young Rachel. She intends to care for her and provide a good life, but this too is thwarted when Charlie tells her that the family that has taken him also wants to bring up Rachel. Lyddie cannot deny her young sister a chance for a good family life and home, and reluctantly she lets her go. Lyddie is alone once again.

Lyddie's chance for escape from her dreary existence comes in a most unexpected way. She receives a letter from her former neighbor in Vermont, Quaker Luke Stevens. He asks her to return to the Vermont farm, which his family is trying to purchase, as his wife. Lyddie knows young Luke is kind and gentle, but she does not love him.

Lyddie goes to a meeting of Diana's radical group intending to sign a petition for better working conditions, but she is too late. The petition has already been sent to the legislature. Lyddie learns that her friend Diana is in trouble; she is pregnant and must leave Lowell so that she does not bring dishonor on the association. Once again Lyddie is alone.

Lyddie befriends young Brigid at the mill and when she passes the building one evening, she hears her friend's cries. Lyddie rushes in to find Brigid being attacked by the mill supervisor, Mr. Marsden. Lyddie hits him with a bucket and the girls escape.

Lyddie realizes she will be fired and, indeed, the next day the mill agent calls her in and tells her that she is a troublemaker and will therefore be terminated. Lyddie asks what trouble she has caused—after all, she has been employed at the mill for a year, has never been in trouble, and as far as management knows, has never signed a petition or been involved in radical meetings. The agent hesitates and calls in Marsden. Asked about the charges against Lyddie, Marsden says she is guilty of moral turpitude. She is dismissed without a certificate of honorable discharge, which means she can't get another job in any company in Lowell.

Lyddie does not know what moral turpitude means, so she spends some of her hard-earned money on a dictionary. With great glee, she learns that she has not been called vile or shameful. True, she was ignorant of the meaning of the word, but what sin is there in that?

Lyddie decides to leave Lowell. Before she does, she confronts Marsden and tells him that if he causes Brigid to lose her job, she—Lyddie—will inform Marsden's wife of what goes on with the young workers in the weaving room.

From Lowell, Lyddie travels to Boston to see Diana. She had planned to stay with her and help her with the baby, but Diana has found her own new family, and there is no need for Lyddie. She then travels through New Hampshire to Vermont, for one last look at her beloved farm.

It is November again as she stands at the door of what was once her home. Suddenly she hears a voice. It is Luke Stevens. He asks her to come stay with his family for the night and he apologizes for writing the letter asking her to marry him—but where will she go, he asks? Suddenly, Lyddie knows what she will do. "I'm off to Ohio," she tells him, "to a college that will take a woman just like a man."

Lyddie knows in her heart that it may be years before she returns to Vermont. However, she will return, and not because she has been beaten down with nowhere else to go. She will not be a slave, even to herself. Yet, as she looks at the kind face of Luke Stevens, she thinks that this gentle Quaker is the man she will one day love. Perhaps, just perhaps, he will wait.

### Thematic Material

This is in many ways a grim story of the hard life endured by children in factories and farms in early America. But Lyddie is painted as a resourceful, believable heroine whose determination to succeed overcomes all obstacles. Life may be hard, the story warns, but there is always hope for a better future. Lyddie's strength and devotion to family and friends make her an inspiring role model.

### Book Talk Material

Incidents on the farm and in the factory provide a good contrast in this story of the deplorable conditions in many working towns in early America. See: the bear intrudes at the Vermont farm (pp. 1–4); Lyddie and Charles make it through the winter (pp. 7–9); Lyddie feels like a slave at the tavern (pp. 18–26); Lyddie goes to Lowell and the mill (pp. 53–61); and Lyddie meets Diana (pp. 68–73).

### Additional Selections

In Patricia Beatty's *Turn Homeward, Hannalee* (Morrow, 1984, $12.95), a family of mill workers—two girls and their mother—seek employment in Indiana during the Civil War. In its sequel, set during the Reconstruction, *Be Ever Hopeful, Hannalee* (Morrow, 1988, $12.95), the heroine and her family move back home to Georgia in search of work.

In *Breaker* (Houghton, 1988, $13.95) by N. A. Perez, a teenage boy enters the mines in 1902 Pennsylvania when his father is killed in an accident. *One Special Year* (Houghton, 1985, $12.95) by the same author tells of a girl's coming of age in an upstate New York town in 1900.

An orphaned fourteen-year-old girl becomes a servant in Pennsylvania during pioneer days in Robin Moore's *The Bread Sister of Sinking Creek* (Harper, 1990, $14.95).

Nelda, the daughter of migrant workers, faces a bleak future during the Great Depression in Pat Edwards's *Nelda* (Houghton, 1987, $12.97).

On the wide Nebraska prairie, young Louisa forms a friendship with a doctor's wife who can't cope with the lonely existence in Pam Conrad's *Prairie Songs* (Harper, 1985, $12.95; pap., $3.50).

In *The Dancing Madness* (Delacorte, 1980, $8.95), by Mildred Ames, Mary's sister enters a dance marathon to help her family through the Depression.

**About the Book**
*Booklist*, January 1, 1991, p. 920.
*Center for Children's Books Bulletin*, February 1991, p. 151.
*Horn Book*, May 1991, p. 338.
*Kirkus Reviews*, January 1, 1991, p. 49.
*New York Times Book Review*, May 19, 1991, p. 24.
*VOYA*, April 1991, p. 34.
See also *Book Review Digest*, 1991, p. 1443; and *Book Review Index*, 1991, p. 704.

**About the Author**
Chevalier, Tracy, ed., *Twentieth-Century Children's Writers* (3rd ed.). St. James, 1989, pp. 758–60.
Commire, Anne, ed., *Something about the Author*. Gale, 1978, Vol. 13, pp. 176–77; updated 1988, Vol. 53, pp. 118–29.
Estes, Glenn E., ed., *American Writers for Children since 1960: Fiction* (Dictionary of Literary Biography: Vol. 52). Gale, 1986, pp. 296–314.
Garrett, Agnes, and McCue, Helga P., eds., *Authors and Artists for Young Adults*. Gale, 1989, Vol. 1, pp. 203–14.
Harte, Barbara, ed., *Contemporary Authors*. Gale, 1970, Vols. 23–24, p. 322.
Holtze, Sally Holmes, ed., *Fifth Book of Junior Authors and Illustrators*. Wilson, 1983, pp. 236–38.
Kirkpatrick, D. L., ed., *Twentieth-Century Children's Writers* (2nd ed.). St. Martin's, 1983, pp. 603–4.
Nasso, Christine, ed., *Contemporary Authors* (First Revision). Gale, 1977, Vols. 21–24, p. 662.
Senick, Gerard J., ed., *Children's Literature Review*. Gale, 1984, Vol. 7, pp. 224–43.
Ward, Martha, ed., *Authors of Books for Young People* (3rd ed.). Scarecrow, 1990, p. 551.
*Who's Who in America: 1986–1987* (44th ed.). Marquis, 1986, Vol. 2, p. 2160.

---

**Rostkowski, Margaret I.**   *After the Dancing Days*
Harper, 1986, $13.89 (0-06-025078-X); pap., $3.95 (0-06-440248-7)

---

This is the author's first novel for young adults. It deals with the tragic aftermath of World War I and how the effects of this war radically changed the lives of a midwestern family and a badly scarred veteran. It is a first-person narrative, told from the point of view of thirteen-year-old Annie Metcalf. The author's second novel, *The Best of Friends* (Harper, 1989, $12.89), deals with another war, the Vietnam conflict, and the various reactions to it by three high school students who are close friends. The point of view shifts from those of a brother and sister, both of whom are against the war, to that of their friend, who, facing an uncertain future, enlists. It is suitable for both junior and senior high readers, whereas *After the Dancing Days* is recommended for readers in grades 6 through 9. Its title comes from lines in an Irish folk song that succinctly point toward the antiwar theme of the book: "Where are your legs that used to run/When first you went to carry a gun?/I fear your dancing days are done/Johnny, I hardly knew you."

**Plot Summary**

On a warm day in April 1919, Annie Metcalf and her mother are at the railroad station in Kansas City awaiting the arrival of the afternoon train from New York City. They have traveled the twenty-five miles from home in their new Model T to greet Annie's father, Dr. Lawrence Metcalf, who is returning after a year and a half working in an army hospital in New York. The war has been over for five months, but the effects are still being felt. Annie has not accepted the death of her mother's younger brother, her beloved Uncle Paul MacLeod, who was killed less than a year before fighting in France. To Annie, Paul was always special. She idolized this charming, considerate man who escorted her to her first opera, *La Bohème,* and allowed her to be the first passenger on the motorcycle he bought just before he enlisted.

After the regular passengers leave the train, they are followed by a group of wounded soldiers who are being sent to St. John's, the local army hospital. Most are bandaged, some sightless, others without legs or arms, and a few horribly disfigured by burns. For Annie, it is the first glimpse of the reality of war and the sight of these maimed and mutilated young men haunts her for months.

Finally Father appears and the three return home for a family reunion at the home of Grandfather and Grandmother MacLeod. There the Metcalfs are joined by other members of the MacLeod clan. It is a joyous occasion, marred only by the continual remembrance of the absent Paul.

Much to the disappointment of Annie's mother, Father has decided to continue his work with the war veterans and practice medicine at St. John's rather than return to the more prestigious County Hospital. When Grandfather learns that Timothy Lewis, a local boy whom he remembers, is suffering from temporary blindness caused by combat wounds, he volunteers to visit the hospital daily as a reader. One day at the beginning of summer vacation, a somewhat reluctant Annie consents to accompany Grandfather. There, seated on a park bench, she sees a man so disfigured by burns that he has only scar tissue for a face, punctuated by two deep brown eyes and a slit for a mouth. His hands are swathed in bandages. At first Annie recoils in horror but she must retrieve her book bag. This time, she summons up the courage to utter one word, "good-bye," before rejoining her grandfather.

Summer progresses and Annie's life is leisurely, punctuated by such events as a visit to Kansas City with her Sunday School class to see Lillian Gish in *Broken Blossoms*, and a wonderful Fourth of July picnic with her loving family.

Annie is still haunted by the sights at the hospital but nevertheless returns with her grandfather, whose own health has been of increasing concern to the family. Once more she meets the man without a face, who introduces himself as Andrew Crayton. They talk together, and, though Andrew tries to be sociable, it is apparent that not only his body but also his mind and personality have been scarred by his war experiences. Grandfather feels so weak that Annie's mother is summoned to bring them home. When she sees Andrew, she rudely refuses to acknowledge his presence and, instead, hurries Annie and Grandfather to the car. Annie is mortified at her mother's rudeness.

Grandfather suffers a minor heart attack, and after his partial recovery, it is decided that Annie's mother and grandmother should take Grandfather to Estes Park in Colorado for a few weeks of recovery. Before they leave, Mrs. Metcalf tells Annie that she is too young to be exposed to all the ugliness and misery at the hospital and forbids her to return there. But Annie has already secretly promised Grandfather that she will continue to read *Ivanhoe* to Timothy.

She visits the hospital faithfully but never mentions this in her letters to her mother. Andrew joins Timothy for her readings and soon she forms a strong bond of understanding and love with him; his reserve of bitterness and hate is gradually broken down. They confide in each other. He tells her about the mustard gas attacks during which he suffered the painful wounds to his face and hands and she describes the terrible emptiness caused by her Uncle Paul's death. One day, Andrew cynically shows Annie the war memento he possesses in addition to his wounds; his Purple Heart. Annie wonders why Uncle Paul was not awarded one even though the family was told he died a hero's death in battle.

One day at the hospital Annie meets Mrs. Crayton, Andrew's mother, who explains that his father, a farmer in a rural area of Kansas, refuses to visit Andrew. He believes that Andrew is to blame for his condition because he joined the army even though farmers' sons were exempt from the draft.

There is some good news from the hospital. After protracted treatments, Timothy's eyesight is restored. Further operations have eased some of the pain that Andrew suffers and have allowed him greater use of his hands. The changes in both his health and his attitude are shown when he begins assisting the nurses with their ward duties.

With the help of Andrew, Annie locates men at the hospital who remember her Uncle Paul in France. She has made arrangements to question Lieutenant Owen concerning the particulars of Paul's death, when her mother and grandparents suddenly arrive back from Colorado. The happy homecoming is marred by Annie's confession about her hospital visits. She loves and respects her mother and this is the first time she has ever lied to her. There is a terrible scene in which Annie tries to explain to her mother how important the hospital and particularly Andrew are to her. The following morning, after sleepness nights for both mother and daughter, Mrs. Metcalf restates the disappointment she feels at Annie's behavior but allows her to continue to go to St. John's.

The interview with Lieutenant Owen is devastating for Annie because she learns that Paul did not die heroically in battle as the family had been told, but of a severe case of measles. She now realizes fully the terrible wastefulness of war. She tells her mother and the rest of the family what she has learned, but they decide that the grandparents should be spared the truth.

Accidentally, Annie learns during a visit with Mrs. Crayton that Andrew has accepted a position working in a veterans' hospital in Toledo. In disbelief, Annie races to Andrew, who tells her that he feels that he can now accept the responsibility of being on his own. He had planned to tell Annie the news at their next meeting.

Annie feels betrayed and abandoned, but in the days before Andrew's departure she gradually accepts the situation and realizes it is best for her friend. One evening, the Metcalfs invite Andrew to dinner. He is so impressed with Mrs. Metcalf's piano playing that he asks if she will play for the veterans at the hospital on the evening of Armistice Day, November 11, the day before he leaves. To the amazement and delight of Annie and her father, she accepts.

Annie takes Andrew to the town's outdoor ceremony on Armistice Day. His presence is a reminder to all of the reality and the legacy of war. The evening's concert goes well, but Annie is filled with dread about tomorrow's parting.

The following morning, Annie and her father go to the station to say good-bye to Andrew. Before entering the train, he kisses Annie gently on the cheek, and, promising that he will never forget her, gives her a small box containing his Purple Heart.

**Thematic Material**

On the dust jacket of the hardcover edition of this novel, the author, a high school teacher, states that her students are "deeply interested in the issues of war and peace and duty to country and where one finds true heroism." From these concerns came this novel, which offers a powerful antidote to those who believe war is all glory and valor. The waste and suffering of war and the agony endured by its surviving victims are movingly portrayed. Although it is technically a historical novel and does give some insights into life after World War I, it concentrates on universal human feelings and conflicts that transcend any particular time period. It could actually be dealing with the aftermath in America of any twentieth-century war. Annie's gradual maturation and passage to self-discovery are logically developed. Loving, wholesome family relationships built on mutual trust and respect are well depicted, but the point is made that parents must allow for the gradual development of responsible independent behavior and decision making in their children. The inadvisability of unduly protecting children from life's realities is also an important theme. Annie is a believable, sensitive heroine who finds, as many youngsters do, that it is sometimes necessary to defy authority in order to do what one considers right.

### Book Talk Material

A discussion of the novel's title and its setting should interest readers. Some particularly important passages are: Annie meets her father's train and sees the wounded veterans for the first time (pp. 1–6); Dr. Metcalf talks to his daughter about the patients at the hospital (pp. 22–24); Annie remembers riding on the motorcycle and attending an opera with her Uncle Paul (pp. 27–35); Annie's first visit to St. John's and her encounter with Andrew (pp. 43–49); a family Fourth of July (pp. 63–69); Annie's second meeting with Andrew and her mother's interruption (pp. 70–79); Annie recalls receiving news of Uncle Paul's death and Andrew shows her his Purple Heart (pp. 104–9).

### Additional Selections

Set in post–World War I Berkeley, California, *The Private World of Julia Redfern* (Dutton, 1988, $13.95; pap., Penguin, $4.95) by Eleanor Cameron features fifteen-year-old Julia who, while trying to become an author, must adjust to family problems, including her father's death. Earlier books in this series include (for a younger audience) *Julia's Magic* (Dutton, 1984, $10.95) and *Julia and the Hand of God* (Dutton, 1977, $12.95).

A family of Jewish immigrants spend World War II in California and face many hardships and family crises in Sonia Levitin's *Silver Days* (Atheneum, 1989, $13.95), a sequel to *Coming to America* (pap., Aladdin, 1977, $3.95).

A fine collection of poems that depict the waste of war and the blessing of peace is found in *Peace and War* (Oxford Univ. Pr., 1989, $17.95), edited by Michael Harrison.

Through his experiences during World War I, a fourteen-year-old Polish boy becomes a pacifist in Rudolf Frank's *No Hero for the Kaiser* (Lothrop, Lee & Shepard, 1986, $13.00).

In Milton Dank's *Khaki Wings* (Delacorte, 1980, $8.95; pap., Dell, $1.95), a teenage boy becomes a mechanic for the air corps in France during World War I.

During the Great Depression, Josh must assume responsibilities beyond his years in Irene Hunt's *No Promises in the Wind* (pap., Berkley, 1987, $2.75).

Two histories dealing with America's part in World War I are Don Lawson's *The United States in World War I* (Harper, 1963, $12.95) and *The Yanks Are Coming* (Macmillan, 1986, $15.95) by Albert Marrin.

### About the Book
*Booklist*, October 15, 1986, p. 356.
*Center for Children's Books Bulletin*, January 1987, p. 97.
*Horn Book*, January 1987, p. 61.
*Kirkus Reviews*, October 1, 1987, p. 1519.
*School Library Journal*, December 1986, p. 121.
*VOYA*, April 1987, p. 32.
See also *Book Review Digest*, 1987, p. 1611; and *Book Review Index*, 1986, p. 625, and 1987, p. 658.

### About the Author
Commire, Anne, ed., *Something about the Author*. Gale, 1990, Vol. 59, pp. 175–76.
Holtze, Sally Holmes, ed., *Sixth Book of Junior Authors and Illustrators*. Wilson, 1989, pp. 249–50.

---

**Sutcliff, Rosemary.** *The Shining Company*
Farrar, 1990, $14.95 (0-374-36807-4)

---

The historical novels of Rosemary Sutcliff have become synonymous with superior quality in writing style, richness of detail, and an amazing ability to re-create the color, action, passion, and living conditions of a particular period in British history. In *The Shining Company*, she returns to the time and setting of some of her finest books for young adults, post-Roman Britain. This novel is based on an early Welsh poem, "The Gododdin," and tells in a first-person narrative the story of Prosper, a boy in training with the Shining Company, a group of young warriors preparing to fight the Saxons. The novel is suitable for better readers in both junior and senior high school.

### Plot Summary
Set in A.D. 600, this tale concerns 300 young warriors, the Companions, and their shieldbearers, who function something like squires. The

king of the Gododdin, Mynyddog, houses these young men and trains them into a fighting brotherhood at his tribal capital of Dyn Eidin, on the site where the city of Edinburgh, Scotland, now stands. After a year, they are ready to fight the invading Saxons of what later became Yorkshire and Northumberland. One of the few survivors of their epic battle was the poet Aneirin, whose work, "The Gododdin," was intended as an elegy for all the warriors who died. *The Shining Company* is the story of what might have happened in that battle, told through the eyes of one young shieldbearer, named Prosper.

At the story's opening, Prosper is not yet fourteen. He is the second son of Gerontius, lord of a half-ruined villa near the sea in the southwest of what is now Great Britain. His mother died giving birth to him and his father cares only for the older son, Owain. Prosper, however, is content with other boys his own age for friends, with his kinswoman Luned, who is about his age, and with his body servant, Conn, given to him by his father on Prosper's twelfth birthday. Prosper was sorely disappointed that day because he wanted a puppy; besides, Conn was damaged goods, having a wounded and infected knee. Still, the knee heals and, despite himself, Prosper grows fond of his servant, who is dismayed to learn that he may spend his life in servitude.

When Prosper nears the age of fourteen, Prince Gorthyn arrives in the area. He is the son of King Urfai, overlord to Prosper's father. The prince cares for little in life but hunting and he has come in search of a white hart. Unknown to anyone else, Prosper, Conn, and Luned have seen this unusual and beautiful beast and have vowed to keep it secret. Prosper goes with the hunting party, intending to kill the hart himself rather than let it be attacked by the hounds. Gorthyn sees his intention and calls off the hounds. Young Prosper senses that this would be a good man to follow and asks to ride with the prince, but Gorthyn says that Prosper is too young; he must wait a year or two.

True to Gorthyn's word, when Prosper is in his sixteenth year, he is summoned to join the prince at King Mynyddog's fortress at Dyn Eidin. The king is forging a band of 300 men—the Companions—and their 600 shieldbearers, who will train for a year and then will battle the invading Saxons. Gorthyn needs a second shieldbearer and has not forgotten his promise to Prosper.

With Conn following him, Prosper heads for Dyn Eidin. There they find the king, who is ill from a past battle during which he took an arrow in the ribs. The medical skills of the queen have kept him alive, but will the king be able to lead these men in battle? The king assures them that other kingdoms in northern Britain will join their cause. Warriors and shieldbearers alike take the Great Oath: "If we break faith with you, may the green earth gape and swallow us, may the grey seas roll in and overwhelm us, may the sky of stars fall upon us and crush us out of life forever."

So begins a year of training for the coming battle. During this time Prosper persuades Conn to learn the trade of the smithy so that he may return to Prosper's father and become a free man. One of the highlights of the year is the great three-day feast that King Mynyddog calls at midwinter. On the second night, one of the warriors, Cynan, whom Prosper admires, and his brothers ride their horses into and through the hall to show off their fine saddles, received as gifts from the king. The brothers spill not so much as a mead jar in the crowded hall. However, what starts off in jest becomes a wild battle, which is stopped only by the appearance of the queen.

After the feast, the warrior Fosterling is named Captain of the Companions, who are now judged ready for battle. They set out to attack the Saxon stronghold at Catraeth. During the trek, Prosper and the warrior Cynan capture a Saxon whom they believe to be a spy. Cynan kills him, and that is Prosper's first and lasting memory of war.

In the battle at Catraeth, the Saxons are taken by surprise. The Companions settle down to await reinforcements from the nearby kingdom of Elmet. But while they wait for aid that does not come, the Saxons regather their forces and encircle them. Prince Gorthyn is killed. Now there are fewer than 100 of the original company and fewer than 200 shieldbearers. The Companions realize that the king has failed to bring kingdoms together to fight the Saxons, but they vow to continue the fight themselves. Although outnumbered, they will attack the Saxons. They choose the bard Aneirin to tell the king what they have done. He will have three escorts, Prosper's former body servant, Conn, among them. The two say good-bye, and Prosper tells Conn to return to his father as a smith, not a bondsman, and to marry Luned, for Prosper has long known that the two love each other.

Prosper now becomes shieldbearer to Cynan. The battle is hideous and fierce. Cynan is gravely wounded, and it becomes Prosper's duty to save him if he can. He manages to get the bleeding Cynan on a horse and leads him away from the battle. Prosper heads north with the wounded warrior and is fortunate enough to meet Aneirin and Conn. It is a long, slow journey back to the king at Dyn Eidin with the ailing Cynan. The small party meets a scout who tells them the king had indeed received their call for reinforcements, but he disbanded those who would ride to join them.

When they reach Dyn Eidin, the king is brought into the hall, looking ten years older than Prosper remembered him. Aneirin tells the king what happened and Prosper describes the last ride of the Shining Company. He also repeats the scout's words telling of the king's dismissal of troops that could have saved the company.

"Why did they never come?" Aneirin asks the king gently. The king replies that the other northern kingdoms refused to answer his call. He was left with only his own small war bands and he judged that to send them would have meant their death as well as those of the Shining Company. By not sending them, at least he lost only the men of the Shining Company. That was the king's terrible decision.

In time and with the queen's help, Cynan recovers. The king tells Cynan that as the one warrior who returned from Catraeth, he is welcome to stay. But Cynan says he cannot live where he sees in men's eyes that he was the only one to survive. He has another, silent, reason, which the king, Prosper is certain, knows: Cynan believes the king betrayed them. The king tells Cynan to leave.

Prosper decides to travel with Cynan wherever that takes him—unknown roads and strange lands. "Make ready," says Cynan with a laugh. "Constantinople, here we come!"

**Thematic Material**

Through the eyes of a young boy, the grim reality and horror of battle come alive for the reader in this fascinating, swiftly moving tale of life in England long, long ago. Truth, friendship, and duty, as well as the terrible decisions that leaders face in battle, are presented as the laws by which those of honor are bound to live their lives.

**Book Talk Material**

A number of scenes will serve as an excellent introduction to this look at England in A.D. 600. See: Prosper meets his body servant (pp. 4–12); seeing the white hart (pp. 32–39); taking the Great Oath (91–93); Prosper tells Conn to go free (pp. 105–7); and the feast in the hall (pp. 139–50).

**Additional Selections**

In feudal Japan, an indigent sumurai thwarts a plan by rebels to invade a small island in Lensey Namioka's *Island of Ogres* (Harper, 1987, $13.95).

In the 1500s, fifteen-year-old Miguel accompanies his godfather and 200 Spanish soldiers on a search for a golden temple in Mexico in Jose Maria Merino's *The Gold of Dreams* (Farrar, 1991, $13.95).

Anxious for war action, Eben, a thirteen-year-old southern boy during the Civil War, joins the Confederate team working on the *Merrimack* in Patricia Beatty's *Eben Tyne, Powdermonkey* (Morrow, 1990, $12.95). The northern counterpart of Eben is the hero of the same author's *Charley Skedaddle* (Morrow, 1987, $12.95; pap., Troll, $2.95).

Barbara Dana brilliantly re-creates the daily life of Joan of Arc before she leads the French army in *Young Joan* (Harper, 1992, $17.95).

With her village destroyed during the Norman Conquest, Juliana, a Saxon thane's daughter, must fend for herself in Eloise McGraw's *The Striped Ships* (McElderry, 1991, $15.95).

Colin, his father, and fifty other men leave the Scottish highlands to fight for Bonnie Prince Charlie in 1745 in James D. Forman's exciting *Prince Charlie's Year* (Scribner, 1991, $13.95), and in Frances Mary Hendry's *Quest for a Kelpie* (Holiday, 1988, $12.95), a twelve-year-old girl in eighteenth-century Scotland becomes involved in the intrigue surrounding Bonnie Prince Charlie.

**About the Book**

*Booklist*, June 15, 1990, p. 1970.
*Center for Children's Books Bulletin*, July 1990, p. 275.
*Horn Book*, September 1990, p. 609.
*Horn Book Guide*, January 1990, p. 250.
*Kirkus Reviews*, June 1, 1990, p. 803.
*School Library Journal*, July 1990, p. 56.
VOYA, October 1990, p. 220.
See also *Book Review Digest*, 1991, pp. 1809–10; and *Book Review Index*, 1990, p. 790, and 1991, p. 880.

**About the Author**

Block, Ann, and Riley, Carolyn, eds., *Children's Literary Review*. Gale, 1976, Vol. 1, pp. 182–92.
Chevalier, Tracy, ed., *Twentieth-Century Children's Writers* (3rd ed.). St. James, 1989, pp. 938–40.

Commire, Anne, ed., *Something about the Author.* Gale, 1986, Vol. 44, pp. 188–97.
Fuller, Muriel, ed., *More Junior Authors.* Wilson, 1963, pp. 200–1.
Harte, Barbara, and Riley, Carolyn, eds., *Contemporary Authors* (First Revision). Gale, 1969, Vols. 5–8, p. 1119.
Kirkpatrick, D. L., ed., *Twentieth-Century Children's Writers* (2nd ed.). St. Martin's, 1983, pp. 744–46.
Ward, Martha, ed., *Authors of Books for Young People* (3rd ed.). Scarecrow, 1990, p. 683.

## Westall, Robert. *The Machine Gunners*

Greenwillow, 1976, $11.88 (0-688-80055-6); pap., McKay, $3.50 (0-679-80130-8)

*The Machine Gunners*, first published in England in 1975, won the Carnegie Medal for excellence in literature for older children. It gives an authentic picture of World War II as experienced by ordinary adults and children. This was Westall's first novel for young readers, but he has subsequently written almost thirty additional titles including *Fathom Five* (pap., Knopf, 1990, $3.95), in which he returns to some of the characters he created in *The Machine Gunners*. Both novels are enjoyed by junior high school readers.

### Plot Summary

It is 1941 in Garmouth, England. The British are bombarded daily by German bombers and there are rumors of an imminent invasion by Nazi forces. Like his friends, fourteen-year-old Chas McGill has grown used to spending nights in an air raid shelter. His out-of-school hours are usually spent looking for bits of shrapnel and other litter left from the air raids.

After one particular raid, Chas comes upon a bit of luck—a German Heinkel has been shot down in a wood near town. The dead pilot is still in his plane, and the pilot's hand is still on an intact machine gun. What a prize for his collection! It takes some effort, but Chas is able to wrest the gun from its pinnings.

A plan forms in Chas's mind: Instead of turning in the gun, he will use it to shoot at the hated German hit-and-run bombers. Such a scheme requires careful planning. Where can he put the gun? How can he conceal it from the authorities? Chas first carefully removes the cartridge cases, wraps the gun in cloth, and stows it in the end of a huge hot-water pipe in his father's greenhouse.

It doesn't take the British authorities long to realize that someone has· removed the machine gun from the German plane. They even suspect that it might be some boys up to mischief. But suspicions are one thing; finding the gun and proving the suspicions are quite another.

After the roof is bombed off his grandparents' home—luckily they are unharmed—Chas is more determined than ever to fight the Germans with his hidden weapon. He and his friends decide that the place to make an encampment for the gun is the garden of Sicky Nicky, because nobody ever goes there and it's private. Sicky Nicky is the boy everyone teases, and he is at first quite surprised to find himself the object of so much attention.

Chas and his friends build the secret encampment. When they finally shoot at a German bomber, the plane isn't hit but the pilot is startled, to say the least. The Messerschmitt is hit by three Spitfires. Its rear gunner, Sergeant Rudi Gerlath, parachutes to safety but injures his ankle. He lands in a garden and crawls into a shed. The boys of course think it is their gunfire that has blown up the German plane.

When a woman in the area later reports that someone has been firing on her mother and the police discover that the bullets are German, they realize that someone nearby has the missing machine gun. But who? And where is it?

A few days later Rudi leaves his garden shed and wanders in search of food. He chances on an abandoned house where he figures he can live for weeks. As luck would have it, he stumbles right into the machine gun encampment of the young Britishers!

Both Rudi and his captives are terrified. They realize he's a Nazi; he realizes they are just youngsters. He also realizes that they have a real gun. While Chas and the others try to decide what to do, Rudi, in his dazed state, simply goes to sleep.

For the next few days, Rudi is aware only that he is being tended by a girl-child, one of the group, who spoon-feeds him medicine and soup. Slowly Rudi and the children begin to communicate. They learn that he was a rear gunner, and so he would be able to repair the machine gun which they discover is damaged. Rudi agrees to mend the gun if they will get him a boat in return. Rudi reasons that they can't possibly get him a boat so he won't actually be aiding the enemy.

Rudi doesn't know these English youngsters. They convince Nicky to let them have his father's boat, arguing that the Germans are soon coming, according to the adult conversation they hear, and that they must have the gun for defense.

Soon the whole Garmouth area is in turmoil with the news that the Germans are about to invade. Even Chas's grandparents arm themselves. In the midst of the confusion, the boys get Rudi into the patched-up boat. Nicky asks to go with him, for he has grown fond of the German and has no home life of his own, but Rudi gently tells him no and heads away from the English shore to meet his German comrades. It doesn't take him long to realize that there is no invasion, that this is all hysteria. With nowhere to go, Rudi turns the boat around and heads back to his encampment in Garmouth.

By the next morning the Garmouth citizens also realize that there is no invasion. However, the boys, in their encampment, don't know this. When they see a corps of foreign soldiers—in this case Polish—marching toward them, they fire. In the confusion, the English official sees a German waving a white flag. It is Rudi Gerlath, Sergeant, Luftwaffe, giving himself up. He tells the bewildered official that six schoolchildren are back in the encampment.

The missing machine gun is located, Rudi is taken prisoner, and Chas and his friends are going to receive a very stern warning from their parents. However, they are promised that perhaps, just perhaps, they will be able to write letters to their friend Rudi.

**Thematic Material**

This is a wonderful offbeat story of youngsters and grown-ups in war. All of the characters, children and adults, are portrayed in a most realistic, understandable way, showing them caught up in the hysteria of wartime but reaching out to each other as people and friends. It is a fast-paced, wartime adventure story that is also a tribute to the unflappable British spirit and will.

**Book Talk Material**

A number of incidents can be used as an introduction to this lively adventure. See: Chas finds the machine gun (pp. 7–9); Chas and his friends go back to the wood (pp. 17–20); Chas hides the gun (pp. 25–26); and the roof goes off Nana's house (pp. 51–57).

**Additional Selections**

A family adopts a baby squirrel while they spend time during World War II on a country farm away from London and hope for their father's return from the war in Nina Bawden's *Henry* (Lothrop, Lee & Shepard, 1988, $13.95; pap., Dell, $3.25).

In Peter Hartling's *Crutches* (Lothrop, Lee & Shepard, 1988, $12.95), a young boy who is searching for his mother in post–World War II Vienna is befriended by a former German officer on crutches.

Fifteen-year-old Rod McKenzie escapes an unhappy home life by joining the Australian army during World War II in Michael Noonan's *McKenzie's Boots* (Orchard, 1988, $13.95).

When the Germans begin rounding up Jews in occupied Denmark, Lisa and her family seek aid from the Resistance in Carol Matas's *Lisa's War* (Scribner, 1989, $12.95; pap., Scholastic, $2.75).

In *Visiting Miss Pierce* by Pat Derby, a ninth-grade boy gains insights into his own concerns when he visits an old lady in a local nursing home (Farrar, 1986, $11.95).

Robert Westall has written five short stories about people caught up in war and its effects. They are collected in *Echoes of War* (Farrar, 1991, $13.95).

A young English girl who spent World War II in the United States is not happy when she returns to Britain in Michelle Magorian's *Back Home* (Harper, 1984, $14.95).

**About the Author**

Chevalier, Tracy, ed., *Twentieth-Century Children's Writers* (3rd ed.). St. James, 1989, pp. 1027–29.

Commire, Anne, ed., *Something about the Author*. Gale, 1981, Vol. 23, pp. 235–36.

Estes, Glenn E., ed., *American Writers for Children since 1960: Fiction* (Dictionary of Literary Biography: Vol. 52). Gale, 1986, pp. 374–79.

Holtze, Sally Holmes, ed., *Fifth Book of Junior Authors and Illustrators*. Wilson, 1983, pp. 322–24.

Kirkpatrick, D. L., ed., *Twentieth-Century Children's Writers* (2nd ed.). St. Martin's, 1983, pp. 812–13.

Metzger, Linda, and Straub, Deborah A., eds., *Contemporary Authors* (New Revision Series). Gale, 1986, Vol. 18, pp. 480–82.

Sarkissian, Adele, ed., *Something about the Author: Autobiography Series*. Gale, 1986, Vol. 2, pp. 305–23.

Senick, Gerard J., ed., *Contemporary Authors* (New Revision Series). Gale, 1987, Vol. 13, pp. 235–36, 242–60.

# 5

---

# Sports Fact and Fiction

SPORTS is one of the principal interests of adolescents—both as spectators and as participants. These seven books explore sports in fact and fiction. The former is represented by a biography of an outstanding athlete, the story of an amazing basketball team, and unusual facts about the Olympic Games. The novels deal with young athletes whose involvement with sports has produced a particular moral dilemma or an unusual ethical choice.

---

**Biracree, Tom.** *Wilma Rudolph: Champion Athlete*
Chelsea House, 1988, $16.95 (1-55546-675-3); pap., $9.95 (0-7910-0217-9)

---

The story of Wilma Rudolph is an inspirational one of a woman who overcame severe physical and social handicaps to become one of the world's great athletes. The author has re-created both the personal and the professional life of this amazing person with vivid accuracy and caring detail. Biracree has also written a number of general nonfiction works for adults, including one on social security and another offering tips for successful parenting. This biography is suitable for junior high readers and perhaps some reluctant readers in senior high school.

**Plot Summary**
One blistering hot day in 1960, a young black American won the title of the "fastest woman in the world." The event was the Summer Olympic Games, held in Rome, Italy. A shy twenty-year-old known as the "Tennessee Tornado" became the first American woman to win three track events in a single Olympics. Her name was Wilma Rudolph.

Wilma earned her third gold medal, the highest Olympic honor, on that September day. It was an incredible feat for any runner. It was an especially incredible feat for this one, for Wilma Rudolph was stricken with polio at the age of four, and for several years it was doubtful that she would ever walk without the aid of a brace. No one thought she would run—and certainly no one thought she would run faster than anyone else.

This is a story of bravery, talent, dedication, hard work, belief, and love, all wrapped up in one inspiring woman from Clarksville, Tennessee.

Wilma was born on June 23, 1940. She was the twentieth of twenty-two children born to Blanche and Ed Rudolph. Her mother took in laundry and sewing; her father was a handyman and railroad porter. Their house had no bathroom, and the Rudolph children rarely saw "store-bought" clothes.

It was a time of racial discrimination. Most of Clarksville's 40,000 residents were white. Blacks could not drink from their water fountains, eat in their restaurants, or go to their schools. The town had only one black doctor. That was most unfortunate for Wilma, a sickly child who always seemed to have a cold. When she was four, after having had mumps, measles, and chicken pox, she nearly died from pneumonia and scarlet fever. After she recovered, there was something wrong with her left leg. It was crooked. The doctor said polio must have caused it.

Polio is a virus that attacks the muscles. Today children are inoculated against the disease, but in the 1940s those who got polio usually died or were paralyzed to some degree. The doctor thought Wilma would never walk. Her mother said she would. Until she was twelve years old, Wilma wore a heavy leg brace. Twice a week she and her mother traveled the fifty miles by bus to Nashville for physical therapy. These sessions finally paid off. One day in the local church, the congregation was shocked to see Wilma walking painfully down the aisle without her brace.

By the time she entered Clarksville's all-black Burt High School, Wilma's still skinny body had grown tall, and she now moved with surprising grace. She became a star on the girls' basketball team, scoring thirty-two points in her first game. It was astonishing to think she had been wearing a heavy metal brace just two years before.

The team made it to the state tournament in Nashville. They lost in the second round. Wilma was crushed, but she needn't have been. One of the referees that night was Ed Temple, the women's track coach at Tennessee State University in Nashville. His team, known as the Tigerbelles, was one of the top in the nation. Wilma's long, powerful legs and ease of movement made Temple think that he had found not a basketball player, but a runner.

With Temple's encouragement, Wilma, now six feet tall, entered many track meets during her high school years. Temple invited her to try out for the 1956 Olympic Games with his Tennessee girls. In the 200-meter race, she tied Olympic veteran Mae Faggs and earned a spot on the Olympic team. This youngest member of the U.S. team, now sixteen years old, this poor black girl from rural Tennessee, was going to Australia.

Wilma did not win an individual race at the 1956 Olympics, although she and her teammates won a bronze medal, the third-place prize, in a relay race. Wilma felt she had let everyone down by her performance and vowed that she would train harder than ever for the next Olympic Games.

Wilma entered Tennessee State College in September 1958 on a full athletic scholarship. She was still very shy and in many ways unprepared for the world beyond Clarksville. She had already learned a hard lesson in how unprepared she was when, as a high school senior, she learned that she was pregnant. Both she and her long-time boyfriend, Robert Eldridge, as Wilma later admitted, knew very little about sex and were both surprised and ashamed to learn of her pregnancy. Wilma's daughter, Yolanda, was born shortly after she graduated from high school. At first, the baby lived with Wilma's older married sister in St. Louis; later the child was brought up in the Rudolph household in Clarksville until Wilma could care for her.

Although Wilma made the team at Tennessee State in her freshman year, she began to lose races regularly in 1960. Then a doctor discovered that she had a long-lasting tonsil infection. After her tonsils were removed, Wilma began to win again.

Wilma and her teammates arrived in Rome for the 1960 Olympics, and almost immediately she sprained an ankle. After all the months of training, would she be able to compete? She followed her doctor's orders and was ready for her first race—the 100-meter dash. Wilma won easily. She was so relaxed after the race that she stretched out on the infield and, to the surprise of her teammates, fell asleep.

Wilma won her second gold medal in the 200-meter dash. In the 400-meter relay race, she nearly cost the U.S. team the win by almost dropping the baton, but in a great burst of speed, she beat all her competitors. The U.S. team won the race, and Wilma won her third gold medal.

When Wilma Rudolph returned home, the town of Clarksville honored her with a celebration—the first integrated event in the town's history. Wilma Rudolph, the shy girl from Tennessee, was now a national celebrity.

Wilma went on to graduate from Tennessee State with a degree in elementary education. She competed in a number of track events, to the delight of her many fans. She met John Kennedy, then president of the United States. She traveled to foreign countries.

Wilma Rudolph ran her last race in 1962, with U.S. athletes competing against those from the Soviet Union. She returned home to Clarksville, where she became the track coach at her old high school and an elementary schoolteacher. She also found Robert Eldridge still waiting. They were married in 1963 and later had a second daughter and two sons. When their oldest child, Yolanda, became a teenager, she received a scholarship to Tennessee State, training under Coach Temple as her mother had done.

Wilma Rudolph continues to be a goodwill ambassador. In 1981 she started the Wilma Rudolph Foundation to help train young athletes. Its headquarters is in Indianapolis.

Once the "world's fastest woman," Wilma Rudolph remains a role model for young women today, especially young black women, although she herself says, "I don't know if I'm a role model or not. That's for other people to decide."

**Thematic Material**

This is a straightforward biography of an outstanding athlete. It conveys a sensitive picture of what it was like to be gifted, physically handicapped, poor, and black, especially in a time of overt discrimination. It sends a powerful message that shows what hard work, determination, and a family's love can accomplish. Wilma Rudolph is shown as a strong role model.

**Book Talk Material**

The descriptions of the challenge young Wilma faced in trying to heal her crippled leg paint a strong picture of her own inner strength and her mother's unfailing belief in her eventual success (pp. 32–39). Young sports enthusiasts will be especially interested in the retelling of Wilma's triumphs at the Olympic Games (pp. 13–25, 77–85). Reading about the extent of racial discrimination during Wilma Rudolph's childhood can help young people gain a greater understanding of the many obstacles this black girl had to overcome on the way to victory (pp. 29–32).

**Additional Selections**

The life of the black heavyweight champion who defended his title twenty times is told by Robert Jakoubek in *Joe Louis* (Chelsea House, 1990, $17.95).

In Leonard Todd's humorous novel *Squaring Off* (Viking, 1990, $13.95), a thirteen-year-old boy obsessed with fighting and beautiful girls asks Champ, a young black boxer, to teach him to fight.

The stories of seven championship runners are told in Nathan Aaseng's *World Class Marathoners* (Lerner, 1982, $7.95).

The story of the black athlete who upset Hitler's master race theory at the Olympics is told in *Jesse Owens: Champion Athlete* (Chelsea House, 1990, $17.95) by Tony Gentry.

Biographies of many famous contributors to several sports are given in George Sullivan's *Great Lives: Sports* (Macmillan, 1988, $22.95).

In the novel *Fox Running* (pap., Avon, 1977, $2.50), by R. R. Knudson, Kathy and an Apache girl find friendship and inspiration in their love of running.

Gail longs for a social life but must make sacrifices if she hopes to be an Olympic gymnast in Mark McCrackin's novel *A Sense of Balance* (Westminster, 1975, $7.50).

**About the Book**
*Booklist*, August 1988, p. 1911.
See also *Book Review Index*, 1988, p. 78.

---

**Crutcher, Chris.** *Running Loose*
Greenwillow, 1983, $9.50 (0-688-02002-X); pap., Dell, $3.25 (0-440-97570-0)

---

This is Chris Crutcher's first novel for young adults. In its first-person narrative, Louis, a sensitive young man, is placed in an untenable position by a dishonorable, bullying coach. As in his other novels, sports, though an integral part of the plot, are secondary to substantive questions involving honor, principles, and decency. Two of Crutcher's other successful novels for the same age group are: *Stotan!* (Greenwillow, 1986, $10.25; pap., Dell, $3.25; condensed in *Juniorplots 3*, Bowker, 1987, pp. 238–43), about a grueling athletic program endured by a high school swimming team, and *The Crazy Horse Electric Game* (Greenwillow, 1987,

$10.25; pap., Dell, $3.50; condensed in *Seniorplots*, Bowker, 1989, pp. 55–59), in which a debilitating accident changes the life of a young athlete. These novels are recommended for both junior and senior high school readers.

**Plot Summary**

"I learned a lot this year, in spite of the fact that I was going to school. I learned some about friendship and a whole lot about love and that there's no use being honorable with dishonorable men." That sums up the senior year in high school for Louie Banks in this story of a young man dealing with love, honor, death, and sportsmanship as he nears manhood.

As the school year begins in the small Idaho town of Trout, Louie figures he has the world by the tail. His grades aren't too bad; he's been running all summer with his best friend so he's earned a starting spot on the championship eight-man football team; his relationship with his parents is pretty good; he's got a part-time job and a pickup truck; and his girlfriend is Becky Sanders, the source of every boy's dreams at Trout High. Of course, there is always a fly in the ointment. In Louie's case, it's Boomer Cowans, also on the football team, always a better athlete than Louie, and forty times as mean.

Still, Louie figures he can stay clear of Boomer, so life looks pretty good. And it is—until the upcoming game against Salmon River. During a pregame lecture, Coach Lednecky warns the Trout team about Salmon River's star, a transfer student from California. He's good, very good, says the coach, better than anyone they've faced. He's also black. To Louie's amazement, the coach seems somehow to be implying that the Trout team should *get* this black student, play dirty if they have to, just get him out of the game. The coach doesn't want a championship season spoiled by some black guy who's not even a native son.

During the game, Boomer Cowans does see to it that the Salmon River star is injured and taken from the field. Trout wins. Louie loses his cool. He tells the coach what he thinks, is thrown off the team for insubordination, is suspended from all sports, and is nearly thrown out of school.

Even so, life isn't so bad. Louie's parents understand and support him. Becky is proud of him, and Louie figures he's really not that great an athlete anyway. He can live without sports.

So Louie works at his part-time job, takes up cross-country skiing by himself, and his relationship with Becky grows even closer. They almost—but not quite—get to the point of sex. Louie figures when they're ready, that will happen, too.

Then, while at work one day, he is told that Becky has been in a car accident. She swerved to miss some children and her car went into the river. She is dead.

Louie begins the painful process of dealing with the loss of a loved one. He decides that he cannot go to Becky's funeral, but at the last minute he does. When he hears the preacher—someone who didn't know her—talking about Becky, he shocks everyone by losing his composure and screaming aloud.

Louie later apologizes to his parents, and to Becky's father and the preacher. Then he plunges himself back into school and work, keeping the warm memories of Becky in his heart. In the springtime, the assistant coach at the high school approaches Louie about running on the track team. Louie explains that he's been banned from all sports activities. Assistant coach Madison persists, and eventually—with Louie largely keeping his mouth shut—a deal is worked out with Head Coach Lednecky and Principal Jasper. Louie will run "unofficially" on the track team.

Although Louie still believes that the head coach and the principal are wrong and unprincipled, he is slowly learning that sometimes there are compromises one must make in life. You can still keep your honor by knowing when to remain silent.

At the fourth track meet of the season, Louie learns that the school will plant a tree and erect a plaque in Becky's honor. Louie likes the idea of the tree, but he is outraged when he reads the plaque and sees that it is personally signed by Principal Jasper, a man Louie feels is without honor. That night Louie returns to the school, knocks the plaque off its concrete base, and throws it in the river.

Principal Jasper isn't fooled. He immediately calls Louie to his office and accuses him of the deed. Louie's attitude is, more or less, "prove it!" Of course, the principal can't.

Coach Madison tells Louie that his opponent for the upcoming two-mile race will be none other than Washington, the black student from Salmon River who was knocked out of the football game back in the fall. On the day of the race, Louie and the Salmon River star meet each other. Washington says that he heard about Louie's outburst and what happened to him after the football game. He says Louie has his respect, but he's still going to try to beat him.

Coach Madison tells Louie, "Just run *your* race." In the race of his life, Louie breaks the tape just before Washington. He wins the two-mile and collapses from exhaustion.

Louie finishes fourth in the regional track meet. Since only the top three spots go on to the state meet, his track career is over—but Louie can live with that, too. The principal even calls him in and tells him to forget about the plaque; they're putting up another one anyway. Louie suggests that this time perhaps the principal shouldn't sign it.

Graduation comes, and on that night Louie's father tells him, "I wish there were some way I could tell you how proud I am." That really causes Louie to burst into tears—right in the gym in front of everybody. However, he has learned that that's all right, too.

Louie figures he has come out of the year okay. Not with Becky's loss, of course; that pain will always be a part of him. He has learned that you can do almost anything if you have people who care about you, and he has learned that you must be responsible for your own actions and stand up for what you believe in.

On the other hand, he is quick to realize that he hasn't learned everything yet. A new plaque is put up beside Becky's tree, and it is exactly like the old one—signed by Principal Jasper. The principal wasn't taking any chances; he camped out overnight by the plaque with his shotgun for a week waiting for the destroyer to show up.

Louie has learned patience. The principal went home tonight.

**Thematic Material**

This is a familiar but warm and well-done story of a young man bouncing along a rocky road to manhood. Louie Banks is a likable teenager whose visions of fair play and sportsmanship are abruptly challenged. When he is confronted with the pain caused by the death of someone he loves, he lashes out. He is expected to be accountable for his actions, but he doesn't always know how. Young boys, and girls, too, will like Louie as he struggles to make sense of a world he doesn't always understand. An important theme of the book is the love and strength Louis receives from his parents.

**Book Talk Material**

Young people can empathize with Louie's reactions to the events of his senior year in high school. The following situations in the book can lead to discussions of how other teenagers might have handled these problems. What else could Louie have done? Would other actions have made things easier for him? See the following: Louie reacts at the Salmon River football game (pp. 61–64); Louie chops down a tree after Becky's death (p. 127); the scene at Becky's funeral (pp. 136–37); Louie destroys the plaque (pp. 174–76).

**Additional Selections**

Profiles of twelve coaches, including Knute Rockne and Vince Lombardi, are given in Hank Nuwer's nonfiction *Strategies of the Great Football Coaches* (Watts, 1988, $12.90), a companion volume to *Strategies of the Great Baseball Managers* (Watts, 1988, $13.90).

In Thomas J. Dygard's *Halfback Tough* (Morrow, 1986, $12.95; pap., Penguin, $3.95), Joe Atkins tries to forget his troubled past when he joins the football team in his new school. Two other Dygard favorites are *Quarterback Walk-On* (Morrow, 1982, $13.65; pap., Penguin, $3.95) and *Forward Pass* (Morrow, 1989, $11.95; pap., Penguin, $3.95).

Randy Powell's *My Underrated Year* (Farrar, 1988, $12.95; pap., $3.95) tells of Roger's sophomore year when a newcomer usurps his place on the varsity football team.

In Jim Naughton's *My Brother Stealing Second* (Harper, 1989, $13.98; pap., $3.95), Bobby grieves for his baseball-star brother who was killed in a car accident and becomes self-destructive until his classmate Annie helps him and he returns to his baseball team.

Gary Madden receives help from an unusual English teacher when he is paralyzed after a football injury in Robin Brancato's *Winning* (Knopf, 1976, $12.95; pap., $2.50).

An excellent anthology of sports stories by both adult and young adult authors is L. M. Schulman's *The Random House Book of Sports Stories* (Random, 1990, $15.95).

Fifteen-year-old Brandon persuades his sister to join his high school varsity football team where she becomes a star in Paul Baczewski's *Just for Kicks* (Harper, 1990, $13.95).

**About the Book**
*Booklist*, April 1, 1983, p. 1019.
*Center for Children's Books Bulletin*, May 1983, p. 165.
*Horn Book*, August 1983, p. 451.
*Kirkus Reviews*, April 15, 1983, p. 161.
*School Library Journal*, May 1983, p. 80.

*VOYA,* April 1983, p. 36.
See also *Book Review Digest,* 1983, p. 356; and *Book Review Index,* 1983, p. 131.

**About the Author**
Commire, Anne, ed., *Something about the Author.* Gale, 1988, Vol. 52, p. 31.
May, Hal, ed., *Contemporary Authors.* Gale, 1985, Vol. 113, pp. 107–8.

---

**Duder, Tessa.**   *In Lane Three, Alex Archer*
Houghton, 1989, $13.95 (0-395-50927-0); pap., Bantam, $3.50
(0-553-29020-7)

---

Tessa Duder has won many prizes for her writing in her native New Zealand, but only recently has come to the attention of American readers. This first-person narrative set in New Zealand in the 1950s combines sports drama with a coming-of-age story. It is told by Alex, a strong, self-absorbed girl who is also particularly vulnerable because of the deaths of both her grandmother and her boyfriend. The author communicates the belief that young people should be more concerned with important career goals than with superficialities of dress and appearance. Interwoven with these serious themes are scenes of swimming meets re-created authentically by the author, who was herself an Empire Games Senior Medalist. This interesting novel is suitable for young readers in grades 7 through 10.

**Plot Summary**
"I have always known that in another life I was—or will be—a dolphin. I'm silver and grey, the sleekest thing on fins, with a permanent smile on my face. I leap over and through the waves. I choose a passing yacht to dive under and hear the shouts of children as I emerge triumphant close to the boat."

So begins the story of fifteen-year-old Alex Archer. It is 1959, in New Zealand. Alex is a popular teenager, a good student, tall, striking looking if not pretty, with a keen sense of humor, a warm, loving family, and a very special friend, Andy. In addition, Alex is a swimmer, a truly outstanding freestyle swimmer, who has been training for six years.

It hasn't all been easy. Sometimes Alex is terrified as she stands poised at the edge of the pool, ready for the race. She often feels caught in a surge of ambition and longing to win. Still, she loves it; this is where she belongs.

Life would be easier, of course, without Maggie Benton. Maggie has been Alex's rival—and sort-of friend—since she was twelve, when Maggie arrived from Singapore. Not nearly as tall as Alex's five feet ten plus, Maggie is fast and strong. When the two are paired against each other, Maggie often wins. She also gets much better press because Alex has a bad habit of shooting off her mouth with reporters.

Now the rivalry between the two swimmers has assumed greater importance than ever. The Olympic Games will be held in Rome in 1960. Alex wants to represent New Zealand in the freestyle swimming events. So does Maggie.

Life becomes a series of training schedules with her swim coach, Mr. Jack, and swim meets, competitions, and school—and some unexpected events, too. Alex is invited to a dance given by Maggie. She and Andy attend, she in her first formal gown, he in a suit, tie, and pink carnation.

Alex also continues to play hockey at school, against the advice of Mr. Jack. One day she is hit by a ball at close range, fracturing a bone in her leg. The leg goes into a cast. It will be two months before Alex can get in the water to practice again. She will never beat Maggie now.

Mr. Jack has other ideas. He asks Alex how badly she wants to get to Rome. If she is willing to work as she has never worked before, perhaps she has a chance. Alex begins a program of weights until the cast comes off. She is also busy with the school's production of *The Wizard of Oz*. Alex plays the Tin Man.

She plunges into the training regimen so rigidly that her parents decide they all need to take a few days off at the beach. Alex is not too keen at the thought of a break until her mother tells her that Andy is invited, too. They spend three days during which Alex feels suspended in time.

Back home, Alex resumes training in earnest. Everything points toward peak form for the nationals to be held in Napier starting in February. Alex does not perform well at her first invitation club meeting. Maggie does. Andy tells Alex she's getting "too earnest again."

Then, quite suddenly, Alex's world falls apart. Andy, her dearest friend, the boy she is beginning to love, is killed by a hit-and-run driver. After the tears and the unbearable pain of the loss, Alex resolves: "I'm going to Rome. For him. I'm going to Rome."

For Andy, Alex decides that she will train harder than she has ever trained in her life. Every meet she attends will receive maximum effort, and in the end, at the nationals at Napier, she will beat Maggie. That she vows. When her name is announced among the Olympic nominations, it will be her silent memorial to Andy.

Training is still as hard as before, but now Alex has an added purpose. Her times are faster. At a meet soon after school finishes, Alex beats Maggie. Her rival still has a faster unofficial time, but Alex knows she can do it.

Finally, all the training is over and the nationals are at hand. The night before the big race at Napier that means so much, Alex cannot sleep. She feels she must go for a swim or go mad.

The pool where the championships are held is closed at this time of night, but as Alex walks by, she runs into the pool manager and asks him to open the pool for her for a short swim. He hesitates, but then allows her a few minutes. Alex swims a few laps in the dark and feels cleansed, then thanks the manager and returns the one block to her motel.

The next morning Alex's coach and her father greet her with the news that everybody knows about her "midnight escapade" with a man. There's talk of disciplinary action. Alex may be made ineligible for the Olympics. She is speechless. Then Maggie tells her that it was Maggie's mother who reported that Alex was "out" with the pool manager.

Alex realizes that no matter what the outcome of the meet, she and Maggie have reached an understanding they have never had before. Shortly afterward, Maggie swims to a national record—65.6 seconds. It is Alex's turn. Suddenly, as she stands at the pool's edge, she is as angry as she has ever been. She is angry about the jealousy and gossip that may ruin her chances. She hits the water like a clap of thunder and outswims her opponents in a fury. Her time—65.2. She has broken Maggie's record.

Hours later Alex learns that the complaint against her has been dropped. The pool manager corroborated her story of a midnight swim. It was foolish perhaps, but she did nothing wrong. She will be allowed to compete.

That night she will swim against Maggie once more. Her coach thinks they will both break the record again. Alex wonders if her life will always be like this. Will she always attract attention and trouble as her ambition takes her forward? No matter, she is strong and she is invincible. She is at peace with herself. She can face family and friends and reporters. She will go to Rome.

Lead on, Andy, she thinks. I'm ready.

**Thematic Material**

This sports story vividly portrays the pressures that talented young people undergo as they try to achieve their dreams. Young Alex is torn between her driving ambition and love of swimming and her desire and need to live a normal life. It also shows how young lives can be manipulated by these pressures as inexperienced youngsters are thrown into the arena of public scrutiny. This is also a story of learning to lose—a competition or a loved one.

**Book Talk Material**

Alex is a talented swimmer, a fact that sets her apart from other teenagers (see pp. 9, 16–21, 28–29, 58, 63–65). She is also a young girl with normal interests; see the formal dance (pp. 35–47) and Alex and Andy on the beach (pp. 106–10). Contrasting these two sides is a good introduction to the pressures of growing up in the mid-twentieth century when talent pulls one way and the need to be like everyone else pulls another, and when young women were not quite so independent.

**Additional Selections**

Overweight sixteen-year-old Mike Thatcher goes on a diet and reluctantly joins the school swim team, where he finds he has talent for diving in Nancy J. Hopper's *Wake Me When the Band Starts Playing* (Lodestar, 1988, $13.95).

A movie star's son helps a shy, insecure teenager achieve success as a runner on the school's track team in Nancy Rue's *The Janis Project* (pap., Good News, 1988, $7.95).

In *Anything to Win* by Gloria D. Miklowitz (Delacorte, 1989, $14.95; pap., Dell, $3.25), about the dangers of steroids, Cam Potter, a high school football player, can probably win a scholarship if he puts on thirty pounds quickly.

Kirstin creates a school controversy when she drops out of the basketball team in favor of taking advanced algebra in Nadine Roberts's *These Are the Best Years?* (pap., Juniper, 1989, $2.95).

In *Separations* (Viking, 1990, $13.95) by Robert Lehrman, Kim's life, including her tennis game, is changed by her parents' divorce.

The limits to which one will go to win is explored in Rosemary Wells's tennis novel *When No One Was Looking* (Dial, 1980, $14.95; pap., Scholastic, $2.95; condensed in *Juniorplots 3*, Bowker, 1987, pp. 253–57).

In *Flip City* by Spring Hermann (Orchard, 1988, $13.95), four girl-friends face personal problems while improving their gymnastic skills.

### About the Book

*Book Report,* May 1990, p. 46.
*Booklist,* November 1, 1989, p. 540.
*Center for Children's Books Bulletin,* November 1989, p. 54.
*Horn Book,* January 1990, p. 68.
*Horn Book Guide,* July 1990, p. 76.
*School Library Journal,* January 1990, p. 120.
*VOYA,* February 1990, p. 342.
*Wilson Library Bulletin,* September 1990, p. 13.

### About the Author

Chevalier, Tracy, ed., *Twentieth-Century Children's Writers* (3rd ed.). St. James, 1989, pp. 299–300.

---

**Frommer, Harvey.** *Olympic Controversies*
Watts, 1987, $11.90 (0-531-10417-6)

---

Harvey Frommer has successfully combined a career of teaching writing at the college level with an absorbing interest in sports. In addition to a biography, *Jackie Robinson* (Watts, 1984, $12.90), he has in print a volume in the First Book series, *Baseball's Hall of Fame* (Watts, 1985, $10.40). *Olympic Controversies* gives a general history of the Olympics with a concentration on the political events, tragedies, follies, quarrels, and general controversy surrounding the games. It begins with the marathon race of 1908 and ends with the 1984 meeting of Mary Decker and Zola Budd in the 3,000-meter race. This book is popular with readers in grades 6 through 9.

### Plot Summary

Every four years, millions of sports fans, as well as those who would otherwise never pay attention, eagerly await what is perhaps the most exciting of all modern athletic spectacles—the Olympic Games. In theory, these are the most noble of sporting events, the coming together in peaceful competition, under the fairest of circumstances, of the best athletes from all countries of the world.

Despite the fact that the Olympic Games have provided some of the most exciting sports moments ever recorded, they have also been plagued with woes. Harvey Frommer takes a through-the-years look at controversies that have marred both the summer and winter games and discusses some provocative questions. Do the Olympics really provide international competition at its best? Have they become too influenced by nationalism or television? Should they continue?

The book begins with a brief look at the transition from the ancient games, which date from races held in Greece 3,000 years ago, to the modern Olympics, beginning in 1896. The ancient games were highly important to Greek life, but they were abolished in A.D. 394, after the Roman conquest. Credit for their revival goes to Baron Pierre de Coubertin, a French aristocrat who made it his life's work to restore the ancient games, reasoning that sports competition would lead to international friendship. The first of the modern games was held in Athens, Greece, in 1896, with fourteen nations competing. It was agreed that they would be held every four years as in ancient times, but that the competition would be in modern sports; that only amateurs (male at the time) could compete; and that the location would change from city to city.

Chapter 2 looks at general controversies that continue today—over the opening ceremonies, for instance. Through the years, especially with more and more extensive television coverage, the opening ceremonies have grown more grand and more spectacular. From the colorful ritual that was intended, the ceremonies have sometimes become a boastful way to extol national pride or exhibit the most expensive uniforms. Some attending nations will not recognize other nations. Winning gold medals (the medals actually are not gold but only covered with a thin sheet of it) has become a matter of national pride instead of an honor for the athlete him- or herself.

Other continuing problems involve television coverage, which costs millions of dollars and can influence an audience's choice of sports equipment or vacation plans, and the whole question of commercialism. Today's winners may be seeking not just a medal, but real gold—the gold in a lucrative "after-the-games" career. American speed skater Eric Heiden, who won five gold medals in the 1980 games, turned down commercial endorsements because he didn't want to "cash in" on his Olympic feats. But for every Heiden, there are many who seek medals for the real cash they bring.

And there is the serious and continuing problem of drugs, usually in the form of steroids taken to enhance performance. A number of contestants have been barred from Olympic competition through drug testing, which is now a permanent part of these games.

Chapters 3 through 7 cover specific periods in the Olympic Games. The 1900 games, with more than 1,100 athletes, including 11 women, competing, were held in Paris to honor Baron de Coubertin (Chapter 3, "The Olympics from 1900 to World War I"). They were so poorly run that, in all the confusion, the baron's name was not mentioned once by the journalists who covered the event. The first U.S. Olympics was held in St. Louis in 1904 with 617 competitors, but 500 were from the United States. The games were marked by a low rather than a high point when American Fred Lorz finished the marathon run and then later admitted that along the way he had hitched a car ride because he was tired. The 1908 Summer Games were held in London and boasted more then 2,000 athletes. The U.S. team was angry at the opening ceremonies because the British had somehow "forgotten" to include an American flag. So, when the U.S. team, carrying small flags, marched past the reviewing stand that held King Edward VII, the American standard bearer refused to dip the flag as was the custom. To this day, American teams do not dip the flag when marching past the host country's reviewing stand. In the 1912 Summer Olympiad at Stockholm, native American Jim Thorpe became the first international sports hero with his tremendous track and field wins. Six months later, Thorpe, one of America's greatest athletes ever, was stripped of his medals because he had earlier played minor league baseball for a North Carolina team. It was not until 1983, twenty-one years after Thorpe's death, that his feats were reinstated in Olympic statistics and the medals were returned to his family.

Chapter 4, "The Olympics between Two World Wars (1920–1936)," witnesses the feats of such sports heroes as American swimmer Johnny Weissmuller (1924 and 1928 Olympics), who later became the movie Tarzan; the first Olympic female star, fifteen-year-old Sonja Henie, who won three gold medals in figure skating in 1928 and went on to a career in Hollywood; and one of America's greatest athletes, Mildred "Babe" Didrikson. More than for any other event, this period is remembered for the 1936 games in Berlin. Adolf Hitler intended the Olympics to be a showcase for the Nazi party and its anti-Jew, anti-black policies. The hero who emerged from the competition was a black American and the grandson of slaves, Jesse Owens, who won four gold medals and set a long-jump record of 16 feet, 5 ¼ inches, which was not broken until 1960.

There were no games from 1937 to 1947 due to World War II, but when they resumed, politics began to play an important role, as evidenced by events discussed in Chapter 5, "The Olympics of the Cold War Years (1948–1960)." The 1952 games in Helsinki, Finland, became a contest between the United States and the Soviet Union, as though the highest number of gold medals would indicate which political system was better. The end result was the Soviets 71, the Americans 76. Real conflict emerged at the Summer Olympiad in Melbourne, Australia, in 1956. Soviet troops and tanks had put down a revolt in Hungary, causing some nations to withdraw from the games. A near riot broke out when the Soviet and the Hungarian teams met in a water polo match, which Hungary won.

Chapter 6, "From Tokyo to Montreal (1964–1976)," continues the story of politics and sports. This period of the games is best remembered for two events. At the 1968 Summer Games in Mexico City, black American runners Tommie Smith, gold medal winner, and John Carlos, bronze medal winner, stood on the podium while the U.S. national anthem was played and raised black-gloved fists in a "Black Power" salute as a political statement. They were suspended from the games. Terror took over at the 1972 Summer Olympiad in Munich, Germany, as Arab terrorists burst into the Olympic Village and murdered two members of the Israeli team. Crowds demanded that the games be called off, but Avery Brundage, president of the International Olympic Committee (IOC), declared that "an end to the Games would mean a victory for terrorism." The games continued.

Chapter 7, "Boycotting the Olympics (1980–1984)," discusses whether the purpose of the games is to join in international competition or to use the Olympics as a political arena. During this period, both the United States and the Soviet Union boycotted the games. Moscow was chosen as the site for the 1980 games. In 1979 Russian troops invaded Afghanistan. U.S. President Jimmy Carter angrily denounced the move in January 1980 and declared that U.S. athletes would not compete; sixty-one other nations also boycotted. It was the Russians' turn in 1984 at the summer games in Los Angeles. The U.S.S.R. refused to send a team, claiming it was concerned about the athletes' safety; actually, the Soviets were "paying back" the Americans for boycotting the games in Moscow.

So it goes—amid the grace and beauty, the superb feats of endurance and skill, the sheer joy of athletic competition, the controversies continue in this showcase of international sport. Future troubles seem more focused on commercialism and drug use than on politics, but, for sure, the next grand and glorious spectacle will be on display to an eager audience.

## Thematic Material

This is a serious although not somber look at the woes that have continued to plague the modern Olympic Games. The author includes the feats of many Olympic heroes, as well as international and political conditions that have impinged on the integrity or spirit of the games as intended at their revival in 1896. Sports fans especially should be interested in these accounts of controversies, some slight, others more serious.

## Book Talk Material

Various incidents concerning the games can lead into discussions of values. With so much emphasis on winning medals, can contestants truly live up to the Olympic oath they take (p. 21)? Is it right for medal winners to capitalize on their Olympic fame as a way of demanding huge salaries when they turn pro or go into some other career (pp. 25–27)? Should American athletes have used the Olympic medal ceremony for their Black Power salute in the 1968 Games, and was the Olympic Committee justified in suspending them (p. 86)?

## Additional Selections

Janet Mohun, in *Drugs, Steroids and Sports* (Watts, 1988, $11.90), discusses what drugs athletes use and why, two problems faced by officials in the Olympic Games.

There are over 150 poems on a variety of sports from baseball to swimming in *American Sports Poems* (Orchard, 1988, $15.95), edited by R. R. Knudson and May Swenson.

Shirley Glubok and Alfred Tamarin trace the origins of the games in *Olympic Games in Ancient Greece* (Harper, 1976, $13.89).

Many sports and their players, rules, and plays are featured in Edward F. Dolan, Jr.'s *The Julian Messner Sports Question and Answer Book* (Messner, 1984, $10.79; pap., Wanderer, $8.95).

A compendium of myth and superstition that helps explain the unusual behavior of some coaches and players is told in Kathlyn Gay's *They Don't Wash Their Socks!* (Walker, 1990, $14.85).

In R. R. Knudson's *Zan Hagen's Marathon* (Farrar, 1984, $10.95; pap.,

NAL, $2.25; condensed in *Juniorplots 3*, Bowker, 1987, pp. 243–46), a young runner fulfills her greatest dream of running in the marathon during the Los Angeles Olympic Games.

An explanation of how such scientific principles as gravity and momentum are applied in sports is explored in Robert Gardner's *Science and Sports* (Watts, 1988, $11.90).

**About the Book**
*Book Report*, January 1988, p. 56.
*Booklist*, January 15, 1988, p. 850.
*School Library Journal*, January 1988, p. 91.
*VOYA*, February 1988, p. 295.
*Wilson Library Bulletin*, December 1987, p. 67.
See also *Book Review Digest*, 1988, pp. 594–95; and *Book Review Index*, 1988, p. 283.

**About the Author**
Commire, Anne, ed., *Something about the Author*. Gale, 1985, Vol. 41, pp. 86–87, 148–49.
May, Hal, ed., *Contemporary Authors*. Gale, 1989, Vol. 26, pp. 148–9.

---

**Jones, Ron.**   *B-Ball: The Team That Never Lost a Game*
Bantam, 1990, lib. bdg., $17.95 (0-553-05867-3); pap., $3.50 (0-553-29404-0)

---

In this humorous, often moving account of work with a team of physically handicapped basketball players, the author draws on his own experiences over the years as coach of the Special Olympics basketball team. This book covers in an episodic fashion events that span several years. It is a very personal story of patience, persistence, love, and achievement. It is enjoyed by readers in junior high.

**Plot Summary**
It is year one of the San Francisco Special Olympics basketball team. Lifelong basketball fan and coach Ron Jones faces his team for the first time—all four of them. His heart sinks. Out the window quickly fly his dreams of pressure defense and a fast-break drill, of feet nimbly flying down the court, and basketballs perfectly arced to the hoop. It is, instead, quite possible that these would-be athletes standing hopefully in front of

him might have extreme difficulty just learning to hold a basketball, much less shoot it.

There is Michael, tall enough to play center, with a bell-shaped body, a singsong voice, and a toothless grin. There is Joey, with no voice and one arm that doesn't work. There is tall, strong Leonette with a Magic Johnson smile, who dashes off for the bathroom at odd times, and there is Audwin, who can run very fast—sideways.

Jones is supposed to teach basketball to these four young people, all classified as mentally disabled. They cannot go to school or hold a job or live on their own. Joey and Audie live with their mothers. Michael and Leonette are boarders, with a history of being on the street.

This unlikely foursome and the dubious coach go to work. Every week they practice at the city gym. Little by little, Coach Jones figures out ways to help these young people learn the fundamentals of basketball. He tapes Xs on the floor to show Michael and Leonette where to shoot from. He uses tape on Joey's hands to show him how to hang on to the ball.

By year three, the San Francisco Special Olympics basketball team is ready to play a game. The Recreation Center for the Handicapped is building a gymnasium. Jones has actually found some more players. The team's first test is in Los Angeles at the Special Olympics. They lose the first game, 16–2. They lose the second, 58–6. They win game three on a forfeit because the opponent team's bus breaks down. Game four they win on their own, 42–12.

It is year five, and now everyone wants to join the team. Jones discovers that is partly because his players have been telling everyone that they won the championship—instead of just one game in Los Angeles—but then, he reasons, if you think you're a champion, you play like one.

Year five includes a trip to the Mid-State Basketball Tournament. It is there that Coach Jones calms down his overexcited players with the "Pizza Defense." They break the huddle with the world's first pizza yell— "Piizzzzaaa!!" It is also at this game that Coach Jones truly realizes that the ultimate champion in the Special Olympics is the game itself, "the challenge and the opportunity it affords everyone who wants to play."

The San Francisco Special Olympics began when some families of disabled children got together to organize athletic competitions. These people realized that children who could not walk or run normally or did not speak well or at all or could not count or spell needed praise and love and recognition just like any other children. They got local businesspeople and organizations to sponsor the awards, the food, the bands.

Now Coach Jones sees that the Special Olympics is growing, perhaps too much. It is threatened by professionalization, the idea of the state taking over, providing "official medals," the competition getting tougher and tougher. Perhaps the emphasis will turn to a quest for medals instead of the thrill of participating. Jones decides to look around for other teams to play that will encourage participation by everyone.

Finally, the coach challenges any team in the San Francisco Bay Area to play his Special Olympics basketballers. His newspaper release reads in part: "Warning: The San Francisco Special Olympics basketball team is undefeated with a record of 35 wins and 0 defeats! We have players that sometime shoot at the wrong basket and sometimes are known to hug their opponents." Wonder of wonders, within one week Jones has a twenty-three-game schedule. All sorts of teams respond—the San Francisco Police Department, a mental hospital, county jail prisoners, high schools, and an all-girl prep school team. Each game usually results in a "hug attack."

Now the coach comes up with the idea of taking his team to China. He gets his high schoolers in Palo Alto, California, where he teaches history, interested in the project. They actually rig up a line and get to talk for fifteen minutes to the minister of education in Communist China.

Jones doesn't get his group to China, but China comes to them. A group of disabled Chinese, stopping over in San Francisco on their way home, wish to see the Special Olympics basketball team. A game isn't scheduled between the two groups, but a wonderful and memorable contest follows. It is a moment Coach Jones and his players never forget.

Jones was to spend ten years as coach of the basketball team that never lost a game. He becomes Michael's legal guardian and teaches him to make pizza. Leonette gets a job for the first time, as a waitress. Audie no longer plays basketball, but has learned how to dial a telephone. Joey remains with his mother and is as sweet and kind as ever.

**Thematic Material**

Disabled youngsters are the heart of this story of the San Francisco Special Olympics basketball team that never lost a game, and the theme is sport. Sport, perhaps, as it should be played, for the pure joy and fun of athletic competition. The handicaps of these boys and girls are not ignored or minimized, but they are accepted as part of their world and they are incorporated into the game as they must play it.

**Book Talk Material**

An introduction to the four original members of the basketball team is a good beginning to this book (pp. 3–7). Readers can gain understanding of what the Special Olympics means to its players from the team's first tournament, in Los Angeles (pp. 32–45). The coach's fears about professionalizing the Special Olympics can lead to a discussion of what happens when professionalism invades any sport (pp. 86–90).

**Additional Selections**

In Brian R. Ward's *Overcoming Disability* (Watts, 1988, $12.90), there is a discussion of the nature of various disabilities and of how people can be helped to cope with them.

Frederick Drimmer covers the stories of seven people, such as Tom Thumb and the Elephant Man, who conquered birth defects and led productive lives in *Born Different: Amazing Stories of Very Special People* (Atheneum, 1988, $14.95).

From 1890 through 1989, a chronological history of basketball highlights is given in William S. Jarrett's *Timetables of Sports History: Basketball* (Facts on File, 1990, $17.95).

A description of sports in which handicapped people can participate is given in Anne Allen's *Sports for the Handicapped* (Walker, 1981, $10.95).

All sorts of physical handicaps are explored with stories of how they have been overcome in Connie Barron's *The Physically Handicapped* (Crestwood, 1988, $10.95).

The would-be captain of the wrestling team finds he has diabetes in V. T. Dacquino's novel *Kiss the Candy Days Goodbye* (Delacorte, 1982, $11.95; pap., Dell, $2.25).

A physically handicapped girl finds she has a male admirer in Susan Sallis's *Only Love* (Harper, 1980, $12.95).

**About the Book**
*Book Report,* November 1990, p. 63.
*Booklist,* July 1990, p. 2080.
*Horn Book Guide,* January 1990, p. 306.
*School Library Journal,* April 1991, p. 148.
*VOYA,* June 1990, p. 126.
*Wilson Library Bulletin,* January 1991, p. 3.

**Klass, David.** *Breakaway Run*
Dutton, 1987, $13.95 (0-525-67190-0)

In this novel, Tony, a teenager whose parents are divorcing, spends five months as an exchange student in Japan. While there he records his experiences both on and off the soccer field and his general adaptation to the country in a journal, which is part of this novel. The author uses his own experiences as an English teacher in a Japanese high school to give validity to this and another novel, *The Atami Dragons* (o.p.), in which Jerry's trip to Japan with his father becomes more interesting when he meets members of the Atami Dragons baseball team. Both books are popular with sports enthusiasts in grades 7 through 10.

**Plot Summary**

What makes a bright, talented teenager decide to spend months away from home—far away in a strange country—as an exchange student? Why go to Japan if you have never shown any interest in things Japanese and do not speak the language?

Even Tony Ross, of Stockton, New Jersey, doesn't have all the answers. It's not just that he likes to play soccer, which he does. It's not just that his well-to-do parents don't get along, which they don't. And it's not just that he can't seem to control his temper any longer, that fights with his peers are more and more frequent.

Perhaps it's all of these things, Tony thinks, as he travels to the town of Atami near Tokyo. There he will spend the next few months of the school year with the Maeda family. The father is a lawyer, the mother a homemaker who speaks no English. There is the young son Taroo and the English-speaking, shy, and lovely daughter, Yukiko.

Tony vows to apply himself and benefit from this time away from home in a new culture, but he is unprepared for the total strangeness of it all. He must learn the unfamiliar formal customs of the Maeda family. Most difficult of all is learning to adjust at school. Besides the problem of the language barrier, Tony finds it hard to fit in. He especially has problems with Tanaka, the well-muscled team leader. Tony's reaction to Tanaka is, at first, much like his reaction to his peers back home when he was angry: He wants to fight.

Slowly, Tony begins to adjust. He learns a few Japanese words. His school studies go more smoothly. He gets to play a little soccer. He even has a few conversations with the shy Yukiko.

Soon Tony hears from his mother that his parents are divorcing. Although not shocked, he is hurt and angry. His father has been unfaithful, his mother says, and she has returned to her parents' home in Boston, where Tony is welcome. She tells him to leave Japan immediately if he wishes.

However, Tony decides to stay in Japan to finish his school year. He does not hear from his father for some time. Then one day he is surprised to find that his father has come to Japan for a medical conference. They spend a few days together and his father tells him that the divorce is the best for all of them.

Little by little, Tony makes headway with his peers at school. He feels that he is gaining some respect through his athletic ability. He even makes friends with Tanaka. Although he does not always agree with the Japanese system of doing things, he begins to understand it more. He sees how important, for instance, seniority is on a sports team in Japan. No matter how talented the freshman player, he or she watches from the sidelines. In sports as in many things Japanese, you must pay your dues by showing respect and patience.

Just when things seem to be settling into a good routine for Tony, he gets another letter from his mother, talking about the divorce just obtained in Mexico. Tony feels as though the love and closeness of his family never existed. In his hurt and anger, he dashes out of the Maeda house into the rain. He soon discovers that Mrs. Maeda has followed him, trying to coax him back to the house. She reaches out and in his unthinking anger he pushes her away and she falls.

Mrs. Maeda is not hurt, but Tony is horrified at his behavior toward this woman who has shown him only affection and caring. He takes a train to Tokyo and calls Yukiko. He asks her to meet him. When she does he explains what has happened. Yukiko is shocked at his behavior, but when Tony asks her to spend the night with him because he does not want to be alone, she agrees.

Nothing physical happens between the two young people, but Yukiko's understanding and affection calm Tony and make him see that he must go back to the Maeda household to apologize.

Tony returns to Atami and the Maeda home with a huge bouquet of flowers. He discovers that Mrs. Maeda has not told anyone what happened between them. He apologizes, and he knows she forgives him. That evening Tony realizes that he has a lot to learn from Mrs. Maeda— about being self-contained, holding a family together, and not getting angry even when you're pushed.

When it is time to go back to America, Tony feels real regret at leaving his Japanese family. He even hugs the formal Mrs. Maeda. As for Yukiko, they will write while they are both away at college and he hopes she will come to see him.

Tony goes to live with his mother and grandparents. They agree that he will attend a prep school near Boston the next year. Tony decides he will like it. If he could adjust to school in Japan, he can adjust to anything.

He also visits his father, who seems to be growing younger. Dr. Ross drives a Porsche with a Playboy insignia hanging from the rearview mirror and he dates a nurse in her late twenties. When, during his visit, Tony gets into a soccer game that erupts into a fight, instead of losing his temper, he keeps his cool. His father, with a little resentment, asks who taught Tony this new behavior. "Nobody taught me," Tony tells him. "I learned some things by myself."

**Thematic Material**

This is a story of growing up and of adjustment—adjustment to a breakup in the family, adjustment to a strange land and strange customs, adjustment to young love. Tony is portrayed as a likable but troubled youth. His way of dealing with the trouble in his family is to lash out at his peers whenever he is challenged. The book nicely contrasts the differences in American and Japanese cultures without criticizing or extoling either one. The importance of respect for family and peers is shown as a strong stabilizing factor in Japanese life.

**Book Talk Material**

Young people will especially be interested in how Tony reacts and tries to adjust both to a strange new family and a strange new school life. See: Tony meets Mr. Maeda and Taroo (pp. 11–14); Tony meets the rest of the Maeda family (pp. 15–19); the first day at the new school (pp. 19– 28); Tony's reaction to his peers in his conversation with a teacher (pp. 30–31); his first soccer game (pp. 32–35); and his race with Tanaka (pp. 50–62).

**Additional Selections**

Ted Bell enters the major leagues and finds he still must learn a lot about baseball in Thomas J. Dygard's *The Rookie Arrives* (Morrow, 1988, $12.95; pap., Penguin, $3.95). A soccer-based novel by the same writer is *Soccer Duel* (pap., Penguin, 1990, $3.95).

Roger is amazed when his school produces a winning basketball team under the leadership of a new coach in Thomas Hoobler's *The Revenge of Ho-Tai* (Walker, 1989, $15.95).

To the horror of Eric Delong, Mousie Potter joins the school's wrestling team, of which he is the star member, in Jerry Spinelli's *There's a Girl in My Hammerlock* (Simon & Schuster, 1991, $13.00).

In Gary Soto's *Taking Sides* (Harcourt, 1991, $15.95), Linc works out many of his personal problems by succeeding on his school's basketball team.

Jack, who is sincerely trying to fit into his new school, tries out for the football team in Robert McKay's *The Running Back* (pap., Ace, 1979, $1.95; condensed in *Juniorplots 3*, Bowker, 1987, pp. 246–49).

In Doris Buchanan Smith's *Karate Dancer* (Putnam, 1987, $13.95), a fourteen-year-old boy faces problems with his interest in karate and with his growing up.

In Randy Powell's *My Underrated Year* (Farrar, 1988, $12.95; pap., $3.95), a sophomore's interest in tennis and football is distracted by his love for his rival's sister.

**About the Book**

*Book Report,* January 1986, p. 33.
*Booklist,* August 1987, p. 1937.
*Center for Children's Books Bulletin,* January 1987, p. 191.
*New York Times Book Review,* July 16, 1987, p. 24.
*School Library Journal,* August 1987, p. 96.
*VOYA,* February 1988, p. 281.
See also *Book Review Digest,* 1988, pp. 147–48; and *Book Review Index,* 1987, p. 425, and 1988, p. 453.

**Lipsyte, Robert.** *The Brave*
Harper, 1991, $14.89 (0-06-023915-8)

This novel is described as a sequel to the author's prize-winning *The Contender* (Harper, 1967, $12.89; pap., $2.95; condensed in *More Juniorplots*, Bowker, 1977, pp. 66–69), in which a young black Harlem teenager, Alfred Brooks, finds direction for his life through boxing. In *The Brave*, the central character is Sonny Bear, who has a white father and an Indian mother. He is another man seemingly headed for tragedy on the New York City streets. When he is picked up by the police, he is questioned by Sergeant Alfred Brooks, who sees in the boy's plight similarities to his own situation several years before. However, it is Sonny's gradual journey to self-control and a more focused life that is the heart of this novel. The boxing scenes throb with hard-hitting energy and authenticity. *The Brave* joins *The Contender* as a fine addition to libraries serving both junior and senior high school readers.

**Plot Summary**

His full name is George Harrison Bayer. His mother named him for a Beatle. His last known address is the Moscondaga Reservation and he boxes under the name of Sonny Bear.

Sonny is seventeen years old and tough. His Uncle Jake thinks he's got the makings of a great heavyweight fighter, except for the monster. The monster is the anger, the uncontrolled anger, that Sonny Bear feels most of his days, especially in the ring. He's an outsider, half white, half Indian. His father is gone, his mother is off somewhere. She's always off somewhere. Just for a few weeks, Sonny, she says. I'll send for you, just give me a few weeks.

Uncle Jake says that if Sonny could learn to control the monster, he could be great. But Sonny doesn't know how to control his anger. He lashes out and usually gets himself in trouble.

After one bad night in some mountain town where the referee tries to give the fight to the local bozo, the monster takes over and Sonny kayoes the bozo like a sack of grain. He and Uncle Jake barely get out of town alive, and certainly leave without pay. Sonny decides he's had enough. He says good-bye to a reluctant Jake and heads for the big city—New York. That's where his mother is, currently.

Sonny Bear steps from one mess right into another, from a mountain town to a dope war in New York's Times Square. His feet hardly hit the city pavement before he's picked up by two hustlers, Stick and Doll, robbed of his money, and in trouble with the police for fouling up a drug bust—because of the monster. However, luck steps Sonny's way in the form of a New York City cop, an ex-boxer from Harlem named Alfred Brooks.

Brooks tries to convince Sonny that his newly found hustler friends are trouble, that they deal in crack and crack is trouble, that letting the monster take control is definitely trouble. Brooks also sees that Sonny has the makings of a fighter.

Sonny is reluctant to accept Brooks's help. He can take care of himself, he thinks. The New York City cop has a plan. Uncle Jake comes north and Brooks finds a gym where Sonny can train in Harlem. He'll come up through the amateur ranks the right way, says Brooks. Sonny Bear has never known training as he now begins to experience it. All he feels is pain, in every part of his body. But Uncle Jake is there to urge him on and so is the policeman.

When it seems as though there may finally be some order coming into Sonny's life, his mother arrives on the scene: in a limo, with a new man and lots of money. They are on their way to Phoenix, and Sonny's mother wants him with her. Since Sonny is only seventeen, Jake knows she can legally take him, so he helps Sonny get away. For the time being, his mother goes to Phoenix without him.

Brooks tells Sonny that the time has come to make a commitment to himself before he can make one to someone else. He must decide to have pride, to act smart, to take control of his life. He also tells Sonny that the monster is a fire inside. It's not good or bad, just something Sonny must control. The great champions, says Brooks, are the ones that turn that fire, which is fear, into fury when they need it. "You learn to do that," advises Brooks, "and you can beat anything, anywhere."

Sonny goes back to training in earnest. After what seems an eternity, it is time for an amateur boxing match. Control, control, Sonny keeps hearing in his corner. And it works. First fight, first win.

There are other fights, a few setbacks, more wins. Sonny is slowly learning to take control. Then comes the bad news. Brooks has been shot on the city streets while on duty. He is paralyzed. Sonny rushes to the hospital, where he thinks he hears Brooks whisper just one word to him: win.

When Sonny turns up for his next match, however, he discovers that he can't win for Brooks after all. He has been disqualified. The boxing commission has been informed that Sonny boxed in a few fights upstate for which he had taken money. The commission says he's not an amateur.

Once again Sonny's world crashes down around him, and once again the monster takes over. He heads back to Manhattan and Times Square, back to his old hustler pals, Stick and Doll. Stick points a shotgun at his chest and asks what Sonny wants. Sonny says he's come to kill him and accuses Stick of turning in the information about the upstate fights. Stick denies it.

Sonny catches Stick off guard and grabs the shotgun. The monster is begging him to get rid of this drug-dealing creep, but then he begins to think—about Brooks, about Jake, about taking control. He makes a decision.

Weeks later, it is fight time once more, at the bottom once again, the bottom of the pro circuit. The Hillcrest lodge hall looks like a place for has-beens and wanna-bes. Sonny has seen it all before.

Once more it is time for control, Sonny says to himself. He puts on his boxing trunks and begins to warm up, feeling the warmth spread through his body. He will not think about Brooks, who has been in a hospital bed for three weeks now, staring at the ceiling because he will never walk again. He will not think about his mother coming back from Arizona with a lawyer to see if she can take him with her. He will not think about Stick, whom he turned in for drug dealing and who will go on trial, a trial at which Sonny will have to testify.

He will think only about this fight. He is a pro now. Control. You take what you got to take till your time comes. And he does—a knockout in 2:21 of the third round. Sonny Bear, The Tomahawk Kid. He's going straight to the title.

**Thematic Material**

This is a gritty, no-holds-barred story of life in the tough lane. The emphasis here is on the torment of a young man divided between two worlds with no anchor in either one. It has relevance for any teenager largely left alone in a confusing world, without the guidance of caring family or other adults. The monster in Sonny Bear is his fear and his inability to control his life or even to understand it. This novel points out the slow and painstaking journey that young people take on the road to maturity. It also stresses how the intervention of even one caring adult can make a tremendous difference.

**Book Talk Material**

The description of Sonny's fight against the monster in himself can serve as an excellent introduction to this story of a young man's inner struggle for maturity; see fighting the bozo (pp. 6–13) and the fight in Times Square (pp. 29–30). Young readers will also be interested in the harsh look at life alone on the streets of a big city; see Sonny hits New York (pp. 22–27); in the police station (pp. 31–36); and Sonny gets involved with Stick and the drug scene (pp. 43–48).

**Additional Selections**

Jack Rummel in his *Muhammad Ali* (Chelsea House, 1988, $17.95; pap., $9.95) covers the boxing career of the heavyweight champion with an emphasis on his most important fights.

Fred fights cancer, local water pollution, and local drug dealers in Robert Lipsyte's *The Chemo Kid* (Harper, 1992, $14.00).

Through the help of a tough former NBA player, Lonnie becomes a fine basketball player and gains a chance to leave Harlem in Walter Dean Myers's *Hoops* (Delacorte, 1981, $13.95; pap., Dell, $2.50; condensed in *Juniorplots 3*, Bowker, 1987, pp. 249–53). In a New York City tenement, a young black boy, Jimmy Little, is accosted by a sick escaped convict who claims to be his father in *Somewhere in the Darkness* (Scholastic, 1992, $14.95), also by Myers.

In *The Throwing Season* (Delacorte, 1980, $8.95) by Michael French, a half-Indian high school boy is being bribed to lose at shotput.

A young Indian boy leaves his pueblo home to live with his grandmother and to understand his roots in Luke Wallin's *Ceremony of the Panther* (Macmillan, 1987, $11.95).

In Andre Norton's science fiction novel *The Sioux Spaceman* (pap., Ace, 1985, $2.50), a descendant of Sioux warriors uses his heritage to help others.

**About the Book**

*Booklist*, October 15, 1991, p. 429.
*Center for Children's Books Bulletin*, November 1991, p. 68.
*Horn Book*, March 1992, p. 209.
*Kirkus Reviews*, September 15, 1991, p. 1225.
*School Library Journal*, October 1991, p. 146.
*VOYA*, December 1991, p. 314.

**About the Author**

Chevalier, Tracy, ed., *Twentieth-Century Children's Writers* (3rd ed.). St. James, 1989, pp. 597–98.

Commire, Anne, ed., *Something about the Author.* Gale, 1973, Vol. 5, p. 114.

Evory, Ann, and Metzger, Linda, eds., *Contemporary Authors* (New Revision Series). Gale, 1983, Vol. 8, pp. 329–30.

Holtze, Sally Holmes, ed., *Fifth Book of Junior Authors and Illustrators.* Wilson, 1983, pp. 196–98.

Ward, Martha, ed., *Authors of Books for Young People* (3rd ed.). Scarecrow, 1990, pp. 441–42.

# 6

---

# Biography and True Adventure

I<small>N</small> this section the reader explores the world from the standpoint of five entertaining lives, three of contemporary people who represent the diverse fields of humanitarianism, literature, and exploration. The other two are biographies of great American presidents who were separated by almost 200 years of U.S. history.

---

**Bober, Natalie S.** *Thomas Jefferson: Man on a Mountain*
Atheneum, 1988, $14.95 (0-689-31154-0)

---

Thomas Jefferson, the third president of the United States, was truly a Renaissance man. He was not only a great politician and an intellectual who wrote the Declaration of Independence but also an accomplished inventor, architect, farmer, and educator. All of these aspects of his amazing career are touched on in Natalie S. Bober's distinguished biography. Using a chronological approach and generous amounts of quotations— from contemporaries, letters, and documents—plus family stories, the author re-creates the life of both the private and the public Thomas Jefferson. There is ample coverage of the frequent sorrows in his family life and his bouts of self-doubt. This book is intended for readers in grades 7 through 12.

### Plot Summary

This is an in-depth look at the life of a very real human being—a brilliant thinker, a practical statesman, a loving husband and father, a notable champion of freedom, an outstanding president, and one of the most revered of this country's leaders.

Lanky, shy, and red-headed, Thomas Jefferson grew up in the colony of Virginia. At the time of his birth in 1743, the colony stretched from the Atlantic Ocean to the Mississippi River and north to the Great Lakes.

Young Tom was the third child and first son of Peter Jefferson, a surveyor with a meager education but a fine mind, and Jane Randolph Jefferson, of the Virginia aristocracy.

Tom enjoyed a happy childhood until his fourteenth year, when his father died. Peter Jefferson's dying wish was that his son have a "classical education," and so Tom lived with a tutor for the next few years, going home on weekends.

By the time he was seventeen, Thomas Jefferson was over six feet tall, which was unusual in that time, not handsome but likable, well-mannered, and shy. Just before his seventeenth birthday, March 25, 1760, he was admitted to the College of William and Mary, founded 1693, in Williamsburg, Virginia.

After college, Jefferson wanted to study law. As there were no law schools in Virginia at the time, young men "read" law under an established attorney. Jefferson read with George Wythe, a distinguished young Virginia jurist.

When Jefferson was twenty-one, in 1764, the first sounds of unrest against the royal government of England were rumbling in the Virginia colony. He listened spellbound to the eloquent speeches of his friend Patrick Henry, who had been elected to the Virginia Assembly. In 1767, just after his twenty-fourth birthday, Jefferson took his examinations and became a lawyer.

Also at that time, he began work on what would become his beloved lifelong home, on land left to him by his father. Jefferson called his estate Monticello, which is Italian for "little mountain." He would not merely live on this beautiful site, but he would build his home himself. He knew nothing about building, so in his customary organized way, he turned to books on architecture and taught himself mechanical drawing. For nearly all the rest of his life, Jefferson worked on Monticello; to him it would never be finished. There was always something to add or change. This lovely two-story house with its beautiful view is a favorite tourist site today.

In 1770, Thomas Jefferson fell in love with Martha Wayles Skelton, a twenty-two-year-old widow with a young son. They were married on New Year's Day 1772. Jefferson was now a successful lawyer and a member of the Virginia House of Burgesses. The young couple began their married life at Monticello. A daughter, Martha, known as Patsy, was born that September. A second daughter, Jane, followed in 1774. Jefferson was delighted with his children and with his wife.

Thomas Jefferson would gladly have spent all of his time at Monticello, but the colonies were stirring with unrest and cries for change. In March 1775 Jefferson sat in on a meeting of the second Virginia Convention and heard his friend Patrick Henry declare: "I know not what course others may take; but as for me . . . give me liberty or give me death!" Shortly thereafter the American Revolution began.

It was some time before Jefferson was able to return to Monticello for a short stay between sessions of the Continental Congress. Shortly after his arrival, his baby daughter Jane died. Jefferson began to worry about his wife's fragile health but was forced to leave Monticello for Philadelphia where he began laboring over what would become his most famous contribution to the United States of America. It was entitled "A Declaration by the Representatives of the United States of America in General Congress Assembled." History knows it simply as the Declaration of Independence.

A son was born to Martha and Thomas Jefferson in 1777, but the baby died a short time later. Daughter Mary was born in 1778. The following year, on June 1, Jefferson stood in powdered wig and fancy dress in the House of Delegates and took the oath of governor of Virginia. He, Martha, and the girls moved to the capital city of Richmond in 1780. Daughter Lucy was born that year, but she died five months later. More fearful than ever for his wife's health, Jefferson decided he would retire from public life at the end of his second term.

The American Revolution ended in October 1781. The following year the Jeffersons had another daughter, also named Lucy. But Martha was now dangerously ill. She died on September 6, 1782, and a distraught Jefferson vowed he would never marry again.

Life now seemed meaningless to Jefferson. Still, the following June he was elected to Congress. He felt he could not take his children to Annapolis, Maryland, where the government met at the time, so he began the first of many letters to his daughters that would continue throughout his lifetime. They show his deep love and concern for them.

In 1784 Jefferson was named minister to France. He took his oldest daughter, Patsy, abroad with him. He would not return to Monticello until 1789, having lived through the fall of the French government and an unrequited love affair.

Back home and wishing only to stay with his daughters at Monticello, Jefferson nevertheless could not refuse the request of the country's first president, George Washington. So, in 1790, Thomas Jefferson became secretary of state. He was immediately at odds with the secretary of the treasury, the brilliant young Alexander Hamilton. Jefferson feared that Hamilton wished to return the country to monarchy.

When Jefferson returned to Monticello in 1793, he was certain his days in government were over. He was fifty years old and sick of politics. He spent the next three years redesigning his home and enjoying his family. "The length of my tether is now fixed for life from Monticello to Richmond," he wrote to a friend.

Alas for him, this was not so. On March 4, 1797, Thomas Jefferson became the vice president of the United States. However, he played no part in the work of John Adams's administration and divided his time between Monticello and Philadelphia, then the seat of the national government.

The government moved to Washington, D.C., in 1800, and the following March 4 Jefferson strolled to the Capitol where he was inaugurated as the third president of the United States. The Louisiana Purchase is considered the single greatest achievement of his presidency, in which the United States bought 828,000 square miles of land west of the Mississippi from France.

In 1802 a scandal broke out charging President Jefferson with being the father of several children by a slave girl named Sally. Jefferson would never reply to these charges—partly, it is believed, because he knew that Sally was a half-sister to his wife, Martha. Most historians believe that such behavior would have been inconsistent with Jefferson's morality, but the accusations haunted him for the rest of his life.

When Jefferson finally retired from office, he returned to Monticello, where he enjoyed his estate and seeing his daughters, now married, and his grandchildren. One of his last great acts was to donate his entire library of books, more than 6,700 volumes, to replace the congressional library that had been destroyed in the War of 1812. It marked the beginning of a great national library, which became the Library of Congress.

Not content to remain idle during retirement, Jefferson laid plans for what became the University of Virginia at Charlottesville, chartered in 1819. In his seventies, he designed the university buildings and saw to their construction, wrote the curriculum, recruited the faculty, and supplied the library with books. The school was, Jefferson said, "the last service I can render my country."

In 1826 Thomas Jefferson was eighty-three years old. He had been remarkably healthy throughout his life, but now he became ill. He died on the nation's birthday, July 4. On that same day, the second president of the United States also died. The last words of John Adams, who, of course, had not heard of Jefferson's death a few hours earlier, were "Thomas Jefferson still survives."

**Thematic Material**

This is a warm biography that reads like a work of fiction, for Thomas Jefferson's passion, his intellect, and his dignity shine through along with his love of family and his belief in the dignity of the people. The reader can only marvel at his accomplishments. Jefferson steps from these pages as a man of his time, with the beliefs of his time. He appears not as a great intellect or a great president, but as a man of warmth, intelligence, and character doing his best in his time. This is an excellent nonfiction work.

**Book Talk Material**

Jefferson's younger years, not written about much in history books, may serve as a good introduction to the third president of the United States. See: young Tom and his relationship with his father (pp. 9–11); Tom meets Patrick Henry (pp. 14–15); Jefferson's first "unproductive" months at William and Mary (pp. 20–24); Jefferson's violin playing (pp. 26–27); and Jefferson's "first love" (pp. 33–38).

**Additional Selections**

Two other recommended biographies of Thomas Jefferson are: Rebecca Stefoff's *Thomas Jefferson: 3rd President of the United States* (Garrett, 1988, $17.26) and Joyce Milton's *The Story of Thomas Jefferson: Prophet of Liberty* (pap., Dell, 1990, $2.95).

The story of how Jefferson planned, built, and lived in his beautiful Virginia home is told in text and extraordinary illustrations in *Monticello* (Holiday, 1988, $14.95) by Leonard E. Fisher.

The first eight years of our federal government are covered in *The Birth of a Nation* (Scribner, 1989, $13.95) by Doris Faber and Harold Faber.

Jean Fritz re-creates the life of another great president, our fourth, in *The Great Little Madison* (Putnam, 1989, $15.95).

Jefferson's brilliant and complex life, filled with both success and failure, is re-created accurately in Milton Meltzer's *Thomas Jefferson: The Revolutionary Aristocrat* (Watts, 1991, $15.95). Another title by Meltzer is

*The Bill of Rights: How We Got It and What It Means* (Harper, 1990, $14.95), which traces the history of the Bill of Rights and discusses the concerns involving civil liberties in a democracy.

Through letters, diaries, journals, and other accounts, the true story of Revolutionary times is told in Meltzer's *The American Revolutionaries: A History in Their Own Words, 1750–1800* (Harper, 1987, $13.95).

In Stan Hoig's *A Capital for the Nation* (Dutton, 1990, $15.95), the story of the long and arduous task of building Washington, D.C., is retold.

In Ann Rinaldi's novel *Wolf by the Ears* (Scholastic, 1991, $13.95), the central character is Harriet Hemings, the daughter of Sally, a slave who may have been Jefferson's mistress.

**About the Book**

*Book Report*, May 1989, p. 49.
*Booklist*, January 15, 1989, p. 854.
*Kirkus Reviews*, September 1, 1988, p. 1319.
*School Library Journal*, November 1988, p. 134.
*VOYA*, October 1988, p. 197.
See also *Book Review Digest*, 1989, p. 165; and *Book Review Index*, 1988, p. 86, and 1989, p. 85.

---

**Cleary, Beverly.** *A Girl from Yamhill*
Morrow, 1988, $15.95 (0-688-07800-1); pap., Dell, $3.95 (0-440-40185-2)

---

Beverly Cleary is one of the most beloved and honored of contemporary writers of literature for young people. Among her many awards is the 1984 Newbery Medal for *Dear Mr. Henshaw* (Morrow, 1983, $12.95; pap., Dell, $3.25) and the Laura Ingalls Wilder Award for her total contributions to children's literature. Among the lasting characters she has created are Henry Huggins and his dog Ribsy, the daredevil mouse, Ralph, and cat named Socks, and the Quimby family including Beezus and the irrepressible Ramona. For a middle-school audience there are novels like *Jean and Johnny* (Morrow, 1959, $12.95; pap., Dell, $2.95) and *Fifteen* (Morrow, 1956, $12.95; pap., Avon, $3.50). This autobiography takes Beverly Cleary from early childhood to her departure for college after high school graduation. It is suitable for readers in grades 6 through 12.

**Plot Summary**

One of Beverly's earliest memories is the joyful sound of all the bells of Yamhill pealing together in celebration. It is the end of World War I and she is two years old.

Her father, Lloyd Bunn, came from hardy pioneer stock that had moved west in the mid-nineteenth century and settled in the town of Yamhill, Oregon, south of Portland in the rich Willamette Valley to the east of the Coast Range. Her grandfather had been a farmer and at his death, Lloyd, the only one of five sons who had any interest in farming, inherited the large family house and eighty-two acres of farmland.

Her mother, Mabel, born and educated in Michigan, left home while still young and moved to Oregon with two female cousins to accept teaching jobs. Later Beverly's other set of grandparents moved to Oregon and opened a general store in the town of Banks. While visiting her parents there, Mabel met Lloyd and they married in 1907.

For her parents, life on the Bunn farm is one of isolation, toil, and hardship, but for the young girl it is a time of instruction and wonder. She marvels at all the farm animals and enjoys the fruits and grains that supply a scant livelihood for her parents. She also enjoys the great beauty of the wildflowers and other vegetation on the farm. Her mother is strict and requires absolute obedience to her many rules. Beverly tries her best to be a respectful and compliant daughter but, because she is curious and seemingly fearless, sometimes causes enough trouble to be spanked. Mabel finds some diversion by crusading successfully to found a town library. From its many treasures, she shares with her only child such delights as the books of Beatrix Potter.

In spite of working from dawn to dusk at farm chores, her parents are barely able to make ends meet. Discouraged by this and the many sacrifices and deprivations of farm life, they decide to move to Portland. Here they rent a home in the city, Lloyd secures a job as a night watchman at a bank, and Beverly prepares to enter the first grade. Her first year at school is a disaster. The teacher, Miss Falb, is a tyrant who terrifies Beverly into complete silence. Bouts with chicken pox and later smallpox cause her to lose so much school time that she is only conditionally promoted to second grade. Her mother is so ashamed of her daughter that she will not allow Beverly to show her report card to others. Things are somewhat better the next year under the more benign tutelage of Miss Marius. When Lloyd is promoted to day lobby manager at the bank, the family moves to better quarters and, in spite of constant nagging from her mother, Beverly begins to blossom. By the fourth grade she develops an insatiable love of reading and enters, and wins, some essay-writing contests. When her father sells the family homestead, the Bunns revel in a few months of prosperity: Beverly is sent to an orthodontist for braces to correct her horribly twisted teeth, Lloyd buys a Model A Chevrolet, and they take a mortgage on a five-room house complete with breakfast nook, attic, and half basement. At school, Beverly is encouraged in her writing endeavors by the librarian/reading teacher Miss Smith and she forms an enduring friendship with Claudine Klum, whose mother, a jolly, affectionate woman, seems to Beverly the antithesis of her own. On a trip to visit her Aunt Dora and Uncle Joe, Beverly, who is still sexually naive, is both confused and horrified by her uncle's attempts at molestation. When she tells her parents, they support her and vow not to see these relatives again.

It is now the summer of 1930 and Beverly is anticipating entering high school in the fall, when her father suddenly loses his job. The country has been decimated by the effects of the Great Depression and even food becomes scarce in the Bunn household. Every morning her father goes out looking for a job, and every evening he returns discouraged and dejected. His bouts of sullen depression cause arguments in the household and Beverly's mother often takes out her frustrations on her daughter. Miraculously, when they seem to have lost everything, Lloyd finds a menial job managing a bank vault. Nevertheless, the grinding poverty continues to take a toll on their family relationships and there are frequent quarrels. For Beverly, these economic woes are complicated by her need as an adolescent to be active socially. Even a request to wear lipstick creates major problems with her mother. Beverly gets some relief from the drabness of her home life through frequent visits to Claudine's. Together the two girls share some carefree moments, principally because each has a well-developed sense of humor. In addition, Beverly's success in such writing ventures as school plays, skits, and short stories plus the encouragement she receives from some of her teachers has given some direction to her life—she has decided to devote herself to writing, however impractical it might seem.

When she is in the tenth grade, Beverly is enrolled in a ballroom dancing class and there meets Gerhart, a serious young man six years her senior. He begins visiting the Bunn household regularly and Beverly is at first flattered by this attention. Surprisingly, her mother promotes this friendship even though the two youngsters have nothing in common. At his job, Gerhart earns the same amount as Beverly's father and is able to buy items like a radio and an automobile, luxuries that her own family can't afford. They date frequently, although Beverly becomes increasingly annoyed with his demands and his unwanted attentions. In spite of her polite efforts to break off this relationship, he persists, to the point of proposing marriage during her junior year. She refuses, but, partly because of her mother's encouragement, he remains friendly and gets some solace from his growing attachment to the Jehovah's Witnesses.

Graduation approaches and all of Beverly's friends are making plans for the future. Most are going to college and others to various kinds of technical schools. Beverly can afford neither. Unexpectedly, a letter arrives from a distant relative, Verna, who is librarian at Chaffey Junior College in Ontario, California, offering Beverly free room and board at her home if she would like to attend her tuition-free institution. Her mother dismisses the invitation as impractical, but her father thinks differently and decides that this would be a splendid opportunity for his daughter. Gradually Mabel is won over, although she tries to thwart the scheme.

After graduation, Beverly spends the summer at home making preparations for leaving and also visiting with Claudine and her family at Puddin', their summer camp. She is glad to kiss Gerhart good-bye but has mixed feelings about leaving her friends and family. On departure day, she slowly climbs aboard her Greyhound bus, takes a window seat, and waves good-bye to her parents. Within moments she is on her way to California and new opportunities.

**Thematic Material**

Readers may be surprised to find that Beverly Cleary's life did not contain the same amount of joy and warmth that characterizes so many of her books. However, many incidents and characters in her real life appear in various guises in her stories and it is interesting to note them. For example in *Ramona and Her Father*, Mrs. Swink describes making stilts out of tin cans, an activity that Beverly engaged in as a child. This autobiography is essentially the story of the formative years of an adventuresome, intelligent, and lovable girl and of the influences that gave direction to her life. It chronicles the joys and sorrows of everyday rural and urban life in America in the 1920s and 1930s. At times it is a painful memoir— particularly when describing the relationship between mother and daughter. The author candidly portrays a mother who, with the best of intentions, unfairly dominated and manipulated her daughter and a daughter who continually tried to please and was wracked with guilt when it was necessary to disobey. How they gradually grow apart because of misunderstandings and the mother's rigidity is well portrayed. In another sense the real villain of this account is the Great Depression and its dehumanizing and degrading effects on a single family. It is also a story of personal courage, determination, resourcefulness, and dedication.

**Book Talk Material**

After one identifies the author and her accomplishments, some of the following incidents could be read or retold: Beverly's father and his family (pp. 10–16); her mother and family (pp. 17–22); Beverly is taught not to be afraid (pp. 39–42); her mother's campaign for the library (pp. 60–63); the first grade and Miss Falb (pp. 75–83); and seventh-grade teachers including Miss Smith (pp. 143–53).

**Additional Selections**

The life of one of America's fine writers and the story of her work with needy children is told in Ann LaFarge's *Pearl Buck* (Chelsea House, 1988, $17.95).

Tony Gentry's *Paul Laurence Dunbar* (Chelsea House, 1989, $17.95; pap., $9.95) is the biography of the great black poet who was a forerunner of the Harlem Renaissance.

The life of another important black writer is examined in *Langston Hughes* (Chelsea House, 1989, $17.95), by Jack Rummel.

This author is also dealt with effectively by Milton Meltzer in *Langston Hughes: A Biography* (Crowell, 1988, $13.89).

Mr. Meltzer tells about his own genesis as a writer in *Starting from Home: A Writer's Beginnings* (Viking, 1988, $13.95).

In the autobiography *Chapters: My Growth as a Writer* (Little, Brown, 1982, $15.95), the celebrated mystery story writer Lois Duncan tells of her career.

M. E. Kerr writes delightfully of her childhood and her life until selling her first story to *Ladies Home Journal* in *Me Me Me Me Me* (Harper, 1983, $12.95; pap., NAL, $3.50).

Some other autobiographical writings by authors popular with young readers are: Jean Little's *Little by Little: A Writer's Education* (Viking, 1988, $13.95); Cynthia Rylant's *But I'll Be Back Again: An Album* (Watts, 1989, $12.99); and Roald Dahl's *Boy: Tales of Childhood* (Farrar, 1984, $13.95;

pap., Penguin, $4.95) and sequel *Going Solo* (Farrar, 1986, $14.95; pap., Penguin, $5.95; condensed in *Seniorplots*, Bowker, 1989, pp. 281–85). The beloved author of the Little House Books, Laura Ingalls Wilder, writes of an arduous journey in *On the Way Home: The Diary of a Trip from South Dakota to Mansfield, Missouri, in 1894* (Harper, 1961, $12.95; pap., $2.95).

**About the Book**
*Book Report*, May 1988, p. 35.
*Booklist*, June 1, 1988, p. 1672.
*Center for Children's Books Bulletin*, March 1988, p. 133.
*Horn Book*, May 1988, p. 369.
*School Library Journal*, May 1988, p. 115.
*VOYA*, June 1988, p. 100.
See also *Book Review Digest*, 1988, p. 321; and *Book Review Index*, 1988, p. 156.

**About the Author**
Chevalier, Tracy, ed., *Twentieth-Century Children's Writers* (3rd ed.). St. James, 1989, pp. 209–10.
Commire, Anne, ed., *Something about the Author*. Gale, 1986, Vol. 43, pp. 53–61.
Estes, Glenn E., ed., *American Writers for Children since 1960: Fiction* (Dictionary of Literary Biography: Vol. 52). Gale, 1986, pp. 85–91.
Fuller, Muriel, ed., *More Junior Authors*. Wilson, 1963, pp. 49–50.
Kirkpatrick, D. L., ed., *Twentieth-Century Children's Writers* (2nd ed.). St. Martin's, 1983, pp. 182–84.
Metzger, Linda, ed., *Contemporary Authors* (New Revision Series). Gale, 1985, Vol. 8, pp. 34–62.
Riley, Carolyn, ed., *Children's Literature Review*. Gale, 1976, Vol. 2, pp. 44–51.
Senick, Gerard J., ed., *Children's Literature Review*. Gale, 1985, Vol. 8, pp. 34–62.
Ward, Martha, ed., *Authors of Books for Young People* (3rd ed.). Scarecrow, 1990, p. 132.

---

**Clucas, Joan Graff.** *Mother Teresa*
Chelsea House, 1988, $16.95 (1-55546-855-1); pap., $9.95 (0-7910-0602-6)

---

If a poll were taken on what contemporary world figure is the most deserving of sainthood, without a doubt the most frequently cited would be Mother Teresa. Her life of simplicity, dedication, and sacrifice has been an inspiration to all. This well-illustrated account gives information

on her childhood and early missions but concentrates on her work in the
slums of Calcutta. It is intended for readers in grades 8 through 10.

**Plot Summary**

During the Christmas season of 1991, a frail, eighty-one-year-old Catholic nun was admitted to a hospital in southern California. There were
grave doubts about her recovery, for she had suffered heart complications
before. However, in early 1992, Mother Teresa, winner of the Nobel
Peace Prize in 1979, founder of the Missionary Sisters and Missionary
Brothers of Charity, tireless worker for the world's destitute and helpless,
recovered and set out once again to bring her message of peace and hope
to a troubled world. This is a remarkable story of a remarkable woman.

She was born Agnes Gonxha Bojaxhiu on August 27, 1910, the youngest of three children of Albanian parents. Her birthplace was a tiny
town in Macedonia, then part of the Ottoman Empire, across the Adriatic Sea from Italy. Her father, a rather well-to-do merchant, died suddenly in 1918 and her mother became a seamstress to support the family.

Perhaps because of her mother's religious devotion or her own quiet
nature that found comfort in prayer, young Agnes, at the age of eighteen, decided to become a nun. Not only would she become a nun, but
she would join the Loreto Order, which worked in India. In 1928 she
traveled to Dublin, Ireland, where she studied English at the Loreto
Abbey. She never saw her sister or mother again.

After six weeks of training, young Agnes reached Calcutta, India's
third-largest city and the site of her first teaching assignment as Sister
Teresa. She chose the name after Sister Therese, a nineteenth-century
nun from France who believed that God could best be served by leading
a life of goodness and simplicity. She took her final vows in 1937.

Sister Teresa had pledged her life's work to the Loreto Order, but in
1946 she became convinced that God wanted her to leave the order and
work in the slums to aid the poor. She applied to Rome for a decree that
would allow her to keep her vows as a nun but be free to travel anywhere
she wished to aid those in need. To the surprise of many, the request was
granted.

In 1948 Sister Teresa took off the dress of the Loreto Order and
donned a simple white cotton sari, a long robe worn by Indian women,
with a blue border. This costume would become the habit of her new
congregation. In December she began her work in the appalling conditions among the destitute of Calcutta.

In 1949 the first of Mother Teresa's former students arrived in India to aid in her work. In 1950 the Missionary Sisters of Charity was formed, with Sister Teresa as the mother superior. The new order was dedicated to compassion and love of the poorest of the poor. In 1954 the order opened a home so that the poor could at least die in dignity instead of in the streets. In 1955 the sisters opened a home for abandoned children, of which there were many in India. Under Mother Teresa's guidance, they began a food-distribution program for the needy. In 1957 she started a program to aid the thousands of people suffering from leprosy in Calcutta. From that beginning eventually came the leper community of Shanti Nagar, which means Town of Peace. About 400 families live there today and they are largely self-sufficient, thanks to the skills taught by Mother Teresa and the sisters.

By 1962 Mother Teresa's order had grown to 119 sisters. They worked from southern India north to the snowy Himalayas. Contributions began to sweep in from wealthy Indians and people in other countries. Mother Teresa made her first trip to the United States in 1960, speaking in Las Vegas, Nevada; Peoria, Illinois; Washington, D.C.; and New York City, including the United Nations.

In 1963, Mother Teresa was a key figure in bringing about the Missionary Brothers of Charity. The brothers do work with young boys similar to that of Mother Teresa and her group. By 1965 the Vatican had granted Mother Teresa's order official recognition, which meant that her mission could expand around the world. The first work outside India was in Venezuela, in Cocorote, a village so tiny it is not listed in any atlas. By the 1970s ten new missions had been established in South America.

Mother Teresa's work was gaining worldwide notice, inside the church and out. She was awarded the first Pope John the Twenty-Third Peace Prize in 1971. Her work in war-torn Bangladesh in 1972 earned her India's Nehru Award for peace. By the mid-1970s hers was a familiar face as she traveled to establish communities for the destitute in the most remote and devastated locations, as well as in more familiar sites in the Middle East, Australia, the Pacific islands, Mexico, and even the South Bronx, New York. It is said that she has never turned down a request to work with the poorest of the poor on any continent.

After twenty-five years of work, in 1976 Mother Teresa had established about 350 missions to help the needy. About 2,500 young women were now part of her order. In 1979, she traveled to Oslo, Norway, where she was presented with the Nobel Peace Prize. Along with the award, she received a check for $190,000. This small, frail-looking woman in her white sari, her brown face creased with lines, said in her thirty-minute speech that "people must love one another, so that no one feels unwanted, especially the children." Mother Teresa did not attend the traditional dinner banquet honoring the prize winner, but requested that the $6,000 for the dinner be given to the poor. Three months later she was awarded her adopted country's highest civilian honor, the Jewel of India. She has held Indian citizenship since 1949.

Mother Teresa carries on her work today—in the Middle East, in China, among AIDS victims, anywhere in the world she can help those in need. In early 1992 in Rome, at the age of eighty-one, she was hospitalized once again. Doctors said this tireless fighter was simply working too hard.

Mother Teresa has never led a nation or held public office, yet she is a world leader in the fight to alleviate suffering and poverty. She has saved thousands of lives and touched millions more.

**Thematic Material**

This is a simple, straightforward biography that is made dramatic by the dedication of its subject. It shows how the quiet determination of one person can make a difference in a world that so often seems uncaring and uninvolved. Regardless of one's religious beliefs, the reader can only marvel at the accomplishments of this largely unschooled woman who has truly saved the lives of so many of the world's unwanted people.

**Book Talk Material**

There are many interesting passages that show Mother Teresa's unswerving determination to carry out what she believes to be her life's work; see Young Agnes decides to become a nun in India and leaves her family (pp. 27–30); as Mother Teresa, she determines to set up her own mission (pp. 35–37); she expands the work of the Missionaries of Charity (pp. 75–79).

**Additional Selections**

The life of another whose life changed the future of India is told in Michael Nicholson's *Mahatma Gandhi: The Man Who Freed India and Led the World in Nonviolent Change* (Stevens, 1988, $12.95).

Two more books about the inspirational leader of nonviolent opposition to British rule in India are Glenn Alan Cheney's *Mohandas Gandhi* (Watts, 1983, $12.90) and Doris Faber's and Harold Faber's *Mahatma Gandhi* (Messner, 1986, $9.79).

The story of India's first prime minister after the departure of the British is told in *Jawaharlal Nehru* (Chelsea House, 1987, $17.95) by Lila Finck and John Hayes.

In Gwendolyne Arbuckle's *Paul: Adventurer for Christ* (pap., Abingdon, 1984, $5.50), the story of St. Paul's life is told from his conversion through his many journeys preaching the gospel.

Hinduism is the main religion in India. An alphabetically arranged guide to it is found in Patricia Bahree's *Hinduism* (Batsford, 1985, $19.95).

Some books that give an introduction to the land, culture, and people of India are: *India . . . in Pictures* (Lerner, 1989, $9.95), P. P. Karan's *India* (Gateway, 1988, $16.95), and James Traub's *India: The Challenge of Change* (Messner, 1985, $10.29).

In James Haskins's *India under Indira and Rajiv Gandhi* (Enslow, 1989, $15.95), the history of modern India under this powerful mother and son is covered.

**About the Book**
*Booklist,* June 15, 1988, p. 1733.
See also *Book Review Index,* 1988, p. 158.

---

**Freedman, Russell.** *Franklin Delano Roosevelt*
Clarion, 1990, $16.95 (0-89919-379-X)

---

Russell Freedman's writings for young readers have made significant contributions in the areas of both science and history. As examples of the former, there are such titles as *Animal Superstars* (pap., Prentice Hall, 1984, $5.95) and *Can Bears Predict Earthquakes?* (Prentice Hall, 1982, $10.95). Among the latter are several books on American history including two explorations of life on the frontier, *Children of the Wild West* (Clarion, 1983, $14.95) and *Cowboys of the Wild West* (Clarion, 1985, $15.95). His biography *Lincoln* (Clarion, 1987, $16.95; pap., $7.95) won the 1988 Newbery Medal, one of the few nonfiction books so honored. It is subtitled "A Photobiography," which could also be an appropriate description of this biography because almost every one of its 200 pages contains an illustration. Although most are black-and-white photographs, there are a few political cartoons. Complementing the main text are sections on places to visit that are associated with Roosevelt, a brief bibliography of other books about him, and a special section of photos about his family life. This biography, like the books mentioned above, is suitable for readers in grades 5 through 9.

### Plot Summary

Franklin Delano Roosevelt was a man surrounded by contradiction and controversy. Although he is known as a leader of great strength, his legs were so weak that he was unable to take a single step without leg braces. He fervently defended the rights of the common people, yet he was born a patrician. Vilified by members of his own class, many of whom considered him a traitor, he was adored by people with whom he had little in common.

He held office longer than any other U.S. president and during that time guided the country through two of its greatest crises, the Great Depression and World War II. He forged America's position as a world leader, and, at home, initiated such social changes as social security and the minimum wage. Yet debate still surrounds the man and his accomplishments. Was he a savior or a dictator? A fearless leader or a gifted egomaniac? Regardless of the ultimate evaluation, his life and his presidency changed forever the quality of American life.

Franklin Delano Roosevelt was born on January 30, 1882, the only child of James and Sara Delano Roosevelt. Home was the family mansion outside Hyde Park, New York, except in summers, when they moved to Campobello Island, New Brunswick. For the first fourteen years of his life, he remained at home under the watchful eye of his domineering mother, who carefully supervised his education. In 1896, he entered Groton, the fashionable Massachusetts preparatory school, where he excelled in a number of activities and fell under the influence of the dynamic headmaster, the Reverend Endicott Peabody. Upon graduation, he attended Harvard University and became involved in a number of outside activities, including editing the university newspaper, the *Crimson*. One of his greatest scoops was a front-page interview with his cousin, then Vice President Theodore Roosevelt. Soon he began courting his fifth cousin, Eleanor Roosevelt, and shortly after Franklin entered Columbia Law School (and in spite of Mama's objections), the two were married. Politics, rather than law practice, beckoned and when he was only twenty-eight he campaigned successfully as a Democrat for a seat in the New York State Senate previously held by Republicans. His great success here led to an appointment by President Wilson as assistant secretary of the Navy, a position Roosevelt held during World War I.

His marriage produced several children and appeared stable when, in 1918, Eleanor discovered that her husband was having an affair with Lucy Mercer. Fortunately, through the intervention of Sara and some close friends, the marriage was saved. A further personal crisis occurred in 1921 when Franklin was stricken with a crippling attack of polio that left his legs paralyzed. Only through herculean effort was he able to recover sufficiently to walk with the aid of leg braces.

During the 1920s, Roosevelt emerged as a powerful force in the Democratic party, although the Republicans maintained national power, first under Coolidge and then under Hoover. When the country sank into a morass of unemployment, privation, and failed businesses after the stock market crash of 1929, Roosevelt led the Democratic party to an outstanding victory in 1932 and, promising the American people a "new deal," took the oath of office as president of the United States in March 1933.

The New Deal attempted to bring relief and recovery to a stricken country. New agencies were created, laws were passed regulating business, legislative reforms were initiated, and thousands of government-sponsored work projects were begun. During Roosevelt's second term, opposition to many of these drastic measures became organized and Roosevelt faced increasing criticism from the Supreme Court and big business. Sometimes he acted ruthlessly in his attempts to circumvent these reversals.

As war clouds thickened in Europe during the late 1930s, Roosevelt faced the problem of trying to provide material support for the forces of democracy in Europe and Asia in spite of the predominantly isolationist attitudes of the American people. After the attack on Pearl Harbor in December 1941, Roosevelt encountered the second greatest challenge of his political career—to lead an ill-prepared, almost defenseless country to victory against the vastly superior might of the Axis powers. He accomplished the superhuman task of transforming America so successfully that by the end of 1943 the United States was able to take the offensive against the enemy. Though Roosevelt is much admired for his leadership during this period, critics point out that the shameful treatment of Japanese Americans and the feeble attempts to save European Jews during the Holocaust are two blots on his record.

The heavy burden of work and stress gradually took its toll on Roosevelt's health. Although he tried to find time to relax and restore his dwindling physical resources during brief sojourns at the summer White House he had created at Warm Springs, Georgia, these stays became less frequent.

After his fourth inauguration, in January 1945, he traveled to Yalta in the Crimea for eight days of intensive and exhausting negotiations with Churchill and Stalin concerning the political fate of Europe and Asia after the war. At the end of March, he returned to Warm Springs for a much-needed rest. It was there that he suffered a massive cerebral hemorrhage and died on April 12, only two and a half months after his sixty-third birthday.

As the funeral train traveled from Georgia to Washington and then on to the burial plot at Hyde Park, an entire nation, indeed an entire world, filled with a sense of grief and loss, stopped to pay homage to the memory of a great American.

**Thematic Material**

This highly readable biography re-creates both the public and private lives of President Roosevelt while also accurately recording the important national and international events that helped shape his career. The portrait is an accurate one that treats both strengths and accomplishments along with shortcomings and failures. Many quotations and excerpts from firsthand accounts supply a feeling of authenticity, immediacy, and involvement. What emerges is a portrait of a complex man of extraordinary ability, energy, and compassion. Some themes that emerge from a study of his life are courage, dedication, the power of initiative, the nature of leadership, and the meaning of democracy. Roosevelt's struggle against his physical disability and his reliance on the support of Eleanor and his family supply human dimensions to his greatness.

**Book Talk Material**

Showing some of the excellent photographs is an effective way to introduce the book to small groups. With others, one could use some of the famous quotations associated with Roosevelt to review the highlights of his career. Some samples: "There is nothing I love as much as a good fight" (p. 33); "The moment of defeat is the best time to lay plans for future victories" (p. 43); "I pledge you, I pledge myself, to a new deal for the American people" (p. 82); "The only thing we have to fear is fear itself" (p. 88); "A date which will live in infamy" (p. 146); and "The only limit to our realization of tomorrow will be our doubts of today" (p. 175). An excellent summation of Roosevelt's career is given on pages 1–5. Some passages that deal with his early life are: his childhood (pp. 7–11); life at Groton (pp. 13–18) and at Harvard (pp. 18–23); courtship and marriage (pp. 26–28); and his first political campaign (pp. 30–33).

**Additional Selections**

Two other fine biographies of Franklin Roosevelt are John Devaney's *Franklin Delano Roosevelt, President* (Walker, 1987, $13.85) and Jeffrey H. Hacker's *Franklin D. Roosevelt* (Watts, 1983, $12.90).

Rachel Toor's *Eleanor Roosevelt* (Chelsea House, 1989, $16.95) tells the inspiring story of one of our country's greatest humanitarians, first ladies, and diplomats.

The lives and accomplishments of presidents' wives are recounted in Rae Lindsay's *The Presidents' First Ladies* (Watts, 1989, $14.90).

Another excellent photo-history by Russell Freedman is the story of two men who taught the world to fly, *The Wright Brothers: How They Invented the Airplane* (Holiday, 1991, $16.95).

The causes of the Great Depression as well as the struggle to overcome it are told in Bruce Glassman's *The Crash of '29 and the New Deal* (Silver Burdett, 1986, $14.96; pap., $5.95).

Milton Meltzer has produced a masterful history of the Great Depression using many original documents in *Brother, Can You Spare a Dime?* (pap., NAL, 1977, $3.95).

Jean Fritz has written an enthusiastic and accurate portrait of the other Roosevelt president, *Bully for You, Teddy Roosevelt!* (Putnam, 1991, $15.95).

**About the Book**
*Booklist,* October 15, 1990, p. 438.
*Horn Book,* March 1991, p. 213.
*Kirkus Reviews,* September 15, 1990, p. 1324.
*New York Times Book Review,* March 17, 1991, p. 38.
*School Library Journal,* December 1990, p. 116.
*VOYA,* April 1991, p. 54.
See also *Book Review Digest,* 1991, p. 639; and *Book Review Index,* 1990, p. 276, and 1991, p. 311.

**About the Author**

Commire, Anne, ed., *Something about the Author*. Gale, 1979, Vol. 16, pp. 115–16.
Holtze, Sally Holmes, ed., *Sixth Book of Junior Authors and Illustrators*. Wilson, 1989, pp. 89–90.
Senick, Gerard J., ed., *Children's Literature Review*. Gale, 1990, Vol. 20, pp. 71–89.
Straub, Deborah A., ed., *Contemporary Authors* (New Revision Series). Gale, 1988, Vol. 23, pp. 151–52.
Ward, Martha, ed., *Authors of Books for Young People* (3rd ed.). Scarecrow, 1990, p. 244.

---

**Peck, Robert McCracken.** *Headhunters and Hummingbirds*
Walker, 1987, $14.95 (0-8027-6645-5)

---

This account of an arduous scientific expedition into the land of the Jivaro Indians in Ecuador is exciting, graphic, and at times harrowing. The author is no stranger to expeditions in exotic locales. In 1980 he conducted a survey of the national parks and wildlife refuges of Kenya and in 1983 he participated in a 300-mile trek through the Himalayas of north central Nepal as part of a research and collecting expedition. The expedition dealt with here appears to surpass the previous two in danger and daring. This account is enjoyed by readers in grades 7 through 10.

**Plot Summary**

This is the story of an adventure undertaken by journalist and photographer Robert Peck along with ten scientists and their porters in the jungles of Ecuador in 1984. Its objective is to study the birds and other natural phenomena of the unexplored Cordillera de Cutucu, an Andean mountain ridge in southern Ecuador.

The South American country of Ecuador lies on the Pacific coast between Colombia and Peru. The expedition starts out from the capital city of Quito in the north. Officials warn the team not to enter Jivaro, or Shuar, land as the inhabitants are the most warlike of all the Ecuadorean Indians. Bob Ridgely, an ornithologist and expert on South American birds, assures the officials that they only want to pass through the Jivaro lands, not conquer them. "I understand," an official says, "but I'm not sure they will believe it. You have our permission, but you'll have to get theirs. The Indians call the shots in the Cutucu."

Suitably warned, after a two-day trip to the base town of Logrono, the party, with their porters, mules, horses, and supplies of all types, sets off on an ever-narrowing jungle path that takes them deeper and deeper into the Cutucu.

Just one day out, the expedition comes upon a small, well-constructed but deserted cabin in the middle of the jungle. Who built it? Where are the builders? They decide to spend the night there, but the scientists become uneasy when one of them uncovers a long lock of human hair tucked under the eaves. They agree to keep this find secret from the others as there is dissension between the first group of porters, who are Indians, and the second group, hired in Logrono, who are white colonists, or *colonos*. Neither group trusts the other and each accuses the other of stealing. The scientists agree to try to keep the two groups apart as much as possible.

At the next camp the men string out nets to attract the birds they wish to study. Most birds are photographed and released, but some are shot and preserved for long-term study of rare species.

After a week in the jungle, the mule drivers declare that the trails have become too dangerous and difficult, and they return to Logrono. All the supplies must now be carried, which causes more trouble among the porters.

The next campsite shows signs of previous use—it is probably a Shuar hunting camp, say the natives. This makes everyone uneasy and the scientists discuss whether they should cut the expedition short. They decide that they have enough food to stay put for a while but they worry about the increasing friction among the porters.

And indeed, within a day the two groups are fighting in earnest and the *colonos* decide to leave the expedition.

As the expedition waits for new porters, they continue to find and photograph bird species. They also hold halting conversations with their Shuar guides and learn about their ancient culture—their instruments, music, dances, musicians.

When six new porters arrive, the expedition, now numbering nineteen, continues. After a month of nearly constant rainfall, half of the expedition must leave. Peck remains with the rest. One day alone on the trail, he is photographing butterflies and other insects and foliage. He becomes so engrossed in his work that he doesn't realize it is nearly nightfall. When he realizes how late it is, Peck starts to hurry back toward the camp. Suddenly he is aware that the huge root on which he is about to step is moving! With horror, he sees that it is a giant brown-and-black snake, the bushmaster. A single drop of its venom can kill a child. It is one of the most feared of poisonous snakes, its bite nearly always fatal. Peck's only choice is to get out of there before it can strike. His left foot lands in the center of the snake's back and Peck is off like a shot!

The routine of camp life is further interrupted when the Indian porters announce that the Shuar leaders in the area do not believe the men are looking for birds. They believe the expedition is after gold. The word is out that the group will be attacked and driven from the mountains or killed.

How could this be true? How could such a message have been passed through the dense jungle? Some of the remaining scientists refuse to believe it. After some discussion, they decide to go deeper into the Cutucu, farther away from Shuar settlements. They have about two more weeks of food supplies and once the decision is made, food becomes their biggest concern. To save what supplies they have, they eat broiled bodies of tiny birds, moldy noodles, and maggots. They also run into teacup-size tarantulas!

In the final week, they are indeed confronted by young Shuar warriors. One of the scientific party claims to have a deadly contagious disease and the warriors back away. Later, on the trail, Peck is ambushed by a Shuar. In the struggle, the Shuar is knocked over the edge of the mountain.

The expedition returns to the base camp at Logrono, where they have much to discuss: tarantulas and brilliant mountain flowers, headhunters, and hummingbirds.

**Thematic Material**

This is an exciting nonfiction adventure that reads like an action-packed novel. The descriptions of the flora and fauna of the dense Ecuadorean jungle are fascinating as are those of the customs of the native people.

**Book Talk Material**

The rare nature species as well as some of the unusual food delicacies should delight young readers. See: birds in the web (pp. 23–27); monkey for breakfast (pp. 53–58); the butterflies (pp. 65–66); the bushmaster (pp. 71–74); conserving food (p. 84); and the tarantulas (pp. 88–90).

**Additional Selections**

In *Exploring the Titanic* (pap., Scholastic, 1988, $5.95) by Robert D. Ballard, both the tragic voyage and the many efforts to explore the wreckage area are covered. On this subject, W. John Hackwell's *Diving to the Past: Recovering Ancient Wrecks* (Scribner, 1988, $14.95) is also recommended.

The life of another adventurer is depicted graphically and with suspense in Rhoda Blumberg's *The Remarkable Adventures of Captain Cook* (Bradbury, 1991, $18.95).

Christopher Columbus is the subject of two recent excellent biographies: Kathy Pelta's *Discovering Christopher Columbus* (Lerner, 1991, $14.95) and Milton Meltzer's *Columbus and the World around Him* (Watts, 1990, $14.90).

The account of a seven-member American team climbing Gongga Shan in China is told in Joseph E. Murphy's *Adventure beyond the Clouds* (Dillon, 1986, $12.95).

Profiles of various adventurers such as Edmund Hillary and Jacques Cousteau are given in Hillary Hauser's *Call to Adventure* (Bookmakers, 1987, $14.95).

A pictorial introduction is given in *Ecuador . . . in Pictures* (Lerner, 1988, $9.95).

Two collections by Don L. Wulffson of true stories involving such villains as war, jungles, and thirst are *Incredible True Adventures* (Dodd, 1986, $8.95) and *More Incredible True Adventures* (Dutton, 1989, $12.95).

One of the greatest true adventures of all time is Thor Heyerdahl's *Kon Tiki: Across the Pacific by Raft* (pap., Pocket, 1987, $3.95).

**About the Book**
*Kirkus Reviews,* January 1, 1987, p. 64.
*School Library Journal,* June 1987, p. 112.
*VOYA,* August 1987, p. 139.

**About the Author**
May, Hal, ed., *Contemporary Authors.* Gale, 1985, Vol. 112, pp. 391–92.

# 7

Guidance and Health

THE four nonfiction books in this section deal with concerns and problems that are either unique to adolescence or explore these areas from the teenager's point of view. They deal with such topics as stress, suicide, substance abuse, and the process of maturation.

**Bell, Ruth.** *Changing Bodies, Changing Lives*
Random, 1987, $19.95 (0-394-56499-5); pap., $10.95 (0-394-73632-X)

This is a revision of the 1981 book that bore the subtitle *A Book for Teens on Sex and Relationships*. Since its first appearance, it has become a classic in its field, offering several experts' combined knowledge on teenage sexuality and the emotional, social, and physical changes that occur during adolescence. It is a valuable book for junior and senior high school readers.

### Plot Summary

This book, written with members of the Boston Women's Health Book Collective and boys and girls of the Teen Book Project, is noted for its specific, reliable information and its honesty and compassion for its audience. The basic underlying idea is that the more honest and complete information teenagers have about their changing bodies, and therefore their lives, the more they will be able to make responsible choices about their actions. And actions based on responsible choices are less likely to result in casual sex, unwanted pregnancies, and sexually transmitted diseases.

*Changing Bodies, Changing Lives* is divided into seven sections. It is well illustrated with photos, diagrams, and drawings. Throughout the book are comments and vignettes from teenagers themselves, who share their feelings, their worries, and their ideas with the reader.

Section I concerns changing bodies. It deals with the physical and obvious changes that occur during puberty, generally starting in the early teen years. After assuring the reader that change is normal and that everyone goes through it, the authors detail the specific changes that occur in the bodies of both boys and girls, including the proper terms (and slang) for body parts, the function and care of the genitals, ejaculation, menstruation, growth of hair, changes in breasts, and tips on the importance of hygiene during these years.

Section II deals with changing relationships—with parents and the family, with peers and friends: What to do about wildly changing moods, how to handle the discipline that parents may want to enforce and teenagers fight; how to fit in with the group, to accept yourself and accept others as well; how to handle opposite-sex friendships and dating; how to handle falling in love.

Sections III to V cover aspects of sexuality. "Exploring Sex with Yourself" discusses learning about sex, including guilty feelings that teenagers may experience. It talks about sexual fantasies and masturbation, about sexual response, and about orgasm. "Exploring Sex with Someone Else" covers the all-important aspect of making decisions about whether to have sex, what it means, what the consequences might be. What about teen pressures to have sex? What about saying no? If the decision is made to have sex, what goes on beyond petting? What about intercourse? It also discusses the problems that may occur if the decision is made to have sex during the teenage years. The chapter looks at homosexuality as well. The chapter "Sex Against Your Will" deals with facts about rape and what to do if it happens to you. It also discusses the crime of incest.

Section VI makes the reader aware that changes occurring during puberty are not changes merely to the physical you but to the emotional you as well. Teenagers are often a jumble of beautiful, frightening, mixed-up emotions. This is normal, but it can be upsetting, too. What is the best way to handle these strange feelings and these mood swings? How do you ask for help if you need it? From whom? Sometimes these emotional changes during the teenage years bring on feelings of helplessness and powerlessness, resulting in the frightening rise in teenage suicide. This section frankly discusses suicide among teenagers, warning that the best way to cope with such feelings in you or someone you know is to get help. How do you find someone to talk to? What about professional help? When is it needed? What can one expect?

Emotional health care also involves intelligent choices about the use of alcohol and drugs. This section discusses drinking and such drugs as barbiturates, hallucinogens, and narcotics and what they do to mind and body. It warns the teen that if the decision is made to indulge in any of these, the results can go beyond "bad trips" and the teenager can become entangled in legal problems. There is also a section on eating disorders such as bulimia and anorexia nervosa, which can be a problem for teenagers, particularly girls.

Section VII talks about physical health care. It is important to form good health habits early in life. This section discusses the importance of medical checkups, including what a typical medical examination entails and where to go for one if you can't afford a private physician. It talks about birth control for those who have made the decision to have intercourse—the types of birth control available, the right one for you, how to go about getting birth control devices, how they work, their effectiveness.

Birth control is not foolproof, so this section covers pregnancy as well, including pregnancy tests, what to do if you suspect you might be pregnant, the boy's role, talking to parents, the question of abortion and what happens if that is the choice, the choice of adoption or keeping the child. It also deals with feelings of guilt, depression, anger, fear, and many others that become part of this difficult process.

The section ends with a frank discussion of AIDS and other sexually transmitted diseases. How can you protect yourself? Where do you go for help if you suspect you have contracted a sexually transmitted disease? What about your partner?

The issues that involve the changing bodies and changing lives of the teenage years have always been challenging to those who are living through them, as well as those who love them, and perhaps even more so in the 1990s. Teenagers are faced with some very serious choices about their sexual and emotional conduct. *Changing Bodies, Changing Lives* helps to sort out the jumble of changing emotions that can be so troublesome. It does so with straightforward talk and compassion, and with facts that help and do not add to the confusion.

**Thematic Material**

This book recognizes that the teenage years can be a difficult time for boys and girls. It is a comprehensive, straightforward guide to surviving puberty that is both reassuring and nonjudgmental. It offers reliable information that will help the teenager make responsible choices about matters that can profoundly affect their future.

## Book Talk Material

Depending on the specific area of concern, the following sections may be of special interest: physical changes in boys' bodies (pp. 9–19); physical changes in girls' bodies (pp. 19–41); masturbation (pp. 81–83); making decisions about sex (pp. 88–97); and dealings with emotions (pp. 137–53).

## Additional Selections

Another volume that explores the physical and emotional changes during adolescence is *You'll Survive: Late Blooming, Early Blooming, Loneliness, Klutziness, and Other Problems of Adolescence* (Scribner, 1986, $12.95) by Fred Powledge.

Carol Weston writes candid advice for adolescent girls in *Girltalk: All the Stuff Your Sister Never Told You* (pap., Harper, 1985, $7.95).

A discussion of various aspects of teen pregnancy including family planning clinics, abortion, and sex education is provided in Cathryn Jakobson's *Think about Teenage Pregnancy* (Walker, 1988, $14.85; pap., $5.95).

Fifty teens talk about the decision whether or not to drink in Wayne R. Coffey's *Straight Talk about Drinking: Teenagers Speak Out about Alcohol* (pap., NAL, 1988, $8.95).

In *Alcohol: Uses and Abuses* (Enslow, 1988, $16.95) by Margaret O. Hyde, there is a discussion of the medical and social problems caused by alcoholism and how to get help for alcoholics and for young people living with alcoholics.

Sara D. Gilbert describes the problems of growing up and suggests some solutions to ease the pain in *Get Help: Solving the Problems in Your Life* (Morrow, 1989, $12.95).

Another classic sex education text for young adults, which also discusses human relationships, is Eric Johnson's *Love & Sex in Plain Language* (pap., Bantam, 1988, $3.95).

Susan Kuklin talked with a number of pregnant teenagers about their future plans and reported on these findings in *What Do I Do Now?* (Putnam, 1991, $15.95; pap., $7.95).

In Jay Gale's *A Young Man's Guide to Sex* (Holt, 1984, $14.95), the fundamentals of sex education are covered from a male point of view.

**About the Book**
*Booklist*, June 1, 1988, p. 1663.
*School Library Journal*, June 1988, p. 121.
See also *Book Review Index*, 1988, p. 64.

---

**Francis, Dorothy B.**   *Suicide: A Preventable Tragedy*
Dutton, 1989, $13.95 (0-525-67279-6)

---

The tragic increase in teen suicide rates has been affecting every part of the United States. This book, while introducing the subject generally and supplying guidance for survivors, concentrates on the causes of suicide and methods of prevention, with material on types of suicidal behavior and what to do when one sees them in friends and classmates. The author has written other fine books on contemporary problems: *Shoplifting* (Dutton, 1979, $11.75) and *Vandalism* (Dutton, 1983, $11.95). These books are intended for both junior and senior high school readers.

**Plot Summary**

Suicide is a subject no one likes to discuss, especially when the subject is teen suicide. Yet, the author urges, it is time to throw out the myths and face the facts. The suicide rate for young people in the United States has tripled over the past thirty years, and every ninety minutes a young adult or teenager commits suicide. It is the third-largest killer of young people, after accidents and homicide.

Who tries to or does commit suicide? Why? What can be done to lower the incidence of teenage suicide in America? Can it be stopped altogether? The author argues that suicide among teenagers is a preventable tragedy.

Although the first step in prevention may be to identify the teenager who might be a potential suicide, author Dorothy Francis makes it clear that this is not easy to do. More than 20 percent of all male suicides in the United States are young men, and young black men have the highest suicide rate in the country. Young women account for 15 percent of U.S. female suicides. The Southwest, in such states as Nevada, Arizona, and New Mexico, has the highest U.S. suicide rates, possibly because of the high incidence among the native American population. Low suicide rate states are in the Midwest and the East Coast: Nebraska and Indiana, for instance, and South Carolina and New Jersey. According to Francis, someone who tries suicide probably has family problems and is usually suffering from depression and hopelessness. Youths who join cults may be at high risk for suicide. Overachievers who don't meet their own expectations may also be at high risk. Those who are successful at taking their own lives usually have easy access to weapons such as guns.

The youngster who attempts suicide may be quiet and seemingly untroubled. Or he may be the six-year-old boy who deliberately runs out into the traffic because he thinks he will go to heaven or the eleven-year-old girl who swallows a bottle of aspirin because she has lost her best friend.

If it is so difficult to determine who will attempt suicide, perhaps a better way to prevent it, says the author, is to learn *why* youngsters take that drastic route.

According to Francis, there are many reasons why young people attempt suicide. Overall, they are all unhappy in some way, and teenagers and other young people are generally inexperienced at dealing with severe unhappy feelings. They haven't yet learned that these feelings generally do not last forever, or even for very long. They see no solutions. More than half of all adolescent suicides are drug-related. And some people may have chemical abnormalities in the brain that predispose them to suicide.

There are many and varied reasons why anyone tries suicide, but the one fundamental reason, which the author stresses, is depression. Everyone suffers from depression to one degree or another at some time and some teenagers feel it more than most. Social and school pressures can lead to depression, as can the death of a loved one or friend. How can one tell if depression calls for professional treatment? Most doctors feel that if an adolescent experiences severe gloomy feelings for longer than two weeks, this is a symptom of abnormal depression.

Is suicide contagious? The startling and sad answer seems to be yes, although the reasons are not certain. Sometimes a youngster commits suicide following the self-inflicted death of a friend in order to capture the same outpouring of attention. Or a teen may feel that his own death will bring the immortality that a friend's death failed to achieve alone.

Many teen suicides could be prevented if people such as parents, teachers, and friends were trained to recognize the warning signs. The following actions, says Francis, might be reason to be concerned:

• A young person suddenly gives away her most prized possession, such as a record collection.

• A teen stops eating or suddenly increases his food consumption drastically.

• Your daughter starts telling you she can't sleep. Your son seems to want to sleep all the time. Both can be signs of impending suicide.

• Schoolwork suddenly declines. A good student who is thinking about suicide no longer cares about grades.

• Your teenager suddenly withdraws from family, friends, and regular activities. He is bored with everything and everyone.

Rebellious or violent behavior can be warning signs. The youngster who runs away from home may be troubled enough to contemplate suicide. Body language can be a warning sign—an empty face, a listless posture. And strong warning signals are sent by such statements as "I wish I'd never been born," "Nothing matters anymore," or "I won't be a problem to you much longer." Parents should be especially aware of the frequency of this kind of remark.

Many mental health specialists believe that most teenage suicides can be prevented if people close to those who are troubled listen to the warning signs and take action. Many young people will turn first to friends rather than family if they are in trouble. Friends must have the emotional courage to act. They must talk and listen and focus on the exact problem. They must keep no secrets, ask hard questions, and take action.

Part of this book deals with what schools can do to help. The State of New Jersey, for instance, is funding three pilot programs in conjunction with Columbia University of New York City to find out if suicide education in schools is of benefit. Muscogee County in Georgia has a school health program that is becoming a national model. Students spend an average of two hours each week on health-oriented topics in all grades. Many of these classes have segments aimed at suicide prevention. Pilot programs in schools in California are informing students about depression. And schools must crack down on students who bring any kind of weapons to classrooms.

Families must be more alert, cautions the author. It is sometimes easy to overlook the problems of their bothersome teenager. "He's just going through a phase." "All teenage girls are like that." It may not be true in either case. Parents should try to find out how the troubled youth is really feeling. Ask. Talk. If it seems like a good idea, question his or her friends. Perhaps bring up the idea of counseling. And, above all, listen.

Many churches, communities, and state institutions are setting up suicide prevention centers in an effort to wipe out the high incidence of suicide among teenagers and young adults. In 1985 the National Committee on Youth Suicide Prevention (NCYSP) was founded in New York. It acts as a national clearinghouse to give information and referrals to prevention groups and organizations all over the country so that they can share insights and data in an effort to prevent death. The more people work together on this problem, the more potential victims can be saved.

**Book Talk Material**

The myths, the sobering statistics, and the warning signs of potential suicide are good introductions to this guide. See: myths and truths about those who commit suicide (pp. 4–6); who commits suicide in America? (pp. 11–19); and learn to heed the warning signs (pp. 49–56).

**Additional Selections**

Patricia Hermes in *A Time to Listen: Preventing Teen Suicide* (Harcourt, 1987, $12.95) explores the tragedy of teen suicide through interviews with friends, families, counselors, and teenagers who have survived suicide attempts.

In a revision of the 1985 title *Teenage Suicide* (Messner, 1990, $11.95; pap., $5.95), Sandra Gardner and Gary B. Rosenberg continue to supply a straightforward account of the causes of teen suicide, the danger signals, and strategies for prevention.

In the novel *Tunnel Vision* (pap., Dell, 1980, $2.95) by Fran Arrick, friends and family examine past behavior to find an answer to Anthony's suicide.

The strong bond of friendship between two boys and a girl is destroyed when one commits suicide in Richard Peck's touching story *Remembering the Good Times* (Delacorte, 1985, $14.95; pap., Dell, $2.95; condensed in *Juniorplots 3*, Bowker, 1987, pp. 90–94).

A boy feels guilty after the suicide of a younger brother in Elizabeth Harlan's *Watershed* (Viking, 1986, $12.95).

In Janet Kolehmainen and Sandra Handwerk's *Teen Suicide: A Book for Friends, Family, and Classmates* (Lerner, 1986, $9.95), types of suicidal behavior are discussed with advice on what to do if they are seen in friends.

Case histories, interviews, and background information highlight Arnold Madison's *Suicide & Young People* (Clarion, 1978, $13.95).

**About the Book**
*Kirkus Reviews,* May 1, 1989, p. 690.
*School Library Journal,* August 1989, p. 156.
*VOYA,* August 1989, p. 172.
See also *Book Review Index,* 1989, p. 279.

**About the Author**
Commire, Anne, ed., *Something about the Author.* Gale, 1976, Vol. 10, p. 46.
Straub, Deborah A., ed., *Contemporary Authors* (New Revision Series). Gale, 1988,
Vol. 24, pp. 192–93.

---

**Ryan, Elizabeth A.**    *Straight Talk about Drugs and Alcohol*
Facts on File, 1989, $16.95 (0-8160-1525-2)

---

Problems involving substance abuse continue to plague the teen segment of the population. This is a straightforward, powerful account
delivering the facts about drugs and alcohol. In addition to providing
information on how they affect the body, this work discusses methods of
treatment and includes a directory of treatment centers. Other titles in
this series by Elizabeth A. Ryan are: *Straight Talk about Parents* (Facts on
File, 1989, $15.95) and *Straight Talk about Prejudice* (Facts on File, 1992,
$16.95). This series is valuable for both junior and senior high school
readers.

**Plot Summary**
Although the teen years have never been regarded as an easy period,
today's teenagers face a host of pressures not encountered, at least to
such a degree, by their parents and others before them. This is especially
true regarding drugs and alcohol. The modern teen lives in a society in
which an overwhelming number of adults drink or take drugs. Depending on where they live, these young people may have been offered drugs
as children. They may have at least one friend who drinks or is on drugs.
They may have had a friend who committed suicide, with the involvement of drugs or alcohol. Probably a family member uses one or the
other to some degree.

Even if the teenager does not drink, smoke, or use drugs, he or she is
surely surrounded by many who do and by many who not only use but
abuse them. This is a pressure-filled world. It can also be a frightening

world for the soon-to-be adult who must make some very hard decisions about involvement with drugs and/or alcohol. How does one decide what is right for the individual?

Offering no pat answers, only straightforward facts, this book encourages teens to take a serious look at drugs and alcohol, the truths and the myths, and make informed choices about actions that will surely influence the rest of their lives.

"The Addictive Society." The young reader is often in the midst of a puzzling world of drinking and drugs. Society frowns on teenage drinking or drug use. But why, the teenager asks, is it okay to stay up all night before an exam and drink coffee? Why is marijuana wrong at a teenage party in Our Town, USA, but okay at a swanky Hollywood bash? Such questions are confusing to many teens, and the answers are never easy.

In this chapter the author asks the young boy or girl to use judgment before making decisions. Look at the whole picture, she urges. How do you really feel about taking chemicals into your body? Do you want to smoke or drink just to show your parents that you can ignore their rules now? The young reader is encouraged, instead, to look beyond such feelings and realize that the individual eventually is responsible for his or her own actions. Look at your behavior—both good and bad—when alcohol and drugs are involved, advises the author. Do you want to drink at a party because you're too shy to talk to people otherwise? Discovering the real reasons for one's behavior can help one make intelligent decisions about use or nonuse.

"Everybody's Doing It . . . Or Are They?" Sometimes a teen feels isolated just by deciding not to get involved in drugs or alcohol. After all, *everybody else* is. This chapter takes a close look at teenage drinking, which may be a far more serious problem than teenage drug use, and the pressures that can lead to abuse.

"Hard Facts about Drinking." What happens when you take a drink? This chapter discusses the physical assault by alcohol on the mouth and throat, stomach, intestines, liver, pancreas, and heart. Drinking often results in upset stomach, diarrhea, anemia, skin problems, and overall decreased fitness.

"Hard Facts about Drugs." Any drug exerts a five-step action on the body. Absorption is the way the drug enters the body, most by being swallowed. The method of absorption affects how quickly or slowly the drug causes a reaction. Distribution is the process that occurs after absorption. Sometimes the drug goes to a part of the body that stores it for a long time. Some researchers say, for instance, that marijuana is stored in the body for lengthy periods and that this long-term storage can have dangerous later effects. Action is what happens when the drug interacts with a specific part of a cell called a "receptor." Some medications may interact in good ways, for instance, causing an irregular heartbeat to function normally. Drugs also can interact badly, causing depression, hallucinations, and worse. Metabolization is the process by which the body tries to neutralize the effect of any drug. With some drugs this happens quickly, with others slowly. This explains why the effects of some drugs last far longer than others. Excretion is the process of eliminating the drug from the body, usually filtered through the kidneys and passed out in the urine, which is why urine testing is so often used for detecting the ingestion of drugs.

This chapter also looks at common categories of drugs and their effects on the body. How long does marijuana, for instance, stay in the body? How does it influence a person driving a car? What can happen when you mix alcohol and pot? Sometimes the worst effects of a drug are not physical, but emotional. How great are the possibilities for addiction?

"Making Choices." In this chapter the teenager is encouraged to take a realistic look at his or her own feelings about use and nonuse of alcohol and drugs. Do you suffer from denial—pretending you don't have a problem when you really do? *When* is drinking a problem? The author offers tough questions to answer about alcohol use—about personality change, about needing alcohol to get through the day, about drinking in the morning, about hiding liquor. The same kind of scrutiny applies to drug use, with an added stress factor. In many situations in society, the use of alcohol within some limits is accepted, at least for adults. But in most situations, the use of drugs such as cocaine, marijuana, and crack is not accepted, by adults or anyone else, and there can be very real legal penalties for getting involved with them.

If some of the questions asked in this chapter cause the young reader to decide that he or she may need help, the author offers advice about the kinds of people available for counseling and aid.

"Families with Problems" deals with the real-world fact that, although a teenager may not personally be involved with either drugs or alcohol, someone in his or her family *is*. What to do in that case? First, the problem must be recognized. How does the problem drinker or drug user in the family affect you? Again, a list of questions helps to define the situation and opens a path for help. The author offers some practical suggestions, some adapted from Al-Anon, an organization for family and friends of problem drinkers, to help the teenager cope with a family member who is causing stress with the abuse of alcohol or drugs.

An appendix lists places state by state to find help: drug and alcohol facilities; Alcoholics Anonymous intergroups; and Al-Anon or Alateen, a division of Al-Anon for teenagers.

**Thematic Material**

This is a serious guide to serious teenage concerns. As the title implies, it is straight talk without preachiness. It presents the facts concerning the consequences of alcohol and drug use without moralizing. The author repeatedly urges young readers to learn the facts and make judgments for themselves and not to blindly accept the actions of parents or peers. The best choices, she says, are informed choices. Throughout the book, teenagers are presented with a number of difficult issues and choices and are then asked to consider the consequences of their decisions. This is must reading for all teenage boys and girls in today's society.

**Book Talk Material**

Getting the facts straight is often the best way to start on the road to intelligent decision making. See: alcohol, drugs, and the teen factor (pp. 6–12); are teens really into drugs and drink? (pp. 14–22); if you decide to drink, know what it does to your body (pp. 23–33); and a hard look at the effects of drug intake (pp. 39–46).

**Additional Selections**

In *Drug Abuse, the Impact on Society* (Watts, 1988, $12.90) by Gilda Berger, there is a well-organized overview of the use of illegal drugs in the United States.

Case studies of how drugs have ruined young people's lives and how rehabilitation is possible are covered in Essie E. Lee's *Breaking the Connection: How Young People Achieve Drug-Free Lives* (Messner, 1988, $13.95; pap., $5.95).

A well-organized overview of alcohol and its effects is given in Jane Claypool's revised *Alcohol & You* (Watts, 1988, $12.90). See under Ruth Bell's *Changing Bodies, Changing Lives* in this section for more titles on alcohol.

Subtitled "An Honest and Unhysterical Guide for Teens," *What You*

*Can Believe about Drugs* (Holt, 1988, $12.95) by Susan Cohen and Daniel Cohen is a straightforward account that separates myth from fact.

Nine young alcoholics and drug addicts tell their stories in Susan Newman's *It Won't Happen to Me* (pap., Putnam, 1987, $8.95).

**About the Book**
*Booklist,* April 1, 1989, p. 1367.
*School Library Journal,* May 1989, p. 132.
*VOYA,* January 1989, p. 128.
*Wilson Library Bulletin,* May 1989, p. 110.
See also *Book Review Index,* 1989, p. 714.

**About the Author**
Commire, Anne, ed., *Something about the Author.* Gale, 1983, Vol. 30, p. 183.
Evory, Ann, ed., *Contemporary Authors* (First Revision Series). Gale, 1982, Vol. 7, p. 419.

---

**Van Wie, Eileen Kalberg.** *Teenage Stress: How to Cope in a Complex World*
Messner, 1988, $13.98 (0-671-63824-6); pap., $6.95 (0-671-65980-4)

---

The maturation process that occurs during adolescence produces a number of problems and concerns unique to this period. Although many involve finding suitable social relationships with peers, others revolve around getting along with adults, achieving financial security, and succeeding at school. All of these pressures can result in stress for the teenager. In this book, the causes of stress are examined, the various types are enumerated, and advice on how to lessen these tensions is given. This book is suitable for junior and senior high school readers.

**Plot Summary**
For most boys and girls, the onset of puberty is a difficult time. As their bodies and emotions change, as they gain more freedom and ability to make decisions for themselves, they often face confusion and stress. The confusion and stress are in turn compounded by the pressures of today's society, where they must learn to deal with competitiveness, changing family structures, drugs and alcohol, and the complexities of life in the late twentieth century.

This book is especially directed toward helping teenagers to cope with stress, and therefore better control their own lives. As each idea for handling an aspect of stress is discussed, it is followed by exercises to help the reader learn the new skill and apply it to his or her daily life. The exercises concern physical appearance, school and family life, dating, physical fitness, privacy, and other areas that most often present problems in the teenage years.

*Teenage Stress* is divided into two parts. Part One deals with stress factors. In chapter 1, the author discusses the general topic of stress in the teen years, explaining that it is the body's response to demands, threats, and changes, called stressors. There are three categories of stressors, and the book deals with each: personal, social, and environmental. Stressors can trigger both physical and emotional responses. The reader is asked to complete a stress symptoms chart to ascertain how his or her responses compare with those of the group of 200 teenagers contacted for this book.

Chapter 2 covers personal stressors. School is a big one. How important, the author asks, do you believe it is to learn? How fearful are you of failing? A learning-styles inventory is included to help the reader discover the pressures he or she feels about school.

Concerns about physical appearance often create stress during the teenage years. The author assures the young reader that wanting to look good is normal and presents exercises to help the teenager better understand feelings and actions concerning physical appearance.

In chapter 3, social stressors come under the spotlight. In family relationships, anger and conflict are often normal reactions. A questionnaire helps the reader evaluate his or her true feelings about family life. The stresses of friendship and dating are discussed, including gossip, competition, embarrassment, and the frequent teenage worries about sex.

Chapter 4 deals with environmental stress. How important is the teenager's need for privacy? What are the stressors when you must start in a new school? How do you adapt? How do you feel when you stay for a time in the home of a friend or relative?

Part Two covers ways in which young boys and girls can cope with the stresses discussed in Part One. Chapter 5 offers a method to ease the difficulty of making decisions—SOLVE: State your problem; Outline your response; List your alternatives; View the consequences; Evaluate the results. This method helps identify the problem situations in your life. Also discussed are brainstorming, story writing, goal setting, and leisure-time decisions.

Learning skills are important in the management of stress: study time, note taking, memory training, and test taking. Another way to cope with stress is through constructive thinking: Keeping a thoughts log and relabeling destructive thoughts are two suggested methods. The reader is also reminded that dealing with stress involves physical as well as emotional changes. Methods are discussed to relax both the mind and the body, including exercises: yawn and sigh, natural breathing, bending, stretching, tension/relaxation interaction, and the quieting reflex.

Chapter 6 covers practical social coping skills. Communication styles are all-important. Are you passive, aggressive, or assertive? The passive style means that you let others make decisions and assume control of your life. With the aggressive style, you put others down by blaming or criticizing. The assertive style means that you are considerate of others and of yourself. The author suggests how to acquire this style. How does one initiate or send assertive communication? How does one respond to and receive it? Such topics as giving compliments, asking questions, making requests, saying no, and dealing with criticism are covered. Also included is an exercise in personal communication style and an important section on humor. Learning to laugh at oneself is an excellent way to deal with stress.

Another good way is by coping with the environment. This section helps the teenager assess food habits and eating practices. Included are dietary guidelines from the U.S. Department of Health and Human Services, as well as calorie charts and desirable-weight lists, and a section on the nutritional needs of teenage athletes.

A major way to deal with stress during any period of life is through exercise. In fact, the author thinks that exercise is probably the best method of all. Covered in this section are the foundation of a fitness program, which is aerobic exercise, and ways to prevent injury.

Another important way to deal with stress in the teenage years is just by looking good. There are many ways in which young adults can improve their appearance. It is easier to cope with stress of any kind if you feel good about the way you look. The author discusses posture, face and skin care, the dreaded acne problem, suntanning and sunburn, and how to use color to enhance your wardrobe. A wardrobe planning worksheet is included.

Adequate privacy should not be overlooked if you feel the pressures of coping with stress. How do you provide yourself with adequate privacy at home? Sometimes it is a matter of redecorating your room to better suit your needs. Sometimes you must learn to deal better with sharing your room with a brother or sister.

### Thematic Material

This clearly written, practical guide offers helpful ways in which today's teenager can cope with the stress factors that abound in modern society. Besides dealing with the important aspects of life that can present problems to the young adult, it offers charts and exercises for evaluating one's own stress factors and ways in which to deal with them in a reasonable, workable manner.

### Book Talk Material

Most young readers will find the exercises and charts of special interest. For example, see: how to judge your own stress symptoms (pp. 11–16); evaluating your destructive thinking (pp. 17–19); taking inventory of your personal learning style (pp. 24–28); evaluating the stresses in your home life (pp. 38–41); and Ten Questions of Sex (pp. 64–71).

### Additional Selections

One cause of stress is competition. The positive and negative aspects of this factor in adolescent life are explored in Susan Cohen and Daniel Cohen's *Teenage Competition: A Survival Guide* (Evans, 1986, $13.95). The Cohens also discuss the nature of stress, how it can be avoided, and how it can be lessened in *Teenage Stress* (Evans, 1983, $10.95).

Failure in school is another cause of stress. *How to Be School Smart: Secrets of Successful Schoolwork* (pap., Lothrop, Lee & Shepard, 1988, $6.95) by Elizabeth James and Carol Barkin is a fine guide to improving study skills, time management, attitude, and test taking.

Through the use of case studies, the various types and causes of teenage depression are discussed and treatments suggested in *Coping with Depression* (Rosen, 1990, $12.95) by Sharon Carter and Lawrence Clayton.

Many practical tips on how to do better in school are given in Maria Orlow's *A Student's Guide to Good Grades* (pap., Wayside, 1990, $10.50).

The world of emotions and how to understand and control them are discussed in E. LeShan's *You & Your Feelings* (Macmillan, 1975, $9.95).

In the *Teenage Survival Book* (pap., Times, 1981, $12.95) by Sol Gordon, the important worries and concerns of adolescents are addressed.

**About the Book**

*School Library Journal,* November 1988, p. 139.
See also *Book Review Index,* 1989, p. 843.

# 8

# The World Around Us

As adolescents reach maturity, they are able to reach out beyond their immediate experience and explore the world outside. In this section, the books highlighted help open up this world to readers exploring the disciplines of history, science, and the arts.

---

**Blanco, Richard L.**   *The Luftwaffe in World War II: The Rise and Decline of the German Air Force*
   Messner, 1987, $10.29 (0-671-50232-8)

---

The roots of the world's current political and economic situation can, in many cases, be traced directly to the results of World War II. Not only was it a period of heroism and tragedy, it was also a time in history during which the powers of evil and oppression almost completely controlled the civilized world. This account tells how the World War II German Air Force emerged, how it became an important part of Hitler's war machine, and the causes of its decline and fall. It is a valuable book for both junior and senior high school students.

**Plot Summary**
The German Air Force, the Luftwaffe, was perhaps the best, and certainly for a time the most advanced, air force in World War II. Its pilots were brilliant and daring, its aircraft the latest in technology, its commitment to Hitler and the Nazi cause total. In 1939, when Germany marched across Europe into World War II, the Luftwaffe had at its command more than 3,700 combat planes and over two million men.

This book is two fascinating stories in one—the building of perhaps the most powerful air arsenal ever created and the story of its downfall, led by a man increasingly out of touch with reality and unwilling to accept defeat.

At the end of World War I (1914–1918), the terms of the treaty imposed on Germany by the victorious Allies outlawed a military air force, permitting operation of only three passenger airlines. Soon after the treaty was signed, however, German designers and engineers began work in secret on new aircraft technology. When Adolf Hitler came to power in 1933 as head of the National Socialist party (the Nazis), he authorized the building of the Luftwaffe (German Air Force). By 1938 the Luftwaffe had 2,000 planes and many aircraft factories working at full speed. To those Germans who were fearful as Hitler began to demand more and more territory, the Nazi leader declared that no foreign country would dare to oppose the growing German air might. The führer was correct.

At the head of the Luftwaffe was Reichsmarschall Hermann Göring, the "Iron Man." A World War I ace, former head of the notorious gang of thugs known as the storm troopers, and a codeine addict (he used codeine to mask chronic pain from an accident), Göring was an arrogant man totally devoted to Hitler, whom he regarded as a genius. Although the pompous Göring later became a subject of ridicule, even among his own people, the Luftwaffe also boasted many brilliant engineers and strategists.

The Luftwaffe's first World War II assignment was to knock out Poland's air power, which it did in just five days. The method stunned the world, for the Luftwaffe operated in a series of sudden, swift strikes by combined land and air forces. It gave a new word to the language of battle—the blitzkrieg, or lightning war. One after another, the small nations of Europe fell. By the spring of 1940, the German advance was so total that thousands of Allied troops found themselves trapped on the French coast at Dunkirk, with the North Sea before them and the Germans surrounding them.

Göring was ecstatic. Encouraged by the success of his air battles, he declared that the Luftwaffe would "wipe out the British on the beaches." However, Göring did not reckon with bad weather and a British Royal Navy and RAF (Royal Air Force) that more than made up in courage and determination what they lacked in numbers. With motorboats and naval vessels, tugboats and trawlers, and with Hurricanes and Spitfires taking on the mighty Luftwaffe, some 366,000 Allied soldiers were rescued and landed safely in Britain. The victory was sweet but almost overshadowed by other events. By June 14, 1940, Paris had fallen and the Germans marched on. Few took note that the Luftwaffe had suffered a rather devastating defeat.

Next, Hitler turned his air power to the Battle of Britain. The plan was for massive aerial attacks to break down the defenses of the British Isles in preparation for the landing of German troops. The Luftwaffe outnumbered the RAF 2,600 planes to 700. From July 1940 until the following May, the planes of the Luftwaffe pounded Britain with increasing fury. Time after time they were met in the skies by the pilots of the RAF. Göring grew increasingly furious as his losses mounted. He berated his pilots as incompetent. But in the end, the Battle of Britain was another defeat for Hitler, Göring, and the Luftwaffe.

Göring made many tactical mistakes in his handling of the Battle of Britain campaign and he ignored his available radar technology. Nevertheless, the victory really came from the courage of the British people and the bravery of the RAF pilots, about whom Prime Minister Winston Churchill eloquently said, "Never in the field of human conflict was so much owed by so many to so few." There was glory yet ahead for the Luftwaffe, but the Battle of Britain changed the tide of the war.

However, World War II raged on for three more years. The Allies fought the Axis powers in the Mediterranean, North Africa, on the Russian front. The power of the German Air Force was awesome, and Allied losses were tremendous. Yet, little by little, inch by inch, the edge went to the Allies. The United States entered the war after the Japanese surprise attack at Pearl Harbor on December 7, 1941. American B-17s and Liberators joined the British in bombing raids over Germany and its conquered lands.

By early 1944 the Allies were gaining in air and ground superiority. But the Luftwaffe, now outnumbered and with aging equipment that the crumbling Nazi war machine could not replace, would not be driven from the skies. Grimly, the German pilots hung on, encouraged by talk of Hitler's "new secret weapon" that would change the fortunes of war.

Instead, the fortunes of war were changed by the Allies on D-Day, June 6, 1944. In a maneuver such as the world had never seen, a million troops were landed on the French seacoast by early July, 1.5 million by early August. The Allied invasion was on.

Where was the mighty Luftwaffe? Because the German leaders had been uncertain about where the Allies would land, the Luftwaffe had only about 1,000 planes available at the Normandy beachhead. They were outnumbered ten to one. The Allied forces established a firm foothold on the French shore and marched inland. Paris was liberated on August 25, 1944.

The war was not yet over, however. From June 1944 until the following March, the long-awaited new German secret weapon was deployed— the V-1 rocket. About 10,000 were fired on England. They were soon followed by the V-2, the first modern missile. Had these weapons been ready earlier, as Hitler had claimed they would be, they would at least have delayed the Allied victory.

The might and fury of the combined Allied forces now turned full blast against Germany. On one day in January 1945, the Luftwaffe lost 250 pilots, its greatest single-day casualty list. The German Air Force had not given up, however. Soon after that devastating loss, three new jets joined the Luftwaffe arsenal. However, the new planes had too many bugs, arrived too late, and were too few. Courageous and daring they may have been, but the Luftwaffe pilots were doomed. So was the Third Reich. Germany surrendered on May 7, 1945.

The Luftwaffe lost 44,000 pilots in World War II; another 27,000 were captured or listed as missing. This once awesome aerial force was destroyed.

And what of its vainglorious leader, the strutting chief of the elite German Air Force? By war's end, Göring had grown impossibly fat and increasingly lazy. He was rarely at the front. He repeatedly called his pilots cowards. He seemed far more interested in adding to his stolen collection of priceless art objects than in directing the young men who so steadfastly gave their lives for the cause of the Third Reich.

It is said that as the war drew to its end, Göring became more and more detached from reality. He rarely left his estate. On April 24, 1945, he wrote a letter to Hitler and told him to resign, requesting that he— Göring—be appointed head of the Third Reich. Instead, a few days before he committed suicide, Hitler ordered Göring arrested for treason.

Göring escaped to the Americans, who took him prisoner, apparently to his surprise. From late 1945 to October 1946, Göring stood among the Nazi war leaders at the Nuremberg trials, accused of crimes against humanity. He was found guilty and sentenced to hanging. Instead, Göring obtained a vial of cyanide and committed suicide on October 15, 1946. Both the Luftwaffe and its infamous leader were gone.

**Thematic Material**

This smoothly written, unemotional account details the building of one of the world's most awesome air forces. It is also a look beyond the facts of history into the personalities that helped to shape the direction and outcome of World War II.

## Book Talk Material

History buffs and aviation fans will be most interested in the stories of the air battles that made a difference in the outcome of World War II. See: the Luftwaffe stuns the world with the blitzkrieg (pp. 25–28); the RAF and the Royal Navy at Dunkirk (pp. 42–44); the Battle of Britain (pp. 55–77); the Luftwaffe and Russia (pp. 91–101); the Luftwaffe at the D-Day invasion (pp. 185–86).

## Additional Selections

Another aspect of the horror and waste of World War II is told in two books by Milton Meltzer: *Never to Forget: The Jews of the Holocaust* (Harper, 1976, $13.89; pap., Dell, $2.50) and *Rescue: The Story of How Gentiles Saved Jews in the Holocaust* (Harper, 1988, $13.95; pap., $6.95).

In the novel *The Man from the Other Side* (Houghton, 1991, $13.95) by Uri Orlev, a teenager helps his father smuggle food through the filthy Warsaw sewers to help the ghetto Jews during World War II.

A matter-of-fact biography of the German dictator is given in Albert Marrin's *Hitler* (Viking, 1987, $14.95). Another recommended biography is Joshua Rubenstein's *Adolf Hitler* (Watts, 1982, $12.90).

A fine overview of World War II from its causes to Hiroshima is given in *The Second World War* (Silver Burdett, 1987, $14.96) by Michel Pierre and Annette Wieviorka. Two other accounts that are heavily illustrated are Robert Leckie's *The Story of World War II* (Random, 1964, $13.99) and Dorothy Hoobler and Thomas Hoobler's *An Album of World War II* (Watts, 1977, $13.90).

An account of the last seven months of the war in Europe is given in Edward F. Dolan, Jr.'s *Victory in Europe: The Fall of Hitler's Germany* (Watts, 1988, $12.90).

The story of the invasion of Europe in June 1944 is graphically told in Milton Dank's *D-Day* (Watts, 1984, $12.90).

## About the Book

*Booklist,* June 15, 1987, p. 1585.
*School Library Journal,* August 1987, p. 89.
See also *Book Review Index,* 1987, p. 76.

---

**Dwiggins, Don.** *Hello? Who's Out There? The Search for Extraterrestrial Life*
Dodd, 1987, $10.95 (0-396-08842-2)

---

One of the questions that tantalize humankind is the possibility of life on other worlds. Fired by films, television series, and science fiction, the interest in this question continues to grow. This book provides a reasonably complete description of the scientific efforts to determine if extraterrestrial life exists. It begins with the ancient Greeks and moves to the present, giving a wealth of interesting information in simple, lucid, nontechnical language. It is enjoyed by readers in both junior and senior high school.

**Plot Summary**

One of the most fascinating of scientific questions concerns life on other planets. Are we alone, or do other intelligent beings live on distant planets? Are the reported sighting of UFOs "proof" of visitors from other worlds?

Some scientists do believe that intelligent life can, and indeed does, exist elsewhere. Even those who don't believe in extraterrestrial life would like to find out for sure. This book by a veteran aerospace reporter traces the history of human concern with life beyond the Earth and what we are doing to try to find the answers.

Humans have been asking whether we are unique in the universe since the beginning of recorded time. It was not until 1609, when Galileo invented the telescope, however, that scientists had a workable tool for exploring the heavens. Even with Galileo's crude instrument, mountains were found on the moon and satellites circling Jupiter. The scientific search for extraterrestrial life began in the nineteenth century with the work of French chemist Louis Pasteur, who drilled into a meteorite in search of biological activity. He found none, and no scientist yet found any evidence that extraterrestrial life exists. But the question continues to intrigue us all, and scientists continue to try to find an answer.

The search for life on Mars began in 1971 with the *Mariner 9* spacecraft launched by the United States. A more detailed analysis was completed in 1976 by *Viking 1* and *Viking 2*, but still no conclusive evidence was found for any life form on the so-called Red Planet.

One of the main problems in searching for extraterrestrial life is the mind-boggling distances involved. If there is no life on the other planets in our solar system, which in itself is only a tiny speck in the giant Milky Way galaxy—estimated to contain about 100 billion stars, then the search must go beyond our solar system. But the closest star cluster that we could reasonably expect to contain planets that might support life may be thousands of light-years away. One light-year is the distance light waves travel in one year—or about six trillion miles—a long way to go for the answer to "Who's out there?" Even if a space vehicle flew at the speed of light, which is 186,000 miles per second, it would take a decade for a round-trip voyage to the nearest star beyond our sun.

Scientists decided on a better way—radio waves. They have been used to send signals since 1894 when a German scientist, Henrich Hertz, jumped a spark across two electrically charged points. This produced electromagnetic waves that moved at the speed of light. In 1931, radio waves coming from outer space were noted. If these were signals from a distant planet, how could we contact the inhabitants? Perhaps the best way to make contact, some scientists reasoned, was simply to listen. Since that time there have been many attempts to contact and to listen for signs of intelligent life elsewhere.

In 1983 the SETI (Search for Extraterrestrial Intelligence) program was launched, managed by NASA's Life Sciences Offices and conducted by the Ames Research Center in Mountain View and the Jet Propulsion Laboratory (JPL) in Pasadena, both in California. The idea was to conduct a search over an outer space area ten million times greater than covered before.

Using radio telescopes fitted with the latest techniques, the SETI program performs a microwave search of the heavens. The first search used an eighty-five-foot dish antenna and covered 80 percent of the sky. It was looking for a signal source, from anywhere.

In 1985, the SETI program began operating a new channel receiver at Harvard's Oak Ridge Radio Observatory. Movie producer Steven Spielberg, of E.T. fame, donated $100,000 for the receiver. This and other giant telescopes around the world are in operation, eavesdropping on the universe party line.

While the SETI program, and the rest of the world, waits for a signal from anywhere, three communications from Earth have actually been sent, like a note in a bottle, winging off into the blackness of space. In 1972 the spacecraft Pioneer 10 was sent hurtling across space with a metal plaque attached to its side. The plaque shows diagrams of the solar system, figures of an Earth man and woman, hydrogen atoms, and pulsar radio frequencies. Earth scientists figure that intelligent life elsewhere could intercept these messages. *Pioneer 10* flew past Neptune in 1986 and on into space.

*Voyager 1* and *2* blasted off in 1977 carrying golden phonograph records. After about a 40,000-year journey to the nearest star, the records will tell someone all about life on planet Earth—if that someone can figure out how to play them. The records, each running about two hours, contain whale grunts, coded photographs of such things as the Golden Gate Bridge in San Francisco, and lots of music, including a Chinese folk tune and Beethoven's String Quartet in B flat, No. 13.

**Thematic Material**

This is a straightforward, easy-to-read account of the search for extraterrestrial life. It covers history and some of the known and little-known scientists who have contributed—some in a lighthearted way—to the search for other life forms. Not an in-depth look, but of interest to any young reader with even a passing interest in this fascinating scientific area.

**Book Talk Material**

The unbelievably vast distances that must be covered in order to contact possible other life forms should serve as a good introduction to this book (see pp. 10–12). Also of interest are the early scientists who paved the way for the scientific experiments of today (pp. 12–16). Is life possible on any other planet in our solar system (see pp. 16–19)?

**Additional Selections**

*UFOs, ETs, and Visitors from Space* (Putnam, 1988, $11.95) by Melvin Berger discusses both the possibilities of life on other planets and the best-known recent sightings of unidentified flying objects.

David E. Fisher conveys a sense of both wonder and delight when he tries to answer questions about how our universe was created in *The Origin & Evolution of One Particular Universe* (Atheneum, 1988, $14.95).

The possibility and practicality of finding out if life exists outside our planet is also explored in William G. Gutsch's *The Search for Extraterrestrial Life* (Crown, 1991, $14).

In Margaret Poynter and Michael J. Klein's *Cosmic Quest: Searching for Intelligent Life among the Stars* (Macmillan, 1984, $11.95), there is an account of the international SETI (Search for Extraterrestrial Intelligence) program.

In nontechnical language, Thomas R. McDonough describes the search for possible life in outer space in *The Search for Extraterrestrial Intelligence* (Wiley, 1987, $19.95).

UFOs, Bigfoot, and Easter Island are only three of the mysteries explored in Catherine O'Neill's *Amazing Mysteries of the World* (National Geographic, 1983, $8.50).

Daniel Cohen has written two fascinating books about UFOs: *The World of UFOs* (Harper, 1978, $13.70) and *Creatures from UFOs* (Putnam, 1978, $8.95).

**About the Book**
*Booklist*, June 1987, p. 1599.
*Center for Children's Books Bulletin*, September 1987, p. 6.
*Kirkus Reviews*, May 15, 1987, p. 794.
*School Library Journal*, October 1987, p. 132.
See also *Book Review Digest*, 1988, pp. 480–81; and *Book Review Index*, 1987, p. 481.

**About the Author**
Commire, Anne, ed., *Something about the Author*. Gale, 1973, Vol. 4, pp. 72–73.
Evory, Ann, and Metzger, Linda, eds., *Contemporary Authors* (New Revision Series). Gale, 1988, Vol. 23, pp. 132–33.
Straub, Deborah A., ed., *Contemporary Authors* (New Revision Series). Gale, 1988, Vol. 23, pp. 132–33.

---

**Fritz, Jean.**   *China's Long March: 6,000 Miles of Danger*
Putnam, 1988, $14.95 (0-399-21512-3)

---

Jean Fritz is usually thought of as the writer who has helped breathe life into American history for middle-grade youngsters in a series of delightful biographies, such as *Will You Sign Here, John Hancock?* (Putnam, 1982, $9.95) and *Bully for You, Teddy Roosevelt* (Putnam, 1991, $15.95). Although her roots are in America, she spent her childhood in China. She tells of this part of her life in *Homesick: My Own Story* (Putnam, 1982, $13.95). Her love of this country and sympathy with its people are apparent in *China's Long March*. Before writing, she researched both English and Chinese sources, collected pertinent documents (from which there are ample quotations), and conducted interviews with survivors. In addition to this scholarship, this account reveals the mark of a true storyteller in its heroic tale of people fighting against impossible odds. It is intended for a reading audience in grades 6 through 9.

**Plot Summary**

This is a compelling account of the Communist army's incredible 6,000-mile journey across China in 1934 and 1935. It is written by an author with firsthand knowledge of China and great compassion for its people.

In the early 1930s, China was waiting to boil over with trouble. For centuries the Chinese people had lived under the rule of emperors and empresses. The last one was overthrown in 1911, but in the following years there was much unrest. Chiang Kai-shek's Nationalist government was now recognized by most as the ruling power. However, the Chinese Communists, whose strength was growing, were determined to take over.

In 1934 segments of the Communist army were grouped in the southeastern province of Jiangxi. Chiang Kai-shek's troops began to surround them, hoping to cut them off from supplies and squeeze them out of existence. The Communists' only hope was to leave the area while they could, perhaps to join up with other Red forces scattered around China.

The Communist, or Red, army, which began its march on October 15, 1930, numbered about 86,000 men, most of them in their early twenties. In addition, there were porters, horses, and hundreds of teenagers who traveled with the army as messengers and water and equipment carriers. The average soldier had no idea where he was going, only that his life was in danger if he remained. There were rumors that they would join other divisions of the Red Army stationed elsewhere in China, but certainly none of the foot soldiers really knew.

So began the Long March, which would end a year later, in October 1935, 6,000 miles away at the other end of China, crossing twenty-four rivers, eleven provinces, and a thousand mountains. The army stretched out in single file for sixty miles as it traveled through the countryside by night and rested under the trees by day to stay out of sight of the Nationalist troops.

Chiang Kai-shek had apparently decided that the outnumbered Communists were no longer a threat—or else his own troops were busy with the Japanese, who had attacked China in the north. At any rate, the Red

Army managed to snake slowly, painstakingly through narrow mountain trails in the cold of winter. The man in charge, and presumably the only one who knew where they were going, was a German, Otto Braun, who had been sent from Shanghai by the Communist party there.

By late November, the Red Army had reached the Xiang River, where they ran into 300,000 Nationalist troops. The battle lasted a week until both sides simply quit fighting. It was estimated that the Communists lost half their men.

Most of the blame for the heavy losses was placed on Braun's leadership. Instead of being dispirited, however, the army turned angry. Before there had been talk of turning back; now there was renewed enthusiasm for joining other parts of the Red Army and defeating the Nationalists. The voice of one of the Communist leaders, Mao Zedong, was heard more and more as he began to edge out Braun in the leadership role. Mao suggested that the army march west, where the Nationalist troops were weaker. The Long March headed west.

In January 1935, the Reds reached and crossed the wide and wild Wu River and by January 8 had taken the city of Zunyi from the Nationalists. Mao led the march of the victorious Communists into the city. Apparently, he had by this time informally taken over the leadership.

By January 15 the Communist leaders held a formal meeting in which they ousted Braun and installed Mao as the man in charge. He would be called Chairman Mao.

Slowly, day by day, mile by mile, battle by battle, the Long March was changing the young Chinese troops from unhappy, complaining soldiers into a unified army intent on ousting the Nationalists and taking control of China. The actions of Chairman Mao's wife, He Zizhen, demonstrate the determination of these young Communists. She gave birth to a baby boy during the march, but because she was a soldier, committed to the army and the cause, there was no time for the baby, no time even to name him. So Mao and He Zizhen wrapped the baby in cloth and gave him, along with a few silver dollars, to a peasant couple along the way. Any other members of the Long March would have done the same.

In February the Red Army gained a great victory over the Nationalists at Lousahn Pass, capturing about 3,000 of the enemy. The Communists suffered losses too, at this battle and at others, but their enthusiasm for their cause only grew stronger. This strength and determination, in turn, drew many of the Chinese peasants to the cause. The Reds seemed invincible. The peasants began to offer them food and supplies as they passed through the countryside. More and more, Chiang Kai-shek and the Nationalists began to worry about this ever-moving, unstoppable force.

By springtime the Red troops were marching north through fields of flowers. Mao headed for the city of Huili to give his army, now down to about 20,000, a rest and to plan strategy. By June, Mao was certain that the Fourth Front Army, with whom he wanted to join forces, was only about one hundred miles north. In order to reach them, his soldiers would have to cross the still snow-covered mountains known as the Great Snowies. The highest peak was about 16,000 feet. Most of the troops wore only cotton suits and thin sandals. They were warned that if they sat down on the march through the high mountains, they would freeze before they could stand up again.

Many died, most suffered unbelievable hardship, but they succeeded. A few days later they joined the Fourth Front Army. Chairman Mao and his young forces were no longer alone.

There were still many miles to travel and battles to win, but by the end of 1935 the Long March was over. It ended in the northern province of Shaanxi. Mao now commanded only 6,000 troops. Few of them could explain how they had managed to survive such hardships.

Mao never lost sight of their cause. They had reached a part of China where they could now regroup and expand their forces. They would defeat the Nationalist Army. They would drive the Japanese out of China. They had survived the Long March; they could survive anything.

On many counts, Chairman Mao was correct, even though not quite in the way he had envisioned. To throw the Japanese out of China, the Communists and Nationalists had to unite. Japan's defeat, however, came at the hands of the Allies at the end of World War II. Four years later, the Communists drove the Nationalists out of China to the island of Taiwan, where Chiang Kai-shek set up his government. Mao Zedong proclaimed the new government of the People's Republic of China on October 1, 1949.

Mao was intent on building a China to fit his vision of a land where the common good was always above personal interest. As he became more and more impatient with the slow realization of his dream, he became more and more repressive. In 1966 he instituted the Cultural Revolution, a ten-year period during which innocent people were imprisoned, intellectuals were humiliated, and schools were closed. The teachings of

Mao became the bible of the people. The Cultural Revolution faded only with Mao's death in 1976.

There may be few people in China today who reflect with pride on the years of the Cultural Revolution, but there are still a number who are survivors of the Long March, a feat of which they are justly proud.

**Thematic Material**

This is a personalized look at a dramatic period in Chinese and world history by an author who lived in China and has great compassion for its people. It is an amazing true story that reads like fiction as the incredible hardships of a 6,000-mile march are detailed through brief looks into the lives of ordinary (and for the most part young) people who grew, not only in determination and bravery, but in the justification of their cause. The fact that the society they fought for became more and more repressive does not lessen the wonder of their endurance.

**Book Talk Material**

Readers will best gain a sense of the incredible hardships of this journey by the glimpses the author provides of what these young people endured. See: the troops begin the Long March (pp. 17–18); Kang Kequing, girl combat soldier (pp. 23–24); four-foot-eleven Liu Ying, who kept up the porters' spirits (pp. 25–26); crossing the Wu River (pp. 36–41); Mao and his wife give up their baby (pp. 49–50).

**Additional Selections**

A more recent aspect of China's history is dealt with in Wendy Lubetkin's biography *Deng Xiaoping* (Chelsea House, 1988, $17.95).

Twenty Chinese folktales have been collected and retold by Laurence Yep in *The Rainbow People* (Harper, 1989, $13.95) with a special introduction that links them to Chinese life and culture.

A history of China since World War II is told with many excerpts from original sources in Stewart Ross's *China since 1945* (Bookwright, 1989, $12.90).

This biography by Sean Dolan, *Chiang Kai-Shek* (Chelsea House, 1988, $16.95), tells about this leader's life as well as covering the history of twentieth-century China.

In *Zhou Enlai* (Chelsea House, 1986, $17.95) by Dorothy Hoobler and

Thomas Hoobler, the story of the life of this Chinese leader is told in text and pictures.

Two interesting biographies of Mao Tse-tung are Hedda Garza's *Mao Zedong* (Chelsea House, 1987, $16.95) and Frederick King Poole's *Mao Zedong* (Watts, 1982, $12.90).

Another account of the Long March is Don Lawson's *The Long March: Red China and Chairman Mao* (Harper, 1983, $12.89).

A general introduction to China is given in John S. Major's *The Land & People of China* (Harper, 1989, $14.89).

**About the Book**
*Booklist*, May 1, 1988, p. 1179.
*Center for Children's Books Bulletin*, April 1988, p. 155.
*Horn Book*, May 1988, p. 370.
*Kirkus Reviews*, January 15, 1988, p. 39.
*School Library Journal*, May 1988, p. 198.
*VOYA*, June 1988, p. 100.
See also *Book Review Digest*, 1988, p. 595; and *Book Review Index*, 1988, p. 285.

**About the Author**
Chevalier, Tracy, ed., *Twentieth-Century Children's Writers* (3rd ed.). St. James, 1989, pp. 363–64.
Commire, Anne, ed., *Something about the Author*. Gale, 1982, Vol. 29, pp. 79–84.
de Montreville, Doris, and Hill, Donna, eds., *Third Book of Junior Authors and Illustrators*. Wilson, 1972, pp. 94–95.
Estes, Glenn E., ed., *American Writers for Children since 1960: Fiction* (Dictionary of Literary Biography: Vol. 52). Gale, 1986, pp. 84–91.
Evory, Ann, ed., *Contemporary Authors* (First Revision). Gale, 1985, Vol. 5, pp. 201–2.
Kirkpatrick, D. L., ed., *Twentieth-Century Children's Writers* (2nd ed.). St. Martin's, 1983, p. 303.
Metzger, Linda, and Straub, Deborah A., eds., *Contemporary Authors* (New Revision Series). Gale, 1986, Vol. 16, pp. 125–29.
Riley, Carolyn, ed., *Children's Literature Review*. Gale, 1976, Vol. 2, pp. 79–83.
Sarkissian, Adele, ed., *Something about the Author*. Gale, 1986, Vol. 2, pp. 99–109.
Senick, Gerard J., ed., *Children's Literature Review*. Gale, 1988, Vol. 14, pp. 102–23.
Ward, Martha, ed., *Authors of Books for Young People* (3rd ed.). Scarecrow, 1990, p. 249.

**Haskins, James.** *Black Music in America: A History through Its People*
Crowell, 1987, $12.89 (0-690-04460-7)

Jim Haskins is a black writer who has developed many facets of his people's history and culture in a number of distinguished volumes. This book not only traces the evolution of black music and musicians in America but also shows how black music has influenced and changed the general trend in American music. There are many brief biographies of famous composers and performers in this account, which begins with the story of Elizabeth Taylor Greenfield, an operatic soprano of the 1850s, and ends with the blossoming career of Wynton Marsalis. Two companion volumes are *Black Dances in America* (Harper, 1990, $14.95) and *Black Theater in America* (Harper, 1982, $12.95). All are suitable in both junior and senior high school.

**Plot Summary**

This is a history of black music in America told through the lives of black people who made it. From the early spirituals and songs of the slaves to the blues, modern jazz, and beyond, the influence of black music on America and on the world cannot be calculated. This panoramic overview from the early 1800s to the present day describes how the changing social climate both hindered and aided the black musician.

"They Came Against Their Will: Early Slave Music" (Chapter 1) tells of the ways in which slaves kept their music alive on the dreadful journey to the New World. Ship captains were mostly unaware that slaves used music to do more than just express their fears and sorrows. Their drum rhythms often communicated rebellion; there were more than fifty revolts aboard slave ships. When the captains finally realized what was happening, drums were outlawed. Then the slaves used their feet.

Once on the plantations, the slaves would often sing, play, and dance, and many southern whites began to respond to their music and to enjoy it. Of course, to the whites this was not an art form, but it *was* entertainment.

The blacks who managed to achieve some success in music during the early years of the nineteenth century were mostly women, presumably because they were regarded as a lesser threat than black men. One of them was Elizabeth Taylor Greenfield, born to slave parents in Mississippi in 1809. Their mistress was a Quaker who moved with them to Philadelphia, where Elizabeth and her parents were freed. In 1851, Greenfield moved to Buffalo, New York, and made her debut as a soprano. Thereafter she was billed as "The Black Swan." In 1853 she studied and performed in London, becoming the first black American concert singer to gain acclaim on both sides of the Atlantic.

"Way Down South: Black Music Gains a Wider Audience" (Chapter 2) follows the period when black music began to influence what became two distinctly American forms of music: the musical comedy and popular ballads. The Fisk Jubilee Singers were part of this period. Fisk University was founded in Nashville, Tennessee, in 1866 to educate the brightest black youth. The school's musical director, George L. White, chose eighteen singers to go on the road giving concerts. The group, named for the year of the emancipation, started out singing popular songs, but more and more the public began to demand spirituals. The Jubilee Singers toured the United States and Europe. Fisk University sponsored the group until 1878, and then a second professional group from 1898 to 1911. Today the Fisk Jubilee Singers is a student group.

"Ragtime and the Blues: The First Age of Black American Music" (Chapter 3) boasts some famous names, among them Scott Joplin. Born in Texas in 1868, Joplin learned the piano from local teachers and struck out on his own at the age of twenty. Traveling through the Mississippi Valley, he heard and became fascinated with the peculiar syncopated piano playing that came to be known as ragtime. He formed his first band in Chicago in the 1890s and was soon composing pieces that would become classics, such as "Maple Leaf Rag," written in 1899. Joplin became popular for his piano playing, but wanted to be respected for his music. He spent the last years of his life trying to get his ragtime opera, *Treemonisha*, produced. Joplin died pretty much forgotten in 1917 at the age of forty-nine. In the 1970s he enjoyed a great revival on Broadway and elsewhere when *Treemonisha* was produced.

"Jazz: The Second Age of American Black Music" (Chapter 4) tells of the music that grew out of ragtime and the blues. The names are legend, such as Jelly Roll Morton, Ma Rainey, and, of course, Louis Armstrong. Nicknamed "Satchelmouth" by Londoners because of the way his cheeks puffed out when he played (the name was later shortened to Satchmo), he was born in New Orleans in 1898 or 1900. Satchmo, who was taught to play the cornet in the Colored Waifs Home, would grow up to become one of the world's most popular entertainers.

"Black Renaissance: 1920 to 1940" (Chapter 5) highlights New York in the 1920s with its own explosion of jazz and black music and one of the greatest of all musical names—Edward Kennedy "Duke" Ellington. He was born in Washington, D.C., in 1899, the son of a White House butler. He won a scholarship to Pratt Institute of Fine Arts in Brooklyn, New York, and composed his first music, "Soda Fountain Rag," when he was sixteen. Ellington came to symbolize the cooler, sophisticated jazz that matured in the 1930s. His musical legacy is almost endless— "Sophisticated Lady," "Solitude," "Take the A Train" are just three of his famous titles.

Another great of the era was singer Billie Holiday, born Eleanora Fagan in 1915 in Baltimore, Maryland. Her father thought she was a tomboy and called her Bill, hence the stage name. She began to perform professionally at age fifteen. Her incredible sense of rhythm and the unique timbre of her voice set her apart and influenced countless other singers down to the present day. But the trauma of her early childhood and her loneliness brought her to drugs and alcohol, and Billie Holiday died of lung congestion in 1959 at the age of forty-four.

"War and Remembrance: The 1940s" (Chapter 6) recalls such great names as Charlie "Yardbird" Parker, Mahalia Jackson, and the unforgettable Nat "King" Cole, who died in 1965 but whose voice and songs are as familiar today as when he was alive. His daughter, singer Natalie Cole, rose to great popularity in the early 1990s, partly through singing the tunes her father made famous.

"Rhythm, Blues, and Arias: The 1950s" (Chapter 7) talks of people like Bo Diddley and Miles Davis, the innovative jazz musician who died in 1992, and opera star Leontyne Price, famed as "the voice of the century." "Soul: The 1960s" (Chapter 8) features James Brown, Aretha Franklin, and the Motown sound. "New Directions: The 1970s and Today" (Chapter 9) covers contemporary musicians and talents including Stevie Wonder, Tina Turner, Quincy Jones, and Wynton Marsalis.

This look at black American music through the eyes of those who made and continue to make it underscores how heavily indebted twentieth-century America is to black music and black music makers.

**Thematic Material**

This is a fascinating, intimate look at talented black musicians through the years and how they influenced American musical history. It is also a very real and readable history lesson, for it shows how the changing social climate influences the music and the lives of musicians. Rich reading for anyone who has ever tapped a toe to a musical beat.

**Book Talk Material**

Depending on one's particular area of interest, individual biographies will serve as an excellent introduction to this upbeat musical history lesson. See the Civil War era's "Blind Tom—Musical Prodigy with Wonder Powers as a Pianist" (pp. 14–16); W. C. Handy and the blues (pp. 42–48); William Grant Still, the musical genius behind countless Hollywood scores, such as *Pennies from Heaven*, and television series, such as *The Perry Mason Show* and *Gunsmoke* (pp. 96–101); and one of the greatest of all musical success stories, the rise of Michael Jackson, born in 1958, winner of many music awards and the idol of countless teenagers (pp. 166–69).

**Additional Selections**

Sam Tanenhaus's *Louis Armstrong* (Chelsea House, 1989, $16.95) is a biography of the great black musician and performer that does not spare the details of his deprived childhood.

Such fundamentals of music as sound, pitch, and tone are explored as well as musical instruments, voices, and recordings in Melvin Berger's *The Science of Music* (Harper, 1989, $13.95).

In *Great Composers* (Bantam, 1989, $20.95), Piero Ventura gives interesting profiles of composers from ancient times through the Beatles.

Jan Greenberg and Sandra Jordan give an excellent introduction to basic elements of art and design in an examination of contemporary American painting in *The Painter's Eye* (Delacorte, 1991, $20.00).

In Janet Nichols's *American Music Makers: An Introduction to American Composers*, the lives of ten composers, including George Gershwin and Philip Glass, are examined.

The story of the grand ragtime composer and his amazing life are told in Katherine Preston's *Scott Joplin: Composer* (Chelsea House, 1988, $16.95).

The life story of another great black performer and composer is covered in Ron Frankl's *Duke Ellington: Bandleader and Composer* (Chelsea House, 1988, $16.95).

**About the Book**

Book Report, September 1987, p. 51.

*Booklist,* July 1987, p. 1168.

*Center for Children's Books Bulletin*, March 1987, p. 125.
*New York Times Book Review*, September 13, 1987, p. 48.
*School Library Journal*, June 1987, p. 106.
*VOYA*, April 1987, p. 45.
See also *Book Review Digest*, 1987, p. 804; and *Book Review Index*, 1987, p. 332.

**About the Author**
Commire, Anne, ed., *Something about the Author*. Gale, 1976, Vol. 9, pp. 100–1.
Holtze, Sally Holmes, ed., *Sixth Book of Junior Authors and Illustrators*. Wilson, 1989, pp. 115–17.
Sarkissian, Adele, ed., *Something about the Author*. Gale, 1987, Vol. 4, pp. 197–209.
Senick, Gerard J., ed., *Children's Literature Review*. Gale, 1978, Vol. 3, pp. 63–69.
Ward, Martha, ed., *Authors of Books for Young People* (3rd ed.). Scarecrow, 1990, p. 312.

---

**Myers, Walter Dean.**   *Now Is Your Time! The African-American Struggle for Freedom*
Harper, 1991, pap., $10.95 (0-06-446120-3)

---

Walter Dean Myers, the distinguished writer of fiction for young adults, has turned to nonfiction in this account of African Americans from slavery through the civil rights movements of the 1960s and 1970s to the present. Interwoven with the general account are stories reflecting episodes in the author's own family history. Scattered throughout this well-researched book are interesting short biographies. The use of quotations from letters and diaries adds realism to this account of struggle, despair, achievement, and sometimes hope. It is beautifully illustrated and contains an excellent bibliography. Both junior and senior high school students will find this book fascinating.

**Plot Summary**
"What we understand of history is what we understand of ourselves." From that premise comes a history especially intended for African Americans presented from a black perspective; a way, states the author, "for young people to identify with historical figures as strongly as they identify with his [the author's] fictional characters." So begin these true stories of the African-American experience, told in twenty-three chapters.

In "The Land," the author speaks of North America, the incredibly beautiful, incredibly rich land stretching between two oceans. For Europe in the 1400s, North America offered a promise of adventure to many. When colonies began to prosper in the New World, many people were needed to do work. At first "indentured servants" seemed to fulfill the need. Prisoners, criminals, debtors, and others were offered passage to the colonies and their freedom after they had worked as servants for a specified number of years. Eventually even indentured servants could not solve the labor problem, and so the practice of slavery prospered. West Africa became a source of slave labor for America for some 236 years.

"To Make a Slave" details how the slave system in America was made to work. It became obvious as more and more slaves were imported into the colonies that keeping order would become a problem, so the patrol system was created. Whites on horseback patrolled the roads in areas where Africans were held against their will. Any African found away from the plantation was stopped. If the slave could not furnish proof that he or she had permission to be away, the slave was returned to his or her master. African hairstyles and religious rituals were made taboo in an effort to maintain complete control over the slaves and to change the way in which blacks thought about themselves. Family structures were often ignored. If owners did allow their slaves to marry, they also thought little of separating the families if economic need so dictated. Destroy the family unit and you destroy the strength of the individual.

For the most part, the system worked for the slave owners. But not all captives took their loss of freedom without rebellion. In "Fighting Back," the author discusses resistance by captured Africans. In 1839, for instance, Africans who had been captured and taken to Cuba as the property of a pair of Spaniards broke their chains on board ship and revolted. The captain, cook, and two sailors were killed. The Spanish owners were spared because they said they would sail the captives back to Africa. Instead they sailed to New York harbor. But local abolitionists backed the Africans, who were allowed to go free and who returned to Africa in 1842.

In 1831, Nat Turner led fellow slaves in a raid on a white plantation, killing fifty-six people. He was executed, but he changed forever the idea that slaves were content with their lot. Some Africans were able to buy their freedom. Some ran away. Some were aided in their escape by black and white free Americans who believed that slavery was wrong.

Over the years, a number of American lawyers brought cases to court in an effort to free the slaves. The most famous of these was the so-called

Dred Scott case in the mid-1800s. Dred Scott was an uneducated black man, the property of an army surgeon named John Emerson. The doctor took Scott with him when he traveled to Fort Snelling in territory that had been declared free by the Missouri Compromise of 1820. In the court case that followed, Scott's lawyer argued that because he had been taken to live in a free state, he had become a free man.

In 1850, Dred Scott won the case and was declared free. Dr. Emerson appealed. The U.S. Supreme Court reversed the decision, 7–2, in 1857, declaring that a slave was not a citizen of the United States and could not become one. A group of whites later purchased Dred Scott's freedom, but the case only served to intensify the debate on slavery between the North and the South.

Another famous name in connection with slavery belongs to a white man, John Brown. Born in Connecticut in 1800, Brown migrated to Kansas in 1855. The area was in a bitter battle between pro- and antislavery forces. Brown joined the antislavery side with a vengeance. Leading a group of armed men against a proslavery settlement, he captured five men and hacked them to pieces. Then he decided to capture the arsenal at Harpers Ferry, Virginia. He thought that this attack by his force of twenty-one men, sixteen white and five black, would rally others—black and white—to their cause. The raid failed, and he did not garner the support he had hoped for. Brown was tried and executed in 1859.

The story of a remarkable American heroine is told in the section on "Ida B. Wells." The Civil War was over. Slavery was dead. African Americans were free—but what was to be done with them? Most were poor and uneducated. So were lots of white Americans. How would they all survive? When the Civil War ended, young Ida Wells lost her mother and father in a yellow fever epidemic in rural Mississippi. She was left with the care of her brothers and sisters. Ida Wells became a schoolteacher and devoted her life not only to educating young blacks but to fighting for the rights of blacks and of women. Armed only with a keen mind and boundless courage, she became a crusader against the injustices of bigotry and racism.

Another fighter for the rights of black Americans and all people was Martin Luther King, Jr., the leader of the modern civil rights movement. The Reverend King came to national prominence in the 1960s when he quietly protested segregation by sit-ins and other nonviolent demonstrations. His tireless work and that of many others, both white and black, eventually led to the passage of civil rights legislation, ending school segregation and protecting voting rights. King was assassinated in Memphis, Tennessee, on April 4, 1968, but his dream lives on.

## Thematic Material

This book presents remarkable stories of men and women of courage who fought injustice and bigotry against overwhelming odds. It is also a simple yet dramatic look at U.S. history through the perspective of African Americans whose lives and perceptions are forever shaped by the color of their skin.

## Book Talk Material

Some of the individual stories in this book can lead to a discussion of how devastating and widespread are the ways in which slavery and injustice permeate the lives of black Americans. See: the story of Abd al-Rhaman Ibrahima (pp. 11–27); the life of James Forten (pp. 53–63); and the heartbreak of Maria Perkins (pp. 74–75).

## Additional Selections

The trial of a twenty-year-old black man that galvanized the United States a decade before the Civil War is narrated in Virginia Hamilton's *Anthony Burns: The Defeat and Triumph of a Fugitive Slave* (Knopf, 1981, $11.95).

The story of the charismatic black leader who was shot at age thirty-nine is told in Jack Rummel's *Malcolm X* (Chelsea House, 1989, $16.95).

The 150-year story of the struggles of the first black union, the Brotherhood of Sleeping Car Porters, is told in *A Long Hard Journey* (Walker, 1989, $14.95) by Patricia McKissack and Fredrick McKissack.

The traumatic childhood of the brilliant black novelist and anthropologist Zora Neale Hurston is told in Mary Lyons's *Sorrow's Kitchen: The Life & Folklore of Zora Neale Hurston* (Scribner, 1990, $13.95).

In the revised edition of Patricia McKissack and Fredrick McKissack's *The Civil Rights Movement in America from 1865 to the Present* (Children's Pr., 1991, $39.93), there is an excellent overview of this topic, which includes sections on Mexican Americans and other Hispanics and coverage of the Bush administration.

A photo-history of the African-American struggle from slavery to the 1990s is given in James Haskins's *The Day Martin Luther King Jr. Was Shot* (pap., Scholastic, 1992, $5.95). In *One More River to Cross* (Scholastic, 1992, $13.95), the same author presents brief biographies of twelve black

Americans, beginning with Revolutionary War hero Crispus Attacks, who have made important contributions in spite of facing terrible odds.

Susan Altman has written a book containing thumbnail sketches of important blacks in *Extraordinary Black Americans: From Colonial to Contemporary Times* (Childrens Pr., 1989, $30.60). Its companion volume, *Extraordinary Hispanic Americans* (Childrens Pr., 1991, $30.60), helps fill the need for information on multicultural achievers. From another publisher there is a collection about fourteen significant Asian Americans in Janet Nomura Morey and Wendy Dunn's *Famous Asian Americans* (Dutton, 1992, $15.00).

**About the Book**
*Booklist*, November 1, 1991, p. 504.
*Horn Book*, March 1991, p. 217.
*School Library Journal*, March 1991, pp. 263–4.
*VOYA*, February 1992, p. 398.

**About the Author**
See entries under *Scorpions,* in Chapter One, Teenage Life and Concerns.

---

**Stwertka, Eve, and Stwertka, Albert.**   *Genetic Engineering*
Watts, 1989, $12.90 (0-531-10775-2)

---

Since the discovery of DNA and the unraveling of the mystery of the genetic code, the possible manipulation of life forms through genetics has become an area for both scientific exploration and philosophical debate. After preliminary background information on genetics and molecular biology, this book covers both the scientific elements in DNA techniques and applications and the ethical and humanistic issues involved. The account is exciting and upbeat and stresses the positive elements in genetic engineering. It is suitable for better junior high school and senior high school readers.

**Plot Summary**
Genetic engineering is concerned with the manipulation of the molecules that make up the innermost structure of living matter, in other words, the hereditary information carried by cells. It is based on the science of molecular biology, which has been around since the early 1950s.

To the uninitiated, genetic engineering sounds mysterious and somewhat frightening. It should be neither. This new technology means advances in our ability to use microorganisms to improve life. For instance, in 1982 scientists inserted the gene that produces human insulin into a microorganism known as *E. coli*, which lives in human intestines. This produced insulin, which is used all over the world to treat people with diabetes. This is a technique of genetic engineering.

The somewhat frightening aspect comes from the fact that genetic engineering can be used to change life forms as we know them. Scientists have already used genetic engineering to produce a "supermouse," twice the size of its twin brother. Would it be possible for scientists to develop a pill that would make children grow to seven feet and taller? Does that mean that some misguided adults could turn five children into their own supercolossal professional basketball team?

The proper use of genetic engineering is of vital concern to all the world's scientists and all the world's people. To make sure that they make the right decisions concerning it, scientists need to know all they can about how the cell functions.

Until the mid-nineteenth century, no one really knew much about reproduction and heredity. No one really knew how the human body grows or what happens during conception or why children don't always physically resemble their parents. Then, in 1886, Gregor Mendel, an Austrian monk, published his five-year study of heredity in garden peas. Mendel's work started scientists on the way to understanding how the cell functions. He found that a tall plant crossed with a short plant, for instance, did not produce a medium-size plant as one might expect. Instead, the plants from tall and short plants were all tall. Mendel found that some traits, such as tallness in the pea plants, were dominant, and some traits were recessive. His work opened the door to our greater understanding of cell function, although today we know that human inheritance is very complicated; human skin color, for instance, is the result of several genes, not just one.

The next major discoveries that would open the way to genetic engineering occurred in the twentieth century. In 1903 a German zoologist, Theodor Boveri, and an American graduate student, Walter Sutton, both independently discovered that chromosomes, the threadlike structures in the nuclei of all cells, pair off during cell division. By 1944 Oswald Avery and associates at Rockefeller University in New York City proved that the gene is made up of DNA, deoxyribonucleic acid. Avery became convinced that DNA played a key role in influencing the heredity of a cell.

Many scientists worked to unravel the mysteries of DNA, believing that unlocking its secrets would enable them to understand life, and if they could do that, they would be able to create or alter it. In 1953 James Watson and Francis Crick announced their now-famous double-helix model of the DNA molecule.

From this knowledge came the basics of genetic engineering. By the early 1970s scientists could split the DNA of a gene, remove parts of it, and splice them to the DNA of other genes. At such places as the Cold Spring Harbor Laboratory on Long Island, New York, research on DNA continues. One of the aims of this research is to cure diseases caused by a defective gene. If it is possible to insert a functioning gene into a cell to correct a faulty gene, such diseases as sickle-cell anemia or dwarfism may be conquered.

Genetic engineering has started a number of new "biocompanies." One of the first and best known in the United States is Genentech, which was started in 1975 by some young scientists and entrepreneurs in San Francisco. Other established companies such as Johnson & Johnson and Eastman Kodak have also recognized that genetic engineering offers a market for new products. Genentech is credited with being the first to apply new genetic techniques in making interferon, a protein that promises to be helpful in fighting cancer, the first to produce a blood clot–dissolving agent to fight heart attacks, and the first to offer Factor VIII, a blood-clotting agent that treats hemophilia, whose victims suffer from uncontrolled bleeding because their own blood does not clot normally.

Genetic engineering has become vital to the production of vaccines that fight all kinds of diseases. When the first Salk vaccine was introduced in the 1950s, there was always the danger that the monkey cells used for growing the vaccine carried an unwanted virus. Although no one, as far as we know, got sick from being injected with the polio vaccine, all vaccines that are grown from cells carry the dead or weakened virus for the disease they are meant to fight. So there is always the danger that, once in the body, the virus will trigger some kind of serious or deadly reaction. Genetic engineering avoids that complication because scientists can now bypass the process of culturing live bacteria and then disabling them. They clone only the proteins that stimulate a system to make a specific antibody.

The Cetus Corporation of California, begun in 1971, produces Interleukin-2, which enters the body of a person afflicted with cancer and seeks out and kills the cancer cells. It is still in the testing stage, but the results are encouraging. Cetus is also working on DNA probes for more reliable detection of such diseases as cancer and AIDS.

New chemicals have been created through genetic engineering techniques. Scientists at Genentech are working on a way to design bacteria that will convert garbage and human waste into combustible fuels. Some bacteria are already at work cleaning up oil spills and chemical dumps.

Other genetic engineering scientists are working on a "green revolution," genetically engineered grains, fruit and vegetables, and animal medicines. They hope to produce plants that are more resistant to or free of disease and that offer bigger and better yields.

No area of genetic engineering so attracts—and worries—the general public as does the idea of manipulating the human cell, of "changing" or "cloning" people. Work of this kind has been going on for years. There are tests today to determine if an unborn baby has a chromosomal abnormality. There are tests that determine if potential parents are carrying a gene that would cause deformities in their children. In time, genetic engineering may wipe out such disorders as Down's syndrome or sickle-cell anemia or Tay-Sachs disease, which strikes Jews of Eastern European descent, and many other abnormalities.

There is much debate even among scientists over the question of manipulating human embryos. Some think it is morally wrong, others that it is dangerous. Some scientists say it would be morally wrong *not* to use genetic engineering to cure genetic defects. Others say we should not be in the business of making "perfect humans." Some say scientists are "playing God." Molecular biologist Robert Sinsheimer of the University of California at Santa Cruz is one of those who thinks that human beings are not yet wise enough to direct their own evolution. Others reply that humans have been disturbing evolution for a long, long time and that, rather than playing God, we are fulfilling our destiny.

The research and the discoveries go on. It will be up to future generations to direct the course genetic engineering will take.

**Thematic Material**

This is a fascinating, easily read look at a complicated area of scientific research and engineering. In many ways it reads like an adventure story. The authors are neither preachy nor judgmental but present the facts of scientific discovery in an interesting, lively way that will intrigue most young readers with even a passing interest in the subject.

**Book Talk Material**

There are numerous items of interest here to spark a lively conversation on the merits of scientific research of this type. See: Mendel's work on dominant and recessive traits, and how it applies to humans (pp. 15–19); the race to unlock the mysteries of DNA (pp. 25–31); the story of growth hormone (pp. 56–57); manipulating the human gene (pp. 68–75); and the moral questions (pp. 114–27).

**Additional Selections**

For more advanced readers, another book that deals with this problem and controversy is an anthology edited by William Dudley, *Genetic Engineering* (Greenwillow, 1990, $15.95).

The story of how we evolved from single cells to complex humans is told in David Peters's exciting *From the Beginning: The Story of Human Evolution* (Morrow, 1991, $14.95).

In the novel *Anna to the Infinite Power* by Mildred Ames (Macmillan, 1981, $11.95), twelve-year-old Anna discovers she is part of a genetic engineering project.

The worlds of brainwashing, hypnosis, and behavior modification are explored in Melvin Berger's *Mind Control* (Harper, 1985, $12.70).

Cloning and other forms of manipulating genes are discussed in John Langone's *Human Engineering: Marvel or Menace* (Little, Brown, 1978, $12.95).

Isaac Asimov gives a simple introduction to the history of gene biology in *How Did We Find Out about Genes?* (Walker, 1983, $10.95).

An explanation of the genetic code and its implications and applications is given in Alvin Silverstein and Virginia Silverstein's *The Genetics Explosion* (Macmillan, 1980, $12.95).

**About the Book**

*Book Report,* January 1990, p. 55.
*Booklist,* January 15, 1990, p. 990.
*Horn Book Guide,* July 1989, p. 108.
*School Library Journal,* February 1990, p. 116.
*VOYA,* April 1990, p. 57.
See also *Book Review Digest,* 1990, pp. 1782–83; and *Book Review Index,* 1990, pp. 787–88.

# AUTHOR INDEX

Author and titles fully discussed in *Juniorplots 4* and those listed as "Additional Selections" are cited in this index. An asterisk (*) precedes those titles for which full summaries and discussions appear.

371

# TITLE INDEX

Titles fully discussed and summarized in *Juniorplots 4* as well as those listed as "Additional Selections" are cited in this index. An asterisk (*) precedes those titles for which full summaries and discussions appear.

# SUBJECT INDEX

This brief listing includes only those titles fully summarized and discussed in this book. Additional titles relating to these subjects can be found in the "Additional Selections" that accompany the discussion of the books listed here. Unless otherwise noted with the label nonfiction, the subject headings refer to fictional treatment of the subject.

# CUMULATIVE AUTHOR INDEX

This index lists all the authors and titles fully discussed in *Juniorplots* (J), *More Juniorplots* (M), *Juniorplots 3* (J3), and *Juniorplots 4* (J4).

# CUMULATIVE TITLE INDEX

This index lists all the titles fully discussed in *Juniorplots* (J), *More Juniorplots* (M), *Juniorplots 3* (J3), and *Juniorplots 4* (J4).

413

# CUMULATIVE SUBJECT INDEX

This index lists only the titles fully summarized and discussed in *Juniorplots* (J), *More Juniorplots* (M), *Juniorplots 3* (J3), and *Juniorplots 4* (J4). Additional titles relating to these subjects can be found in the "Additional Selections" that accompany the discussion of the books listed here. Unless otherwise noted with the label nonfiction, the subject headings refer to fictional treatment of the subject.

George, Jean Craighead. *Julie of the Wolves*, M-213
Gipson, Fred. *Old Yeller*, J-133
    *Savage Sam*, M-217
Hinton, S. E. *Taming the Star Runner*, J4-45
Kjelgaard, Jim. *Big Red*, J-135
London, Jack. *White Fang*, J4-154
Morey, Walt. *Gentle Ben*, M-220
Peck, Robert Newton. *A Day No Pigs Would Die*, M-16
Phipson, Joan. *Birkin*, J-95
Rawls, Wilson. *Where the Red Fern Grows*, M-223
St. George, Judith. *Haunted*, J3-149
Steinbeck, John. *The Red Pony*, J-195
Street, James. *Goodbye, My Lady*, J-50
Swarthout, Glendon. *Bless the Beasts and Children*, M-226
Westall, Robert. *The Cats of Seroster*, J3-131

**Animal Stories—Nonfiction**
Foster, Rory C. *Doctor Wildlife*, J3-258
North, Sterling. *Rascal*, J-45
Peck, Robert McCracken. *Headhunters and Hummingbirds*, J4-322

**Arizona**
Koertge, Ron. *The Arizona Kid*, J4-57
Swarthout, Glendon. *Bless the Beasts and Children*, M-226

**Arkansas**
Dragonwagon, Crescent and Zindel, Paul. *To Take a Dare*, J3-36

**Art**
Oneal, Zibby. *In Summer Light*, J3-82
Trevino, Elizabeth Borton de. *I, Juan de Pareja*, J-170

**Athletes—Nonfiction**
Biracree, Tom. *Wilma Rudolph*, J4-272
Gooden, Dwight with Woodley, Richard. *Rookie*, J3-262

**Australia**
Aldridge, James. *A Sporting Proposition*, M-204

Park, Ruth. *Playing Beatie Bow*, J3-186
Phipson, Joan. *Birkin*, J-95

**Authors—Nonfiction**
Cleary, Beverly. *A Girl from Yamhill*, J4-308
Hamilton, Virginia. *W. E. B. Du Bois*, J3-265
Kerr, M. E. *Me Me Me Me Me*, J3-270

**Automobiles**
Cormier, Robert. *The Bumblebee Flies Anyway*, J3-23
Felsen, Henry Gregor. *Hotrod*, J-128
Gault, William Campbell. *The Oval Playground*, M-134

**Badgers**
Eckert, Alan W. *Incident at Hawk's Hill*, M-210

**Ballet**
Bennett, Jay. *The Haunted One*, J4-135

**Baseball**
Allison, Bob and Hill, Frank Ernest. *The Kid Who Batted 1.000*, J-61

**Baseball—Nonfiction**
Gooden, Dwight with Woodley, Richard. *Rookie*, J3-262

**Basketball**
Brooks, Bruce. *The Moves Make the Man*, J3-235
Carson, John F. *The 23rd Street Crusaders*, J-64
Frick, C. H. *Five Against the Odds*, J-88
Myers, Walter Dean. *Hoops*, J3-249

**Basketball—Nonfiction**
Jones, Ron. *B-Ball*, J4-290

**Bears**
Morey, Walt. *Gentle Ben*, M-220

**Biography**
Biracree, Tom. *Wilma Rudolph*, J4-272
Bober, Natalie J. *Thomas Jefferson*, J4-303

**Boy-Girl Relationships—Nonfiction**

**Factories**
Paterson, Katherine. *Lyddie,* J4-253

**Families—Nonfiction**
Bell, Ruth. *Changing Bodies, Changing Lives,* J4-326
Biracree, Tom. *Wilma Rudolph,* J4-272
Francis, Dorothy B. *Suicide,* J4-330
Kerr, M. E. *Me Me Me Me Me,* J3-270
Killilea, Marie. *Karen,* J-90
Palmer, Francis. *And Four to Grow On,* J-165

**Family Stories**
Armstrong, William H. *Sounder,* M-1
Bagnold, Enid. *National Velvet,* J-32
Banks, Lynne Reid. *Melusine,* J4-131
Bell, Thelma Harrington. *The Two Worlds of Davy Blount,* J-152
Benary-Isbert, Margot. *The Ark,* J-125
Blume, Judy. *Just as Long as We're Together,* J4-6
*Then Again, Maybe I Won't,* M-179
Booth, Esma Rideout. *Kalena,* J-106
Brancato, Robin F. *Come Alive at 505,* J3-5
Brooks, Bruce. *No Kidding,* J4-193
*The Moves Make the Man,* J3-235
Carter, Alden R. *Up Country,* J4-10
Cleaver, Vera and Cleaver, Bill. *Where the Lilies Bloom,* M-128
Collier, James Lincoln. *Outside Looking In,* J4-19
Cone, Molly. *Reeney,* J-158
Cresswell, Helen. *Bagthorpes Abroad,* J3-32
*Bagthorpes Haunted,* J3-32
Crutcher, Chris. *Running Loose,* J4-276
Deaver, Julie Reece. *Say Goodnight, Gracie,* J4-33
Doherty, Berlie. *Granny Was a Buffer Girl,* J4-37
Duder, Tessa. *In Lane Three, Alex Archer,* J4-281
Duncan, Lois. *Locked in Time,* J3-125
*Twisted Window,* J4-141
Eyerly, Jeannette. *The Phaedra Complex,* M-4

Fitzhugh, Louise. *Harriet the Spy,* J-178
Fleischman, Paul. *The Borning Room,* J4-244
Fox, Paula. *One-Eyed Cat,* J3-214
Freedman, Benedict and Freedman, Ruth. *Mrs. Mike,* M-153
Garfield, Leon. *The Sound of Coaches,* M-86
Gates, Doris. *Blue Willow,* J-69
Gilmore, Kate. *Enter Three Witches,* J4-215
Guy, Rosa. *The Disappearance,* J3-129
Hall, Barbara. *Dixie Storms,* J4-42
Hamilton, Virginia. *The House of Dies Drear,* J4-148
*The Mystery of Drear House,* J4-148
Hamner, Earl, Jr. *You Can't Get There from Here,* M-7
Head, Ann. *Mr. and Mrs. Bo Jo Jones,* M-157
Highwater, Jamake. *The Ceremony of Innocence,* J3-218
Hinton, S. E. *Taming the Star Runner,* J4-45
Hunt, Irene. *Across Five Aprils,* J-181
Ik, Kim Yong. *Blue in the Seed,* J-92
Kerr, M. E. *Gentlehands,* J3-48
*I Stay Near You,* J4-51
Klass, David. *Breakaway Run,* J4-294
Klein, Norma. *Mom, the Wolfman and Me,* M-10
Konigsburg, E. L. *Father's Arcane Daughter,* J4-62
Landis, J. D. *Daddy's Girl,* J3-56
Lasky, Kathryn. *Pageant,* J3-59
L'Engle, Madeleine. *A Ring of Endless Light,* J3-63
Lowry, Lois. *Rabble Starkey,* J4-71
Lyle, Katie Letcher. *I Will Go Barefoot All Summer for You,* M-160
McKay, Robert. *The Running Back,* J3-246
Mahy, Margaret. *The Changeover,* J3-132
Marino, Jan. *The Day That Elvis Came to Town,* J4-81
Miklowitz, Gloria D. *The War between the Classes,* J3-78
Mohr, Nicholasa. *Nilda,* M-13

**Parents—Nonfiction**
Helmuth, Jerome. *Coping with Parents*, J3-283

**Pennsylvania**
Crawford, Charles P. *Letter Perfect*, J3-28
St. George, Judith. *Haunted*, J3-149
Sorensen, Virginia. *Miracles on Maple Hill*, J-146
Spinelli, Jerry. *Maniac Magee*, J4-108

**Photography—Nonfiction**
Sufrin, Mark. *Focus on America*, J3-274

**Physical Disabilities**
Butler, Beverly. *Gift of Gold*, M-103
   *Light a Single Candle*, J-86
Frick, H. E. *Five Against the Odds*, J-88
Hunter, Mollie. *The Stronghold*, M-109
Konigsburg, E. L. *Father's Arcane Daughter*, J4-62
Lee, Mildred. *The Skating Rink*, M-115
Ney, John. *Ox*, M-199
Phipson, Joan. *Birkin*, J-95
Robinson, Veronica. *David in Silence*, J-99
Rostkowski, Margaret I. *After the Dancing Days*, J4-258
Stolz, Mary. *In a Mirror*, M-201
Vinson, Kathryn. *Run with the Ring*, J-101

**Physical Disabilities—Nonfiction**
Biracree, Tom. *Wilma Rudolph*, J4-272
Hocken, Sheila. *Emma and I*, J3-306
Jones, Ron. *B-Ball*, J4-290
Killilea, Marie. *Karen*, J-90

**Physical Fitness**
Crutcher, Chris. *Stotan!*, J3-238

**Physics—Nonfiction**
Fleisher, Paul. *Secrets of the Universe*, J3-300

**Pittsburgh, Pennsylvania**
Konigsburg, E. L. *Father's Arcane Daughter*, J4-62

**Pole Vaulting**
Frick, C. H. *The Comeback Guy*, M-189

**Police**
Carter, Alden R. *Up Country*, J4-10
Lipsyte, Robert. *The Brave*, J4-298

**Polio**
Frick, C. H. *Five Against the Odds*, J-88

**Polio—Nonfiction**
Freedman, Russell. *Franklin Delano Roosevelt*, J4-317

**Political Activism**
Ames, Mildred. *Who Will Speak for the Lamb?*, J4-1
Lasky, Kathryn. *Pageant*, J3-59

**Politics**
Nixon, Joan Lowery. *A Candidate for Murder*, J4-158

**Politics—Nonfiction**
Freedman, Russell. *Franklin Delano Roosevelt*, J4-317

**Poverty**
Armstrong, William. *Sounder*, M-1
Clarke, Tom E. *The Big Road*, J-67
Cleaver, Vera and Cleaver, Bill. *Where the Lilies Bloom*, M-128
Collier, James Lincoln. *Outside Looking In*, J4-19
Gates, Doris. *Blue Willow*, J-69
Hamilton, Virginia. *M. C. Higgins, the Great*, M-195
Highwater, Jamake. *The Ceremony of Innocence*, J3-218
Mazer, Norma Fox. *Silver*, J4-85
Mohr, Nicolasa. *Nilda*, M-13
Myers, Walter Dean. *Hoops*, J3-249
   *Scorpions*, J4-90
Richard, Adrienne. *Pistol*, M-69
Sebestyen, Ouida. *Far from Home*, J3-98
Shotwell, Louisa A. *Roosevelt Grady*, J-76
Taylor, Mildred D. *Let the Circle Be Unbroken*, J3-226

## Roosevelt, Franklin Delano
Freedman, Russell. *Franklin Delano Roosevelt*, J4-317

## Runaways
Bunting, Eva. *If I Asked You, Would You Stay?*, J3-12
Clarke, Tom E. *The Big Road*, J-67
Cole, Brock. *The Goats*, J4-14
Dragonwagon, Crescent and Zindel, Paul. *To Take a Dare*, J3-36
Lasky, Kathryn. *Pageant*, J3-59
Macken, Walter. *The Flight of the Doves*, M-137
Spinelli, Jerry. *Maniac Magee*, J4-108
Wier, Esther. *The Loner*, J-52
Zindel, Paul. *Pardon Me, You're Stepping on My Eyeball!*, M-47

## Running
Crutcher, Chris. *Running Loose*, J4-276
Knudson, R. R. *Zan Hagen's Marathon*, J3-243

## Running—Nonfiction
Biracree, Tom. *Wilma Rudolph*, J4-272

## Sailing
Paulsen, Gary. *The Voyage of the Frog*, J4-163

## St. Francis of Assisi
O'Dell, Scott. *The Road to Damietta*, J3-222

## Sandburg, Carl
Sandburg, Carl. *Prairie-Town Boy*, J-167

## School Stories
Ames, Mildred. *Who Will Speak for the Lamb?*, J4-1
Blume, Judy. *Just as Long as We're Together*, J4-6
*Then Again, Maybe I Won't*, M-179
Brancato, Robin F. *Come Alive at 505*, J3-5
Brooks, Bruce. *The Moves Make the Man*, J3-235

Conford, Ellen. *Genie with the Light Blue Hair*, J4-202
*We Interrupt This Semester for an Important Bulletin*, J3-20
Cormier, Robert. *The Chocolate War*, M-28
Crawford, Charles P. *Letter Perfect*, J3-28
Crutcher, Chris. *Running Loose*, J4-276
Duder, Tessa. *In Lane Three, Alex Archer*, J4-281
Frick, C. H. *The Comeback Guy*, M-189
Kerr, M. E. *Is That You, Miss Blue?*, M-35
Klass, David. *Breakaway Run*, J4-294
Klass, Sheila Solomon. *The Bennington Stitch*, J3-52
Konigsburg, E.L. *(George)*, M-112
Korman, Gordon. *A Semester in the Life of a Garbage Bag*, J4-67
Landis, J. D. *Daddy's Girl*, J3-56
McKay, Robert. *The Running Back*, J3-246
Miklowitz, Gloria D. *The War between the Classes*, J3-78
Petersen, P. J. *Would You Settle for Improbable?*, J3-94
Rodgers, Mary. *Freaky Friday*, M-19
Sleator, William. *The Duplicate*, J4-233
Stolz, Mary. *In a Mirror*, M-201
Tchudi, Stephen. *The Burg-O-Rama Man*, J3-106
Zindel, Paul. *A Begonia for Miss Applebaum*, J4-121

## School Stories—Nonfiction
Cleary, Beverly. *A Girl from Yamhill*, J4-308
Kerr, M. E. *Me Me Me Me Me*, J3-270

## Science
Zindel, Paul. *A Begonia for Miss Applebaum*, J4-121

## Science—Nonfiction
Dwiggins, Don. *Hello? Who's Out There?*, J4-348
Fleisher, Paul. *Secrets of the Universe*, J3-300